How Geography and Institutions Shaped the Development of Nations

This book provides a concise and informative introduction to how geography and institutions shaped the development of nations, showing that while the role of institutions for the development of nations is indisputable, the role of geographic factors remains underexplored and underestimated.

Drawing on rich empirical material from the history and modernity of different continents and nations, *How Geography and Institutions Shaped the Development of Nations: Across Countries and Continents* seeks to show not only the importance of geographical explanations of development but also their extraordinary diversity. This book is divided into two parts. The first part examines the main contributions to the understanding of development under the influence of geographic and institutional factors, as well as states' geographic attributes and borders as geographic institutions. The second part immerses the reader in empirical material, presenting various cases on different continents in different historical periods.

This book is an essential read for researchers in a broad range of areas, including international organizations and practitioners involved accelerating national development. It will also be of interest to scholars and students in development studies and, more broadly to, geography, comparative politics, and regional studies.

Irina Busygina, Research Fellow, Davis Center for Russian and Eurasian Studies at Harvard University, USA.

Routledge Studies in Human Geography

This series provides a forum for innovative, vibrant, and critical debate within Human Geography. Titles will reflect the wealth of research which is taking place in this diverse and ever-expanding field. Contributions will be drawn from the main sub-disciplines and from innovative areas of work which have no particular sub-disciplinary allegiances.

Object-Oriented Cartography
Maps as Things
Tania Rossetto

Human Geography and Professional Mobility
International Experiences, Critical Reflections, Practical Insights
Weronika A. Kusek and Nicholas Wise

Geographies of the Internet
Edited by Barney Warf

Locating Value
Theory, Application and Critique
Edited by Samantha Saville and Gareth Hoskins

Spatialized Islamophobia
Kawtar Najib

Over Researched Places
Towards a Critical and Reflexive Approach
Edited by Cat Button and Gerald Taylor Aitken

How Geography and Institutions Shaped the Development of Nations
Across Countries and Continents
Irina Busygina

For more information about this series, please visit: www.routledge.com/Routledge-Studies-in-Human-Geography/book-series/SE0514

How Geography and Institutions Shaped the Development of Nations

Across Countries and Continents

Irina Busygina

Routledge
Taylor & Francis Group
LONDON AND NEW YORK

First published 2025
by Routledge
4 Park Square, Milton Park, Abingdon, Oxon OX14 4RN

and by Routledge
605 Third Avenue, New York, NY 10158

Routledge is an imprint of the Taylor & Francis Group, an informa business

British Library Cataloguing-in-Publication Data
A catalogue record for this book is available from the British Library

ISBN: 978-1-032-80408-8 (hbk)
ISBN: 978-1-032-80410-1 (pbk)
ISBN: 978-1-003-49673-1 (ebk)

DOI: 10.4324/9781003496731

Typeset in Times New Roman
by Apex CoVantage, LLC

Contents

Acknowledgments *vi*

Introduction 1

PART I 15

1 Development, institutions, and geography: how do they fit together 17

2 Modern states and their geographical attributes: size, shape, and location 39

3 Borders as geographical institutions 56

PART II 71

4 Europe 73

5 Asia 102

6 Africa 124

7 Latin America 147

8 North America 168

9 Oceania 194

10 Russia 212

11 Conclusion 237

Index *244*

Acknowledgments

I am eternally grateful to Dr. Alexandra Vacroux, Prof. Eve Blau, Prof. Timothy Colton, Cris Martin, Laura Sargent, and all my dear friends and colleagues at the Davis Center of Russian and Eurasian Studies at Harvard University. Without their constant support and help, this book would never have been finished. I started working on this book in Russia. After the beginning of the Russian war against Ukraine in early 2022, I resigned my positions at the Higher School of Economics and left Russia. I took my unfinished book with me and was able to finish it at the Davis Center. The environment at the Davis Center, which I consider unique, allowed me to work productively and once again appreciate the value of human and professional relationships. This gratitude to the Davis Center will be with me forever.

Introduction

In their article for *Foreign Affairs* of June 12, 2024, Dev Patel, Justin Sandefur, and Arvind Subramanian argued that

> as early as the fifteenth century, formerly prosperous societies from Mesoamerica to China suffered reversals of fortune, falling – or being pushed – behind the West. With the advent of the Industrial Revolution, growth rates in rich and poor nations diverged even further. But as the Cold War drew to a close, this grim historical pattern broke, and developing countries started growing faster. Within another decade, they began catching up, albeit slowly, with living standards in the rich West.

Convergence instead of previous long, long divergence – this is what occurred between the fortunes of rich and poor countries between 1990 and 2020. The main driver of this unprecedented change was, according to Patel, Sandefur, and Subramanian, hyperglobalization – exponential rise of the international trade flows due to a rapid decline in the cost of transporting goods and communicating, the turn of political leaders to more globalization-friendly policies, and the end of the Cold War that promised an international environment with lower risk of war and geopolitical confrontation. Importantly, this was a chance not for individual countries like China and India but for the plurality of developing countries – "as a group, they started reversing their previously bleak economic fortunes to a plurality of developing countries." But this unique chance was not taken, "after experiencing their greatest era of economic flourishing, developing countries turned inward." Patel, Sandefur, and Subramanian called the architects of the world's economic future to

> take a moment from their hyperfocus on great-power competition to look at things from developing countries' perspective. The stunning nature of convergence illuminates the enormity of what has been lost: developing countries, as a group, broke from a 500-year pattern of development; then, for a few brief decades, that historical trend was arrested. Global inequality fell, and the consequences for human welfare were enormous.

DOI: 10.4324/9781003496731-1

If these renowned experts are right and the chance of hyperglobalization has been missed, what does this mean in terms of the gap between rich and poor nations? The "natural" way has not worked, but it makes deliberate strategies, policies, and instruments aimed at narrowing this gap even more important. The first thing that comes to mind is aid flowing from international organizations and richer nations to the poorer ones. Nothing new: for decades, richer countries and international organizations have been trying to develop "aid industry" to the poor. Nobody would claim that this aid was completely useless, of course, but so far it has failed to deliver sustainable economic development and poverty reduction. The main recipient of aid – sub-Saharan Africa remains the poorest region in the world. Frustration led to calls for a radical change in the principles and mechanisms of aid or even to put an end to the project altogether. For instance, Dambisa Moyo in her book *Dead Aid: Why Aid Is Not Working and How There Is a Better Way for Africa* (2009) asked, "What if, one by one, African countries each received a phone call, telling them that in exactly five years the aid taps would be shut off – permanently?" The shock would force them to create a new economic plan that phases in alternative financing mechanisms as aid is phased out, she argued. Moyo fiercely called for a move away from aid dependency of developing nations. It is not clear, of course, whether Moyo's calls if converted into new policy decisions would improve the gap situation or if they would lead to new frustrations. These frustrations – and this is what this book focuses on – may be the result not only of the gap between poor and rich countries per se but of its spatial pattern that has not changed for decades. Both the poorest and richest nations are spatially clustered.

So, to move forward, it is critical to get our expectations right, and to get them right we need to work on adequate and competent explanations for the spatial unevenness of world development. Explanations first and only then the policy recommendations. Indeed, someone who would explain territorial differences between countries in terms of development would be doing humanity an invaluable service.

Importantly, the problem of differences in levels of development is not only that some countries are "rich," and their people enjoy life, while others are "poor," and the citizens are preoccupied with survival and do not have the opportunity to experience freedom. Notably, these differences often coincide with significant economic, social, and political challenges and risks. In poorer countries in particular, these disparities fuel populist discourses criticizing institutions of market economy and globalization and calling for an immediate reshaping of the world order sometimes by brute force.

Besides that, discussing development we must pay special attention to the problem of inequality. According to Ros (2013: 341), the societies of developing countries are more unequal than those of developed countries. High degree of inequality and maintaining this degree over time create incentives for different social groups to engage in rent-seeking behavior and leads to social unrest. The resulting uncertainty may reduce the rate of growth. Rodrik (1999) argued that high inequality weakens the institutions of conflict management, making a country more vulnerable to external shocks, and growth collapses. There are a lot of reasons for inequalities within societies, and each of them deserves serious discussion. In terms of this book, I would like to mention here the point made by Engerman and Sokoloff (2002), who related the degree of inequality to the composition of factor endowments (including climate, soil and density of native population, besides the abundance of land and natural resources). Comparing colonies in North and Latin America, they argued that in the former, factor endowment attracted European immigrants with a relatively egalitarian distribution of human capital. In North America, a system of smaller family farms emerged that were not subject to economies of scale. On the contrary, in Latin America (and also in the US South before the Civil War) a system of large latifundia was characterized by extensive economies of scale that stimulated the concentration of land and the creation of slave plantations. The other factor that also contributed to the high inequality of income and wealth was the abundance of labor with low human capital (slaves in Brazil and West Indies and natives in Mexico and Peru).

If we imagine all the countries of the world as a kind of mythical animal where parts of this animal's body would be groups of countries with different levels of development (high, middle, and low), this would be an animal with a quite small head (high-income countries), an exceptionally large torso (middle-income countries), and a long tail (low-income countries). And this is where the questions arise. Why does the animal look like that? Why is it so extremely difficult for countries to "jump" from the tail to the torso and from the torso to the head and remain there? Why there are so few successful transformations like that? And why does the tail consist of the countries geographically concentrated near the equator? Table 0.1 demonstrates that the ten poorest countries are clustered in sub-Saharan Africa. The only exception is Afghanistan, located in Asia. The same group of countries have very low institutional quality indices. Let us just remember this combination for now: the world's poorest countries with low institutional quality indices are concentrated in one geographic region (and not scattered all over the world map).

This book does not so much offer brand new explanations for the spatial unevenness of countries' development but rather to "return" explanations that were actively and fruitfully discussed until the mid-2010s and then undeservedly overshadowed. Clearly, these explanations do not pretend to be exhaustive; they are fundamentally partial. Moreover, they do not contradict other explanations, for example, the cultural explanation of development. In his book, *Five Families: Mexican Case Studies in the Culture of Poverty* (1975), Oscar Lewis back in the late 1960s has proposed the "culture of poverty" theory, which postulated that sustained poverty generated a set of cultural attitudes, values, beliefs, stereotypes, and practices, and this "culture of poverty" embracing all of them would tend to perpetuate itself over time, even if the structural conditions that originally gave rise to it would change. In other words, the "culture of poverty" is not just a description of a particular community but the driving force that constantly *reproduces* poverty in that community (with the possibility of spilling over to the neighboring ones). Is this theory important when thinking about the development perspectives of this community, the city that contains such communities, and the country where "culture of poverty" is one of the major characteristics of the urban spaces? Yes, for sure. Culture affects economic outcomes (Guiso, Sapienza and Zingales 2006).

Table 0.1 The poorest countries in the world (2021), their institutional quality, and geographical location

Countries	*GNI[1] per capita (in US dollars)*	*Institutional quality index (political institutions)*	*Institutional quality index (market institutions)*	*Region of the world*
Central African Republic	663	172	173	Sub-Saharan Africa
Burundi	686	177	164	Sub-Saharan Africa
Democratic Republic of Congo	796	178	178	Sub-Saharan Africa
Niger	906	113	152	Sub-Saharan Africa
Malawi	1,604	101	146	Sub-Saharan Africa
Liberia	1,078	129	154	Sub-Saharan Africa
Mozambique	1,100	148	165	Sub-Saharan Africa
Madagascar	1,339	123	149	Sub-Saharan Africa
Sierra Leone	1,348	116	168	Sub-Saharan Africa
Afghanistan	1,647	168	166	South/Central Asia

Sources: World Bank World Development Indicators, Institutional Quality Index.

Collier (2017) viewed culture as "building an arsenal or 'toolbox' that people use to formulate action strategies economically." Ignoring cultural differences, both between and within nations, is guaranteed not to achieve the desired outcome in terms of development. Culture matters! – It is simply indecent to deny this (Harrison and Huntington 2001). Thus, cultural explanations of development are an important part of the general "piggy bank" of developmental explanations.

In this book, I focus on other explanations from the "piggy bank" – these are institutions and geography. The idea is to "reclaim" these explanations – not as always independent of each other but as causally related, yet capable of having direct impact on development – motivated the writing of the book. The book takes a broader view on states as complicated multidimensional entities where various systems work together, in combination. The institutional system defines rules and expectations and constrains the choices. The book contends that geographical system – a set of geographical factors, such as borders, territorial size of the countries, their location, and shape – is another important system of states. The geographical system interacts with the institutional one setting a corridor of choices for political and economic actors that can accelerate or hinder a country's development. In addition, it is important that institutional and geographical systems intersect with the formation of "geographical institutes" – these are borders and federalism.

Again, geography as a national system creates its own opportunities and constraints for development. Therefore, the task of national elites would be not only to create or borrow the "right" political and economic institutions but to dock them with national geography. In this case, it would be more reasonable to expect that, mutually supporting each other, they will work for the common goal of accelerating national development (or at least not creating obstacles to it). Both institutions and geography belong to "fundamental" determinants of economic development (Ros 2013: 26).

Here I briefly present the main concepts of the book that are development, institutions, and geography (geographical factors). I will discuss the concepts in more detail in Chapter 1.

The conceptualization of "development" is changing over time; this concept will always remain contentious. For many reasons, it is impossible to imagine a situation where scholars from different disciplines, experts, and practitioners will reach a definitive consensus on what can be considered development and what cannot. The idea of development – not as a historical process that has universal regularities but as a process that can be directed and modeled – became popular in the 1950s, when the former European colonies began to gain independence. At that time, the idea of development was conceptualized mainly as modernization and was associated with scholars like Walter Rostow, who in 1959 has published a highly influential article "The Stages of Economic Development." However, by the 1970s, it became clear that the development pattern of most postcolonial countries did not meet the predictions of the modernization approach; on the contrary, the level of poverty and inequality in these countries was increasing. The alternative – structuralist – approach claimed that the poor countries'

> bad development trajectory was due to the internationalization of the world economy, in which some countries developed at the expense of others. In the 1980s–90s approach to development took a neoliberal turn, which implied a focus on reducing the size of the state, privatization, elimination of price controls, and decentralization. These were the development programs for poorer countries that the experts of the World Bank and the International Monetary Fund elaborated. However, these prescriptions, too, have been extremely limited in their success.
>
> (Moseley and Pandit 2007: 351–352)

From the point of view of the desired outcome, this approach has also proved to be, to say the least, uncontroversial.

Almost all issues related to development are debated. And these discussions are not only about the causes of poor development and ways to improve it but also about language. This is a really sensitive issue: what should we call less well-off countries? The term "Third World" has been routinely used over time. Everyone knew what the term meant – countries that were less well-off, troubled with poverty, inequalities, and violence, where educational and health care systems were weak, and where corruption was flourishing. But the term was a problem being offensive and referring to the period of colonization of some nations by the others. New alternatives appeared.

Many argued that the term "developing nations" was a better choice as it implied a country's trajectory to "improvement." However, this term was also not unproblematic. While the term "developing" brings about a connotation of improving conditions, it also encourages the misconception that countries with big economies did not need to develop. Difficult situation. In 2016, the World Bank announced that the distinction between "developing" countries and "developed" does not adequately catch the nature of the problem.[2] Then, the term "Majority World" was applied reminding the West that the countries of this "World" outnumber Western countries. "Majority World" refers to countries where the most population resides. This term is perfectly correct but unfortunately suffers from a lack of content – it does not indicate development issues in any way. Finally, "Global South" (as opposed to "Global North") was invented and is actively used. The term seems to indicate the geographical location of countries, but it does not. Clearly, the term does not group nations by their geography. For instance, Haiti is in the Global North and Australia is in the Global South. In addition, the "Global South" is increasingly used not to refer to development problems but to the contradictions between the political and economic interests of the "South" and the "North." A consensus term has not yet been found. While gaining correctness, there are losses in substance.

No matter how we define development, narrowly or broadly, as certain values of economic parameters or as an embodiment of the idea of freedom, we intuitively know what we are talking about. And we understand "bad" or "not good enough" development even better than "good" development. Moreover, when assessing a country's development and its prospects, we must remember that development is path-dependent, that is conditioned by previous choices.

A critical important indicator for development is the quality of institutions (recall Table 0.1). Douglas North (1990: 3) defined "*institutions* are the rules of the game in a society or, more formally, are the humanly devised constraints that shape human interaction." According to Faundez (2016: 374),

> North had a major impact on contemporary development thinking. His work was the single most important source of inspiration that led development agencies in the early 1990s to shift their attention from technical economic issues towards broader institutional concerns. This shift, reflected in the World Bank's motto "institutions matter," brought about a substantial increase in the resources that international development agencies allocate to legal and institutional reform.

For Haas, Keohane and Levy (1993: 4–5) institutions are "connected set of rules, norms, and practices that prescribe roles, constraint activity, and shape the expectations of actors." This is an overly broad definition (like this of North) as it embraces many quite different things, excessively big and exceedingly small – regional integration groups, states and markets, property rights, criminal codes, youth organizations, religion, marriages, and so on (Lim 2010: 94). March and Olsen (1984: 738) pointed out that institutions are "autonomous political actors in their own right." "New institutionalism" argues that institutions have *agency*: they are not just something that individuals and groups choose and use but collective actors with their own "interests" and "goals." From this perspective, they should be understood as key independent variable explaining outcomes (Lim 2010: 94).

Institutions are critical to economic development anywhere in the world. They are fundamental to economic development because certain combinations of institutions tend to facilitate mutually beneficial exchange, entrepreneurship, and innovation. Other institutions, on the contrary, may impede economic relations between people or they may direct people to act in socially wasteful manners (see North 1990; Murphy, Shleifer and Vishny 1991; Boettke, Coyne and Leeson 2008). Empirical literature in economics found three elements deemed to be necessary conditions for long-term economic development: a) protection of property rights; b) constraints on the power of the executive; c) absence of vast disparities in incomes per capita. If a country having these conditions are present, sustained economic growth is expected to follow (Portes and Nava 2017), although it is not guaranteed, of course. As Helpman (2004: 39) concluded,

> [C]ountries that start with similar endowments can follow different developmental paths as a result of differences in institutional structures, because institutions affect the incentive to innovate and to develop new technology, the incentives to reorganize production and distribution in order to exploit new opportunities, and the incentives to accumulate physical and human capital.

Thus, institutional factors offer the most compelling explanations for a country's level of development and its progression. Advocates of this viewpoint emphasize the importance of institutions, arguing that institutional path dependence and reforms largely shape a nation's developmental trajectory. But if this were the case, prosperous countries would serve as examples and leaders for others, with the primary task of the latter being to adopt "efficient" institutional practices. However, while this institutional borrowing often occurs, it seldom yields the anticipated results – namely, accelerating development in less affluent countries.

When studying economic history, North (1992: 21) concluded that the root cause of Spain's long stagnation was centralized bureaucracy that tried to spread its control on every aspect of the national economy issuing endless decrees and regulations. He then compared Spain and England explaining different paths taken by their colonies in the Americas. England's colonies in North America were able to adopt inclusive political systems, modeled on England, but Spanish colonies in Latin America reproduced the institutional flaws of their mother country and became centralized states (North 1989: 1329–1330). However, differences in institutional colonial legacies were not the only ones; geographical factors also mattered: the soils in the British colonies were more suitable for grain cultivation than for Latin American lucrative cash crops such as cotton, coffee, or sugarcane (Portes and Nava 2017).

That geographical factors play some role for developmental trajectories of nations has been noted for a long time, long before the study of the impact of institutions on development began. Interestingly, in the past, researchers tended to emphasize unfavorable geographical conditions in regions far from Europe. For instance, in *The Wealth of Nations*, Adam Smith cited inland Africa and the interior of Asia as examples of geographically disadvantaged regions where a lack of natural access to markets resulted in slow growth (Ros 2013). Indeed, various geographical factors influence the course of development – either directly or through institutions (Rodrik, Subramanian and Trebbi 2002; Easterly and Levine 2003). Geography includes physical geographical factors of a country – its climatic conditions, soils, relief, spread of diseases, and so on, which determine the ability of a country to develop. Another important set of geographical factors relate to state territory – its size, shape, and location (neighbors, access to the sea, distance from strategic objects). Finally, there are "geographical institutions" – borders first and foremost and federalism and territorial autonomy.

The constraints that geography imposes on development were beautifully and poetically shown by Maria Amoamo (2016) using the example of the island of Pitcairn, "lost in time and space":

> situated halfway between New Zealand and South America, Pitcairn is often referred to as one of the most isolated islands in the world. Its tiny size, rugged coastline and sheer cliffs offer no safe anchorage for ships that must lie a mile or two offshore. Transport to the island is governed by the skill of local men and their longboats. Due to Pitcairn's remote location, there is no air strip and access to the island is by ship, a journey of 36 hours from Mangareva, French Polynesia's far-flung archipelago of Gambier Islands. The current service operates only four times a year and has continually been a barrier to economic growth. A handful of cruise ships, charter vessels and yachts visit the island annually. Today, Pitcairn's populace is dwindling. Cooperation, coordination, mutual trust, working self-government are critically important here, more than in the communities elsewhere.

In his book *The Mystery of Economic Growth*, Helpman (2004) mentioned interesting studies that were generally aimed at exploring the link between institutions and development but could not ignore geographical factors in their various manifestations. Greif (1993) analyzed the history of medieval traders in the Maghreb region, attributing their economic success to the invention of institutional norms supporting long-distance trade. The solution consisted of the creation and common acceptance of the Merchant's Law that monitored the behavior of trade agents in distant lands and enjoined all merchants to refrain from doing business with an agent who had violated the trust of one of its members. Acemoglu, Johnson, and Robinson (2001) focused on the institutions created by Europeans in their colonial areas. Scholars showed that colonies where Europeans created permanent foundations, managed to develop robust institutional frameworks borrowed from the "mother" countries that, in turn, provided the basis for sustained economic growth. Aware of the endogeneity problem between institutions and development, scholars controlled their main determinant – European settler concentration – on prior-reported death rates among early colonists. They concluded that geographic areas where high death rates were reported among early settlers because of malaria and yellow fever were confined to an extractive role and that only healthier, temperate ones were deemed suitable for European settlement.

Geography has one crucial feature: it has its own language. These are geographical maps, a special means of conveying information about space. This language was used by men long before the advent of writing. The language of maps is a conventional and symbolic form of information transmission. It is impossible to imagine the history of a country's development without the use of maps. In the words of Denis Wood (2010: 1), by enabling us to see the interposition of objects in space, maps become a tool that has the potential to transform human energy into meaningful action.

A political map is a representation of a state. The emergence of many new states on the world map after World War II has dramatically revived interest in atlases as symbols and evidence of a new statehood. Later, the number of national atlases skyrocketed immediately after the process of decolonization: the former colonies turned to cartography as a means of economic and social development and of forming their own political identities. The same happened after the collapse of the Soviet Union in 1991.

Maps are not only the language of geography, but they are also institutions. Maps are humanly devised and constrain the behavior of humans. Official maps of countries and their regions, agreed and approved by the state, are considered in all state actions – reforms, military campaigns, and emergencies. Just as the basic institution – the national constitution – is formulated in words, maps formulate rules in the language of symbols. Each map has a legend that decodes these symbols. The science of mapping (cartography) has undergone an all-out technological revolution, and the revolution continues today. Satellites with special cameras and scanners transmit information to computers, noting the growth of deserts, shrinking glaciers, urban growth, and deforestation. Modern computers are not only able to receive and sort this information but also to reflect it in the form of images (graphically). In turn, this has allowed geographers to make (and continually improve) *geographic information systems* (GIS) that assimilate constantly incoming new information and update maps within seconds (De Blij and Mueller 2010: 4).

Bad maps that "lie" and provide misleading information are like bad institutions, both lead to undesired outcomes. In 1862, during the American Civil War, Northern troops planned to defeat the Southerners by capturing their capital (Richmond, Virginia). However, General McClellan's staff based their plan of attack on sloppy maps, and that slowed the advance of the Army of the North. The Southerners, too, lacked good maps and were therefore left in the dark as to the strategic advantage that had arisen. Another example is during the 1983 invasion of Grenada, US troops were armed with outdated British maps. In one case, this led to the destruction of an uncharted mental hospital in an air attack; in another, the US soldiers themselves were hurt (Monmonier 1996: 45).

By the will of those who create them (or, more accurately, give orders to those who create the maps), maps can deliberately distort information. This task is facilitated by the fact that maps are a form of communication that traditionally enjoys a high degree of trust. While maps are often thought of as objective representations of the world, they are performing political tasks (Fotiadis 2009). In history, maps have repeatedly been used to justify territorial conquests, economic exploitation, and the justification of cultural colonialism. Maps (especially historical maps) are a powerful intellectual weapon in determining the ownership of disputed territory or in delimiting the border. In addition, maps can serve the purpose of political propaganda: depending on the task, maps can present a country (or region) as large and important or, on the contrary, as small and vulnerable to external aggression. For totalitarian regimes, maps served as powerful tools for propaganda and manipulation of public consciousness. The use of maps for political propaganda by Nazi ideologues in Germany deserves special mention. Perhaps no other regime used maps so intensively and "ruthlessly"; the objectives were to increase sympathy for Germany, reduce support for Britain and France, and attempt to keep the United States from intervening in the war on European territory (Monmonier 1996).

When Russian President Putin needed to prove to Russians that Ukraine had never had independent statehood and had no right to it, he turned to maps. A completely anecdotal situation arose.[3] In May 2023 (more than a year after the Russian invasion of Ukraine), the chairman of the Russian Constitutional Court, Valery Zorkin, came to see Putin and told him literally the following:

> It turned out that we have found in the Constitutional Court a copy of a 17th century map drawn up under Louis 14 by the French themselves. Why did I bring it? There is no Ukraine there.[4]

It's not that these two politicians trusted this map, but they calculated that such trust in maps is present in the population. The Russian media were actively discussing this remarkable find: well, look at this . . . so, this is how it really is with Ukraine.

At this point, I would like to briefly discuss a process and a concept that runs through almost all the chapters of the book. This is colonization and colonial (institutional) legacy.

Generally, literature defines legacy as a long-lasting effect of historical events, institutions, and practices. Legacy-type arguments are composed of three key components: an outcome that cannot be fully explained by causes contemporary with that outcome, a preceding cause, and speculative connections between the antecedent and the outcome. The extent to which a study has established a legacy's existence depends on its argument's quality (Wittenberg 2015: 369). Legacy effects are seen in various dimensions and spheres, from culture to politics. For instance, Ken Jowitt's collection of essays provided the first comprehensive analysis of the Leninist legacy, which encompasses the cultural, social, political, and economic heritage inherited by the Eastern European successor regimes and the Soviet Union (Jowitt

1992). Legacy-type arguments are often presented within the theoretic framework of "historical institutionalism" that emphasizes the "path dependence" of institutions.[5]

Colonial rule has left an enduring imprint on the development of colonized nations and was a driver of dramatically divergent income levels across countries (for the overview of the argumentation, see De Juan and Pierskalla 2017). In particular, Acemoglu, Johnson, and Robinson (2001) argued that differences between types of colonial rule explain the variation in income levels across the developing world. While some territories became settler colonies with institutions that protected private property rights limiting government and stimulating innovation and growth, others became extractive colonies where institutional framework enabled a small European elite to monopolize political and economic power. This predatory rule remained in place even after decolonization and significantly increased the chances of the emergence of an autocratic government with a low record of economic development. Mahmood Mamdani in his classic book *Citizen and Subject: Contemporary Africa and the Legacy of Late Colonialism* (1996) convincingly demonstrated that colonial rule created institutional legacies that led to the rise of African despots. Busygina and Filippov (2024) showed that the legacy of the Soviet Union rule and its disintegration plays an important role in the evaluation of real and imaginary threats to the problem of sustaining territorial integrity of the post-Soviet nations.

Although most of the studies support the argument that different effects of colonial legacy are still visible and still largely determine the development trajectory of former colonies, there is an alternative view arguing that the relevance of colonial legacies to institutional quality and economic development is disappearing and that the impact of colonial legacy is not persistent. Maseland (2018) showed that differences in institutional quality or income are explained less and less by colonial legacy while there is evidence that precolonial social and geographical circumstances are becoming more important. A similar argument was made regarding Central Asia: after gaining independence in the 1990s, there was a revival of traditional (pre-Soviet and even pre-Russian Empire) social institutions and practices in these countries.

This introduction is followed by the book chapters. The first three chapters discuss the relationship between development, institutions and geography, geographical parameters states, and the borders. They are followed by chapters on continents, in which I have tried to provide illustrations and situations of the impact on development of institutions and a variety of geographical factors at different historical stages. The chapters deliberately do not follow the same pattern to demonstrate and emphasize different aspects of such influence. I do not and could not pretend to discuss all or most cases of such influences; it is impossible. My aim was rather to show their diversity.

Notes

1 Gross domestic income.
2 https://blogs.worldbank.org/opendata/2016-edition-world-development-indicators-out-three-features-you-won-t-want-miss

3 President Putin has no luck with geography at all. He likes to refer to geographical terms but obviously does not understand their meaning. In September 2022, speaking at an open class for schoolchildren (!) in the city of Kaliningrad, he stated that the purpose of Russia's "special military operation" was to eliminate an anti-Russian enclave that is being created in Ukraine and threatened Russia (Путин назвал целью спецоперации ликвидацию "антироссийского анклава" – РБК (rbc.ru)). Enclave is a state completely surrounded by the territory of the other state. There are a few examples of enclaves on the world map; these are Lesotho, San Marino, and Vatican City. Where Putin managed to find an enclave within Ukraine is completely unclear.

4 Путин заявил, что "никакой Украины не было" до создания УССР – РБК (rbc.ru).

5 Path-dependence of institutions and development are discussed in more detail in Chapter 1.

References

Acemoglu, Daren, Simon Johnson, and James Robinson. (2001). "The Colonial Origins of Comparative Development: An Empirical Investigation." *American Economic Review*, 91: 1369–1401.

Amoamo, Maria. (2016). Pitcairn and the Bounty Story. In *Touring Pacific Cultures*, ed. by Kalissa Alexeyeff and Taylor John, pp. 73–88. Australia: ANU Press.

Boettke, Peter, Christopher Coyne, and Peter Leeson. (2008). "Institutional Stickiness and the New Development Economics." *American Journal of Economics and Sociology*, 67(2): 331–358.

Busygina, Irina, and Mikhail Filippov. (2024). *Non-Democratic Federalism and Decentralization: Lessons from Post-Soviet States*. London, UK: Routledge.

Collier, Paul. (2017). "Culture, Politics, and Economic Development." *Annual Review of Political Science*, 20: 111–125.

De Blij, Harm, and Peter Mueller. (2010). *Geography: Realms, Regions, and Concepts*. Hoboken, NJ: John Wiley & Sons.

De Juan, Alexander, and Jan Henryk Pierskalla. (2017). "The Comparative Politics of Colonialism and Its Legacies: An Introduction." *Politics & Society*, 45(2): 159–172.

Easterly, William, and Ross Levine. (2003). "Tropics, Germs, and Crops: How Endowments Influence Economic Development." *Journal of Monetary Economics*, 50: 3–40.

Engerman, Stanley, and Kenneth Sokoloff. (2002). "Factor Endowments, Inequality, and Paths of Development among New World Economies." *Economia*, 3(1): 41–88.

Faundez, Julio. (2016). "Douglass North's Theory of Institutions: Lessons for Law and Development." *Hague Journal on the Rule of Law*, 8: 373–91.

Fotiadis, Piers. (2009). The Strange Power of Maps: How Maps Work Politically and Influence Our Understanding of the World, School of Sociology, Politics, and International Studies. University of Bristol, Working Paper No. 6.

Greif, Avner. (1993). "Contract Enforceability and Economic Institutions, in Early Trade: The Maghribi Traders' Coalition." *American Economic Review*, 83: 525–548.

Guiso, Luigi, Paola Sapienza, and Luigi Zingales. (2006). "Does Culture Affect Economic Outcomes?" *Journal of Economic Perspectives*, 20(2): 23–48.

Haas, Peter, Robert Keohane, and Marc Levy. (1993). *Institutions for the Earth – Sources of Effective International Environmental Protection*. Cambridge, MA: The MIT Press.

Harrison, Lawrence, and Samuel Huntington. (2001). *Culture Matters: How Values Shape Human Progress*. New York: Basic Books.

Helpman, Elhanan. (2004). *The Mystery of Economic Growth*. Cambridge, MA: Harvard University Press.

Jowitt, Ken. (1992). *New World Disorder: The Leninist Extinction*. Berkeley: University of California Press.

Lewis, Oscar. (1975). *Five Families: Mexican Case Studies in the Culture of Poverty*. New York: Basic Books.

Lim, Timothy. (2010). *Doing Comparative Politics: An Introduction to Approaches and Issues*. Boulder, CA: Lynne Rienner Publishers.
Mamdani, Mahmood. (1996). *Citizen and Subject: Contemporary Africa and the Legacy of Late Colonialism*. Princeton, NJ: Princeton University Press.
March, James, and Johan Olsen. (1984). "The New Institutionalism: Organizational Factors in Political Life." *American Political Science Review*, 78: 734–749.
Maseland, Robert. (2018). "Is Colonialism History? The Declining Impact of Colonial Legacies on African Institutional and Economic Development." *Journal of Institutional Economics*, 14(2): 259–287.
Monmonier, Mark. (1996). *How to Lie with Maps*. Chicago; London: The University of Chicago Press.
Moseley, William, and Kavita Pandit. (2007). "Geography, Development and Underdevelopment: Introduction." In *The Introductory Reader in Human Geography*, ed. by William Moseley, David Lanegran, and Kavita Pandit. Hoboken, NJ: Wiley.
Moyo, Dambisa. (2009). *Dead Aid: Why Aid Is Not Working and How There Is a Better Way for Africa*. New York: Farrar, Straus, and Giroux.
Murphy, Kevin M., Andrei Shleifer, and Robert W. Vishny. (1991). "The Allocation of Talent: Implications for Growth." *Quarterly Journal of Economics*, 106(2): 503–530.
North, Douglass. (1989). "Institutions and Economic Growth: An Historical Introduction." *World Development*, 17(9): 1319–1332.
North, Douglass. (1990). *Institutions, Institutional Change, and Economic Performance*. Cambridge: Cambridge University Press.
North, Douglass. (1992). Transaction Costs, Institutions, and Economic Performance. International Centre for Economic Growth, San Francisco, Occasional Paper No. 30.
Patel, Dev, Justin Sandefur, and Arvind Subramanian. (2024). "A Requiem for Hyperglobalization: Why the World Will Miss History's Greatest Economic Miracle." *Foreign Affairs*, June 12.
Portes, Alejandro, and Jean Nava. (2017). "Institutions and National Development: A Comparative Study." *Revista Espanola de Sociologia*, 26(1): 9–31.
Rodrik, Dani. (1999). "Where Did All the Growth Go? External Shocks, Social Conflict, and Growth Collapses." *Journal of Economic Growth*, 4(4): 385–412.
Rodrik, Dani, Arvind Subramanian, and Francesco Trebbi. (2002). "Institutions Rule: The Primacy of Institutions over Geography and Integration in Economic Development." *Journal of Economic Growth*, 9(2): 131–165.
Ros, Jaime. (2013). *Rethinking Economic Development, Growth, and Institutions*. Oxford: Oxford University Press.
Wittenberg, Jason. (2015). "Conceptualizing Historical Legacies." *East European Politics and Societies*, 29(2): 366–378.
Wood, Denis. (2010). *Rethinking the Power of Maps*. New York; London: The Guilford Press.

Part I

1 Development, institutions, and geography

How do they fit together

Probably, the main concern about the development of mankind is not that nations and societies develop too slowly, but that they develop too unevenly, with increasing disparities and inequalities within nations, among nations, and among the regions of the world. This unevenness has both vertical and horizontal dimensions. The vertical dimension refers to differences between social groups within societies, while the horizontal dimension focuses on differences between spaces, territories, areas, and regions. I focus on the horizontal – spatial – dimension. However, the challenges to development posed by spatial inequalities are not limited to the *existence* of disparities and the fact that the development gap between rich and poor nations is widening (Estes 2019). An added complexity is that spatial unevenness of development tends to be "fixed" or "cemented" in the sense that the group of more rich and advanced nations, on the one hand, and the group of much less well-off and troubled, on the other, remain virtually unchanged in composition with time. The poorest countries in the world are in a large group concentrated in Africa – these are Central African Republic, Malawi, Burundi, Liberia, the DRC, Niger, and Afghanistan. The composition of this list has not principally changed over the decades.

If we zoom in and look not at nations but at macro-regions or climate zones, we will see almost the same gaps. As Gallup, Sachs, and Mellinger (1999) showed, the average income in Africa in the 1990s was roughly equal to the average income in Europe in 1820. According to Przeworski (2004), in 1820, the average per capita income in the tropical zone was 70% of the average income in the nontropical zone, and in the beginning of the 1990s, it was already only 25%. Immediate explanation that almost automatically comes to the minds of many – that is the malicious legacy of the European colonization, which slowed down the development of an entire continent. However, these persistent differences in income could hardly be explained solely by a heavy colonial past. There are states in Africa that were not under colonial rule; still their development trajectories are not much different from those of former European colonies. In addition, more than half a century has passed since decolonization; yet this period of sovereignty has not brought the desired pace of development to most African states. An even more troubling fact is that many of these disadvantaged regions have the highest population growth rates. Such a combination of slow development and increased population growth rates situation has profoundly negative social and political implications.

DOI: 10.4324/9781003496731-3

We need more explanations for the spatial unevenness of development. One possible approach (but certainly not the only one) is to look for these explanations in geography, institutions, and – in geography-and-institutions. Very, very schematically, the difference is made between "institutional hypothesis" and "geographical hypothesis." Acemoglu, Johnson, and Robinson (2001: 1369) laid down the "institutional hypothesis" as follows: "Countries with better institutions, more secure property rights, and less distortionary policies will invest more in physical and human capital and will use these factors more efficiently to achieve a greater level of income." The strong version of this hypothesis is the proposition that institutions not only matter for development but that they are the fundamental cause of long-run economic performance (Ros 2013: 367). "Geographical hypothesis" postulates that large and persistent differences in income per capita between countries are largely attributable to geographical advantages and disadvantages (first, to their location in different climate zones). There is a direct and strong impact of geography on levels of development (Ros 2013: 389). As farming continues to be the world's most important occupation, the differences in agricultural productivity among countries profoundly affect income per capita. Low levels of productivity result from soil formation and erosion, pests and parasites, the effects of outside temperature on plants, and the availability of water. According to Ros (2013: 390),

> The absence of frost in the tropics has adverse effects. Tropical areas are characterized by a wealth of insect life which competes with humans in consuming food crops. This is not the case in countries where frost kills exposed organisms. Frost slows the decay of organic materials (by killing the microorganisms in the soil) and preserves the fertility of the soil. It also helps to control the types of animal diseases that place a heavy burden on tropical agriculture. . . . There is also good evidence that the tropics constitute a bad health environment: the incidence of disease is considerably greater in the tropics than in temperate regions. This is another way in which climate affects income, by affecting the health of people and thus its human capital.

Does it make sense to set these hypotheses against each other? Are the geographical factors affecting development exhausted by climate and related variables? In the following, I discuss the main concepts applied in the book, those of development, institutions, and geographic factors and then turn to their possible interdependencies.

Development

Development is a term which is used indefinitely and generally has a positive connotation although little consensus exists today about what constitutes development. As Peet and Hartwick (2009) argued,

> development is a complex, contradictory, contentious phenomenon, reflective of the best of human aspirations, and yet, exactly for this reason, subject

to the most intense manipulation, liable to be used for purposes that reverse its original intent by people who feign good intentions, the more to gain power.

Indeed, this is not a very life-affirming characterization of development, although it does warn us of the pitfalls related to misuse of the concept. Probably, the simplest (though not necessarily primitive) interpretation of development is *development as economic growth.* Here the term is used as a quantitative concept usually measured by Gross National Product (GNP) per capita or Gross Domestic Product (GDP) per capita.

However, economic development entails growth accompanied by *changes* in the structure of production and employment, generally referred to as structural changes. This implies that economic growth (increase in GDP per capita) can occur without structural changes, as it happened, for instance, in oil-exporting countries like Nigeria, Venezuela, or Russia. Another situation of "growth without development" can arise because of the national authorities' policy of accelerated development of one sector of the economy (in many cases this is the defense-industrial complex), with no spillover effects on other sectors of the economy. This would be the case of today's Russia: the war against Ukraine has created incentives for the Kremlin to put maximum effort into develop the defense-industrial complex using huge amounts of public funds. The number of jobs and the income of those employed in the military-industrial sector are growing, but this comes at the expense of reduced spending on social development and investments in human capital. Can such a trajectory be considered development? Hardly.

To stress the importance of (positive) changes, development could be understood as *modernization.* This approach emphasizes the process of social change which is required to produce economic advancement and examines changes in social and political processes. Recent modernization studies emphasized the special characteristics that a *modern* state must have to be successful in the global world. It must be strong and capable but at the same time limited and accountable. It must be able to commit credibly both to the outside world (investors, international organizations) and to its own society. As I will show in Chapter 6, it is statehood that poses the greatest challenge to the development of African states.

Thus, development is not purely an economic phenomenon but rather a complex multidimensional process. For instance, it is impossible to conclude that the state is developing if we do not know the answers to the question about how state revenues are distributed among different social groups, that is, the question of inequality. Reducing inequalities and empowering marginalized groups are important and integral elements of national development that do not necessarily go hand in hand with the goal of enhanced economic growth. As Seers (1977) formulated, besides providing economic growth and structural changes, "genuine" development should lead to decrease in poverty and malnutrition, decline in income inequalities, and improvement in employment situation. The problem of inequalities has plagued Latin American nations for decades, acting as a powerful barrier to development (see Chapter 7).

Another important question about development would be who and to what extent benefits from the current model of the state and its policies. Are the gains not privatized by individual interests (groups)? Extensive research was devoted to proving that narrow-group interests are largely responsible for the observed differences between countries in productivity levels. These groups do not only just enrich themselves at the expense of the nation but are able and interested in blocking the use of technological innovations that are crucial for development. Parente and Prescott (2000) argued that differences in levels of innovation between countries did not arise as a reflection of some fundamental difference in "stocks of useful knowledge," which differ from society to society. Rather, these differences were the result of policies pursued by each state that limited, in many cases, the use of advanced techniques and technologies. They made the important point that many of the restrictions and barriers are enacted to protect the interests of groups investing in current production processes. These groups supported government regulations that directly or indirectly prevented the effective use of the most advanced technologies. Vested interests may hinder reforms, leading countries to get stuck in the "middle-income trap." This argumentation explains well the situation in today's Russia (see Chapter 10).

How powerful and pervasive vested interests could be was beautifully illustrated by Mancur Olson in his book *The Rise and Decline of Nations* (1982). Olson analyzed in detail how, because of lobbying by interest groups for certain public policies, effective innovation was blocked, resulting in losses for society as a whole. Moreover, Olson hypothesized that external shocks, such as a military defeat (as happened to Germany and Japan in World War II), could create the conditions for subsequent technological breakthroughs. This was because shocks disrupted the existing system of interests that hindered innovation for one simple reason: their rents depended on the use of old technologies. In addition to defeat in war, Olson identified two other mechanisms for destroying the old system of interests: revolutions and integration (e.g., within the European Union, see Chapter 4).

In his book *Development as Freedom* (1999), Nobel Prize winner Amartya Sen emphasized that assessment of development must go well beyond national GNP and income information. These economic indicators

> leave out the question of the distribution of that GNP among the population. It is, of course, possible for a country to have an expansion of GNP per head, while its distribution becomes more unequal, possibly even the poorest groups going down absolutely in terms of their own real incomes.
>
> (Sen 1999: 13)

Then, the real income of a person tells at best the extent of that person's well-being. But what kind of life does this person succeed? To answer that question, a more integral approach is needed, according to Sen.

Sen argued that development is enhanced by democracy and liberalism, especially the protection of human rights. Such rights, especially freedom of the press, speech, assembly, and so forth, increase the likelihood of good governance – honest, clean, and professional. That no democracy has ever experienced famine is due to the governments that have to win elections, face public criticism, and have strong incentives to undertake measures to avert famines and other catastrophes. As a process, development is the expansion of human freedom. It implies the removal of major sources of unfreedom: poverty, tyranny, poor economic opportunities, social deprivation, neglect of public facilities, as well as intolerance or overactivity of repressive states.

Sen's ideas have been instrumental in the thinking of the United Nations Development Program (UNDP) on human development, including the creation of the Human Development Index (HDI), which is a composite index that measures the average achievement in a country in three basic dimensions of human development: a long and healthy life, as measured by life expectancy at birth; knowledge, as measured by the adult literacy rate and the combined gross enrolment ratio for primary, secondary and tertiary schools; and a decent standard of living, as measured by GDP per capita in purchasing power parity in US dollars. While the concept of human development is much broader than any single composite index can measure, the HDI offers a powerful alternative to income as a summary measure of human well-being.[1] All in all, developed societies for Amartya Sen and his numerous followers can consist of only free people. And the way to free people is paved by good institutions.

Development is path dependent (Lipset and Rokkan 1967; North 1990; Skocpol 1979). Most generally, path dependence means that where we go next depends not only on where we are now but also upon where we have been. The key idea here is that in a sequence of events, the later events are not (completely) independent from those that occurred in the past. Two different approaches to path dependence can be described by the images of the "trodden trail" and the "road juncture." While the first view stresses the spontaneous evolution of an institution and its subsequent long-term entrenchment, the second looks at the interdependent sequence of events that structure the alternatives for future institutional changes (Ebbinghaus 2005).

The "trodden path" implies the subsequent repeated use by other actors of the once-chosen path. Once taken, the path stabilizes with a phenomenon called "lock-in." The "lock-in" in path dependence means, in fact, a lock-in to something "bad" or at least a lock-out of something "better." It constitutes an inferior outcome. The irreversibility of this path derives from the fact that actors have already invested in the dominant path and are thus unwilling to switch to an alternative one (Liebowitz and Margolis 1999: 982). This approach therefore suggests that path-dependent processes can reinforce *inefficient paths*. And besides that, such deterministic approach to path dependence necessarily claims the inflexibility of institutions (Ebbinghaus 2005).

The "road juncture" approach to path dependence implies that one of the available alternative pathways must be chosen to continue a journey. According to North, "path-dependence is a way to narrow conceptually the choice set and link decision making through time. It is not a story of inevitability in which the past predicts the future" (North 1990: 98–99). This approach is actively used in historical-institutionalist studies: the concept of path dependence is taken in a broader, nondeterministic sense; "path" does not describe the emergence and persistence of an institution through the repeated uniform basic decisions of individual actors but through the long-term developmental pathway of an institution, or complex institutional arrangement, shaped by and then further adapted by collective actors (Prado and Trebilcock 2009: 14). Unlike the deterministic "trodden path" that assumes chance events will have long-term consequences, the developmental approach focuses on the particular historical origins of institutions. Historical-institutionalists see institutions emerging from not accidental but rather deliberate choices by collective actors at critical junctures. Even if it is often impossible to precisely predict a critical juncture, for instance, the fall of the Berlin wall in 1989, retrospective analysis can reveal the factors leading to the emergence of a new institution as the result of the interactions of collective action by individual and corporate actors in each historical situation (Prado and Trebilcock 2009: 16) Dani Rodrik (2007) has emphasized the role of path dependence in generating the wide diversity of institutions and policies observable around the world, including among developed countries.

Institutions

Douglas North (1990: 3) defined "institutions are the rules of the game in a society or, more formally, are the humanly devised constraints that shape human interaction." North's interest in institutions was preceded by his extensive work in European economic history; his two major books are *The Rise of the Western World – A New Economic History* (1973) and *Structure and Change in Economic History* (1981). According to Faundez (2016: 374),

> [T]he main lesson he draws from this work is that sustained economic growth requires an efficient system of property rights so that individuals can channel their efforts into activities that will bring private returns close to the social rate of return. The way economies move towards achieving better institutions is through a process of adaptive efficiency. The focus of adaptive efficiency is on the rules that shape economic evolution over time and on the willingness of its players to acquire knowledge and skills to develop innovative solutions for resolving problems (North 1990: 80). Adaptive efficiency brings about improvements to the overall institutional structure, but it is also conditioned by it.

As North argued, institutions are established to reduce the obstacles arising from imperfect and asymmetrical information. These obstacles are described as transaction costs. North distinguished two kinds of constraints: formal and informal. Together, these constraints comprise what he called the rules of the game (North 1990: 4). For North, the institutions critical for nation's development are property rights. These rights are secure only when the state can make a credible commitment that it will respect them. Generally, the concept of institutions was a cognitive breakthrough in social sciences which allowed scholars to offer new explanations for many phenomena and processes, including development.

Later, the book of North, Wallis, and Weingast *Violence and Social Orders: A Conceptual Framework for Interpreting Recorded Human History* (2009) became an important contribution to the study of development and, even more important for us, it explicitly linked development with institutions. Let us quote Robert Bates (2010), who in his review of the book summarized its main findings in a few sentences. In his words, the book

> imparts a central lesson: that politics – and, in particular, the use of coercion – determines the quality of life to which people can aspire: the level of prosperity, the degree of security, and the ranges within which they vary. Because of differences in the manner in which power is deployed, some societies collapse in response to shocks whereas others prove adaptive. Over time, those that grow for longer periods and collapse less frequently achieve higher levels of income. Throughout history, the powerful have tried to combine in order to create rents and to restrict access to them – this is the "natural state." But, in a few societies, there is "open entry" and, when combined with other features, *these are the few that develop*. Among the key factors distinguishing "open entry" from "natural" societies, two receive special emphasis: the existence of *impersonal norms* and the emergence of permanently lived organizations. The first facilitates the circulation of elites: all who perform are entitled to be rewarded. The second amplifies the impact of the first while also ensuring continuity: because organizations possess more clout than individuals, they enable citizens to exert influence even when not holding office and, because the lifetime of an organization exceeds that of its members, organizations provide stability where one might otherwise expect flux resulting from the impact of faction. Two other differences stand out. In natural societies, wealth and power are held by the same people and they are armed. Under such circumstances, politics resembles a temporary truce in which small deviations can trigger violent and costly reprisals. Because the military constitutes a profession divorced from politics in open access societies, such deviations are less consequential and, therefore, less unsettling. Secondly, in natural societies, politicians intervene in markets in ways that generate opportunities for rationing, thereby securing the resources with which to grant favors and to build political followings. In contrast, open access societies are based on market-like principles. Ideas compete for adherents and a few barriers limit political entry. When hit by external shocks, then, open access societies are better positioned to adapt, with new leaders coming to the fore or old leaders championing new policies.

These impersonal norms are institutions. There is a fundamental consensus among researchers concerning the recognition of the key role of effectively functioning economic and political institutions for the growth of the population's well-being and the development of the national economies. Institutions determine the real capabilities of the state, its state capacity, and at the same time encourage good governance. On the contrary, weak and corrupt states are responsible for the most serious economic and social problems in many countries of the world.

Importantly, institutions are subject to change over time. Both the Magna Charta and the Glorious Revolution were institutional changes because they substantively changed political power and could not be simply reversed the next day, thereby setting the stage for substantial economic change (Acemoglu and Robinson 2006). And institutions are also the subject of choice though this choice is conditioned by path dependency. Both institutional changes and institutional choices are critical to developmental perspectives of nations.

Every state has its basic institution – a national constitution. Of great importance is the choice of the institutions of the "first order" – between presidency and parliamentarism, between federal or unitary order. A constitutional revision in favor of the presidency or parliamentarianism, if it happens, turns out to be one of the most important institutional decisions in terms of the outcomes. For many researchers, the institutional choice in favor of presidential regimes appeared to be the key explanation for the poor quality of democracy in Latin America and post-Soviet countries and even the collapse of democratic regimes. The opposition between the presidency and the parliamentary decisions has become a classic example of the debate in political science about the "best" institutional form for economic and political development. Research has gone through several stages – from attempts to present one institutional form as "the best in all respects" to identifying the relative advantages and disadvantages of each form, then to recognizing the importance of differences both between institutional regimes and within one type of regime, and finally to recognizing the key role of other, complementary institutions of "lower orders" for understanding how the main institutional differences work. For instance, institutions supporting autonomy of subnational regions (that are the institutions of federalism and decentralization) have a significant positive effect on income, suggesting that strong subnational institutions enhance development when not dominated by national institutions (Mitton 2016).

Today, scholars recognize the fundamental need to consider separately different factors (political system characteristics, such as the course of reforms, democratic development, resilience, polarization, and fragmentation) as depending not only on the type of regime itself (presidential or parliamentary) but also on the interactions of the type of regime with other institutional factors (see Busygina and Filippov 2012, Chapter 7). Importantly, the rules that constrain human interactions are not only formal like presidentialism or federalism. They also span a wide set of informal norms of behavior, shared beliefs, and acceptable means of enforcement.

The role of institutions has become one of the most popular research areas in development economics over the last 30 years. Rodrik, Subramanian, and Trebbi (2002) made an argument about the primacy of institutions over geography and integration in economic development. These are the institutions that regulate property rights, rule of law, and political and economic competition. For instance, research by Acemoglu et al. (2019) suggested that, on average, democratization increases GDP per capita by about 20% in the long run. However, that does not mean that one can just introduce elections and hope to get the observed average boost-effect. Incentives, beliefs, and professional norms – the pillars of state capacity – are crucial to explain differences in institutional performance and policy effectiveness.[2]

According to Acemoglu, Johnson, and Robinson (2002a), the importance of institutions increased with the beginning of industrialization and the acceleration of technological development. Generally, the institution theory implied that differences in institution caused different long-run comparative growth. However, the study of the specific impact of particular institutions on development proved problematic. For instance, Przeworski, without questioning the general importance of institutions, pointed out that вопрос о том, which institutions are important, and in which territories, didn't get a definitive answer.

Perhaps, the most difficult problem to solve in relation to institutions is their endogeneity. The point is that the relationship between the quality of institutions and the level of income is possible both ways – good institutions explain a high level of income, but the level of income itself can serve as an explanatory factor for good or bad institutions. But in any case, institutions matter – and a lot!

The embeddedness of institutions affects the way they function as well as their effect on economic outcomes. Institutions are embedded in a country's social and cultural contexts; but they are also embedded in a country's geography.

Geographic factors

It may seem that it is much easier to discuss geographical factors than institutions. (Because, as economists and political scientists sometimes believe, geography itself is much simpler or perhaps even more primitive than economics and political science.) However, this is not at all true, especially if the question is about the relationship between geographical factors (variables) and development. The question of what exactly we consider geographic factors is not at all simple.

Let's look at geographic factors. I would divide them into three groups.

First, these are the factors that we can call "absolute" – those that Mother Nature itself has provided nations and societies with *(first nature geography)*. These factors include climate, soil, altitude, and topography. This list also includes the spread of diseases, especially malaria (the spread of which significantly complicated and limited colonization processes).

Given by Mother Nature, these factors are still subject to change caused by human activity (often thoughtless), and these changes may cause shifts in approaches to development. As a rule, these changes are not revolutionary (unless we are talking about man-made disasters like Chernobyl), they proceed incrementally. However, they accumulate, and at some point they can no longer be ignored by elites and societies (the awareness of the threats and risks associated with these changes is slow, this awareness is also accumulating gradually). Thus, economic growth may be still central to mainstream economics, but nature pays the price through pollution, waste, and climate change. It was back in the 1970s when economist and pioneer in climate change economics William Nordhaus convincingly justified the necessity of transitioning from a "cowboy economy" to a "spaceship economy" (Nordhaus 1998). In the former, he wrote, "we could afford to use our resources profligately," and "the environment could be used as a sink without becoming fouled." But, in the spaceship economy, "great attention must be paid to the sources of life and to the dumps where our refuse is piled." He added that "things which have traditionally been treated as free goods – air, water, quiet, natural beauty – must now be treated with the same care as other scarce goods." Now, as the climate crisis has become ever harder to ignore, more people are questioning whether infinite economic growth is possible on a planet of finite resources. Mainstream environmentalism is still firmly entrenched in the idea of "green growth." The World Bank, the OECD, and national governments rely on the idea of being able to "decouple" growth from its ecological impact. The general argument for "green growth" rests on the assumption that technology is the solution and salvation. An alternative approach would be degrowth. Proponents of degrowth argue that to date, decoupling has happened only in wealthy economies that have outsourced emissions-heavy sectors like manufacturing to economies like China and that globally the correlation is still strong. "Degrowthers" think that we should reverse the central logic of economic systems that prioritize growth over human and ecological well-being, and then we would not miss the furious activity that is keeping a minority of the human population in must-have products and ever-more material wealth.[3]

Second, this is a group of geographic factors which relate to states built and rebuilt by the rulers and which have emerged during the historical development of mankind (*second nature geography*). These are the attributes of states – territorial size, shape, and geographic location (see Chapter 2). These geographical factors are not institutions: they are certainly "constraints shaping human interaction," although not "humanly devised" constraints in the sense of an institution. However, these factors had a very serious impact on the development prospects of states. For instance, geographic location of the countries could have significant effects on income growth because of the transportation costs (Gallup, Sachs and Mellinger 1999). For centuries, states fought with each other for access to the sea. The number and composition of neighbors condition states' foreign policy.

According to Ros,

> [G]eographical location affects openness to trade, with potentially beneficial effects on specialization, allocative efficiency, and the facilitation of technology transfer. Proximity to the ocean, for example, affects a country's ability to engage in international trade. Distance from the major centers of economic activity also affects a country's openness to trade as transport costs increase with distance from major centers.
>
> (Ros 2013: 392)

Sachs (2012) has emphasized that geographic location was the most important explanation of why landlocked Bolivia has been growing more slowly in recent decades than Vietnam. Long coastline and location in booming East Asia has made Vietnam attractive for foreign direct investments in tourism and manufacturing.

Finally, there is another, *third*, group of factors which I call "geographical institutions." These are institutions (as defined by North), but at the same time they are highly geographical, that is, territorial. Such "geographical institutions" include borders (both between and within states), which I discuss in Chapter 3, as well as federalism and territorial autonomy. Both federalism and territorial autonomy are forms of states' spatial organization that significantly impact their development (Sánchez 2007).

Federalism implies the existence of autonomous territorial communities in the state, ensuring the principle of "unity in (territorial) diversity" and supporting territorial integration in large states. According to Robinson (1961: 1),

> [F]ederation is the most geographically expressive of all political systems. It is based on the existence of regional differences and recognizes claims of the component areas to perpetuate their individual characters. Federation does not create unity out of diversity rather it enables the two to coexist.

Dikshit (1971) considered geography to be the basis of federalism. In his book *The Political Geography of Federalism: An Inquiry into Origin and Stability* (1975: 10), Dikshit has identified two reasons why federalism is the most expressive form of government. The first is that federalism is based on the existence of regional differences or a sense of locality. Second, federalism implies significant regional autonomy, so the regions in federal states remain highly articulated. This means that spatial interactions in a federation are recognized most clearly. A federal solution allows political institutions to be embedded in a national geographical context and thereby stimulate development. In the book, I show how the federal solution has worked in this regard in the United States, Canada, Australia, and elsewhere. In the United States and Canada, the federal solution has made it possible to combine the geographic expansion of the country's territory with the maintenance of a democratic institutional design through different types of federal arrangements.

Territorial autonomy implies specific institutional arrangements between central state and territorially concentrated minority group to accommodate demands for self-governance. These arrangements work in very different ways; some have brought about virtual sovereignty for the entity concerned while others provide for a very limited autonomy (Benedikter 2009: 9). As an option for managing separatism and therefore supporting political and social stability in a country, territorial autonomy is found across world regions, regime types, and levels of development. As Benedikter (2009: 63) argued, geography is not a criterion, but it matters as a driving rationale for autonomy. The forms of territorial autonomy include democratic (like Québec in Canada), post-conflict (Aceh in Indonesia), indigenous autonomy (Nunavut in Canada, Mosquito Coast in Nicaragua), and authoritarian autonomy (Xinjiang, Tibet in China) (Barter 2022).

The developmental outcomes of territorial autonomy are as diverse as its forms. For instance, Mosquito Coast autonomy in Nicaragua did not lead to a reduction but rather to an increase in polarization of the country. Nicaragua is the largest country in Central America but the least developed. Neighboring nations, with similar geographic conditions, demonstrated higher levels of development than Nicaragua. Nicaragua is highly centralized, with the exception of autonomous regions along the Atlantic coast. But autonomy, though officially recognized, remains rather a formality, and these regions highly depend on the center (Sánchez 2007).

What is the role of geography in development?

It would be ridiculous to deny the role of institutions in development. However, it would be as ridiculous to consider institutions "everything" for development. Jeffrey Sachs (2003a) warned against uncritical infatuation with institutions as explanatory for development to the detriment of other factors:

> The vague concept of "institutions" has become, almost tautologically, the intermediate target for all efforts to improve an economy. If an economy is malfunctioning, the reasoning goes, something must be wrong with its institutions. In fact, recent papers have argued that institutions explain nearly everything about a country's level of economic development and that resource constraints, physical geography, economic policies, geopolitics, and other aspects of internal social structure, such as gender roles and inequalities between ethnic groups, have little or no effect.

I would suggest considering this rather harsh judgment of Sachs as an indication that it would be wrong to reduce explanations of the development of countries to an institute hypothesis.

How do geographical factors affect the development of nations? I start with the "first nature" geographical factors.

There is a group of studies supporting the idea of *direct influence* of geographic factors on development (geographical explanation). This is an old idea that could be traced as far back as the work of Montesquieu *The Spirit of the Law* (1748), where he in particular wrote: "Approach the south and you will think you are leaving morality itself, the passions become more vivacious and multiply crimes." Today, this statement sounds like a funny illustration of geographic determinism. But the idea that levels of per capita income and other economic development measurements were strongly correlated with geographic variables such as spread of diseases (in particular, malaria risk), distance from coast, and climate conditions find support today. Jeffrey Sachs gave convincing examples of how "bad" geography may hamper development. He presented evidence that production technology in the tropics has lagged behind temperate zone technology in the two critical areas of agriculture and health, and this in turn opened a substantial income gap between climate zones. The difficulty of mobilizing energy resources in tropical economies was emphasized as another significant contributor to the income gap (Sachs 2001). Besides that, the disease lowers the returns on foreign investments and raises the transaction costs of international trade, migration, and tourism in malarial regions.

In his bestseller *Guns, Germs, and Steel: The Fates of Human Societies* (1997: 405–407), Jared Diamond stressed that "all developments of economically complex, socially stratified, politically centralized societies beyond the level of small nascent chiefdoms were based on food production." He pointed out to "the striking differences between the long-term histories of peoples of the different continents have been due not to innate differences in the peoples themselves but to differences in their environments." Continents differ in many parameters and indicators (in fact, in all parameters one could imagine), but Diamond identified those which appeared to him to be the most important ones for the development of societies. Continents differ in the wild plant and animal species available as starting materials for domestication. This domestication was concentrated first on each continent only in a few small favorable areas. Plant and animal species migrated then to other areas, though the rates of diffusion and migration greatly differed among continents:

> [T]hey were most rapid in Eurasia, because of its east-west major axis and its relatively modest ecological and geographical barriers. Diffusion was slower in Africa and especially in the Americas, because of those continents' north-south major axes and geographic and ecological barriers.

Populated area was also an important factor:

> [A] larger area or population means more potential inventors, more competing societies, more innovations available to adopt – and more pressure to adopt and retain innovations, because societies failing to do so will tend to be eliminated by competing societies. That fate befell African pygmies and many other hunter-gatherer populations displaced by farmers.

Diamond drew parallels between migration of species and of technological innovations and political institutions arguing that "most societies acquire much more from other societies than they invent themselves. Thus, diffusion and migration within a continent contribute importantly to the development of its societies." Generally, this book is a very interesting and comprehensive study that seeks to identify the roots and prime causes of the differences in development between continents.

Other studies focused on more specific cases of relationship between geography and development. Gallup, Sachs, and Mellinger (1998) explored the effects of location and climate on various indicators of economic development through channels of relative transport costs, disease burdens, and agricultural productivity. Masters and McMillan (2000) pointed to the positive impact of winter frost on productivity and thus on the level of economic development in general. And later, Haber (2012) has taken climatological variable and compared tropical "pineapple kingdoms" to the fractionalized nature of agriculture in Europe. In the tropics, many crops like pineapple tended to require larger economies of scale relative to crops in temperate regions. This in turn led to high incentives for more authoritarian control. A similar process occurred in arid climates due to centrally controlled irrigation from large water sources like rivers.

In addition, geographical factors affect not only the development of nations but also the development of regions and localities within them. There could be (and are) significant variations between subnational regions in terms of development, and regional geographies contribute to this variation. Geography, together with institutions and culture, is relevant for local development; it is among the main reasons for persisting development differentials (Crescenzi and Percoco 2013). Mitton studied the determinants of economic development in a dataset covering 1,867 subnational regions from 101 countries, focusing on within-country effects of geography and institutions. He found that several geographical factors had significant explanatory power for within-country differences in per-capita GDP, including terrain ruggedness, tropical climate, ocean access, temperature range, storm risk, and natural resources such as oil, diamonds, or iron (Mitton 2016). Importantly, this is the situation not in poorer nations only but in richer and well-off nations as well. For instance, in the Appalachian region of the United States, the initial geographic conditions were very important for economic development, having significant effects lasting hundreds of years (Cliton and Barrutieta 2006). In Australia, Tasmania is the only federal state that is not located on the Australian mainland; it is separated from mainland by Bass Strait. From the very beginning "islandness" has seriously complicated Tasmania's development (Stratford 2008), and despite the economic uptick of recent years, Tasmania is still the poorest Australian state.

Finally, the effects of geographical factors on economic development can be different (in fact, the opposite) from the global perspective and from the continental one. Nunn and Puga (2012) explored the effects of ruggedness. They found that although rugged terrain hindered trade and most productive activities, negatively affecting income globally, rugged terrain within Africa afforded protection to those being raided during the slave trades. Since the slave trades retarded subsequent economic development, ruggedness within Africa has also had a historic indirect positive effect on income.

In addition to having a direct impact on development, geographical factors can influence development *together* with institutions. Sachs (2003b) explained the effects of *different combinations of institutional and geographic factors*:

> First are the countries, and regions within countries, in which institutions, policies, and geography are all reasonably favorable. The coastal regions of east Asia (coastal China and essentially all of Korea, Taiwan Province of China, Hong Kong SAR, Singapore, Thailand, Malaysia, and Indonesia) have this beneficent combination and, as a result, have all become closely integrated with global production systems and benefited from large inflows of foreign capital. Second are the regions that are relatively well endowed geographically but, for historical reasons, have had poor governance and institutions. These include the central European states, whose proximity to Western Europe brought them little benefit during the socialist regime. For such countries, institutional reforms are paramount. And, finally, there are impoverished regions with an unfavorable geography, such as most of sub-Saharan Africa, central Asia, large parts of the Andean region, and the highlands of Central America, where globalization has not succeeded in

raising living standards and may, indeed, have accelerated the brain drain and capital outflows from the region. The countries that have experienced the severest economic failures in the recent past have all been characterized by initial low levels of income and small populations (and hence small internal markets) that live far from coasts and are burdened by disease, especially AIDS, tuberculosis, and malaria. These populations have essentially been trapped in poverty because of their inability to meet the market test for attracting private capital inflows.

Sachs's diagnosis was that both institutions and geography matter for development.

However, on the world map we see countries for which this direct link, "geography–development," seems not to work. One of them is Australia, which did not have the conducive climate to expect booming agriculture and, besides that, was geographically isolated. Acemoglu and Robinson in "Why Nations Fail?" (2012: 278) told a story of how a country without ideal natural factors was able to achieve high-level economic development. Why? And here come the institutions as "convicts were allowed to become entrepreneurs and hire other convicts." Property rights, rule of law, and low corruption rates were the critical institutions that promoted economic growth and social change.

The "reversal of fortune" argument provides a deeper understanding of the relationship between geography, institutions, development – and also time. A geographical explanation of development postulates that as geography remains the same, income differences should also remain stable over time. Starting factors directly determine economic outcomes. However, this is not the case. Five hundred years ago, the level of development – state capacity, living standards, and technological advancement – was much higher in China (Ming Dynasty) or in the rising Ottoman Empire, than in Europe that was weak, backward, and horribly fragmented. In the late fifteenth century, the fortune of Europe reversed, and by 1914, Europeans had conquered 84% of the globe and surpassed all other political entities in measures of economic development (Hoffman 2015). According to Acemoglu, Johnson, and Robinson (2002a), originally more developed systems were accumulating institutional failures: they adopted inferior institutions, which blocked opportunities to accelerate modernization. On the contrary, the Western European nations advanced in new technologies and social organization. Another example of reversal is the countries that Europe colonized after its own reversal of fortune. Two Americas, the richest civilizations in 1500 at the time of colonization (Aztecs and Incas), have switched places with previously backward civilizations of the North.

As Acemoglu, Johnson, and Robinson (2002a: 1233) wrote,

> [T]he simplest version of the geography hypothesis emphasizes the *time-invariant* effects of geographic variables, such as climate and disease, on work effort and productivity, and therefore predicts that nations and areas that were relatively rich in 1500 should also be relatively prosperous today.

This hypothesis was clearly not supported.

> More sophisticated versions of this hypothesis focus on the *time-varying* effects of geography. Certain geographic characteristics that were not useful, or even harmful, for successful economic performance in 1500 may turn out to be beneficial later. A possible example, which we call "the temperate drift hypothesis," argues that areas in the tropics had an early advantage, but later agricultural technologies, such as the heavy plow, crop rotation systems, domesticated animals, and high-yield crops, have favored countries in the temperate areas.
>
> Another version of the sophisticated geography hypothesis could be those certain geographic characteristics, such as the presence of coal reserves or easy access to the sea, facilitated industrialization.
>
> (Acemoglu, Johnson and Robinson 2002a: 1234)

Acemoglu, Johnson, and Robinson did not find significant evidence that these geographic factors were directly converted into the sources of development and caused industrialization.

Gallup, Sachs, and Mellinger (1998: 29) claimed that effects of geography were *mediated* by policies and institutions: "Good policy and good geography may have a tendency to go together. . . . The result is that natural differences in growth potential tend to be amplified by the choice of economic policies." In other words, their central claim was that geography matters, even when controlled for policies and institutions.

There are other studies that confirmed this mediation effect of geography. McArthur and Sachs (2001) identified several main channels of influence of geographical variables on the level of economic development. *First*, geography affects income directly through institutions. To take Hall and Jones's study (1999) as an example, they showed that during colonization Europeans carried with them institutions, above all secure property rights and the rule of law. Thus, the impact of geographical factors is indirect, acting through institutions. At the same time, in the early nineteenth century, European colonists, learning from bitter experiences, avoided settling *en masse* in regions where tropical diseases were prevalent, and these regions fell under the rigid exploitation mainly by local elites while Europeans preferred to distantly control these administrations. Europeans were simply too few to determine the institutional development of these territories.

Second, geography can influence institutions indirectly, through technology. In this case, climate and/or the spread of disease affects technology, which in turn affects institutions, such as free or slave labor, and institutions affect the level and character of economic development. Engerman and Sokoloff (1997) applied this logic to show how the tropical climate in the Caribbean led to a plantation economy based on slave labor, which in turn seriously stymied market reforms in those countries and the transition to sustainable development.

Third, geography can influence development both through institutions and directly by influencing productivity. Indeed, there are many direct geographic effects – geography affects population health, growth patterns, food production, etc. For example, MacArthur and Sachs (2001) proved the influence of geographical factors on population health. Tropical climates are "laden" with many infectious diseases (above all, malaria), which are much less common and better controlled in temperate zones. Tropical climate zones also show lower agricultural productivity than temperate zones. These are direct effects of geography. Beyond these, an indirect effect of unfavorable geography may indeed be the reason for more extractive and predatory institutions that maximize rents to narrow ruling groups and are detrimental to society.

Acemoglu, Johnson, and Robinson (2002b) provided a remarkable illustration of the importance of institutions and geography to the economic development of nations. We know that from the early sixteenth to the late eighteenth centuries Western Europe has experienced an unprecedented economic boom that made the territory substantially richer than Asia and Eastern Europe. At the same time, the rapid and long-term economic growth was limited to a small number of states – Britain, the Netherlands, France, Spain, and Portugal. All these countries shared the same geographical advantage – they were located at the Atlantic coast, and thus were directly involved in international trade and colonization of new territories. It was the rise of the European Atlantic Europe. Within this group of countries, however, there were significant differences: Britain and the Netherlands developed significantly faster and more steadily than Spain and Portugal. The explanation for this difference in development reflected institutional differences, but the initial condition for such an incredible rise of this group of countries was a favorable geographic location (see more about this in Chapter 4). Favorable geography created premises for accelerated development; some countries were able to promote it through institutional change while the others were not.

The studies mentioned here reflect the difference in the views of scholars but still allow to formulate general ideas:

(1) Both institutions and geography matter for economic development of nations.
(2) Geographical advantages (and disadvantages) are not absolute but relative; they may change over time under factors like technology or globalization.
(3) Geography (location) may create premises for accelerated development, but these are institutions that determine strategic winners among the nations.
(4) Geographical factors may have a direct influence on development or affect development indirectly, influencing the choice of institutions.

Let's now look at "second nature" geography.

As Bosker and Garretsen (2006) argued, geography can contribute to the explanation of the level of economic development in a different way if a country's geography is viewed not as a set of absolute indicators but from a relative perspective. This search for a new perspective on geographic variables has been driven by the low importance that researchers have given to the so-called second nature geography. The studies were primarily focused on absolute variables – distance to the equator, climate, and the spread of disease – with little research on relative variables, such as, for instance, a country's geographic location relative to other countries, that is, the effects of neighborhood.

Several studies explored the channels of influence of institutional design in one country (or group of countries) on its neighbors. Supporters of "new economic geography" argued, among other things, that income of a state, other things being equal, will be higher if that state is located in proximity to other high-income countries, in other words, if these countries are clustered. The European Union would be the best example: its member states are not only clustered, but this clustering also has an institutional framework. Non-European high-income countries are also clustered – Canada and the United States, Japan and South Korea, and Australia and New Zealand.

On the other side, misguided economic policies and low-quality institutions in one country, and the negative economic trends associated with them, negatively affect income levels in neighboring countries (Easterly and Levine 2003). Ades and Chua (1997) found convincing evidence that instability in neighboring states (e.g., the frequency and the number of revolutions and coups) has a negative impact on economic development in the country of study. Instability in the region undermines international trade, an effect that is particularly pronounced in the case of landlocked countries that depend on trade routes through neighboring countries. Moreover, instability and political conflicts that disrupt transit trade routes can have significant consequences for exceedingly long areas. For example, political tensions between Russia and Ukraine (which existed long before the war launched by Russia against Ukraine in 2022) have repeatedly caused panic in the European states, which were overly concerned about the possible disruption of oil and gas supplies from Russia. As Murdoch and Sandler (2002) argued, civil war in a neighboring country leads to disruptions in economic development "at home."

The process of institutional borrowing proceeds more smoothly if institutions are borrowed from a neighboring country. Simmons and Elkins (2004) have shown that countries would, with higher probability, copy or, on the contrary, avoid certain institutional decisions or practices from neighboring countries. Bosker and Garretsen (2006) conducted an analysis on a sample of 147 countries and proved that institutions do matter in explaining a country's level of economic development (as measured by per capita income). However, it is not only a country's own institutions that are important, as it was argued earlier, but also the quality of institutions in neighboring countries. The results of the study once again confirmed that the development of a country does not take place in isolation. When the geography of institutions is excluded from consideration, a skew occurs: the factor of the country's own institutions becomes almost the only explanation of the level of economic development of the country.

Researchers of the regional integration processes have long paid attention to the geography of institutions, more precisely, to the "neighborhood effect" of institutions. For example, one of the motivations for Germany's inclusion to the European Economic Communities (EEC) – the community of democratic nations – in the early 1950s was the expectation that close neighborhood and cooperation with other EEC countries would be an important factor in the political and economic modernization of postwar Germany. And this is what happened. The factor of Germany's membership in the EEC (then EU) is considered to be one of the most important for the German postwar *Wirtschaftswunder* (Razeen 1995; Leigh 1975). Later, a special "neighborhood policy" was developed in the European Union aimed, among other things, at the Europeanization of the neighboring states and creation of a "belt of friends" preventing conflicts and tensions and supporting security at the external borders of the European Union. The idea was to maintain the attractiveness of the "European model" for neighboring countries without offering them prospects for membership but rather by deepening economic and political cooperation. Europeanization was understood as a norm (institutions) transfer from the territory of the European Union to the neighboring countries (Busygina 2018).

The Association of Southeast Asian Nations (ASEAN) is a very different organization. This organization consists of countries with completely dissimilar institutional and political systems with different levels of development. The idea of institutional borrowing of Singapore's successful experience may look attractive in theory, but it is practically impossible, and these fundamental differences in institutional development trajectories are one of the reasons why the depth of ASEAN's integration process is not (and will be not) comparable to that of the European Union.

These research results have important practical relevance, particularly for experts and practitioners from international organizations like the IMF and the World Bank. These results suggest that economic development in one country cannot be stimulated in isolation, without considering what is happening in neighboring countries. Reform assistance efforts in one country are doomed to be very limited or ineffective if that country remains surrounded by states with poor quality institutions. Thus, it would make sense to assist countries not on an individual basis but to think more about elaboration of a consistent and comprehensive strategy for a wider region. This applies first to the efforts of international organizations in the African continent.

In this chapter, I have presented – very schematically – the main concepts of this book and their possible relationships and channels of mutual influence. Geography and institutions influence development through many pathways. The following historical processes on different continents that I present in Part II will allow us to make observations about this variety of situations.

Notes

1 Asian Century Institute – Amartya Sen on development as freedom.
2 Institutions matter for growth and prosperity, today more than ever (worldbank.org).
3 https://www.dw.com/en/climatechange-emissions-fossilfuels-gdp-economy-renewables/a-55089013

References

Acemoglu, Daron, and James A. Robinson. (2006). *Economic Origins of Dictatorship and Democracy*. New York: Cambridge University Press.

Acemoglu, Daron, Simon Johnson, and James A. Robinson. (2001). "The Colonial Origins of Comparative Development: An Empirical Investigation." *American Economic Review*, 95(5): 1369–1401.

Acemoglu, Daron, Simon Johnson, and James A. Robinson. (2002a). "Reversal of Fortune: Geography and Institutions in the Making of the Modern World Income." *The Quarterly Journal of Economics*, 117(4): 1231–1294.
Acemoglu, Daron, Simon Johnson, and James A. Robinson. (2002b). The Rise of Europe: Atlantic Trade, Institutional Change and Economic Growth. National Bureau of Economic Research, Working Paper No. 09378.
Acemoglu, Daron, Suresh Naidu, Pascual Restrepo, and James A. Robinson. (2019). "Democracy Does Cause Growth." *Journal of Political Economy*, 127(1): 47–100.
Ades, Alberto, and Hak Chua. (1997). "Thy Neighbor's Curse: Regional Instability and Economic Growth." *Journal of Economic Growth*, 2: 279–304.
Barter, Shane. (2022). "Understanding Self-Government: A Typology of Territorial Autonomy." Paper presented at Western Political Science Association (WPSA) annual meeting, Portland OR, US.
Bates, Robert. (2010). "A Review of Douglas C. North, John Joseph Wallis, and Barry R. Weingast Violence and Social Orders: A Conceptual Framework for Interpreting *Recorded Human History*." *Journal of Economic Literature*, 48(3): 752–753.
Benedikter, Thomas. (2009). *The World's Modern Autonomy Systems: Concepts and Experiences of Regional Territorial Autonomy*. Bozen/Bolzano: EURAC Research.
Bosker, Maarten, and Harry Garretsen. (2006). Geography Rules Too! Economic Development and the Geography of Institutions. CESIFO Working Paper No. 1769.
Busygina, Irina. (2018). *Russia – EU Relations and the Common Neighborhood: Coercion Versus Authority*. Abingdon, UK: Routledge.
Busygina, Irina, and Mikhail Filippov. (2012). *Political Modernization of State in Russia*. Moscow: Liberal Mission Endowment. [Politicheskaya modernizatsiya gosudarstva v Rossii].
Cliton, Eric, and Alma Barrutieta. (2006). Institutions Versus Geography: Subnational Evidence from the United States. IMF Working Paper No. 169.
Crescenzi, Riccardo, and Marco Percoco. (2013). *Geography, Institutions, and Regional Economic Performance*. Berlin: Springer Verlag.
Diamond, Jared. (1997). *Guns, Germs, and Steel: The Fates of Human Societies*. New York: Norton.
Dikshit, Ramesh. (1971). "Geography and Federalism." *The Annals of the Association of American Geographers*, 61(1): 97–115.
Dikshit, Ramesh. (1975). *The Political Geography of Federalism: An Inquiry Into Origin and Stability*. New Deli: The MacMillan Company of India Limited.
Easterly, William, and Ross Levine. (2003). "Tropics, Germs, and Crops: How Endowments Influence Economic Development." *Journal of Monetary Economics*, 50: 3–40.
Ebbinghaus, Bernhard. (2005). Two Approaches Applied to Welfare State Reform. Can Path Dependence Explain Institutional Change? MPIfG Discussion Paper No. 05/25.
Engerman, Stanley, and Kenneth Sokoloff. (1997). "Factor Endowments, Institutions and Differential Paths of Growth Among the New World Economies." In *How Latin America Fell Behind*, ed. by Stephen Haber. Stanford: Stanford University Press.
Estes, Richard. (2019). "The 'Rich' and 'Poor': The Widening Income and Development Gap between Rich and Poor Nations Worldwide." In *Wealth(s) and Subjective Well-Being*, ed. by G. Brulé and C. Suter. *Social Indicators Research Series*, 76. Cham: Springer.
Faundez, Julio. (2016). "Douglass North's Theory of Institutions: Lessons for Law and Development." *Hague Journal on the Rule of Law*, 8: 373–391.
Gallup, John, Jeffrey Sachs, and Andrew Mellinger. (1998). "Geography and Economic Development." *International Regional Science Review*, 22(2): 179–232.
Haber, Stephen. (2012). "Where Does Democracy Thrive: Climate, Technology, and the Evolution of Economic and Political Institutions." Stanford University and NBER. http://stephen-haber.com/wp-content/uploads/2014/02/Haber-Where-Does-Democracy-Thrive.pdf.
Hall, Robert, and Charles Jones. (1999). "Why Do Some Countries Produce So Much Output Per Worker Than Others?" *Quarterly Journal of Economics*, 114: 83–116.

Hoffman, Philip. (2015). *Why Did Europe Conquer the World?* Princeton: Princeton University Press.

Leigh, Michael. (1975). "Germany's Changing Role in the EEC." *The World Today*, 31(12): 488–497.

Liebowitz, Stan, and Stephen Margolis. (1999). *Winners, Losers, and Microsoft: Competition and Antitrust in High Technology*. Oakland, CA: The Independent Institute.

Lipset, Seymour Martin, and Stein Rokkan. (1967). *Party Systems and Voter Alignments: Cross-National Perspectives*, 7. New York: Free Press.

Masters, William, and Margaret McMillan. (2000). "Climate and Scale in Economic Growth." Center for International Development, Cambridge, MA: Harvard University.

McArthur, John, and Jeffrey Sachs. (2001). Institutions and Geography: Comments on Acemoglu, Johnson, and Robinson (2000). NBER Working Paper No. 8114.

Mitton, Todd. (2016). "The Wealth of Subnations: Geography, Institutions, and Within-Country Development." *Journal of Development Economics*, 118: 88–111.

Murdoch, James, and Todd Sandler. (2002). "Economic Growth, Civil Wars and Spatial Spillovers." *Journal of Conflict Resolution*, 46(1): 91–110.

Nordhaus, William. (1998). *Economics and Policy Issues in Climate Change*. Washington, DC: RFF Press.

North, Douglass. (1981). *Structure and Change in Economic History*. New York: W. W. Norton.

North, Douglass, and R. P. Thomas. (1973). *The Rise of the Western World: A New Economic History*. Cambridge: Cambridge University Press.

North, Douglass. (1990). *Institutions, Institutional Change, and Economic Performance*. Cambridge: Cambridge University Press.

North, Douglass, John Josepf Wallis, and Barry Weingast. (2009). *Violence and Social Orders: A Conceptual Framework for Interpreting Recorded Human History*. Cambridge: Cambridge University Press.

Nunn, Nathan, and Diego Puga. (2012). "Ruggedness: The Blessing of Bad Geography in Africa." *The Review of Economics and Statistics*, 94(1): 20–36.

Olson, Mancur. (1982). *The Rise and Decline of Nations: Economic Growth, Stagflation, and Social Rigidities*. New Haven, CT: Yale University Press.

Parente, Stephen, and Edward Prescott. (2000). *Barriers to Riches*. Cambridge, MA: The MIT Press.

Peet, Richard, and Elaine Hartwick. (2009). *Theories of Development: Contentions, Arguments, Alternative*. New York: The Guilford Press.

Prado, Mariana, and Michael Trebilcock. (2009). Path Dependence, Development, and the Dynamics of Institutional Reform. University of Toronto, Legal Studies Research Paper No. 09-04.

Przeworski, Adam. (2004). Geography vs. Institutions Revisited: Were Fortunes Reversed? http://politics.as.nyu.edu/docs/IO/2800/reversal.pdf.

Razeen, Sally. (1995). "Review: The Economics and Politics of the German Miracle." *Government and Opposition*, 30(4): 541–553.

Robinson, James, and Daron Acemoglu. (2012). *Why Nations Fail: The Origins of Power, Prosperity, and Poverty*. New York: Random House.

Robinson, Kenneth. (1961). "Sixty Years of Federalism in Australia." *Geographical Review*, 51.

Rodrik, Dani. (2007). *One Economics, Many Recipes: Globalization, Institutions, and Economic Growth*. Princeton: Princeton University Press.

Rodrik, Dani, Arvind Subramanian, and Francesco Trebbi. (2002). "Institutions Rule: The Primacy of Institutions Over Geography and Integration in Economic Development." *Journal of Economic Growth*, 9(2): 131–165.

Ros, Jaime. (2013). *Rethinking Economic Development, Growth, and Institutions*. Oxford: Oxford University Press.

Sachs, Jeffrey. (2001). Tropical Underdevelopment. NBER Working Paper No. 8119.

Sachs, Jeffrey. (2003). *Institutions Don't Rule: Direct Effects of Geography on Per Capita Income*. Working Paper Series No. 9490. Cambridge: National Bureau of Economic Research.
Sachs, Jeffrey. (2003). "Institutions Matter, But Not for Everything." *Finance & Development*, June, 38–41.
Sachs, Jeffrey. (2012). "Government, Geography and Growth." *Foreign Affairs*, September/October.
Sánchez, Luis. (2007). "Splitting the Country: The Case of the Atlantic Coast of Nicaragua." *Journal of Latin American Geography*, 6(1): 7–23.
Seers, Dudley. (1977). "The New Meaning of Development." *International Development Review*, 19(3): 2–7.
Sen, Amartya. (1999). *Development as Freedom*. New York: Alfred Knopf.
Simmons, Beth, and Zachary Elkins. (2004). "The Globalization of Liberalization: Policy Diffusion in the International Political Economy." *American Political Science Review*, 98(1): 171–189.
Skocpol, Theda. (1979). *States and Social Revolutions: A Comparative Analysis of France, Russia and China*. Cambridge: Cambridge University Press.
Stratford, Elaine. (2008). "Islandness and Struggles Over Development: A Tasmanian Case Study." *Political Geography*, 27(2): 160–175.

2 Modern states and their geographical attributes

Size, shape, and location

As Jones, Jones, and Woods (2004: 20) poetically expressed it, "rather like the air we breathe, states are organizations that surround us individuals, influencing and, in many ways, offering sustenance to the lives we lead" (Jones, Jones and Woods 2004: 20). Indeed, the very word "state" is so familiar to us, and we pronounce it so often that we rarely think about *what* it is, *how* it works, *how* it emerged, and *how* it changes over time. According to Giddens, a state is "a set of institutional forms of governance maintaining and administrating monopoly over a territory with demarcated boundaries (borders), its rule being sanctioned by law and direct control of the means of internal and external violence" (Giddens 1985: 121). Whether we talk about nation-states or multinational states, all of them have inalienable geographic attributes – territory, shape, and borders. Modern states are the basic units of the world political system, a kind of grid cells of world politics.

The German geographer Friedrich Ratzel called the state "alpha and omega" of political geography. In the early twentieth century, not only the German geographer Ratzel but also the Swedish political scientist Rudolf Kjellen called for overcoming the narrow understanding (and study) of the state as a legal system and moving to the study of "the whole state," which is quite impossible without geography. Kjellen defined geopolitics as the doctrine of the state as a geographical organism or phenomenon in space, of the state as land, territory, area, or, more precisely, as territorial domination (Björk and Lundén 2021). Subsequently, it was this "obsession with state" that led to the development of the ideas of traditional German geopolitics, in particular the idea of the inalienable right of vital states to grow, that is, to territorial expansion. However, another possibility is love for one's country, which motivates the researcher to study it intently. "Obsession with state" is fundamentally different from love of country which Fernan Braudel expressed in his "manifesto":

> I love France with the same passionate, demanding, and challenging love as Jules Michelet loved her. . . . What is France? To give an answer to this question is to grasp the very essence of the problem, to understand France with its own help, to see how it is born from the countless layers that its past has patiently deposited layer by layer, just as a powerful earth crust is formed from the barely visible marine sediments accumulated over many centuries.

DOI: 10.4324/9781003496731-4

> In short, explore the sediment, the alloy, the combinations, and mixtures. To delve into the process, into the country's endless struggle with itself.
>
> (Braudel 1989)

States have *territoriality*, which can be considered in two aspects: (1) states have territory that is important materially or physically as a place of concentration of population, resources, material objects; (2) the territory of the state is of key importance in the political context, partly explaining the nature of government and administration in the state. Territorial control means that within the territorial boundaries of a state, everyone living and/or working there or even passing through must obey the laws of that state. State borders are not just lines on the map, border posts, or checkpoints; these boundaries serve as markers of the political space of state power (Jones, Jones and Woods 2004: 20–21) (on borders, see Chapter 3).

Territorial states (nation-states) owe their birth to Europe. But back in the sixteenth century, the territorial state was by no means the only possible form of political consolidation in Europe; in addition to emerging states, there existed small city-states, such as Florence and Genoa, and extended empires, such as the Holy Roman Empire of the German nation. However, as Spruyt showed, medium-sized states (neither too large nor too small in size) had advantages over the other two forms of territorial consolidation in terms of combining economic and military power (the common reason for consolidation was the need to successfully wage wars). City-states were the centers of production (and consumption) of capital; they probably had enough economic resources to wage war but lacked people to form a powerful combat-ready army. Empires, on the other hand, had large manpower resources to build an army, but they lacked the economic power for large-scale military activities and internal cohesion. Henrik Spruyt argued that to successfully wage a war, a state needed two conditions – cities to produce capital and a military elite to command armies (Spruyt 1994). Consequently, a state was a prerequisite for the success of its military campaigns and, ultimately, its survival.

The task of governing the subordinates was critical for the rulers, and this task demanded a legally homogeneous territory within their borders. This daunting task required a change in deeply rooted local traditions. To solve it, elites had several options:

- to strengthen centralization, when political, economic, and sociocultural norms would spread from the center to the peripheries;
- enter into negotiations with elites of the peripheral regions and share competences between the center and the regions (i.e., create a federation or some form of decentralization);
- to develop the ideology of state nationalism, which could become the basis of the loyalty of the populace to the state and its institutions (Jones, Jones and Woods 2004: 29–31).

The number of states in the modern world is growing while, naturally, their average size is decreasing. At the beginning of the twentieth century, on the world map, there were about 50 independent states, at the beginning of the twenty-first century the United Nations included about 200 member states. In the course of the twentieth century, three "waves" of the emergence of new states on the map can be distinguished: (1) the formation of states in Eastern Europe as a result of the collapse of empires after World War I; (2) the emergence of new states as a result of the collapse of the colonial European empires after World War II; (3) the emergence of sovereign states after the collapse of the Soviet Union in 1991.

Talking about the "birth" of new states, we should not forget about the "death" of states (that is, about their disappearance from the world map as sovereign entities). This process is not comparable in scale with the process of the "birth" of new states; so about half "deaths" of state entities occurred because of the consolidation of Italy and Germany in the nineteenth century. Attempts by large revisionist states to "kill" their smaller neighbors by annexing them (e.g., to restore their empire, as is happening to Russia in relation to Ukraine before our eyes) arouse the fierce and quite just resistance of the latter.

The nation-state – the form of state that in Europe has "won" the competition with other territorial entities – became the basis for the territorial and political organization of territorial space in Western Europe. The expansion of the state as a political organization outside Europe took place either as a result of the movement of this form along with the resettlement of colonists (this is how the resettlement states were formed – the United States, Canada, Australia, New Zealand, South Africa) or as a result of the collapse of European colonial empires and the emergence of brand-new states in South America, Africa, and Asia. However, what was exported was only the form – a territorial state with a system of formal institutions – but not the factors that held the state together and made it capable, effective, and resilient to crises. Attempts of postcolonial nation-building in most of the cases led to formation neither of nations nor of nation-states. Thus, European project – territorial state – was "exported" to other continents when European empires were broken up (like Spanish and Portuguese empires) or dissolved (like British, French, and others), and many new sovereign states were formed in the three continents of South America, Africa, and Asia (Jones, Jones and Woods 2004: 34). Many of these states have faced considerable problems, and several major issues facing Southern states were caused by "bad geography" (for instance, a number of new African states were landlocked as we will see in Chapter 6 on Africa) or "bad institutions" (corruption, patrimonialism) or both.

In the following pages, I discuss three important geographic variables related to states – territorial size, shape of territory, and geographic location. This discussion allows us to formulate several assumptions about the choices of developmental strategies that are *ceteris paribus* feasible for this or that state.

Territorial size

One of the most important parameters of the state, which has a significant impact on many aspects and features of social and political life, is the size of the state's territory. It must be said at once that the territory of the world land is distributed among states *extremely unevenly*. The seven largest states in the world account for more than 48% of the world's land area (excluding Antarctica). Vatican (0.44 square kilometers), Monaco (1.6 square kilometers), Nauru (21.3 square kilometers), and San Marino (61 square kilometers) belong to the group of the smallest countries in the world. African states have the smallest average size of territory in comparison with other continents; they are also the "youngest" in age. Interestingly (and quite unexpectedly), on average, the largest states are located in Oceania – this is the result of the presence of the one very large state – Australia – and a relatively small number of states in this macro-region.

It can be assumed that:

- the larger the state is, the richer and more diverse are its natural resources;
- the presence of a large territory can counterbalance an unfavorable geographical location of a state;
- for large-sized states, in comparison with small- and medium-sized ones, the problem of "overcoming space" is acute, for example, the problem of establishing interregional ties. Infrastructure is critical: a substantial part of the national income is spent on connecting vast spaces. For Russia, for instance, huge distances and the location of more than half of the country's territory in regions that are difficult to live and manage created serious constraints for development (see Chapter 10).

State presence may be uneven across the territory country. Guillermo O'Donnell (1993) has drawn attention to the existence of "brown spots" in the political topography of Latin American states, which he defined as peripheral regions or districts in which the presence of the state was attenuated and more arbitrary forms of power hold sway. Similarly, uneven projections of state authority were visible not only in Brazil's Amazonia, highland Peru, and northwest Argentina but also in Russia in the 1990s and across most sub-Saharan African countries. These "brown spots" can result from the erosion of stateness in the course of a major crisis (for instance, legitimacy crisis). Such unevenness may be also the effect of state-building itself. This was the case in Russia where colonization has reached territories very distant from Saint Petersburg, then-capital of the Russian Empire (the rivers of Amur and Ussuri at the Far East). Being capable of reaching that far, Russian colonizers, however, proved to be incapable of systematically "organizing" and developing them (see Chapter 10).

As Catherine Boone wrote, "geographers' and economists' work on state-building underscores the fact that projection of central state power through space is costly." Rational state-builders weigh the costs (and risks) of power projection against the benefits (and risks) of not doing so. Such an approach predicts that the costs of power projection will outweigh the benefits in (i) peripheral or difficult-to-access regions of the national territory, (ii) zones of low population density, and (iii) where there are few resources for the central state or its principals to exploit. In such areas, states will refrain from investing in the build-up of extensive infrastructural power (Boone 2012). The example of Russia's North is telling. In Russia, the development of the resources of the North gave rise to a focal form of settlement corresponding to the natural conditions of this harsh region. The costs of developing the North were always very high. Thus, the Soviet Union, and after its collapse, Russia, faced a serious dilemma: the cost of developing the North was extremely high, but the factor of its enormous resources "outweighed" these considerations. On the contrary, the availability of resources and the vast spaces themselves created incentives for the Russian state to pursue an extensive path of development, involving ever new (and increasingly less accessible) territories in this process. The extensive way of territory development, artificially ignoring geographical limitations, subsequently led to degradation of communities in regions in the Russian North. The development of the resources of the North gave rise to a focal form of settlement corresponding to the natural conditions of this harsh region. The costs of development of the North were very great. Enterprises, cities, and roads were built by the labor of prisoners. Because of the low technological level of production, the number of people employed in it and the total population of northern cities and towns were much higher than that which would have ensured an equal volume of production with higher technology. Resource cities were doomed to extinction after the depletion of deposits (Lappo 2005: 202).

Traditional geopolitics of the early nineteenth century perceived the size of the territory as a symbol of the viability and power of the state and also as the guarantee of its weight in the international arena. Indeed, a territory is a resource or capital of a state of a special kind, and as such it cannot be replaced by anything. However, as noted earlier, territorial increments (even if to talk only about geographical consequences, ignoring the possibly illegitimate nature of these increments) as such may not solve but rather create problems. First, there are problems with the effective use of the territory and its development. Second, there is the problem of natural constraints (e.g., permafrost), which make the territory extremely difficult for permanent residence.

Territorial "giants" and territorial "dwarfs"

A special group among the countries of the world is *territorial giants*. This group includes Russia, China, the United States, Canada, Brazil, India, and Australia. A giant country certainly has special characteristics, but it by no means equals with a great power or superpower. At the same time, the very factor of the extraordinary size of the territory of the giant countries generates both special opportunities for development and increased risks. Andrei Treyvish identified the following special characteristics of the giant countries:

Geographic

(1) large number of economic regions within one country;
(2) the potential abundance of natural resources;
(3) uneven development and interregional disparities.

Sociocultural

1) ethno-cultural and confessional heterogeneity;
2) social contrasts;
3) low social cohesion.

Economic

1) large domestic market and potential craving for autarchy;
2) developmental inertia.

Political

1) potentially: power and influence in the world, missionary work;
2) a tendency to expansion;
3) the large size of the army and state apparatus

(Treivish 2010: 26)

A giant country has many potential opportunities and just as many risks.

The huge size of the territory determines its inertia, which, in particular, is manifested in the unevenness of developmental reforms throughout the country and the fact that the return from them comes with a long delay. Reforms to accelerate economic development start in the capital and large cities. But it takes a long time before reforms are launched in remote peripheral regions. Taking this inertia into consideration is very important for all reformers when they elaborate reform strategy. Importantly, the factor of territorial size and, consequently, the constraints it imposes on the nature and speed of reforms should be considered before the reform process begins, not after reforms have begun. It is precisely the factor of territory and its political significance that was not considered by Russian reformers in the 1990s. Democrats started the reforms in Moscow, but halfway through they were slowed down in the regions by authoritarian elites who preferred to freeze the reforms at the stage where they benefited the most. Another example would be Australia, where continental size has complicated national consolidation.

The gigantic size of the country is also potentially fraught with centrifugal tendencies and even territorial disintegration, especially in the event of a legitimacy crisis, broken political system, and weakened central institutions. For instance, in the mid-1990s, scenarios and maps of the possible collapse of the Russian Federation (with the subsequent compilation of maps of such a collapse) were the subject of research by some Russian and foreign experts. I will give just one example. In 1997, *Foreign Affairs* magazine published an article by Zbigniew Brzezinski with a map on which Russia was divided into three parts: Russia proper (the European part), Siberia, and the Far Eastern Republic (Treivish 2010: 39).

Western experts were discussing territorial disintegration of Russia, almost at the same time Russian experts were discussing the disintegration of the United States. Igor Panarin in his book *The Collapse of Dollar and Disintegration of the United States* (2009) in the mode of "free scientific inquiry" (his own words) made a conclusion that the United States had no future, and this state was doomed to territorial disintegration. Panarin presented a map of the US disintegration – it was to break up into six territorial "pieces" – the eastern part of the United States (New England) would go to the European Union, the west – to China, the Hawaiian Islands – either to China or to Japan, and Alaska will be integrated into Russia. The rest of the US territory will be divided by its neighbors, Canada and Mexico. However, attempts to create new maps for the collapsed giants remain little more than speculation, and the sheer size of the state provokes them. "Free scientific inquiry" does not allow for reliable predictions. None of the giant states that are now present on the political map of the world show centrifugal tendencies. National identity, culture, history, economic ties, and – not less important – the nature of political institutions work for to the preservation of the territorial integrity of giant countries.

Importantly, territorial size of the country affects the nature of the political regime and the form of government. According to Hiscox and Lake, the size of the country, democracy, and federalism impose mutual restrictions on each other, which leads to the emergence of a predictable equilibrium in each specific case. In the giant countries, federalist decisions can reconcile the requirements of regional autonomy (resulting from the differences of interests of different parts territory of the country/regions) with the benefits of federal control in other areas. Federalism allows the state to provide various services on a different scale, which is optimal and makes it possible both to use the advantages of a large market and security (federal services) and to maintain regional specificity through the implementation of various policies in the regions (regional services). Hiscox and Lake have tested and confirmed the hypotheses that federal states are likely to be democracies and that unitary states will be (as a rule) territorially smaller (Hiscox and Lake 2002: 4–7). And, indeed, all the giant countries are federal democracies, except for China. China is not a democracy, but neither is it a federation though political centralization in the country is combined with high degree of economic decentralization and regional autonomy. This combination is one of the conditions for accelerated economic development of the country (Libman and Rochlitz 2019).

There is another way of looking at the relations between the political regime of a country and its size. Based on the results of theoretical analysis and empirical data, Stepan concluded that a democratic political system in a large and multinational country is possible only based on a federal form of state. Indeed, all large multinational democracies are federal (Stepan 1999). Conversely, none of the modern multinational states that have abandoned the practice of federalism have yet succeeded in democratic development.

At the other end of the spectrum, in terms of territorial size, are small states. Their behavior is motivated, among other things, by a sense of vulnerability – political and economic. Accordingly, the political strategy of small states would be greater (compared to large states) liberalization and greater flexibility and adaptability and a faster learning process. It is the ability to learn and adapt to a rapidly changing world that is extremely important for understanding the high rates of development and the level of well-being of small European states. At the same time, the (forced) economic openness and vulnerability to external challenges as a result of control over relatively small resources increase the likelihood and scale of losses (as a result of a shock or major crisis) for a small state compared to a large one (Katzenstein 2003).

Small states are more inclined to initiate coalitions/alliances or join existing ones. Alliance membership should potentially allow small countries to share the burden of losses among coalition members and/or better respond to external challenges by acting as a group. In other words, by acting as part of a coalition, small countries will be more likely to form and implement successful policies in relation to a changing external environment and to implement solutions that they would not be able to pursue independently. In an alliance that brings together small states and a disproportionately large state, small players will tend to free ride, while most of the costs of maintaining the alliance will be borne by the large player.

Alesina and Spolaore argued that the small size of the state is not only beneficial to its citizens but also "natural" in the global world. Their central thesis is that liberalization of international trade and economic integration are leading to the gradual failure of one of the main advantages of a large country – a large domestic market (Alesina and Spolaore 1997). In free trade, the market for a small country is virtually the whole world (Alesina and Warsziarg 1999). The link between economic boundaries (i.e., market size) and political boundaries disappears, and the "optimal" size of the country shrinks accordingly. Regional, cultural, and linguistic groups can enjoy the advantages of political independence and not share a common agenda, policies, and institutions with groups whose preferences are fundamentally different for the sake of access to a larger domestic market (Alesina, Spolaore and Warsziarg 1997).

Shape of territory

Another important variable is the *shape or configuration of a state's territory*. The shape of the state's territory largely determines the availability of the capital and other large centers from peripheral, remote regions; the effectiveness of the state management system; and the intensity of horizontal (between regions) and vertical (between regions and the center) ties. The nature of the connectivity of territorial cells and the shape of the territory have a significant impact on spatial interactions. This situation is well illustrated by the example of Bulgaria and Cuba: these two countries have approximately equal area (size of territory) but completely different configuration, which affects the peculiarities of the territorial organization of the economy and political processes. Thus, a compact state with a circular shape is the easiest to manage.

The question of the *organic form of the state* has a deep meaning (though not strictly academic), it is especially important for territorially large countries. The question of the natural or optimal correspondence between the state territory and the country has potentially many answers. The "natural" or "organic" form of a country can be realized by several states. So, in addition to Germany itself, in Western Europe, there are several more fully or predominantly German states – Austria, Luxembourg, Liechtenstein, and Switzerland. The German linguistic and cultural space obviously does not coincide with the political space. Perhaps, it was on this path that Germany was able to resolve the notorious "German question" on the state borders and to acquire a territory that would support the internal stability of the German state (Kagansky 2002: 18).

There is a notion of an "ideal" form of the state, which promotes its internal cohesion and is therefore a favorable prerequisite for development. The state with such a form is France – it is a pentagon with the capital in the center, bounded by the seacoast, mountains, and rivers. But there are not many states with such a favorable shape as France. Most states have an irregular shape. Regarding special cases of "territorial distribution," states can be divided into the following:

- Elongated states (Chile, Norway, Vietnam). An elongated or attenuated territorial shape, such as Chile makes it difficult for the central state to govern peripheral areas in the north and south, which are located far from the central capital of Santiago. Vietnam is also an elongated state, which has battled numerous attempts by other countries to divide it, such as the 20-year Vietnam War, where first French and then US forces tried unsuccessfully to keep the southern part of the nation separated from the north.
- Fragmented states, for example, located on archipelagos (Malaysia, the Philippines, Indonesia), or consisting of unconnected parts (Pakistan between 1947 and 1971 consisted of two parts distant from each other);
- States with exclaves (Russia with the Kaliningrad region,[1] Angola and its province of Cabinda);
- States with large natural barriers and hard-to-reach territories (e.g., Peru, divided into two parts by the Andean ridges).

There are also "perforated" states like South Africa, which fully surrounds the state of Lesotho. The surrounded nation of Lesotho can be reached only by going through South Africa. If the two nations are hostile, access to the surrounding nation can be difficult. Italy is also a perforated state; Vatican City and San Marino – both independent countries – are surrounded by Italy. Finally, a protruded, or panhandle country such as Myanmar (Burma) or Thailand has an extended arm of territory. Like an elongated state, the panhandle complicates the management of the country. Myanmar has existed in one form or another for thousands of years, for example, but the country's shape has made it an easy target for many other nations and people, dating to the Nanzhao kingdom in the mid-800s to the Khmer or Mongol empires. (Though it's not a nation, you can get an idea of how hard it would be to defend a protruded country if you picture the state of Oklahoma, which has a prominent panhandle) (Rosenberg 2021).

Geographic location of states

In terms of a state's development trajectory, geographic location can play a fundamentally important role. There is a difference between geographic location (GL) and just location. An analysis of GL gives us the answer to the question: in relation to what? Location answers other questions: where and what is it part of? So the location speaks about the localization of the object (state), and the GL reflects the *relations* in the spatial system. In other words, the GL characterizes the relationship of the object with its external environment. Thus, the location of a state remains unchanged while the geographical position can change quite significantly. For example, Poland is in Central Europe on the continent of Eurasia – this is its location. However, at the same time, Poland is in close proximity to the war zone between Russia and Ukraine – and this is the geographical location of the country, which determines, among other things, its choice of its foreign policy actions.

Let's compare geographic locations of the Great Britain and Germany. Great Britain owed its political stability, moreover, relatively peaceful evolution from monarchy to parliamentary democracy, in particular, to its geographical location. The channel separating Great Britain from the European continent played an important role in the political history of the country; for centuries, it served as a geographical barrier to invasions from outside (the last successful invasion was carried out by the Normans in the eleventh century). This barrier allowed England to distance from conflicts and wars on the continent, so it had a choice whether or not to intervene in the continental political games. And since the threat of invasion was insignificant, the British did not need to create a powerful land army, which potentially (as was the case with many other states) could be a threat to civilian rule. A completely different case was geographical location of Germany, located at the "crossroads" of Europe and not having a natural eastern border. For centuries, the territory of Germany has been a battlefield. Attempts by the Germans to answer the question "Where does Germany end?" have resulted in two world wars.

The benefits of GL could be converted into a resource for the development of the territory. For instance, the location of the tiny state Singapore on the world trade routes has become the most important factor in its prosperity and transformation into an advanced economy. Egypt and Panama have gained significant benefits from the location of canals of global trade importance on their territory. The Suez Canal connects the ports of the Atlantic and Indian Oceans, and the Panama Canal links the Atlantic and Pacific Oceans.

When generally assessing the pros and cons of a state's GL, it is important to pay attention to geographic remoteness. Remoteness and isolation restricting communication and exchange with the outside world generate the emergence of closed communities as this was the case with Japan prior to 1853. Another telling example is Bhutan, which is situated in the eastern Himalayas. This is a small, mountainous, and landlocked country between the People's Republic of China and India. Geographic remoteness is responsible for the limited connection of Bhutan with global markets, and the country is still suffering from its challenging geography.

For centuries, the most important characteristic of the GL was *the access to the seacoast*. Territories with access to the sea have long been considered strategically important; the sea opened the way to the outside world. It is no coincidence that in the eighteenth century Russia waged an active struggle for access to the Baltic and Black Seas. The states that do not have access to the sea find themselves in a vulnerable, dependent position. Currently, there are more than 40 such states on the world map (including three states that have access to the Caspian Sea, which in terms of physical geography is a lake), 16 of them are in Africa. The problem of access to the sea acquired extreme urgency after the collapse of the USSR, since most of the post-Soviet states – Belarus, Moldova, Armenia, and Azerbaijan, all the states of Central Asia – lost access to the seas with the collapse of the Union.

The lack of access to the sea can lead to the dependence of such a state on its neighbors; in general, the importance of the "neighborhood factor" sharply increases for the landlocked states. This dependence may not be fatal for a country belonging to a stable supranational community (e.g., this is the case of Austria, a member of the European Union); however, in other regions, being landlocked can cause an economic crisis in the country. Macedonia suffered greatly when the border with Greece was closed: when Macedonia was part of Yugoslavia, it actively used the Greek port of Thessaloniki. Thus, by controlling the exits of neighbors to the outside world, some states can gain geographical advantages over others.

The answer to the question – Who are your neighbors? – is often critically important for the country and the prospects and trajectory of its development. There are numerous examples: Mongolia, locked between Russia and China, and Mexico, its closeness to the United States is of extreme importance for the country. Geographic proximity to Russia is the most important factor in the foreign policy of the post-Soviet states, in this regard, it would be enough to look at Ukraine.

The competition of major powers for their smaller neighbors can make the lives of the latter quite complicated, making them "hostages" of external interests. Let's have a closer look at the countries located between Russia and the European Union (so-called shared neighborhood (SN)). The differences in Russia's and the EU's approaches to the CN were evident – both in terms of general strategies and in terms of the use of concrete power instruments. Russia's main interest in the CN countries was the need to build a coalition to confirm its aspirations to great power status. The CN countries suit this purpose as Russia has the capacity both to reward and to punish them. Russia needed loyal coalition partners, but the problem was that there were physically not enough potential candidates – countries that would be geographically close, reliable, and that could be firmly and permanently bound to Russia. The dearth of potential coalition partners pushed Russia to perceive each country that could enter a Russia-centered coalition as being of great value. From this perspective, the SN countries appeared exceptionally attractive, given their dependence on Russian energy supplies, as well as the cultural and historical affinities that these states share with Russia. The task of building a coalition around Russia and the apparent "availability" of the CN countries have made the Russian establishment think that these countries are doomed to make a "final choice" between Russia and Western Europe.

Unlike Russia, the European Union has never wanted to include the SN states in any kind of coalition, or to see them soon as members of the Union. Nor has the European Union ever put forward the idea of a "final choice." The key word in the European Union's strategy toward the SN has been "security," which is to be achieved by surrounding the European Union with a "ring of friends." Thus, the European Union's main goal regarding common neighbors was to create a safe neighborhood area. To achieve this goal, the European Union has developed a set of authority instruments based on the conditionality principle, designed to initiate certain reforms in target countries by shifting these societies into a course of Europeanization. The desired stability along the EU border requires changes and therefore creates instability (at least in the short term) in the SN countries. This temporary instability that emerges as a by-product of Europeanization is, however, principally different from the "managed instability" that is part of Russia's larger strategy toward its neighboring countries (Busygina 2018).

The Russia–EU rivalry has led to a deep divide in the "shared neighborhood" between the countries that have joined the Eurasian Economic Union (i.e., Belarus and Armenia) and those that have signed the Association Agreements (AAs) and the Deep and Comprehensive Free Trade Agreements (DCFTAs) offered by the European Union under the Eastern Partnership (i.e., Georgia,[9] Moldova, and Ukraine). Today, Russia is losing Moldova and Georgia, and it has irretrievably lost the most strategically important country – Ukraine.

The centrality of geographic location is an important factor in social and political life and not only in relation to the position of the state in the area but also in relation to the location of the most important objects on the territory of the state. The location of the capital can play an important role, not only economically but also politically. In several states, to level out interregional disparities, reduce the level of conflict, and speed up economic development, the national capital was moved to geographic centers. This was the case with Brazil, where the capital was moved to develop the natural potential of the hinterland from Rio de Janeiro to Brasilia. The capital of Nigeria was moved to Abuja, since the former capital, Lagos, was associated with acute interethnic and interclan conflicts. In 1923, after the collapse of the Ottoman Empire, when Turkey lost most of its territories in Europe, its capital was moved from Istanbul to Ankara.

The transfer of the capital of Kazakhstan from the "Soviet" Almaty, located in the southeast of the country, to the more northern located "Kazakh" Akmola (renamed to Astana) was an important instrument in pursuing the general policy of "Kazakhization" by the country's leadership. This ambitious project has been launched in 1994 and completed in 1998. Officially, the reason for the relocation was purely geographical – the city of Almaty was located in an earthquake zone, and the mountain prevented territorial expansion of agglomeration. In reality, however, the reason was both political and geographic. Relocation has brought national authorities closer to potentially secessionist regions of the north populated mainly by Russians. At the same time, the capital would be distanced from China. As Cummings argued, "the capital's relocation may thus be regarded as a graphic example of the importance of geopolitics in the leadership environment. The move demonstrated an acute awareness of the country's geostrategic location as a landlocked country between China and Russia, and with almost all the bordering regions having a Russian minority" (Cummings 1999: 95). Finally, the capital relocation allowed the then-President Nazarbayev to "free himself" from excessive control by the strong political elites of Almaty. It should be added that the project proved to be extremely expensive: 22% of 2006 GDP was spent on the construction of the new Kazakh capital (Franke, Gawrich and Alakbarov 2009: 130).

The relocation of the national capital can also be motivated by specific historic circumstances. After the collapse of Nazi Germany in 1945, the territory of Germany was divided between the Allies, as was the national capital, Berlin. Moreover, Berlin happened to be surrounded by the Soviet occupation zone, later the German Democratic Republic. Consequently, this excluded Berlin as the capital of West Germany, and the decision was made in favor of Bonn on Rhine as the provisional capital of the country. Bonn had no capital traditions, it was a relatively small, quiet university city, so this has emphasized the provisional character of the decision. After the unification of Germany in 1990, it was decided to move the capital of the state back from Bonn to Berlin.

For a territorially large state, the differences in the geographic location of its internal regions are also important. The degree of peripherality of the regional GP depends on the size of the state's territory, configuration, and the structure of institutions (political and economic centralization). So we can note the peripherality and remoteness of the GL of Eastern Siberia and the Far East of the Soviet Union, comparing it with the GL of the Pacific coast of the United States, where remoteness does not mean peripherality.

The peripheral regions are often located on states' borders risking to become "no man's land." Therefore, for such regions, it is important to look at the neighboring countries and the possibility of turning the regions into a zone of contact with neighboring countries through cross-border cooperation. The experience of the European Union showed that peripheral border regions (e.g., Saarland in Germany) could receive additional impetus for development when a country entered regional integration organization. The location of Saarland was peripheral in Germany; but it turned out to be central in the European Union.

How important are geographical variables in the era of globalization?

The processes of globalization have stimulated vivid debates about the changing role of the states in economic development and good governance promotion.[2] Some experts argued that

> the state itself is in its death throes, we are constantly told. For this is the era of "civil society" and "postmodernity," of "global society" and the transnational market. . . . Wherever we look across the social sciences, the state is being weakened, hollowed out, carved up, toppled, or buried.
>
> (Weiss 1998: 2)

Others claimed that the role of the national state is changing to accommodate new societal and international demands, but there is no reason to expect its domestic dominance to diminish any time soon (Sassen 2003: 241).

Despite globalization, the national state remains the fundamental element of contemporary governance (Gill 2016). Moreover, recent studies suggested that the state was strategically important for accelerated development and success in the global economy. Based on experiences of Brazil and other Latin American countries, Carlos Bresser-Pereira (2010: 2) concluded that "given the competition that characterizes globalization, nation-states have become less autonomous, but, as a trade-off, their role has become more strategic." Under the forces of globalization, the role of government was progressively shifting toward providing an appropriate enabling environment for private (corporate) enterprise (Farazmand 2004, 2017). As Dani Rodrik (2011) argued, the key role of national governments is to minimize transaction costs within national boundaries thus making national economies competitive in global economy. To minimize the transaction cost, the state must be able to provide good governance and be limited and insulated from the political pressures of special interest groups (Bardhan 2016).

Under globalization, economic competition reaches a fundamentally new level, and national economies are becoming more and more dependent both on each other and on global crises and shocks. The growing inability of a modern sovereign state to control the processes of globalization, and even more so to manage them, is becoming a worldwide tendency, and even the largest states are highly dependent on global market forces. The creation of regional integration groups (primarily the European Union) was, at least in part, an attempt by territorially smaller states to respond to the challenges of globalization through market enlargement.

In a globalized world, economic priorities and trends are changing more and more rapidly and increasingly depend on what is happening outside even the largest national economies. Therefore, at the national level, making economic forecasts and making decisions based on past trends are becoming increasingly difficult and unproductive. The role of the state is strategically changing, one of its important tasks is to create favorable conditions for external and internal investors and maintaining an attractive image in the world. The conclusion is simple: in the modern world, to achieve success, the state critically needs to be able to cooperate, as well as to be open to investors, that is, create conditions that attract them.

"Geographical location is no longer destiny," Craig Barrett, Chair of Intel, proudly declared at the Tunis World Summit on the Information Society (WSIS) in 2005 (Barrett 2005). Some scholars would disagree with him. Yes, globalization, and the Internet revolution first of all has made long-distance communication dramatically faster, easier, and cheaper than ever before. But the world still did not transform into a "global village" with "borderless society" where the importance of geographic proximity in social interactions has decreased. On the contrary, while technology has undoubtedly increased the overall level of communication, this increase has been most pronounced for *local* social ties, and the volume of electronic communications is inversely proportional to geographical distance (Goldenberg and Levy 2009). In the words of Kellerman and Paradiso (2008), "geographical location still maintains, even in the information age, its basic dimension as an anchor in space for activities."

Geographic factors are not destiny, but they do matter and will matter – also in the globalized world, and the ongoing Russian war against Ukraine is a telling example. The long-standing argument of Colin Gray (1977: 1) that "geography is the most fundamental factor in the foreign policy of states because it is the most permanent" still holds true today. It is impossible to replace or interchange states' geographic positions. As Mackinder remarked back in 1904, "the most remarkable contrast in the political map of Europe is that presented by the vast area of Russia occupying half the Continent and the group of smaller territories tenanted by the Western Powers." Geographic positions of Russia, the European Union, and the United States largely determine their involvement in the war in Ukraine. For Russia, it is the possibility of military aggression against a neighboring country; for the European Union, it is the perception of Russian aggression as a direct threat to security in Europe; and for the United States, it is the possibility of flexible involvement in the war based on their national interests.

Notes

1 Kaliningrad region is the westernmost region of Russia, the result of the postwar redrawing of the political map of Europe. After World War II, by decision of the Potsdam Conference in 1945, a third of the territory of East Prussia with the city of Konigsberg became part of the Soviet Union. In 1946, the Konigsberg region was formed on this territory, which was soon renamed Kaliningrad. As part of the USSR, the region bordered on the allied Lithuanian SSR and the Polish People's Republic. Already in 1946, a mass arrival of immigrants from Russia and Belarus to the region was organized, which determined the resettlement character of the region. The collapse of the USSR led to a sharp change in the position of the region: it became an exclave, being separated from the main, mainland territory of Russia. The enlargement of the European Union in 2004, the joining of Poland and Lithuania, changed the position of the region for the second time, making it truly unique: Kaliningrad region is a Russian enclave within the political system – the European Union.

2 While the concept of government usually refers to the formal governing processes at the nation-state level, governance is commonly regarded as patterns that emerge from the governing activities of state and non-state actors operating at subnational, national, and international levels. For a review of the concept and the indicators of governance, see Kaufmann and Kraay (2008).

References

Alesina, Alberto, and Enrico Spolaore. (1997). "On Number and Size of Nations." *Quarterly Journal of Economics*, 112(4): 1027–1056.

Alesina, Alberto, Enrico Spolaore, and Romain Warsziarg. (1997). Economic Integration, and Political Disintegration. NBER Working Papers No. 6163.

Alesina, Alberto, and Romain Warsziarg. (1999). "Is Europe Going too Far?" *Carnegie-Rochester Conference Series on Public Policy*, 51: 1–42.

Bardhan, Pranab. (2016). "State and Development: The Need for a Reappraisal of the Current Literature." *Journal of Economic Literature*, 54(3): 862–892.

Barrett, C. (2005). "Keynote Address at the Second Phase of WSIS." World Summit on the Information Society, Tunis, 16 November. http://www.itu.int/WSIS/tunis/statements/docs/ps-intel-opening/1.pdf.

Björk, Ragnar, and Thomas Lundén. (2021). *Territory, State and Nation: The Geopolitics of Rudolf Kjellén*. New York: Berghahn Books.

Boone, Catherine. (2012). "Territorial Politics and the Reach of the State: Unevenness by Design." *Revista de Ciencia Política*, 32(3): 623–641.

Braudel, Fernan. (1989). *The Identity of France: History and Environment*, Vol. 1. New York: Happer & Row.
Bresser-Pereira, Luis Carlos. (2010). *Globalization and Competition: Why Some Emergent Countries Succeed while Others Fall Behind*. New York: Cambridge University Press.
Busygina, Irina. (2018). *Russia-EU Relations and the Common Neighborhood: Coercion versus Authority*. London: Routledge.
Cummings, Sally Nikoline. (1999). "The political elite in Kazakhstan since independence (1991–1998): Origins, structure, and policies." PhD thesis, London School of Economics and Political Science.
Farazmand, Ali, ed. (2004). *Sound Governance: Policy and Administrative Innovations*. Westport, CT: Praeger.
Farazmand, Ali. (2017). "Governance Reforms: The Good, the Bad, and the Ugly; and the Sound." *Public Organization Review*, 17(4): 595–617.
Franke, Anja, Andrea Gawrich, and Gurban Alakbarov. (2009). "Kazakhstan and Azerbaijan as Post-Soviet Rentier States: Resource Incomes and Autocracy as a Double 'Curse' in Post-Soviet Regimes." *Europe-Asia Studies*, 61(1): 109–140.
Giddens, Anthony. (1985). *The Nation-State and Violence*. London: Routledge.
Gill, Graeme. (2016). *The Nature and Development of the Modern State*. London: Palgrave Macmillan.
Goldenberg, Jacob, and Moshe Levy. (2009). Distance Is Not Dead: Social Interaction and Geographical Distance in the Internet Era. *ACM SIGCAS Computers and Society*.
Gray, Colin. (1977). *The Geopolitics of the Nuclear Era*. New York: Crane Russak.
Hiscox, Michael, and David Lake. (2002). Democracy, Federalism, and the Size of States. https://ssrn.com/abstract=1002686 or http://dx.doi.org/10.2139/ssrn.1002686.
Jones, Martin, Rhys Jones, and Michael Woods. (2004). *An Introduction to Political Geography: Space, Place and Politics*. London; New York: Routledge.
Kagansky, Vladimir. (2002). "Insane Space." *Otechestvennye Zapiski*, 6. [Nevmenyaemoe prostranstvo].
Katzenstein, Peter. (2003). "Small States and Small States Revisited." *New Political Economy*, 8(1): 9–30.
Kaufmann, Daniel, and Aart Kraay. (2008). "Governance Indicators: Where Are We, Where Should We Be Going?" *The World Bank Research Observer*, 23(1): 1–30.
Kellerman, Aaron, and Maria Paradiso. (2008). "Geographical Location in the Information Age: From Destiny to Opportunity?" *GeoJournal*. http://dx.doi.org/10.1007/s10708-008-9131-2.
Lappo, Grigory. (2005). "The Results of Russian Urbanization to the End of XX Century." In *Russia and Its Regions at the End of XX Century*. Moscow: OGI. [Rossiya i ee regiony k kontsy XX veka].
Libman, Alexander, and Michael Rochlitz. (2019). *Federalism in China and Russia*. Cheltenham, UK: Edward Elgar.
Mackinder, Halford. (1904). "The Geographical Pivot of History." *The Geographical Journal*, 23(4): 421–437.
O'Donnell, Guillermo. (1993). "On the State, Development, and Some Conceptual Problems: A Latin American View with Some Glances at Some Post-Communist Countries." *World Development*, 21: 1355–1369.
Panarin, Igor. (2009). *The Collapse of Dollar and Disintegration of the United States*. Moscow: Goryachaya Linia. [Krakh Dollara i Raspad SShA].
Rodrik, Dani. (2011). *The Globalization Paradox*. Oxford: Oxford University Press.
Rosenberg, Matt. (2021). "A Country's Shape Can Impact Its Fortunes and Destiny." ThoughtCo, February 16. thoughtco.com/shape-of-the-state-1433558.
Sassen, Saskia. (2003). "The State and Globalization." *Interventions: International Journal of Postcolonial Studies*, 5(2).
Spruyt, Henrik. (1994). *The Sovereign State and Its Competitors: An Analysis of Systems Change*. Princeton, NJ: Princeton University Press.

Stepan, Alfred. (1999). "Federalism and Democracy: Beyond the U.S. Model." *Journal of Democracy*, 10(4).

Treivish, Andrei. (2010). "What Are Giant States and How to 'fight' Them. In *Giant Countries: The Problems of Territorial Stability*, ed. by Irina Busygina, Leonid Smirnyagin, and Mikhail Filippov. Moscow: MGIMO University. [Chto takoe gosudarsva-giganty i kak s nimi "borot'sya. V Strany-Giganty: Problemy Territorial'noi Stabil'nosti. Pod red. Iriny Busyginoi, Leonida Smirnyagina i Mikhaila Filippova. Moskva: MGIMO-Universitet].

Weiss, Linda. (1998). *The Myth of the Powerless State*. Ithaca, NY: Cornell University Press.

3 Borders as geographical institutions

As Newman argued,

> borders create and support difference. The existence of borders enables us to maintain some sort of *order*, both within the spaces and groups which are thus encompassed, as well as between "our" compartment and that of the "other" groups and spaces which are part of a broader system of global ordering.
>
> (Newman 2003: 15)

The concept of boundary (border) can rightfully claim the title of a general scientific concept or even a philosophical category. Border is something located between two objects and separating them, or something lying directly around one object and separating it from the rest, but this "something" itself is usually negligibly small in comparison with the objects, phenomena, and entities being separated. The phenomena to be delimited have names (proper or nominative) or signs substituting them, eventually deciphered in words, while the boundary in most cases has no name, it is recognized through the names of the objects which it delimits (Rodoman 1982: 20). In other words, boundaries are represented but not depicted. The phenomenon of the boundary itself is not expressed on a map.

If you ask a geographer about borders between states, regions, and communities (in general, about any borders that can be shown on a map), he will answer that this is certainly an object of study of geography and only geography. Since a boundary is a spatial object. This is true but not completely true. Borders "belong" not only to geographers but also to all scholars of social sciences. The studies of borders are principally multidisciplinary, they draw together political scientists, geographers, sociologists, anthropologists, historians, economists, international lawyers, and even philosophers. At the same time, the boundaries discussed in this book are geographical institutions. They meet the classical definition of institutions as rules that structure and constrain human behavior. They are drawn across a territory – and, thus, are significant elements of the political–geographical landscape. While states prefer to draw "safe" borders that would minimize uncertainty and costs, it is impossible to anticipate all possible implications of a new border (Carter and Goemans 2011). The solution found may be the most optimal under current

DOI: 10.4324/9781003496731-5

conditions, but changing those conditions may lead to disputed boundaries by one or both parties. The collapse of the Soviet Union is a good example of this.

In the words of the historian Serhii Plokhy,

> the collapse of the Soviet Union, like the disintegration of past empires, is a process rather than an event. And the collapse of the last empire is still unfolding today. This process did not end with Mikhail Gorbachev's resignation on Christmas Day 1991, and its victims are not limited to the three people who died defending the Moscow White House in August 1991 or the thousands of casualties from the Chechen wars.[1]

More than 30 years after the collapse of the Soviet Union, its former republics dispute the borders between them: Azerbaijan expels Armenians from Nagorno-Karabakh, Kyrgyzstan and Tajikistan are unhappy with the demarcation of a common border, Russia claims some Ukrainian territories and, in a war of aggression, pushes its border west and south. According to Dmitry Medvedev, deputy head of the Russian Security Council (and former president of the country), the strategic borders of states depend on their "political strength," sovereignty, and power: "all our adversaries need to firmly and forever understand a simple truth: the territories on both banks of the Dnieper River are an integral part of Russia's strategic historical borders, so all attempts to forcibly change them are doomed."[2] Crimea, Donetsk, and Luhansk People's Republics, Zaporizhzhia and Kherson regions became part of Russia following referendums held there in 2014 and 2022. Ukraine and Western countries do not recognize their results and consider this as annexation.

Importantly, national development is inextricably related to the state-centered cartography defined by borders, in other words, development takes place within the borders of states. There are numerous examples of how boundaries directly affect development. Indeed, if a state is involved in a long-term border conflict, this can significantly slow down its development, diverting resources, exacerbating relations with neighbors, and negatively affecting the reputation of the state's elites. On the other hand, open and transparent borders can contribute to the economic development of small and poorly located states. This is confirmed by the experience of the European Union, where smaller countries benefit from the "four freedoms" governing the movement of goods, persons, services, and capital within the European Union. They are the cornerstones of the Single Market and the common currency. Many see them as the greatest achievement of the European integration project. Besides that, borders can be critical for a successful regime change. Among all the preconditions for the success of democracy consolidation, the most important is the existence of consensus in society about the boundaries of the state and its identity (Schmitter 2010; Linz and Stepan 1996).

Typology and functions of borders

One of the better-known typologies of borders was posited by the American geographer Richard Hartshorne (1959), who described the process of border demarcation in terms of "antecedent," "subsequent," "superimposed," and "natural" borders. *Antecedent* borders were those which had been delimited *prior* to the settlement of the area in question in what was perceived as constituting virgin or unsettled land. As such, the border determined *ipso facto* the creation of separate societies and, in current terminology, difference, between later settlers in the region, contingent upon the side of the border which they chose as their place of residence. *Subsequent* boundaries were those which were demarcated according to the existing settlement patterns and difference, supposedly reflecting the ethno-territorial patterns of the region. *Superimposed* borders were those which were imposed by an outside (usually colonial) power on a region under their control, often with scant regard to the existing tribal and ethnic settlement patterns. The result of such superimposed boundaries was the division of tribal and ethnic territories between more than one state, or the inclusion of numerous ethnic groups in a single territory, giving rise to much of the ethnic strife that has plagued Africa and parts of Asia until today (we have discussed such borders in the chapters on Asia and Africa) (Newman 2006: 174).

Generally, borders are characterized by a duality of functions – barrier and contact. A border divides states and regions by impeding flows of all kinds (goods, people, information), it weakens these flows, filters them, detains them. At the same time, it is the border that connects neighboring territories. The barrier and contact functions, complementing each other, are localized differently. As a bearer of border functions, the border will be bifurcated: the contactor will be the center and the barrier – the contour (the border itself) (Kagansky 1982). Let's look, for instance, at Russia: flows are detained and filtered at its state border, but the main contactor of the country with the outside world is its capital – Moscow.

On the world political map, we see the "jigsaw" of states, each clearly demarcated by a line – the state border – and illustrated in a separate color. We take this picture for granted, as if borders are "eternal." But look, for example, at Europe: all the borders have shifted at some point in history and only ten European states (!) have the same borders today as they did 100 years ago. This means that borders are very much in flux and that their physical appearance changes in both space and time. Wars for territory, of which there are no fewer in the modern world, ultimately have one goal: to move borders, expanding the territory of one state at the expense of another.

There are a lot of unusual borders which reflect specific historical circumstances or situations. In *The Atlas of Unusual Borders*, Zoran Nikolić (2019) provided around 50 illustrated examples. A large proportion of the book focuses on Europe, which is expected given the long and complex history of the many political jurisdictions on the continent, the others are located in Africa and South America. Many of the borders included in the atlas are provided as standalone examples, whereas others are clustered into groups, such as "Unusual capitals" and "Ghost towns." Indeed, it is not uncommon to see the border cutting right through the middle of the streets and even houses. In the small European town of Baarle, parts of Belgium and the Netherlands sit side by side. One can simply waltz between the two countries by stepping over the slabs marked with the letters B and L. While the Belgian area is called Baarle-Herog, the Dutch one is called Baarle Nassau. Another example:

a pair of rocky islands in the middle of the Bering Strait, the Diomede Islands are separated by the International Date Line that marks the border between the United States and Russia. Big Diomede is part of the Russian Federation while Little Diomede is owned by the United States. Since Big Diomede is 23 hours ahead of its Russian counterpart owing to the International Date Line, it is often called Tomorrow Island and Yesterday Isle respectively. And the only quadripoint in the world, the borders of Botswana, Namibia, Zambia, and Zimbabwe, all meet at one place. And then the tri-border shared by the three countries is formed by the natural convergence of two rivers – the Parana River and the Iguazu River. The region of Foz do Iguaçu is where Brazil, Paraguay, and Argentina form a triple frontier.

Interstate borders

Generally, the views on borders at one time or another corresponded to the concept of state (or empire). The focus of the Holy Roman Empire was not on defining their territories in terms of fixed borders but rather on controlling people and settlements. The idea of fixed, immovable borders contradicted the very essence of the empire, which sought territorial expansion. The Peace of Westphalia (1648) introduced a principally different approach, it was the starting point for the modern state system in Europe. Since then, the principle of "nation-state" sovereignty and the right of "national self-determination" has gradually emerged and provided a new understanding of borders (instead of imperial frontiers) dividing not just people but also territory (Haselsberger 2014: 506). Fixed linear borders became to be markers for state sovereignty. However, it was not until the early nineteenth century that exclusive border lines were established instead of the former permeable frontiers. Making and remaking political maps became an important activity of the state, and maps were seen as crucial to the maintenance of state power. According to Haselsberger (2014), this did not mean that

> state borders in Europe were fixed as stable, sealed, and efficient lines separating states. Indeed, the opposite is true. On the one hand, Europe had been through a process of consolidation (driven by the imperatives of territorial aggrandizement) of small states and fiefdoms (like king- and dukedoms) into larger multi-national entities, a process which reached its zenith at the end of the nineteenth century. On the other hand, the twentieth century saw the successive break-up of the great European empires.

In the beginning of the twentieth century, German geopolitics made its contribution to the understanding of the sense of borders in Europe. For instance, Friedrich Ratzel's concept of boundaries followed logically from his view of the state as a living organism. The boundary was the skin of the living state, and like the epidermis of animals and plants it provided defense and allowed exchange with environment to occur (Prescott 1965: 10). Later, the period of the Cold War (1945–1991) must be recognized as the high point of stable, sharply demarcated state borders in twentieth-century Europe. In this period, states achieved an unprecedented degree of control over the economy, politics, and culture of their citizens and a capacity to regulate cross-border flows that can be described as territorial "boundedness" of states. Contemporary Europe has many more state borders than existed in the period prior to the collapse of the Iron Curtain in 1989.

Globalization became a driver for discussions of a "borderless" and "deterritorialized" world. However, today even the "globalization purists" accept that the state (with its borders!) is still in its place, playing a different, but strategically no less important role in the global world.

A *state border* is a line that defines the limits of a state's territory and, accordingly, the limits of state sovereignty. State borders are divided into land, river, lake, sea, and air. Borders can be drawn considering natural objects – mountains, rivers, lakes (orographic borders), or established by drawing straight lines (geometric borders: we find them, for instance, on a map of Africa in the Sahara zone) or conducted by parallels and meridians (astronomical borders: this is a border on a map of North America between the United States and Canada).

The emergence of the concept of state border is associated with the emergence of the institution of the state. State borders are state institutions. The borders of the state marked the territory, which the sovereign protected and from which he collected tribute (taxes).

There are usually two stages in the process of establishing a state border:

(1) Delimitation of the border – the contractual determination of the border line and its mapping;
(2) Demarcation of the border – marking (establishment of special boundary signs) of the border line on the ground in accordance with the agreement on delimitation. (Demarcation lines should be distinguished from state borders. The former could appear because of an armistice following a military conflict. For example, in the twentieth century such lines divided into two states Korea in 1949 and Vietnam in 1954).

Preexisting boundaries never disappear quickly. Or they don't disappear at all. The term "phantom borders" is often used as a synonym for relict borders. Officially not existing, these borders still evoke strong emotions in population, they remain a subject of political discourse and, therefore, can be used in political mobilization, for strengthening or transforming national, ethnic, or regional identities. The most known cases of "phantom borders" include the Great Wall of China, which has become the most recognizable monument in China, or the Berlin Wall (Checkpoint Charlie, in particular), which is one of the main symbols of the Cold War (Kolosov 2020). As Braudel beautifully wrote, "history tends to consolidate borders, which seem to turn into natural folds of the terrain, inherently belonging to the landscape and not easy to move" (Braudel 1989: 274).

It's worth adding that new international (state) borders are rarely brand new. So, when states choose new borders, they usually use previous administrative boundaries to solve a difficult short-term bargaining problem and long-term coordination and accommodation problems. Borders drawn along previous administrative boundaries experience fewer territorial disputes and have a lower risk of militarized confrontation in case a dispute emerges. When the Soviet Union fell apart in 1991 and 1992, the international borders of the new republics were overwhelmingly drawn following the previously existing internal administrative borders of the Soviet Union. As the annexation of Crimea from Ukraine to Russia in 2014 and the war that Russia unleashed against Ukraine in 2022 showed, this did not completely prevent territorial conflicts but postponed their occurrence by 25 years.

Administrative borders

Within the territory of a state, we usually find administrative boundaries separating subnational (internal) regions. An administrative boundary may also separate territorial autonomy from the "mainland." As mentioned earlier, the ideal of nation-building in nineteenth-century Europe was "one nation, one state." However, this ideal was practically unattainable; all European states (except the smallest in terms of territory) contained ethnic minorities. To prevent conflicts between the minority and the majority, *territorial autonomy* (TA) was invented that implied the existence of a certain geographical territory with a special status as compared to other subnational territories. TA implied some legislative powers for the territory but no political autonomy (as in a federation, where the regions – territorial entities of a federation – have political autonomy) (Olausson 2007: 25). The "classical" minorities requiring TA are ethnic minorities, especially in case of their geographically compact settlement; but in some cases, the basis for TA can be a special geographical position – these can be islands, former colonies, and dependent territories (e.g., the Netherlands Antilles, New Caledonia, the Azores, Sicily, and Sardinia). It is important to underline that TA does not imply a requirement of sovereignty for the territory, TA includes only the powers necessary for the autonomy to preserve its cultural identity, such as bilingualism of local authorities, powers of education, culture (including protection of cultural heritage) and media, as well as the development of its own symbols (Benedikter 2009).

Borders that separate the US states from each other are called astronomical. This was President Jefferson who established the "grid system," de facto following the solution adopted by the English crown, based on the geographic coordinate system. Jefferson decided to start with measures taken in the field. The first experimental result was the Mason-Dixon Line between Maryland and Pennsylvania: the first linear boundary, with markers (*milestones*) every mile and special *Crownstones* every five miles. Jefferson's idea was simple and efficient. The Federal Cadaster was simple and already available in the Land Registry in Washington before the pioneers could began taking possession of the Western territories (Bellezza 2023).

Administrative boundaries between territorial entities (states, regions) of a country can become a serious obstacle to national development, modernization, and democratization processes, especially in federal and decentralized states. As Gibson (2012) showed, the democratization of a national government is only a first step in the diffusion of democracy throughout a country's territory. Even after a national government is democratized, subnational (regional) governments create authoritarian "enclaves" and continue to resist the infiltration of democratic practices and institutions from the federal center into their territories. Gibson's theory of "boundary control" captured the conflict pattern between incumbents and oppositions when a national democratic government exists alongside authoritarian regions. His perspective explains subnational variations in democratic institutionalization. According to him, "the existence of a democratic national government alongside a provincial authoritarian government within the nation-state creates a situation of regime juxtaposition. Two levels of government with jurisdiction over the same territory operate under different institutional regimes" (Gibson 2012: 103). In his book, he concluded that the resilience of local authoritarian rule "is a testament to the strategic, economic, and political tools available to local boundary closers, as well as to the national partisan networks that organize and protect them" (Gibson 2012: 146).

Gibson compared the late-nineteenth-century American "Solid South" with contemporary experiences in Argentina and Mexico. However, political developments on the "other side of the world," in Russia in the 1990s, show striking similarities to what Gibson described and analyzed in the Latin American experience. In Russia, during this period, Moscow's efforts to push democratic reforms into the regions were also met with stiff resistance from regional authorities, who resisted the process and closed boundaries. Another reason for closing boundaries was the deep economic crisis, which forced the regions to find ways to survive on their own (Busygina 2016).

Borders as institutions

Like all institutions, borders are a set of internal rules which govern and constrain the behavior of actors; borders are self-enforceable and resistant to change. Border institutions govern the extent of inclusion and exclusion, the degree of permeability, and the laws governing trans-boundary movement – exit from one side of the border and entry into the other side.

Borders are barriers. As Newman argues (2003), "borders prevent the entry of undesired elements – be they people, goods, arms, drugs and – albeit to a much lesser extent than in the past – information. The determination of just what can and cannot move beyond the border is conditioned by the power elites of a given society or country, by their views on the border as an institution which protects those who are on the 'inside' or are 'here' from the (perceived) negative impact of those who have been excluded and are on the 'outside' or are 'there.' At the same time, borders protect the safety of those inside from external threats, be it drugs, migrant labor, competition in the marketplace, and so on. Borders contain external cultural and ideological influence on domestic audience undesirable for national elites."

But equally important is the contact function of borders. Following Newman (2003),

> [F]rom the moment they are established, there are always groups who have an interest in finding ways to move beyond the barrier. They may be seeking

> jobs, visiting family and friends from whom they have been cut off, smuggling goods, drugs, or weapons. . . . To study borders as dynamic institutions, it is therefore important to study the "bottom up" process of change, emanating from the daily practices of ordinary people living in the borderland region, as much as the traditional "top down" approach which focuses solely on the role of institutional actors, notably – but not only – governments.
>
> (Newman 2003)

Carter and Goemans (2011) argued that an institutional perspective on borders suggests that borders have another important function – they

> *coordinate* the expectations and behavior of both international and domestic actors and thereby produce joint gains. While both domestic and international actors may have conflicting preferences over the precise location of the border, the worst outcome is to have no delineated border at all. The result of a failure to agree on a border is both domestic and international uncertainty which at a minimum impedes trade and at a maximum lead to incessant conflict. Internationally as well as domestically, borders delineate relevant jurisdictions and help coordinate economic, social, and military interactions.

Thus, the delineation of international boundaries implies a bargaining process between two parties having both compatible and conflicting interests (this process can also involve the third party, the UN). States have compatible interests regarding the outcome – in drawing a border – because it clarifies jurisdictions. However, the states may (and usually do) conflict the very location of a border because this location means territorial benefits for one party and losses for the other. In other words, both parties want to coordinate but on different outcomes (Carter and Goemans 2011).

Further, Carter and Goemans (2011) considered borders atypical institutions for at least two reasons.

> First, it is difficult to conceive of an institution more salient to a state than its borders. Borders define the state's territorial jurisdiction and control and the identity of its members and thereby affect almost all the state's policies in some respect. Second, the establishment of borders is not subject to a "renegotiation clause." Rather, attempts to revise an established border, imply the very costly outside option of opening a territorial dispute. Recent research has unambiguously established that territorial disputes are economically costly and relatively likely to escalate to militarized conflicts.

Frontier as a geographic institution and a way of life

Frontier is a strip of land that forms the margin of settled or developed territory. It is a specific type of moving border characteristic of communities in the process of expanding their territory. In general, the frontier itself is a process of change. On the frontier, the nature of institutions – political, economic, and social – is determined by the ongoing process of exploration.

Frederick Jackson Turner interpreted the frontier as a border between developed and undeveloped lands, as "the process of meeting, unexpected collision of colonizers, local population and the environment" (Turner 1920: 23–27). Much later, Elizabeth Furniss (2005: 23) defined the frontier as "the point or moment of meeting between savagery and civilization." The frontier has been important to the exploration and development of countries such as Canada, Australia, Brazil, and Russia. However, the frontier has been both celebrated and criticized most in the United States.

As Altenbernd and Young (2014: 127) stated,

> [F]or US scholars, the very word frontier is irrevocably linked to the legacy of historian Frederick Jackson Turner (1861–1932), who, in his 1893 essay "The Significance of The Frontier in American History," cast the frontier as both a moving line of settlement and the well-spring of American individualism and democracy. Today, US scholars reject Turner's "frontier thesis" as inherently ethnocentric and nationalistic and have largely backed away from the idea that the frontier is the locus of US history and culture."

Turner was criticized for painting an idealized picture of the frontier and frontiersman. The land that Turner characterized as "free" was in fact violently taken from Native Americans and, in many cases, westward expansion was more "conquest" than "settlement" (Limerick 1988). Henry Reynolds (2006) pointed out the same features of the Australian frontier.

The frontier was idealized – and then de-idealized. However, I would like to draw attention to something else – the specialness of the frontier as a geographical institution and the fact that, indeed, the presence of a frontier of settlement shaped early US history (see Chapter XX) as well the history of some other countries. The frontier created special communities and a special way of life. According to Bazzi, Fiszbein, and Gebresilasse (2020), the American frontier shaped a culture of rugged individualism that persisted throughout time. They explained the significance of the frontier can be by three factors.

> First, frontier locations attracted individualists able to thrive in harsh conditions. Second, frontier conditions – isolation and low population density – further cultivated self-reliance, and they offered favorable prospects for upward mobility through effort, nurturing hostility to redistribution. Finally, frontier conditions shaped local culture at a critical juncture, thus generating persistent effects.
>
> (Bazzi, Fiszbein and Gebresilasse 2020: 2329–2330)

The world of the frontier was contradictory. For all its harshness and even cruelty, it stimulated voluntary activity, social trust, tolerance of outgroups, and civic protest (Foa, Nemirovskaya and Mostovova 2012). Frontiers in different countries influenced national development in different ways. In the United States, the frontier culture become entrenched at the national level because the frontier has been settled by a significant proportion of the country's population, the population movement was unrestrained, and land was made readily available to newcomers. However, this has been less true historically of Canada, Brazil, and Russia, where settlement of the frontier was a more centralized and a more controlled process. In all these countries, until very recently, "the vast majority of the population has lived not along the frontier but rather in the territories of the Atlantic coast, or in the case of Russia, along the European waterways, the Volga, Don, and Neva. Those who made it to the frontier of Canada, or Brazil, may have lived much as their counterparts have done in the United States, autonomous and self-reliant, with relatively egalitarian and decentralized institutions, only that their numbers were remarkably fewer" (Foa, Nemirovskaya and Mostovova 2012: 38).

Why border disputes?

The history of border disputes is as old as the history of the borders themselves. Political elites of neighboring polities have claimed the same territory and sought to move the border in their favor, believing that they were the first to discover and settle it, especially since the legal establishment of borders began relatively late and was quite conflictual. Another, more practical, aspiration of the elites was to move the border away from the national capital or important strategic sites to guarantee national security.

A frequent case of a territorial (border) dispute is the issue of border demarcation. The subject of disputes between states can be ownership of the border territory or the question of the place of the border line. Kyrgyz–Tajik border conflict is a telling example. Since the breakup of the Soviet Union in 1991, the disputes over border demarcation remained the main issue between Kyrgyzstan and Tajikistan. Border disputes caused multiple conflicts over access and use of natural resources as water for irrigation and pasture grounds for grazing animals. As Tajik and Kyrgyz authorities proved to be incapable of finding a mutually acceptable solution, they avowed the disputed territories neutral (Kurmanalieva 2019). This decision, however, did not bring peace. The fighting along the Kyrgyz–Tajik border in April 2021 came as a shock, despite the clear signs that tensions were building along that border for years. It was the first time since the five Central Asian states became independent in late 1991 that militaries of two countries had engaged in combat against each other. While the skirmishes were over relatively quickly, the fighting was on a scale never seen before in the area, and most casualties were civilians. There have been attempts at reconciliation despite the mutual accusations over who is at fault – and the question of marking the last sections of the Kyrgyz–Tajik frontier has gained new urgency.[3]

Observing the history of border disputes, it is possible to summarize the argumentation of the parties include:

- history and the age of ownership;
- effectiveness of possession, that is, continuous and nonviolent exercise of territorial supremacy over the disputed territory, at least de facto;

- the conduct of the disputing parties (prolonged silence may be taken as consent of the party);
- identity and preferences of the inhabitants of the disputed border territory.

Border disputes and conflicts arise for the following reasons:

- On ethnic grounds (example: in the summer of 1977, Somalia made territorial claims on part of Ethiopia, the Ogaden Desert, on the grounds that the territory was inhabited by ethnic Somalis);
- After the political division of territories along the front lines (example: fighting between North and South Korean border guards);
- As a harbinger of war (example 1: conflicts on the border between the South and the North of the United States before the beginning of the Civil War in the states of Missouri and Kansas; example 2: the modern border conflict between Ethiopia and Eritrea as a harbinger of the beginning of hostilities);
- As a legacy of the colonial period (example 1: territorial disputes between former colonies of Spain in Latin America; example 2: The Falkland Islands (Malvinas) as an object of dispute between Great Britain and Argentina. The origins of the dispute, which in 1982 led to an armed conflict, date back to the colonial period);
- On religious grounds (example: the border conflicts between Saudi Arabia and Iraq: between Sunnis and Shiites);
- On economic grounds (example 1: dispute between Iraq and Iran over the use of the Shatt al-Arab border waterway; example 2: dispute between Venezuela and Guyana over territory transferred to Guyana in 1899. The territory is extremely rich in gold, diamond, and oil);
- Because of incomplete and/or imperfect border delimitation/demarcation. (The longer the border, the more contiguous the states, the more likely the disputed territories are. For example, China's border has many disputed areas, primarily with India and Tajikistan but also with the DPRK and Vietnam. The problem of border delimitation and demarcation was acutely felt by most states of the former Soviet Union in the 1990s.)

Borderlands/border regions

Borders necessarily influence adjacent territories. According to Newman (2006: 180),

> [T]he nature of the border would definitively have an impact on the "borderland." The specific borderland characteristics will vary contingent upon the degree of openness or closeness of the border, enabling or preventing contact and interaction. Borderlands may undergo differential development on each side of the border, dependent on the respective policies exercised by the authorities on each side.

For instance, within the European Union, trans-boundary interaction zones have been actively encouraged as a means of bringing peoples together prior to the ultimate opening and removal of the interstate borders. The European Union has invested a great deal of resources into the creation of trans-boundary activity spaces, creating frontier zones of interaction – or even integrative borderland landscapes (Rumford 2006; Zielonka 2002). The Association of European Border Regions (AEBR) aims to safeguard cross-border cooperation as one of the priorities of European cohesion and regional policy as well as being responsible for the drawing up of the Charter of the European Border and Cross-Border Regions.

Borderland or border region is an area close to the state border, subject to frequent border effects and a territory perceived as border by most of the involved population (Lechevalier and Wielgohs 2013). Borderlands are the territories experiencing "border effects," and these effects manifest themselves in very different ways. This can be, for instance, the effect of "nobody's land" or peripheral effect when border regions become more or less "handicapped" and damaged areas due to their distance from the national capital and large cities, difficult access, and often imperfect infrastructure. Such borderlands become a challenge for national development, requiring constant increased financial redistribution, special programs, or even the relocation of the national capital (as it happened, for instance, in Brazil with the relocation of the capital from Rio de Janeiro to Brasilia).

A different effect of diffusion is primarily manifested due to the borders contact function. In this case, the potential difference, that is the difference between neighboring regions, would stimulate border interaction, contacts, passenger, and freight traffic despite a diverse level of price and quality of goods, services, and opportunities on both sides of the border. It is obvious that the development of transborder cooperation brings along/initiates a simple diffusion effect and processes resulting in the diffusion of neighboring cultures, so-called pull effect, that is, development affected (pulled) by the neighboring region. The exploration of border regions with a special combination of border effects in each case shows that *each border region is unique*.

It is important to add that the development dynamics of borderlands depends very much upon the capacity of a state to which these borderlands belong. If state capacity is low, borderlands start to "live their own lives" trying to survive by making use of their specific geographic location. The forms of such survival may well include various nonlegal activities and the development of special local communities associated with special activities, primarily smuggling. Such communities are typical for, for example, the US–Mexico or Polish–Ukrainian border.

Interestingly enough, de facto states can also turn into borderlands. Let's look, for instance, at Abkhazia and South Ossetia. The two actors that had a decisive impact on the borders, whether de facto or de jure, of Abkhazia and South Ossetia are Georgia and the Russian Federation, being the only two countries that share a border with these de facto states. South Ossetia is in fact landlocked by its two larger neighbors while Abkhazia has an extensive coastline along the Black Sea. In reality, these two territories are not only de facto states but also Russian borderlands. These two perspectives do not contradict each other, they are just different.

While the first one focuses on the deficits in statehood and sovereignty of such political entities, the second is more geographically oriented and focuses on Russia, which in fact has border regions beyond its official boundaries.

In the modern world, borders have proved to remain resilient institutions; states adapt and reinvent border control in different ways (Gülzau, Mau, and Korte 2021). "Borderless world," predicted by Kenichi Ohmae (1990), caused by the free movement of capital and provoked hot discussion, seems not to be emerging. Borders increase in number, including economic ones. Authoritarian rules work on the erection of new borders and the remaking of old ones in their favor, which it suffices to recall Russia's fierce calls for "economic and technological sovereignty," supported by a number of national leaders.

Notes

1 The Soviet Union Is Gone, But It's Still Collapsing (yahoo.com).
2 Медведев рассказал о границах России, которые "шире географических" – РБК (rbc.ru).
3 https://www.rferl.org/a/majlis-podcast-making-sense-of-the-clashes-at-the-kyrgyz-tajik-border/31246182.html

References

Altenbernd, Erik, and Alex Trimble Young. (2014). "Introduction: The Significance of the Frontier in an Age of Transnational History." *Settler Colonial Studies*, 4(2): 127–150.

Bazzi, Samuel, Martin Fiszbein, and Mesay Gebresilasse. (2020). "Frontier Culture: The Roots and Persistence of 'Rugged Individualism' in the United States." *Econometrica*, 88(6): 2329–2368.

Bellezza, Giuliano. (2023). "On Borders: From Ancient to Postmodern Times." ISPRS/IGU/ICA Joint Workshop on Borderlands Modelling and Understanding for Global Sustainability, 5–6 December, Beijing, China.

Benedikter, Thomas. (2009). *The World's Modern Autonomy System: Concepts and Experiences of Regional Territorial Autonomy*. Bolzano: Institute of Minority Rights, EURAC Research.

Braudel, Fernan. (1989). *The Identity of France: History and Environment*, Vol. 1. New York: Happer & Row.

Busygina, Irina. (2016). "How Does Russian Federalism Work? Looking at Internal Borders in the Russian Federation." *Journal of Borderlands Studies*, 32(1): 1–15.

Carter, David, and H. E. Goemans. (2011). "The Making of Territorial Order: New Borders and Interstate Conflict." *International Organization*, 65(2): 275–309.

Foa, Roberto, Anna Nemirovskaya, and Elena Mostovova. (2012). "Internal Empires I: Social Institutions of the Frontier: National Research University 'Higher School of Economics'." *Series: Sociology*, 9.

Furniss, Elizabeth. (2005). "Imagining the Frontier: Comparative Perspectives from Canada and Australia." In *Dislocating the Frontier: Essaying the Mystique of the Outback*, ed. by Deborah Bird Rose and Richard Davis, pp. 23–46. Canberra, Australia: ANU Press.

Gibson, Edward. (2012). *Boundary Control: Subnational Authoritarianism in Federal Democracies*. Cambridge: Cambridge University Press.

Gülzau, Fabian, Steffen Mau, and Kristina Korte. (2021). "Borders as Places of Control. Fixing, Shifting and Reinventing State Borders. An Introduction." *Historical Social Research/Historische Sozialforschung*, 46(3): 7–22.

Hartshorne, Richard. (1959). *Perspective on the Nature of Geography*. Chicago: Published for the Association of American Geographers by Rand McNally.

Haselsberger, Beatrix. (2014). "Decoding Borders: Appreciating Border Impacts on Space and People." *Planning Theory & Practice*, 15(4): 505–526.

Kagansky, Vladimir. (1982). "Geographical Borders: Contradictions and Paradoxes." In *Geographical Borders*, ed. by Boris Rodoman and Boris Ekkel, pp. 7–19. Moscow: MGU. [Geograficheskie granitsy: protivorechya i paradoksy].

Kolosov, Vladimir. (2020). "Phantom Borders: The Role in Territorial Identity and the Impact on Society." *Belgeo: Revue belge de géographie*, 2.

Kurmanalieva, Gulzana. (2019). "Kyrgyzstan and Tajikistan: Endless Border Conflicts." *EUCACIS Online Paper*, 4.

Lechevalier, Arnaud, and Jan Wielgohs, eds. (2013). *Borders and Border Regions in Europe*. Bielefeld, Germany: Transcript Verlag.

Limerick, Patricia. (1988). *The Legacy of Conquest: The Unbroken Past of the American West*. New York: Norton.

Linz, Juan, and Alfred Stepan. (1996). *Problems of Democratic Transition and Consolidation: Southern Europe, South America, and Post-Communist Europe*. Baltimore, MD: Johns Hopkins University Press.

Newman, David. (2003). "On Borders and Power: A Theoretical Framework." *Journal of Borderlands Studies*, 18(1).

Newman, David. (2006). "Borders and Bordering: Towards an Interdisciplinary Dialogue." *European Journal of Social Theory*, 9(2): 171–186.

Nikolić, Zoran. (2019). *The Atlas of Unusual Borders*. New York: HarperCollins Publishers.

Ohmae, Kenichi. (1990). *The Borderless World: Power and Strategy in the Interlinked Economy*. New York: HarperBusiness.

Olausson, Pär. (2007). *Autonomy and Islands, a Global Study of the Factors That Determine Island Autonomy*. Åbo: Åbo Akademi University Press.

Prescott, John. (1965). *The Geography of Frontiers and Boundaries*. London, UK: Routledge.

Reynolds, Henry. (2006). *The Other Side of the Frontier: Aboriginal Resistance to the European Invasion of Australia*. Sydney: University of New South Wales Press.

Rodoman, Boris. (1982). "The Main Types of Geographical Borders." In *Geographical Borders*, ed. by Boris Rodoman and Boris Ekkel. Moscow: MGU. [Osnovnye tipy geographicheskikh granits].

Rumford, Chris. (2006). "Borders and Rebordering." In *Europe and Asia Beyond East and West: Towards a New Cosmopolitanism*, ed. by Gerard Delanty. London: Routledge.

Schmitter, Philip. (2010). "Twenty-Five Years, Fifteen Findings." *Journal of Democracy*, 21(1): 17–28.

Turner, Frederick. (1920). *The Frontier in American History*. New York: H. Holt and Company.

Zielonka, Jan, ed. (2002). *Europe Unbound: Enlarging and Reshaping the Boundaries of the European Union*. London: Routledge.

Part II

4 Europe

Europe is a relatively small peninsula of the huge continent of Eurasia, where people lived in proximity, but – until recently – peacefully. The diversity in Europe for such a relatively small territorial size is amazing. This is in Europe, where advanced social and political institutions were created and later transferred to other parts of the world – with greater or lesser success. In this chapter, I trace the history of the creation of various territorial and political institutional forms, discuss their opportunities and constraints for development, and look at the contribution of geographic factors to this development.

The territorial size of European states is very different, their geographical location and shape greatly vary as well. It is important, however, that Europe (unlike Eurasia) has no hegemonial powers, and this conditions the structure of the European institutions to the most serious extent. Most Western European states have access to the sea, and the most "continental" point of the region (located in the east of Hungary and Slovakia) is 600 kilometers away from the sea. Let's note here the ruggedness of the coastal line of Europe, divided into several large peninsulas – Iberian, Apennine, Balkan, and Scandinavian. This was a premise for European political, social, and cultural diversity and the emergence of different polities in different parts of Europe.

The United Nations recognizes 50 countries in Europe. However, many lists of European countries include territories that could be countries, but which the United Nations does not recognize as such. For example, Kosovo is a territory that many consider independent, but others consider to be part of Serbia. Other country-sized noncountries include the massive island territory of Greenland, which is an autonomous dependent territory of Denmark, and the Faroe Islands, a self-governing overseas administrative division of Denmark. From ten poorest countries of Europe (measured in Gross National Income (GNI) per capita), nine are located outside the European Union; only Bulgaria, the EU member state, ranks tenth. The first place in the list of the poorest countries is occupied by Ukraine[1] (although is it right to put Ukraine on this list along with other countries when it has been systematically destroyed by the aggressive war unleashed by neighboring Russia for already more than two years?). At the other end of the spectrum is the Northern European cluster – Sweden, Finland, Denmark, the Netherlands, and Belgium – the "innovation leaders" of Europe.[2]

DOI: 10.4324/9781003496731-7

The entire history of Europe, from the ancient period to the present day, is full of fascinating evidence of the influence of geography and institutions on the development of territories and societies.

Ancient period

Already in antiquity (before the fifth century AD), Europe gave birth to two competing territorial polities – ancient Greece and Rome, which had fundamentally different territorial structures, different institutions, and constraints on development. It is no exaggeration to say that ancient Greece and the Roman Empire played an exceptional role in the development of mankind.

Scholars explained the miraculous phenomenon of ancient Greece by a special combination of factors; while one of the most important was the geographical one – its location on the shores of the Aegean Sea, the islands and straits of which served as "an ideal nursery for future sailors, merchants, and colonists" (Davis 1996: 71). The golden age of the Greek city-states fell in the eighteenth to fourth centuries BC. In the fifth century BC, Athens was on the rise of over other city-states; however, fierce rivalry in the fourth century put an end to the political hegemony of Athens – Sparta rose, then Thebes. Subsequently, Greece subjugated neighboring Macedonia, a Hellenized country north of Greece, and then the "Greece of cities" became a part of the vast empire created by Alexander the Great. As a result of the conquests of Alexander and his successors, the world of Greek city-states merged with a much larger and mostly non-Greek world. The Greek coastal civilization could not withstand the confrontation with the neighboring mainland states with their huge armies; Greek's extended communications were good for economic "soft" colonization by sea but not for waging wars on land. The army forces of Greece and Rome were highly unequal, and the conquest of Greece by Rome was completed by the end of the Pyrrhic Wars in 266 BC.

The Greek civilization did not "cover" the entire territory of Greece, it did not reach the inner mountainous regions. However, during the Golden Age, the geographical expansion of the Greek coastal policies was impressive. Miniature city-states located on the rocky Aegean coast often did not have sufficient resources to support the growing population (cities did not expand spatially, did not have hinterlands), and active colonization went to Sicily, southern Italy and on the Black Sea coast – Pontus Euxine. Over time, the early colonies became the starting points for further colonization, so that chains or families of cities appeared. The largest of these families was born of the city of Miletus: it included up to 80 cities. "Classic" Greek polis is usually described as a small flat area surrounded and protected by hills. Indeed, the plains immediately surrounding the polis provided it with agricultural products, and the frontier of the polis passed over the hills. The polis was not a geographic concept but rather a community united to govern its territory (Pounds 1973: 28).

The rise of Rome and turning it into the center of a powerful empire brought profound changes to the political history of Europe and beyond. Since the development of Europe has been linked to empires for centuries, let's define this concept.

An empire implied not only special institutions but also a special geography (territorial size and borders). Huge territorial size was an important, but not the only, attribute that distinguished empires from other polities. The empire was a multilevel and multinational political system. According to Motyl's colorful definition, it be could compared with *wheel without a rim*. Within this system, the elite of the core (metropolis) dominated the peripheral elites and societies, acting as intermediaries in their most important interactions and managing resource flows from the periphery to the core and vice versa. Thus, the empire constantly reproduced the model "dominant center – subordinate periphery"; the exchange of resources went through the center. Consequently, vertical connections were much stronger than horizontal ones (Motyl 2001). The boundaries of empires tended to fluctuate; they were dynamic rather than static and preserved remarkable resilience over time.[3]

Josep Colomer (2008, 2017) distinguished between empires and nation-states in the following way:

(1) Empires were vastly larger in territory than states.
(2) Empires lacked fixed or permanent boundaries, whereas a state did.
(3) Empires had a compound of diverse groups and territorial units with asymmetric links with the center, whereas a state had supreme authority over a territory and population.
(4) Empires had multilevel, overlapping jurisdictions, whereas a state sought monopoly and homogenization.

Unlike Greece, Rome was characterized by integrity and cohesion; the various parts of the Roman Empire were linked through control, the main channels of which were the military fortifications in each province; a dense network of roads connecting the provinces with Rome ("All roads lead to Rome"); general principles of law and administration, implemented through a unified army of officials. If Greece was a decentralized, weakly integrated system of policies, then Rome grew out of a single organism. While the Greek world gradually expanded by sea routes, the Roman world gathered around one core through the seizure of more and more territories. Rome and Italy were the "consumption centers" of the wealth and resources of the entire empire. When explaining the phenomenon of Rome, priority is given to the so-called territorial imperative, which means the extremely important role of physical territory – its organization, exploitation, and protection from outside invasions. Greece developed by sea, Rome collected lands.

Rome systematically populated and mobilized vast territories. In the first century AD, the vast Roman Empire stretched from the English Channel to the Sahara and from the Atlantic coast to Mesopotamia. The elites of the metropolis resorted to various means to ensure that the territories contributed to the maintenance of the military machine of Rome. At the same time, a kind of vicious circle arose: the growth of the territory required the growth of the army for its protection, and the growth of the army gave rise to the need for new territories for its maintenance. "A militarized society . . . has developed an insatiable" agrarian appetite "– an appetite for land" (Davis 1996: 117). Limes – a line of border fortifications – was the main feature of the empire's defenses. It marked which lands fell under the jurisdiction of Rome and which did not. Note, however, that within the framework of this general strategy, the actual political institutions in the provinces were remarkably diverse.

The empire was huge in territory but at the same time internally unstable. Gradually, it gave up its position: it "crumbled" at the edges and became demoralized in the center. The connections of the periphery with Rome were weakening; provinces began to demand autonomy. In 395, the Roman Empire was divided into Western and Eastern; Rome ceased to be a political center.

Middle Ages

During the Middle Ages (around the fifth to fifteenth centuries), the era of large empires has continued while the European (Christian) world has been reorganized into new imperial systems: it was this process that became one of the central political–territorial stories of the Middle Ages (Davis 1996: 214). The founding of the empire of Charlemagne in 800 and of the Holy Roman Empire in 962 were the main milestones of the imperial reorganization.

The empire of Charlemagne represented the alliance of the popes with the growing state of the Franks. Despite the weakness of this design, which completely disappeared after 100 years, its influence was significant. Charlemagne pushed the boundaries of the empire in all directions: to the Southern Alps, to Saxony, Bavaria, Carinthia, and beyond the Pyrenees. Interestingly, the empire was ruled by a court that constantly moved from one possession to another, and a network of 300 commitants or counties (the favorite residence of Karl – Kaiserpfalz – was the Aachen standing on the thermal springs). In 843, according to the Peace of Verdun, Charles's empire was divided into three parts among his grandchildren; this laid the foundations for both the future France and the future Germany (between them – the Middle Kingdom, which did not become the center of a stable territorial entity).

The Holy Roman Empire existed from 926 to 1806 (from the end of the fifteenth century to the Holy Roman Empire of the German nation) and included Northern and Central Italy, Bohemia, Burgundy, the Netherlands, Switzerland, and some other territories. The empire was a rather amorphous structure; its fragmentation was constantly growing; the rulers considered themselves the only sources of law in their territories. An interesting feature of the empire was that the political center did not coincide with the economic one: the former gradually shifted to the east due to the dominant role of the Saxon royal house while the latter remained on the Rhine.

Political conflicts within the empire developed along three main lines: between the emperor and the papacy; between the Western and Eastern (Byzantium) empires; between the emperor and individual rulers.

In Western Europe began the process of the formation of large feudal states. Thus, at the end of the fifth century, the Frankish state has been formed, the largest state that emerged on the territory of the Western Roman Empire. The state decisively dissociated itself from the restored Holy Roman Empire. This was the beginning of the creation of a new territorial identity. Initially, the state was often fractured and then united again. The "collecting of lands" was continued by the kings of France in the twelfth, thirteenth, and early fourteenth centuries. A major contribution to the success of the strategy of "collecting of lands" was the rise of the cities: they served as a kind of anchor points for the kings. At the same time, the process of collecting was inspired not only from the center: at first there was a relatively uniform strengthening of the political power of territorial princes (including the king) within their domains, and then the expansion of the royal domain at the expense of large feudal possessions began. The king was able to "overcome" the borders of his domain due to his position as the head of the feudal hierarchy and supreme sovereign over the whole territory of the country (History of France 1972: 77–78, 81, 83). From this time, Paris, the largest political, economic, and cultural center of the country, became increasingly dominant among the French cities.

Geographical factors were crucial for the formation of France. According to Vidal de la Blache, the country's favorable geographical location – a "pentagon" of territory with a fertile plain in the center, bordered by the Atlantic Ocean, the seas, and the Alpine and Iberian Mountain systems – contributed to the early unification of territories around Paris and the development of complementarity and solidarity between the territorial components of the country (Claval 1994: 50). Later, Fernand Braudel wrote: "To live, one must have a home. France exceedingly early acquired its borders, its own home, even before it was formally born" (Braudel 1989: 271). Already in the fifteenth century, France was the most territorially united country in Europe; "waves" of separatist sentiments (explained, in particular, by a deficit of economic ties between the north and south of the country) could no longer affect the general vector of consolidation. In the sixteenth century, France emerged as the largest centralized state in Europe, although several territories had special relationship with the French crown.

A good illustration of the importance of geographic location for good institutions was the Champagne Fairs. In the Champagne region of France, Charlemagne established administrative centers in the towns of Troyes and Provins. Due to their administrative roles and their location at the intersections of old Roman highways, these two towns along with Lagny and Bar-sur-Aube became the sites of an important set of trade fairs that rotated between the four locations. During the eleventh, twelfth, and thirteenth centuries, these trade fairs brought together a gathering of international traders from Crete, Cyprus, England, Flanders, Greece, Genoa, Portugal, Spain, Syria; Tuscany, and Venice. Precious and exotic luxury goods from the Levant and Orient were traded with high-quality textiles from Flanders. There were six fairs annually, and they were rotated between the four locations in the Champagne area. The main factor that led to the success was the very convenient geographic location. The fairs were in an area that lay between economic regions of northern Europe and Italy, making it a good meeting point for traders from the north and the south. The Champagne Fairs were an innovation in international commerce of that era. They linked the two European trading regions together that previously had little contact, and they linked northern Europe to eastern civilizations through the Italians. The Champagne Fairs played an important role in the economic renaissance of northern Europe (Abu-Lughod 1989).

In the tenth to thirteenth centuries, the processes of state formation in Denmark, Sweden, Switzerland, Poland, and Lithuania were underway. Switzerland's political consolidation began in the late thirteenth century, when three "original" cantons – Schwyz, Uri, and Unterwalden – signed a perpetual alliance of defense in 1291, swearing to help one another in the event of external danger. This alliance became the nucleus of unification for the neighboring territories – Lucerne, the imperial city of Zurich, Glarus, Zug, the powerful city-state of Bern. It should be noted that from the very beginning it was a highly decentralized system: apart from the agreement of 1481 establishing a system of mutual obligations, Switzerland had no common institutions. The empire recognized the independence of the Union.

Along with the states in the territory of medieval Europe, alternative forms of statehood were also developing, which in this period acted as competitors to nation-states. These were the city-states – Genoa, Pisa and the so-called Clearest Republic, Venice, which created a network of settlements along the sea route from the Adriatic to the Eastern Mediterranean, capturing several Greek ports. Genoa and Venice took over from Constantinople its role as organizer of maritime trade. It was the city-states that awakened the Italian economy, "dormant" since Roman times. In the cities economic activity developed in the secondary and tertiary sectors: it was said of the Venetian, "he does not plow, he does not sow, he does not gather grapes" (Braudel 1992: 104). On the role of the "strange city" of Genoa in the destiny of Europe, Braudel wrote: "To organize the outside world to preserve it for himself, then to abandon it when it became uninhabitable or unusable; to design another . . . And in the XIX century to unite Italy to his advantage" (Braudel 1989: 161). Like other Italian cities, Genoa masterfully conquered others' economic space, making others' space the basis of its own prosperity. Studies of Italian cities have highlighted the role of geography and institutions as key determinants of urban development. The quality of institutions measured by the experience of free city-state and the presence of a university had a positive effect on urban development, and, besides that, cities located in mountain areas grew less than cities located in lowlands, possibly with access to the sea (Percoco 2013).

With the time, however, the cities of Lombardy and the Rhineland, the textile centers of Tuscany (Siena and Florence) and Flanders (Ghent, Ypres, Bruges) began to rival Italian cities. In European cities, freedom became not a personal but a territorial privilege (!), and the growth of wealthy cities with a constitution, an army, and a civic consciousness became a characteristic tendency, strengthened over time.

In the Baltic and the North Sea, merchants united for mutual protection against pirates. The first such *Hansa* (merchant union or guild) was formed at Visby on the island of Gotland in 1161, under the name of the "Association of Holly Roman Travelers." Gradually, the practice of creating such unions began to spread. In the fourteenth century, the most influential became the *Hanseatic League*, which included smaller unions (Wend-Saxon Quartet, Westphalian Group, Livonian

Group etc.). Delegates from these unions met regularly to formulate common policies; each of the League's member cities had their own dependent towns. Up to 200 towns were members of the Hansa at different times. The Hansa had no formal constitution but formed a whole body of legal institutions and practices (the so-called Lübeck Law). The League dominated trade in the Baltic Sea area and, to some degree, in the North Sea area as well. At one point, it achieved a virtual monopoly on trade with Scandinavia. The League traded in timber, grains, furs, wool, and textiles (Hunt and Murray 1999: 165).

The Hanseatic League fought not only against pirates but also against states, especially Denmark – and quite successfully. But it was no match for such powerful new nations as England and Prussia; the last Hansa congress was held in 1669; Hamburg, Lubeck, and Bremen, the last strongholds of the Hanseatic League, did not join the German customs union until 1889.

The New Age

In the fourteenth and fifteenth centuries, early Modernity (the New Age), the "world-economy," as Braudel defined it, or the axis of development crossed Europe from South to North, began in Venice, passed through the cities of Germany and the Netherlands, and ended in the ports of England (Braudel 1989: 121).

The end of the fifteenth century was both the fall of the Church's reputation and the simultaneous religious revival through Protestantism. Martin Luther – the father of the Reformation of the Church, "the most German man," "the hero of the history of freedom," a man "most accomplished and absolute" – held an incredibly special place in German history and culture. Heinrich Heine considered Protestantism contributing to that purity of morals and that rigor in the performance of duty which is commonly called morality. Luther advocated a direct relationship between man and God, bypassing unnecessary church intermediaries, and he doubted the divine origin of the papacy: the papacy was a man-made institution, so its infallibility could be questioned.

The spread of Protestantism had an expressed geographic dimension. Luther's ideas were directly addressed to the German princes: these ideas reinforced and legitimated their authority. Thus, Luther's teaching was immediately accepted in several principalities – Württemberg, Hesse, Anhalt, the Duchy of Saxony, Pomerania, and most cities in northern Germany. In Denmark, in 1537, Lutheranism became the state religion. The most influential current of Protestantism was founded by Jean Calvin; Calvinism (known as Presbyterianism) became the major religion in Scotland; in France, Calvinism (Calvinists were called Huguenots) spread to the south and west; in the Netherlands it became a major factor in the division between the western Catholic provinces and the United Provinces in the east. Religious differences divided the Christian world into three parts: Catholicism, Protestantism, and Orthodoxy.

In 1555, the Peace of Augsburg established a balance between Catholics and Protestants; each territorial ruler decided on the faith of his subjects separately according to the principle "cujus regio, eius religio." The division into Catholics and Protestants was important for Germany and Central Europe, but to call it a defining line of demarcation ("Catholic South" versus "Protestant North") would be an exaggeration (Busygina 2000).

This period was also characterized by a sharp increase in urbanization: in the sixteenth century Europe already had 14 cities with more than 100,000 inhabitants: Constantinople, Naples, Venice, Milan, Paris, Rome, Palermo, Messina, Marseille, Lisbon, Seville, Antwerp, Amsterdam, and Moscow. Generally, the importance of cities to the development of states is very well argued by Charles Tilly. According to him, through European history, state formation stemmed from the accumulation and concentration of both capital and coercion within cities, which have also long had the potential to disrupt and contest the power of wider state authorities. Power-holders seeking to fight wars to consolidate territorial control had to develop relations with urban elites – including by taxing them to fund these wars in exchange for protection, which in turn fueled the development of state bureaucracies. Thus, the relationship between cities, taxation, and conflict fueled the rise of modern states (Tilly 1992). As centers of government, loci of powerful economic and social organizations, and as *places of geographic importance* (e.g., industrial centers or ports), cities – and particularly capital cities – have been pivotal sites of revolutions, as well as wider forms of contentious politics. Controlling and dominating capital cities have thus been key objects of war, revolutions, and regime changes (Goodfellow and Jackman 2020: 9–10).

Gradually, medieval communities began to disintegrate, giving way to nation-states. The first state of the New Age, the "European miracle" of the seventeenth century, was the United Provinces of the Netherlands. France entered the period of prosperity, which was accompanied by the strengthening of centralized royal power at the expense of the privileges of the provinces. The main rival of France remained the empire, with wars between them acquiring a pan-European scale. With the domination of England, Great Britain came closer to unification: Wales voluntarily joined England, a personal union of Scotland and England was concluded in 1603, Ireland was conquered by Cromwell in 1649–1651 and annexed. The role of leadership was increasingly shifting to England, primarily because of its geographic location (the ability to ignore continental wars and conflicts and its location at the hub of sea routes from Europe to America and India).

The United Provinces lived by trade, and their merchants traveled to the most remote regions. For example, Dutch merchants were making big money in Asia long before the British arrived there; the Dutch East India Company, founded in 1602, practically monopolized the trade in many commodities, from silk to spices. Amsterdam was the richest and most dynamic city in Europe. The Dutch pioneered in creating new institutions crucial to development; they created a system of public debt that allowed the government to borrow money from its citizens at low interest. Moreover, they established a kind of central bank. Their money was reliable and the tax system simple and efficient. Modeled on the East India Company, the English created their own – The East India Company and the famous Hudson's Bay Company (in 1670) – to monopolize the Canadian fur trade (Ferguson 2003: 15–17).

The Thirty Years' War (1618–1648) was the most important stage in the struggle for power on the continent, in which most of Europe's rulers took part. The Peace of Westphalia (1648) determined the foundations of the international order in Europe for more than 100 years. The Peace of Westphalia significantly expanded the rights of feudal princes, it gave them the right to sign international agreements and adopt imperial laws only with the consent of their parliament. The treaty included a provision that the foreign policy actions of princes should not be directed against the empire, but this provision was not taken seriously; the formation of a "national feeling" (*Nationalgefuehl*) was a project for the future (Ferguson 2003: 13).

According to the treaties, the Holy Roman Empire lost considerable lands, mostly to France and Sweden; the independence of the Swiss Confederation was recognized. The empire receded into the background; its interests became secondary to those of the most powerful states – Austria, Bavaria, Saxony – and the growing new power of the future, Brandenburg-Prussia.

The treaties formalized a political–territorial order whose original structures were the free cities of late medieval Europe, the emerging absolutist states, and the principle of "cuius regio, eius religio" within the empire. The Peace of Westphalia was the first stage in the formation of a system of sovereign states because the treaties included recognition of the political autonomy of many territorial units of the empire.

The Westphalian system was formed by territorial polities of different scales:

- The empire;
- Kingdoms or other large polities;
- Principalities (smaller polities);
- Cities.

In fact, the Westphalian system was to ensure the circulation of the only public good – military security. The fundamental norms of the Westphalian world model were territoriality, borders as markers of sovereignty, and the primacy of state interests.

The period from the mid-seventeenth to the mid-eighteenth century saw relatively few changes on the political map of Europe. This period is called the Century of Enlightened Absolutism, but it is noteworthy that absolutist states were not the majority in Europe at this time. Between the highly decentralized Swiss Confederation and the extreme autocracy of the Papacy, there was a range of intermediate options. Venice and the United Provinces had republican form of government parliamentary monarchies at various times England, Scotland, and Sweden; absolutist monarchies were France, Austria, and Spain. Special political systems were represented by the Holy Roman Empire, situated between republic and constitutional monarchy, Prussia – between absolutism and constitutionalism. Even more diverse were the systems of "small states" (*Kleinstaaterei*) – city-republics (Genoa, Geneva), small principalities (e.g., Courland), clerical states (Avignon), etc. It is extremely interesting and important that political systems overlapped territorially, so that rulers had to rule differently in different territories of their state. For example, the Prussian kings behaved differently in Berlin, where they were subordinates of the empire, and in Königsberg, where they were completely independent.

The empire had an extremely complex (and conflictual) institutional order, geographically its core were the territories of modern Germany and Austria, Luxembourg, and Belgium. The basic institution of government was the Reichstag, which consisted of three curiae (councils): the Council of Electors (choosing the emperor), the Council of Dukes, and the Council of Imperial Cities. To function effectively, this complex institution needed the political will for compromise and a political culture of tolerance. In addition, the territory of the empire was divided into imperial districts, and these were united in a variety of associations, mainly to jointly repel a military threat. There was also a so-called corporation of imperial knights, who remained outside both the Reichstag and the district structures. All this indicates the presence of a *multilevel system of government* within the empire. The empire provides rich material for the study of the relationship between centralization, federalism, devolution, and the institutionalization of (shared) sovereignty (Axtmann 2003).

European colonialism

At this time, colonialism began to play an increasingly important role in international relations; European colonies and overseas possessions multiplied, with the circle of colonialist states limited to the maritime powers that initiated the colonial increments; the German states and Austria did not belong to this circle. In Western Europe, the dividing line was drawn between the countries possessing colonies (Spain, Portugal, Britain, France, and the Netherlands) and other countries; in Central and Eastern Europe, land remained the main resource. A European system of international relations was emerging, with the colonies becoming an integral part of this system.

The earliest maritime colonial empires were the Spanish and the Portuguese, then came the time of Holland and England. It should be said that these maritime empires were fundamentally different from continental empires because they connected ports, trading areas, and territories that were separated by vast water distances. However, there were significant differences among the maritime empires as well. Thus, the earliest empires were based on direct military conquests of territory (the actions of Spain and Portugal in Latin America), whereas later maritime empires followed more sophisticated strategies; systematic colonization was based on trade relations, and military force acted more as an additional, supporting tool. Thus, economic exploitation and unequal trade relations became characteristic features of commercial relations between center and periphery and, indeed, one of the foundations of the world order of the time.

Three times in the course of its history, the Portuguese colonial empire had fantastic prospects for expanding its colonies – and realized those prospects but failed to keep them. In 1497–1499, India was discovered by Vasco da Gama's expedition. During the sixteenth century, the Portuguese managed to create a huge "state of India" headed by a viceroy. It included 123 cities and 23 fortresses. At this time, overseas expansion became in fact the national idea of Portugal, expansion has been realized as a great historical mission of the Portuguese people. But the Portuguese metropolis lacked the resources for the full-scale colonization of vast territories; Portugal lost to the more developed Holland and England, and already in the first quarter of the seventeenth century, the Portuguese colonial empire in India ceased to exist. However, the possession of Brazil (discovered as early as 1500 by Pedro Cabral) still allowed Portugal to feel itself a great colonial power. In 1822, however, Brazil declared independence – Portugal was forced to accept it. Africa remained Portugal's "last great hope"; by the beginning of World War I, Portugal had three major colonies on the continent: Guinea, Mozambique, and Angola. The goal was to link the territories of Angola and Mozambique into a huge Portuguese empire (the "Map of Pink" plan). However, the powerful British Empire prevented the plan from being carried out. Officially, Portugal abandoned overseas expansion only in 1974 after the fall of the president Salazar regime.

In the British Isles, the United Kingdom was created in 1707; henceforth the kingdom was ruled by a united parliament, and the British identity began to emerge.[4] On the continent, thanks to its favorable geographic location, large population, and the decline of its main rival Spain, France dominated, a position that remained unchanged until the fall of Napoleon in 1815.

In eighteenth-century Italy, several dividing lines were intertwined: the main rivals were the House of Savoy in Turin, the Austrian Habsburgs in Milan, and the Dukes of Tuscany; in addition, there were the traditional rivalries between the republican cities, the autocratic papacy, and perhaps the main political actor in the region, the Kingdom of Naples of Both Sicilies.

In Central and Eastern Europe, the period was marked by the rapid rise of Prussia and the slow emergence of the superpower, the Russian Empire. Prussia's power was augmented by a remarkably efficient, European-renowned administrative machine and a huge regular army, the backbone of which was an aristocratic officer corp. The special "Prussian spirit" grew out of loyalty to the dynasty and pride in Prussian cultural and educational progress. Beginning with the capture of Silesia in 1740, war became Prussia's chief political instrument. It was a multi-ethnic and multi-confessional entity: by the end of the eighteenth century, Prussia's population was 40% Slavic and Catholic and had a large Jewish community.

Between these giants, Prussia and Russia, the Polish-Lithuanian state was sandwiched. The greatest redistribution of territory in the eighteenth century were the three partitions of Poland – in 1773, 1793, and 1795, committed by the three aggressor powers in their interests – Russia, Prussia, and Austria. "Historical guilt" for this act of arbitrariness against a state incapable of defending its integrity lies with all three states but more so with Prussia, which as a result strengthened its position within the empire and in Europe as a whole. As a result of the partitions, Russia seized more than half of Poland, but these were lands inhabited mainly by Ukrainians, Lithuanians, and Belarussians, who were less economically developed. The original Polish lands were divided between Prussia and Austria.

Three empires that have partied Poland, greatly differed in institutions, culture, and policies toward the Polish territories. Prussia, which was more developed economically, industrialized its Polish part more than both Russia and Austria. The Austrian empire, in contrast to both Prussia and Russia, gave substantial administrative and cultural autonomy to its piece of the Polish territories. Austria was the only empire of the three to allow Poles to participate in local governance. Both Russian and Prussian regimes (unlike the Austrian one) used political and cultural oppression, ultimately aimed, respectively, at Russification and Germanization. Russia was also characterized by the least efficient administrative apparatus and the lowest education spending of the three empires. The partition borders were exogenously imposed on Polish lands. They did not coincide with any of the borders prior to partitions and were driven by the relative military strength of the three Empires.

It is important that the partition of Poland by the three European superpowers in the eighteenth and nineteenth centuries – Russian, Prussian, and Austro-Hungarian empires – continues to exert an influence on contemporary Poland, despite ending a century ago. This influence manifests itself in the differences in intensity of religious practices and in beliefs in democratic principles (Grosfeld and Zhuravskaya 2014).

The Ukrainian lands, annexed to the Russian Empire because of the last partition of Poland, were divided into ten provinces. A policy of Russification was conducted in Ukraine. Historically, there were three centers of Ukrainian political culture – Kiev, Kharkiv, and Lviv, which reflected the presence of three main types of population – Ukrainian proper, the russified residents of the east and south, as well as the population of Western Ukraine, where Germanic, Austrian, and Polish influence was considerable.

The situation on the Balkan Peninsula was different. None of the great civilizational movements of the West – the Renaissance, the Reformation, the Enlightenment, the Scientific Revolution – largely penetrated here. In addition, the long Turkish yoke had a great impact on this region. The borders of a gradually diminishing European Turkey became one of the deepest lines of demarcation on the map of Europe.

In 1806, Napoleon abolished the Holy Roman Empire of German Nation, depriving the German princes of independence, which, among other things, contributed to the growth of German national consciousness. During Napoleon's rule, a total of 112 small territorial entities with a population of three million were abolished, and their territories were transferred to Bavaria, Baden, Württemberg, and Nassau. The "mediatization" – the averaging of the size of the German states – effectively signaled the beginning of the end of the Holy Roman Empire and a certain weakening of Germany's fragmentation (Busygina 2000: 15–16). Outside the Napoleonic transformations remained Britain, Scandinavia, and Russia. At the end of the Napoleonic Wars in 1814, Norway was proclaimed a sovereign constitutional monarchy, ending 400 years of Danish rule.

Napoleon's empire was vast, and it died, to quote the emperor himself, "of indigestion." In the end, the European coalition defeated Napoleon, and it was the Russian campaign of 1812 that was Napoleon's greatest failure, the turning point of the empire's development. In 1815, as France struggled with a returning emperor

("One Hundred Days of Napoleon"), his empire was rapidly falling apart. Napoleon once remarked that history is made of time and space. Over the course of his history, he reshaped European spaces, and although the time of his empire was short, these changes paved the way for the reforms of the nineteenth century.

As Gellner has shown, from 1815 to 1918, Europe began a gradual – in several stages – transition to nation-states. In the first stage, while preserving the former territorial and political structures, "nationalist ideas, formalized as a political principle," appeared. The second stage was characterized by the collapse of multinational empires, and smaller states arose in their place, while each of them declared its intention to lead a special national path for the ethnic group with which it was identified. And since ethnic groups were not compactly settled in much of Europe, virtually all political boundaries were perceived as unfair, at least by certain political groups. And on the territory of Eastern Europe, the formation of a "fair" political map was even less possible. The destruction of empires as "prisons of peoples" led to the creation of new "prisons" for ethnic minorities within smaller states (Gellner 2006).

Tilly also attributed the emergence of nation-states in Europe to the early nineteenth century; the necessary conditions for their emergence, according to his approach, were (1) the ability of the state to trace, limit, and control resources within its own territory, and (2) the willingness of other states to accept the right of that state to regulate these areas. Tilley noted the states were beginning to attach more importance to their border regimes. Whereas many European states had previously lacked strict control over the movement of people, goods, and money across borders, since the nineteenth century, state administrations have paid special attention to this. Registration systems and fee collection systems became more effective (Tilly 1994).

Gellner identified several "time zones" of nation-state formation in Europe (in fact, these were time-geographic zones). To the first zone he attributed the Atlantic coast of Europe. The second belt was to the east of the coast, where the building of nation-states followed the path of unification and there were two developed codified cultures – Italian and German. The main task of state-building was to erect a "unified political roof" over those territories where high culture had already dominated before. So the task of the "roof" was to bring small- and medium-sized states together. The third time zone, further east, was characterized by the most complex geographical and social intertwining of different cultures; political, cultural, and religious boundaries did not coincide. With the collapse of the empires came the daunting task of creating both the cultures and the states that made them up. Finally, the fourth time zone generally corresponded to the territory of the Russian Empire.

Atlantic Europe

The phenomenon of the British Empire deserves special attention. Geographically, it was the largest empire in history which has managed to build a complex system of institutions to hold together vast territories around the world. Britain was relatively late in the race to divide the world; the Spaniards and Portuguese were the first. In the seventeenth century, the British Empire included very few territories, while Columbus had laid the foundations of the Spanish colonial empire more than a century and a half earlier. The Spanish Empire was an autocracy, ruled tightly from the center; the silver from the American colonies made it a real contender for world domination. In England, by contrast, the power of the monarch was not absolute: it was limited by a wealthy aristocracy, later by the two Houses of Parliament. Yet in the relative weakness of the English crown lay the origins of the empire's future power. When the Spaniards conquered Mexico and Peru, they gained access to vast reserves of silver. The English searched for mineral treasures in Canada, Virginia, and the Gambia and found none. In such a situation, the only solution was to rob the Spaniards. From here begins the story of English pirates on ships under the Jolly Roger, and many fortunes were made that way. The relationship between Spain and England was highly conflicted, and in the face of a direct threat, Queen Elizabeth I of England makes the unorthodox decision of legitimizing what already existed. The plundering of Spanish ships by the English out of crime becomes part of England's political strategy, and the sea becomes their first empire (Ferguson 2003).

At sea, the English faced the Dutch. Between 1652 and 1674, the English fought the Dutch three times for control of the sea lanes from Western Europe to India, the Baltic, the Mediterranean, North America, and West Africa. The reasons for the wars were purely commercial interests. As a result of the Glorious Revolution in 1688, Dutch Prince William of Orange became the head of the English executive, and Dutch merchants became major shareholders in the English East India Company. This Anglo-Dutch business "merger" allowed England to adopt Dutch advanced financial institutions: establishing the Bank of England (1694) and creating a system of public debt (Ferguson 2003).

England owed its future imperial greatness primarily to its internal development – the emergence of the world's first mass consumption society – and, beyond that, to its advanced economic and commercial institutions and – *geographic location.* A key to expanding the international trade of Britain was the British East India Company. Established in 1600 as a joint-stock company by traders and investors in London, the company received a royal charter giving it exclusive rights to develop trade with the East Indies. It was one of the first multinational corporations and was responsible for the territorial annexation of Malaya, Singapore, Hong Kong, and much of the Indian subcontinent, which became especially important to the British economy.

France was Britain's main rival in the competition, where global domination was the stakes. Britain's victory came from two things: sheer maritime superiority and borrowing, which accounted for more than a third of the cost of the war. After the victory over France, it was already a vast empire, where "the sun never sets" and whose borders have not yet been marked by nature.

In the nineteenth century, Britain and France held the greatest colonial empires. In contrast to them, Spain and Portugal have been virtually unable to retain their colonies.

"Atlantic Europe" (Britain, the Netherlands, France, Spain, Portugal), by virtue of its geographical position, had obvious competitive advantage and was directly involved in the trade and colonization of new territories. However, there were significant differences within this group of countries: Britain and the Netherlands developed significantly faster than Spain and Portugal. A well-known study by Acemoglu, Johnson, and Robinson concluded that the development of international trade influenced changes in political institutions – the new stratum (merchants) needed stable property rights, which meant limiting the power of the monarchy and groups associated with it. Commercial interests played an increasing political role. (Note, however, that these new institutions certainly did not protect the rights of the entire population and were not democratic. Rather, they could be described as oligarchical since they secured only the rights of wealthy merchants).

However, this process did not develop in countries where Atlantic trade was controlled solely by the crown. In Spain and Portugal, trade was dominated by a single company under the control of the monarchy. In Britain and the Netherlands, by contrast, the main conflict was between the monarchy and its supporters and commercial interests. Thus, the explanation for the long-term growth of these countries lies not in the special culture of these nations but in the special institutions that were developed also by virtue of their geographic location (Acemoglu, Johnson and Robinson 2002).

Twentieth century

The two world wars and their aftermath largely shaped the twentieth century. Already the beginning of the twentieth century in Europe "breathed" a premonition of a major war. The rapid economic growth in Germany, especially the development of the military-industrial complex, caused justified fears in Britain, France, and Russia. In Germany itself, public sentiment ranged from enthusiasm to panic and a sense of the coming "end of the world."

By 1914, the beginning of World War I, Europe was divided into two warring factions, two coalitions of powers: the Entente ("Grand Triangle") and the Central Powers. The configuration of the "Great Triangle" was initially unstable – it consisted of Britain (without a regular army), France, Italy (since 1915), the United States (since 1917), and imperial Russia, which had delayed mobilization and weak industrial capabilities. The Central Powers – above all Germany and Austria-Hungary – were more consolidated and had developed lines of communication. They took up arms to reconsider the territorial and power order of Europe.

Spain, the Scandinavian countries, the Netherlands, and Switzerland managed to remain neutral. The Central Powers were eventually defeated, mainly due to weak state capacity and institutions rather than military defeats proper.

The Continental War ended with a series of peace treaties, the most important of which was the Versailles Treaty (signed by defeated Germany on June 28, 1919). The question of the contours of the political map of Europe is once again of paramount importance; the great powers, while constructing a political–territorial order, considered the system of sovereign states as a kind of "ideal." World War

I led to the disintegration of four empires (Russian, Austro-Hungarian, German, and Ottoman), which had dominated the map of Europe until then; the emergence of new independent states – Finland, Poland, Estonia, Latvia, Lithuania; Austria, Hungary, Czechoslovakia, the Kingdom of Serbs, Croats, and Slovenes (since 1929). Germany had lost Alsace and a part of Lorraine to France, Eupen-Malmedy to Belgium, the northern part of Schleswig to Denmark, and parts of Prussia and Silesia to Poland.

The fate of Austria-Hungary is notable. It was not decided by the Entente states until the spring of 1918. The initial project envisaged the federalization of the empire, but later it was decided to abolish it and create in its place small independent states. This was intended, first, to weaken Germany and, second, to organize a "cordon sanitaire" in the way of Bolshevism to Europe (these ideas were especially strongly supported by France). Thus, after the collapse of the empire, the state of Czechoslovakia emerged. Its borders were drawn in the most approximate way; the very concept of "Czechoslovakia" – geographical or historical – was not known in the dictionaries of that time. The state and its borders emerged first "in the heads" and only then were transferred to the geographical map.

In 1933, the dictatorial regime of the Third Reich emerged in Germany, and its foreign policy response was the elimination of all restrictions on rearmament imposed by the Treaty of Versailles. In March 1938, the Wehrmacht invaded Austria (the so-called Anschluss), which became a province of Germany. In 1938, Czechoslovakia was forced to cede to Germany the Sudetes, where most of the population was ethnic Germans (the border between the states was now 40 kilometers from Prague). In 1939, Germany occupied the Czech Republic and Moravia, and Italy occupied Albania. In the same year, Germany attacked and defeated Poland.

In the same year, Hitler and Stalin divided Eastern Europe into spheres of influence by the German-Soviet Boundary and Friendship Treaty (Molotov-Ribbentrop Pact). The secret protocols attached to the treaty delimited the Soviet and German spheres of interest in Europe: the Soviet sphere included Finland, Latvia, Estonia, and, somewhat later, Lithuania, eastern Poland, and Bessarabia; to the west of the boundary line, Germany gained freedom of action. In September 1939, the Soviet Union and Germany separated Poland, most of it went to Germany.

The Soviet Union began to "master" the sphere of its interests. In the same year, the Red Army crossed the Soviet–Finnish border, which ended in 1940; Finland ceded the strategically important Karelian Isthmus to the USSR (on this territory and the former Karelian ASSR formed the Karelian-Finnish SSR, which existed until 1956). After launching this war, the USSR was excluded from the League of Nations as aggressor. A similar situation developed with the Baltic states: in 1940, after the Red Army entered their territories, the prepared-in-advance plebiscites brought the predicted results, the so-called people's governments were created, and three countries – Latvia, Lithuania, and Estonia joined the USSR as union republics. In addition, Bessarabia and Northern Bukovina were annexed to the USSR.

Germany went on the offensive in the West: after occupying Norway and Denmark, the Wehrmacht entered Belgium, Holland, and France. On June 22, 1941, Germany attacked the Soviet Union without a declaration of war.

A radical turning point in World War II occurred in late 1942 – the first half of 1943. Nazi Germany suffered a crushing defeat. The postwar arrangement of Europe was discussed by the heads of the victorious powers at the Crimean Conference in February–March 1945, and the final questions of the peaceful postwar settlement were resolved at the Potsdam Conference in July–August 1945. Territorial questions were also discussed, such as borders and territory of Germany, the establishment of the Polish–German border on the Oder-Neisse. Compared with 1938, Germany's territory had shrunk by approximately one-quarter. In contrast, the territory of the SS Union grew: in addition to the part of East Prussia, the Ukrainian SSR received Transcarpathia, and in the northwest, the area of Pechenga was incorporated into the Union under the 1947 peace treaty with Finland.

In addition to the territorial changes, the Potsdam Conference determined the displacement of the population. About nine million Germans left the territories of Poland and Czechoslovakia and were subsequently (successfully!) assimilated into Germany. In Königsberg, the place of the displaced Germans was taken by Soviet soldiers and Soviet citizens from all over the country. The Poles who had left Lviv moved to Wroclaw – with their university, mayor, and municipality.

Pretty soon the Allies in the anti-Hitler coalition (the Soviet Union, the United States, France, and Great Britain) were no longer united: the postwar world was developing as a bipolar system, and the confrontation between the two "superpowers" – the United States and the Soviet Union – took the form of the Cold War. Military-political blocs were created. In 1949, the North Atlantic Treaty Organization (NATO), composed of the United States, Great Britain, France, Belgium, the Netherlands, Luxemburg, Canada, Italy, Portugal, Norway, Denmark, and Iceland, was formed first. Greece, Turkey (both in 1952), Germany (1955), Spain (1982), Hungary, Poland, the Czech Republic (all three in 1999), Bulgaria, Romania, Slovakia, Slovenia, Latvia, Lithuania, and Estonia (all seven in 2004), Albania and Croatia (both in 2009) later joined the treaty.

Under the patronage of the Soviet Union, the Warsaw Treaty Organization (WTO) was created in Eastern Europe, consisting of the USSR, Bulgaria, Czechoslovakia, Hungary, GDR, Poland, Romania, and Albania (it withdrew from the WTO in 1968). In Europe, the dividing line between the two political systems was emerging and deepening.

The territory of Germany (and the territory of Berlin) was divided into four occupation zones, according to the number of victorious powers. The eastern part of the country was controlled by the Soviet military administration, and the western zones by the administrations of the United States, Great Britain, and France. Gradually, the split between the Soviet and Western zones grew, while the Western zones formed first what was called "Bizonia" (under a common US–British administration) and then "Trizonia" when the French part joined them. The split manifested itself in the eventual formation of two states: in 1949 the Federal Republic of Germany (FRG) was formed within "Trizonia" with its capital in Bonn, and a month later the German Democratic Republic (GDR) within the borders of the Soviet zone and with its capital in the Soviet sector of Berlin – East Berlin.

This led, among other things, to the "West Berlin problem," when the western part of the city was separated from the Federal Republic of Germany by the territory of the German Democratic Republic. In 1949, the Soviet Union imposed a blockade of West Berlin, which was broken by British and American transport planes making 277,264 (!) flights. West Berlin became a political-geographic "anomaly," its political status was unique: it was not formally part of West Germany as a federal state but was represented in both houses of the German parliament, although its representatives were not elected by the population but were appointed by the city council. The laws of the Federal Republic of Germany were not automatically valid in West Berlin. When the Basic Law of the Federal Republic of Germany was being drafted, even the idea of placing the capital of the state in West Berlin (exclave!) was discussed, but such an exotic solution would have involved enormous inconveniences, and the decision was made in favor of Bonn. The border between West and East Berlin ran through the center of the formerly single city and almost all its length among ruins that neither side was in any hurry to rebuild.

West Berlin survived on massive economic aid from the Federal Republic of Germany: two pfennigs extra for each piece of mail sent to the Federal Republic of Germany – "for Berlin." Until 1961, the border between West and East Berlin was open, and people left the East for the West: in 1961 alone, more than 207,000 people left the GDR. East German authorities accused West Berlin and the FRG of "human trafficking," "poaching" of personnel, and attempts to disrupt economic plans. As the situation around Berlin escalated, the leaders of the OWD countries decided to close the border. The Berlin Wall was built in 1961 and existed until 1989, when it was destroyed, and with it the problem of West Berlin ceased to exist. Reunited Berlin became a federal state and the capital of Germany.

Postwar Europe

In postwar Western Europe, the movement for a united Europe was gaining strength. In May 1948, the Congress of Europe was held in The Hague, where the principle of supranationality was put forward – the need to sacrifice some national sovereignty in the common interest and to preserve peace. In 1951, the firstborn of European integration was the European Coal and Steel Community, which united six states – Germany, France, Italy, Belgium, the Netherlands, and Luxemburg. In 1957, the European Economic Community (EEC) and the European Atomic Energy Community (Euratom) appeared. Today, the European Union unites 28 states – both Western and Central and Eastern Europe.

European states initiated the process of decolonization as the preservation of the old empires is becoming impossible: the elites of the colonial peoples are loudly demanding independence, the ties of the colonies with the metropolis are weakening, and finally, both the United States and the United Nations are opposing the "old" traditional imperialism.

Interestingly, the logic of development of Western and Eastern Europe was opposite: in the East the Soviet Union strengthened the empire within the boundaries embracing the "socialist camp," while in the West the empires, on the contrary, were dismantled.

"The Soviet empire" – the Eastern bloc – despite its propagated internationalism, was essentially divided into separate segments. The bloc included such diverse countries as the GDR, the most bizarre version of "people's democracy," pro-Soviet Bulgaria with its late unfinished modernization, and the least Sovietized Poland, where the Catholic Church was not actually subject to Soviet control. By the early 1980s, the Union had virtually no means of influencing the situation in the Soviet bloc, and the system began to collapse rapidly. As Western Europe was uniting, Eastern Europe sought to disintegrate.

The next stage of redrawing the political map of Central and Eastern Europe began in the late 1980s with the systemic changes in the USSR and then the democratic revolutions in the countries of the subregion. In 1991, the Warsaw Pact Organization ceased to exist. In 1993, the federal Czechoslovakia disintegrated into two sovereign states, the Czech Republic and Slovakia.

Since the early 1990s began the collapse of the Socialist Federal Republic of Yugoslavia (SFRY), resulting in severe chronic conflicts. The geography of communities – confessional and ethnic – is unusually complex throughout the former Yugoslavia. The result of protracted military conflicts on the territory of the former SFRY was the formation of six independent states – Serbia, Croatia, Montenegro, Slovenia, Macedonia, and Bosnia and Herzegovina.

It is worth noting that the collapse of the Eastern bloc not only led to disengagement but also contributed to unification processes. Thus, the most important process of the 1990s, which had a distinct political and geographic dimension, was the unification of the two Germanies after 40 years of separation. In September 1990, the "4 + 2" treaty (the four victorious powers of World War II and two German states) was signed, which provided international support for this process. A united Germany was created as a federation of 16 states, and the capital of the state was moved from Bonn to Berlin.

The European Union: supranational institutions as drivers for the European development

There are many international organizations on the map of Europe, but only one of them has made exceptional progress and, although it does not coincide with "Europe," it is still often associated with it. European integration is one of the most curious and significant phenomena of the twentieth century. In general, the term "integration" has a strong positive connotation among scholars; it is usually associated with *development*, progress, compromises, justice, good governance, and a "healthy community."

The history of the European integration is the history of *institutional development*. The creation and development of the European Union is a multistep process of national leaders of European democracies working together to find mutually acceptable compromises. Compromises – both between countries and between different interests within countries – are a key characteristic of European integration and explain the nature of its institutions. With the signing of the treaty establishing the European Coal and Steel Community (ECSC) in 1951, the first phase of European integration began. During this time, the European Union went the unprecedented way from a free trade zone through a customs union and a single internal market to an economic and monetary union. The number of members of the association increased from six to 27.

Geographical factors are very important for the success of the *beginning* of integration in several ways. *First*, integration starts with geography, as countries located in close geographical proximity to each other are integrated; they form a region (that is why integration is called regional). Indeed, geographic proximity is a big advantage when it comes to infrastructure integration, for instance. *Second*, the composition of the group is important; territorial size is also important. The presence of a hegemonic country in an integration association makes institutional compromises very difficult. *Third*, the integration group is principally open and implies expansion to neighboring countries. Therefore, the nature of these neighbors, their political regime, and foreign policy will play a role. Geography favored the beginning and development of the integration process in Europe. Initially, common institutions were created by small and larger countries, but the *sine qua non* condition was always the absence of a hegemon. Subsequently, the integration process was joined mainly by small countries. In addition, the first expansions (which were among other things a testament to the attractiveness of the European project) were aimed at the west and north of Europe, that is, "problem-free" neighbors.[5]

However, geography only creates prerequisites for regional integration; the choice of institutions is key. The leaders of different EU countries (or even leaders in the same country, succeeding each other) pursued different goals in the integration process. In fact, there has never been unity of purpose beyond the most general declarations; so for the success of the integration process, it was crucial to build an *institutional mechanism* that would make it possible to find compromises and promote integration regardless of contradictions between the participants. In different periods, the basis for compromise was fundamentally different. For example, the initial impetus for integration was the problem of postwar Germany. The states of Europe, especially France, faced a dilemma: how to create conditions for a speedy restoration of Germany without losing control over it? A new form of relations between states in Europe had to be found that would be capable of ensuring that a strong Germany would not once again become a threat to Europe and the world. The immediate (technical) solution was to bring the production of coal and steel, which at the time were the main strategic raw materials, under common control. Subsequently, integration for many years was built around solving purely pragmatic economic problems, such as the stability of monetary policy, the reduction of budget deficits, and the reduction of bloated social guarantees and expenditures. In recent years, there have been increasing calls in Western Europe to promote integration in Europe as a counterbalance to Russia's efforts to bring Eastern European and post-Soviet states back into its orbit using various forms of dependency.

The main problem of any attempt at integration between sovereign countries lies in overcoming the mistrust of the parties. This requires reliable and bona fide guarantees of the implementation of the agreements reached. If the agreements are implemented, the trust of the parties increases over time. The practical difficulty lies in the fact that it is necessary to simultaneously work out a compromise to create sufficiently effective institutions and practices of integration and guarantees for each member state to maintain control over the activities of the European Union. In other words, it is necessary to create and maintain sufficiently strong supranational institutions that would nevertheless remain under the control of national leaders.

The treaty establishing the European Coal and Steel Community (ECSC), the first European association, was signed in Paris in 1951 and entered into force in 1952. In the 1970s, the attractiveness of the integration project was reflected in the first enlargement of the European Union: Britain, Denmark, and Ireland joined it in 1973. However, the process itself came to a standstill, there was a period of "small steps." Nevertheless, the European Union provided political support to the young democracies, admitting Greece in 1981 and Spain and Portugal in 1986, although this enlargement considerably aggravated its structural problems.

A new boost to integration began in the mid-1980s: in 1985, the European Commission published a white paper, which laid out a concrete plan for the creation of a single internal market. The Commission's proposals constituted the Single European Act (SEA), which entered into force in 1987. The SEA widened the scope of integration to include new areas, effectively paving the way for the adoption of treaties in the 1990s.

At the beginning of the 1990s, the European Union underwent an extremely significant transformation, which became a turning point in the development of the European integration processes, and the European Union development strategy was determined both by the practical task of transition to the Economic and Monetary Union and by the changes of political regimes in Central and Eastern European countries, which opened new prospects of spatial expansion of the integration association. The EU opted for a strategy of simultaneous deepening and widening.

The early 1990s marked the peak of the integration's deepening, which was confirmed by the signing in December 1991 of the Treaty on the European Union (the Maastricht Treaty). In 1995, Sweden, Finland, and Austria joined the European Union.

Currently, the European Union consists of 27 states. In 2004, in an unprecedented move, ten states from Central and Eastern Europe, Cyprus, and Malta joined the EU-15, three of which, Latvia, Lithuania, and Estonia, had previously been republics of the Soviet Union. In 2007, during the second wave, Bulgaria and Romania joined the European Union. On June 1, 2013, Croatia became the twenty-seventh member of the European Union. The only member state that has left the European Union is United Kingdom. Among the many reasons that led to Brexit, experts cite the geographical factor: Britain does not belong to continental Europe; it is an island whose surrounding waters have partially isolated it from cultural developments on the continent.[6]

The geographical focus of EU enlargement is now on the Western Balkans: Slovenia and Croatia have already joined the European Union while Macedonia (applied for membership in 2004), Albania (in 2009), Serbia (in 2009), and

Montenegro (in 2008) have got candidate status. The states of the Western Balkans are signatories to the Stabilization and Association Agreement, which is already in effect for Albania, Macedonia, Montenegro, and Serbia and is usually preceded by an application for membership.

A state's membership in the European Union is not only a certain status but also, importantly, a system of institutions and commitments. The question of the geographical scope of this membership (in other words, the question of the EU's external borders) is important not only for the European Union itself but also for the entire international system. While the internal borders between member states of the European Union, thanks to the single internal market and the Schengen zone, are becoming increasingly transparent and are gradually disappearing, the external borders of the association, in contrast, becoming tighter, and a hard border separates member states from non-EU countries. Thus, borders are indeed becoming important political institutions.

It can be assumed that future EU borders will not be rigid and fixed. Rather than a Westphalian "superstate," we will rather see a political system with overlapping governments, divided sovereignty, diverse institutional arrangements, and multiple cultural identities (Zielonka 2002: 13).

In the early 1990s, Marks noted that in the European Union we observe "a system of continuous negotiations among nested governments at several territorial tiers" (Marks 1993: 392). However, it was eight years later that the work of Hooghe and Marks initiated the process of recognition of the multilevel governance approach as a promising analytical perspective (Hooghe and Marks 2001). This recognition could be explained (at least in part) by the apparent limitations of explanatory power of normative theories and, more importantly, by the empirical research on European integration that revealed not a drift of sovereignty from the national to the European level but complex political processes of dividing and sharing competences. Multilevel governance is not just the interplay between national governments and the European Union, but as Benz and Zimmer argue, "attention is focused on multiple actors including regional governments, national governments and parliaments, the European Commission and the European Parliament, as well as on their patterns of interaction, which are described as networks and negotiations" (Benz and Zimmer 2010: 17). A multilevel system of governance is therefore an adaptation of decision-making to the circumstances of territories under multiple jurisdictions, which allows for the reflection of local preferences in decision-making. The Westphalian approach to the issue of sovereignty in international relations was left behind and is not any longer a suitable model for explaining what is happening in the European system of multilevel governance with its multiple shared sovereignties.

Importantly, the European Union is building institutions not only within its territory but also outside its borders in adjacent geographies, seeking to accelerate their development. This is known as "Europeanization." According to Radaelli,

> Europeanization consists of processes of construction, diffusion and institutionalization of formal and informal rules, procedures, policy paradigms, styles, "ways of doing things" and shared beliefs and norms which are first

> defined and consolidated in the EU policy process and then incorporated in the logic of domestic (national and subnational) discourse, political structures and public policies.
>
> (Radaelli 2004)

According to Börzel and Suyatin (2012: 8), Europeanization is "the emergence of new rules, norms, practices, and structures of meaning, to which member – states are exposed and which they have to incorporate into their domestic rule structures" (Europeanization is developed and implemented through conditionality – the method of practicing authority within and outside the European Union. Conditionality means that the European Union sets conditions, which aspiring members must fulfill to receive the reward of EU membership status (Schimmelfenning and Sedelmeier 2004: 669) or participate in other EU institutional initiatives/programs.

The external efforts of the European Union are mostly aimed at the neighboring countries that aspire to EU membership, but not on them only. There are also other institutional initiatives focused on specific geographies – Euroregions, Northern dimension, and Baltic Strategy. *Importantly, these are local and regional institutional forms embedded in geography, and diversity of institutional forms responds to geographical diversity.*

Transborder cooperation: Euroregions

Euroregions are a territorial form of interaction between individual EU member states and neighboring countries. In fact, this is an attempt to create cross-border regional and local governance systems. Euroregions outside the European Union existed even before its last enlargement – on the German-Polish, German-Czech etc. and later on the borders with the republics of the former Soviet Union, including Russia. This is a very common form of interaction: for example, since 1990, only local authorities in Poland have signed 13 agreements of this kind with their external neighbors.

Euroregions are a special form of cross-border agreements linking regional and – especially – local authorities on both sides of the border. Cross-border cooperation within the framework of Euroregions is institutionalized (i.e., develops according to certain, agreed rules, adopted voluntarily by the participants), nevertheless, there is no common tracing stone or model Euroregion. The European Union in this case is represented by the countries concerned, which are guided not by a universal but by a contextual approach, when specific mechanisms and instruments of cooperation are determined by local conditions and let us emphasize, by national preferences.

Northern Dimension

The Northern Dimension (ND) policy aims at supporting stability, well-being, and sustainable development in the Northern Dimension area/region through practical cooperation. This EU initiative was launched by Finland in 1997 and adopted by the

European Commission as an EU strategy in 1999, initially for the period 2000–2003. An essential part of the ND is the development of cross-border cooperation between the neighboring administrative areas of the participating countries. In accordance with the founding documents, it covers the territories of Finland, Sweden, Norway, Iceland, the Baltic States, and Poland, as well as parts of the Russian Northwest.

The ND was primarily an attempt by the northern EU members to overcome the growing divide between the European Union and Russia by addressing practical functional problems together rather than another channel for fighting over "high" politics. Security and political issues were either removed from the agenda or discussed to a very limited extent. The European participants involved have found it a good practice not to raise oil and gas supply issues in the ND; only nuclear safety and energy conservation have been included in the ND Environmental Partnership. It has been repeatedly emphasized that the ND proves that small EU countries can achieve a lot with "smart small policies." The success of the ND can be explained through a multilevel governance approach, which assumes that actors can influence EU decision-making through a variety of channels, from working with European institutions to indirect action through regional, national, and subnational structures. The policies formed in this way are the result of overlapping competences, tensions, and conflicts in a multilevel governance system. Decision-making on private, localized issues are decentralized, that is, dispersed among the various institutional levels – regional, national, and supranational (Busygina and Filippov 2008). Constructivists have a broader vision of the ND: they see it as an apt example of the construction of the new moral language and geopolitical discourse for the enlarging European Union (Moisio 2003).

The Baltic Sea Strategy

The Baltic Sea Strategy affects over 80 million people and eight EU Member States (Estonia, Latvia, Lithuania, Poland, Germany, Denmark, Sweden, and Finland) working together to improve the competitiveness of the region, create new transport and energy connections, protect the environment, promote scientific cooperation and contacts, and ensure the safety of people and the environment. The strategy also makes it possible to involve the countries of the European Economic Area (Norway and Iceland). The strategy was established in 2009. Following the example of the Baltic Sea Strategy, the European Union later developed strategies for the Danube, Adriatic, Ionian, and Alpine regions. The main idea behind such strategies is to unite countries around a common large geographical object. These countries, being in direct proximity to this object, share interests in relation to it and therefore are incentivized in coming up with institutional arrangements that work, with the European Union creating a common framework by supporting the countries' incentives.

Conclusion: territorial–political orders in Europe

For centuries, European nations have been at war with each other. These were long and bloody wars that considerably hindered general development (the wars may have stimulated technical development, though in selected sectors, and encouraged enrichment, though of narrow groups. Overall, societies experienced massive losses from the wars.

Let's call a protracted situation when there are no actors in the system (elites of political entities) who could and/or wanted to challenge the current peaceful status quo *territorial–political order*. Then, looking at European history, we can distinguish several such orders (TPO):

The first TPO can be labeled "imperial solution." That was the attempts to create an "all embracing" structure, empire (the Roman Empire, The Holy Roman Empire of the German Nation), where wars would have been prevented by loyalty to the emperor shared by all territorial units. Besides that, the Holy Roman Empire was based on common value: Christianity. However, the low capacity of the empire, non-centralization, and constant "hunger for resources" have undermined internal stability and weakened empires. The institutions that allowed the empire to maintain governability while simultaneously expanding territorially – primarily non-centralization leading to asymmetries and the dominance of informal institutions – became the sources of its internal weakness and instability. The geographical (territorial) imperative prevented investment in necessary institutional changes. As time went on, it became more and more difficult to develop the empire as a whole; it was more a question of developing its individual parts. Cleavages and splits were growing – between the cities and feudal principalities as well as inside Christianity itself with the advent of the Reformation. The Imperial project proved to be incapable of stopping wars between polities – territorial entities of the empire.

The second TPO relied on a different approach: instead of making one actor, the emperor, "responsible" for maintaining peace and development, it divided responsibility among all participants in the system. It was "Europe of sovereignties" based on the Westphalian model with the fundamental formal norms of noninterference in each other's internal affairs; the principle of territoriality (borders were markers of sovereignty, and they should be inviolable); the primacy of state interests and state sovereignty. However, this attempt has failed since the order did not generate the internal legitimacy and credible commitments of the rulers of numerous territorial units that differed significantly in geographic size, population, and resources (including for warfare).

The third TPO emerged in Europe after the unsuccessful attempt of Napoleon to embody an "imperial solution"; this was the "European concert of powers" constituted by the Congress of Vienna. This was an attempt to lay the responsibility for the non-war on a group of major powers: Russia, Prussia, and Austria entered the "Holy Union" in 1815 to keep order after the Congress, later the "Union of Three Emperors" was created. The gradual polarization of the European political space – the Russian Empire on the East and the Great Britain on the East –, as well as the unification of Germany in 1871 put an end to this TPO. Importantly, the condition for maintaining this order was to preserve the balance of power between the major powers in Europe; the unification of Germany and its accelerated development and militarization changed the balance and made it impossible to maintain the previous order.

The two subsequent world wars represented the other attempts of German Second and Third Reichs to revive the "imperial solution" on the European continent. These attempts failed, and the "imperial solution" for Europe was finally defeated.

After the end of World War II, a process began in Europe of structuring political spaces on both sides of the "Iron curtain" that strictly divided socialist (Soviet) and capitalist (Western) camps – politically, economically, and ideologically. The order then was based on dividing lines in Europe and the principal non-transparency of the "Iron curtain." The two camps were almost simultaneously institutionalized with the creation of NATO and Warsaw Pact Organization (in the security domain) and EEC (EU) and the Council for Mutual Economic Assistance (common market). The Council of Europe was created in Western Europe to defend democracy and human rights – but no institutional response from the socialist camp followed.

The two camps created their own orders, which were separated by an impenetrable border. In Western Europe, the order was based on the institutions of regional integration, while in Eastern Europe it was based on the imperial-like solution under the hegemony of the Soviet Union. After the collapse of the socialist camp and the Soviet Union, there seemed to be a well-founded hope that a common new order for the whole of Europe was possible (and soon!). In this new order, wars between European nations would be excluded, dividing lines would not exist, and all countries would finally be able to commit credibly and trust each other. These hopes proved to be premature.

The competition between the European Union and Russia for the "shared neighborhood" (post-Soviet states located in Eastern Europe and Transcaucasia) became increasingly intense. Nevertheless, a real war in the center of Europe seemed impossible – until Russia launched such a war against Ukraine in February 2022. The crisis and new risks in the region has created a demand and opened a geopolitical dimension to the EU neighborhood policy, which required Brussels to fill a hard security vacuum in its own policies in the neighborhood, which invoked an application of new instruments to deter Moscow and support the European Union's Eastern allies (Nizhnikau and Moshes 2024).

Some experts consider the fundamental reason for Russia's war against Ukraine, embedded in the broader context of the confrontation between Russia and the West, the age-old opposition of land and sea, of continental power and seafaring power. Others draw attention to the new relevance of Halford Mackinder's geopolitical ideas. I am not sure that appealing to old (very old!) ideas with all their fundamentality could contribute much to a better understanding of this war. Rather, it seems useful to remember Robert Kaplan, who predicted the "revenge of geography" and argued that no progress, be it economic or technological in nature, can afford to ignore the principle of territory, because the sum of geographical factors inevitably impacts international processes (Kaplan 2013). According to Klinke, the 2022 invasion of Ukraine challenged geographical conceptualizations of war. The attention was diverting away from the "new," "asymmetrical," and "everywhere" wars that had come to dominate geographical debates in recent years (see Gregory 2011). As Klinke wrote,

> [D]espite an initial rhetoric of cyber- and hybrid warfare, Ukraine has been a remarkably twentieth-century armed conflict, *a war for territory*. Although unmanned aerial vehicles and satellite images are used to significant effect, tremendous loss of life is inflicted by an old-fashioned mode of warfare, by artillery fire.
>
> (Klinke 2023)

The Russian regime's desire to possess new territories as proof of greatness, uninhibited by domestic institutions, gave rise to this war in the center of Europe.

Notes

1 Poorest countries in Europe 2024 (worldpopulationreview.com).
2 These are Europe's top five most innovative countries | World Economic Forum (weforum.org).
3 After elections in Poland in 2023, observers once remarked that Poland's modern electoral maps displayed a familiar pattern: the east voted for the incumbent Law and Justice (PiS) party, whereas the west supported various opposition groups, mostly the liberal Civic Coalition (KO). More remarkable, however, is that rather than following a gradual gradient from east to west, modern Poles' political loyalties remain firm right up to the edge of a historical line that cuts down the middle of the country. This split dates back to the partition of Poland between the three empires in the late eighteenth century. Imperial borders still shape politics in Poland (economist.com).
4 The 1707 Treaty of Union has long been portrayed as a tale of bullying, bribery, and betrayal. "We are bought and sold for English gold. Such a parcel of rogues in a nation," wrote Robert Burns, as he raged against Scotland's loss of independence. So the argument is that the Union was an illegitimate act that shouldn't have happened and that it wasn't Scotland's decision. However, Christopher Whatley and Derek Patrick (2006) have challenged this argument in their book, arguing that a number of Scottish parliamentarians fervently wanted the Union and that that the Scottish parliament has not been forced to make this decision (Whatley, Christopher, and Derek Patrick. (2006). *The Scots and the Union*. Edinburgh University Press).
5 The problems with the United Kingdom, which eventually culminated in Brexit, were very specific.
6 The ultimate causes of Brexit: history, culture, and geography | British Politics and Policy at LSE.

References

Abu-Lughod, Janet. (1989). *Before European Hegemony: The World System A.D. 1250–1350*. Oxford: Oxford University Press.
Acemoglu, Daren, Simon Johnson, and James Robinson. (2002). The Rise of Europe: Atlantic Trade, Institutional Change, and Economic Growth. NBER Working Papers.
Axtmann, Roland. (2003). "State Formation and Supranationalism in Europe: The Case of the Holy Roman Empire of the German Nation." In *Europe without Borders*, ed. by M. Berezin and M. Schain, pp. 118–139. Baltimore, MD: The John Hopkins University Press.

Benz, Arthur Benz, and Christina Zimmer. (2010). "The EU Competences: The 'Vertical' Perspective on the Multilevel System." *Living Review European Government*, 5(1).
Börzel, Tanja, and Digdem Suyatin. (2012). *Europeanization in Turkey: Stretching a Concept to its Limits? KFG, Working Paper*, Vol. 36. Berlin: Freie Universität Berlin.
Braudel, Fernan. (1989). *The Identity of France: History and Environment*, Vol. 1. New York: Harper & Row.
Braudel, Fernan. (1992). *Civilization and Capitalism, 15th–18th Century*, Vol. 1. Berkeley: University of California Press.
Busygina, Irina. (2000). *The Regions of Germany*. Moscow: ROSSPEN. [Regiony Germanii. Moskva: ROSSPEN].
Busygina, Irina, and Mikhail Filippov. (2008). "EU-Russia Relations and the Limits of the Northern Dimension." In *The New Northern Dimension of the European Neighborhood*, ed. by Michael Emerson and Pami Aalto. Brussels, Belgium: Centre for European Policy Studies (CEPS).
Claval, Paul. (1994). "From Michelet to Braudel: Personality, Identity and Organization of France." In *Geography and National Identity*, ed. by D. Hooson. Oxford: Oxford University Press.
Colomer, Josep. (2008). *Great Empires, Small Nations: The Uncertain Future of the Sovereign States*. London; New York: Routledge.
Colomer, Josep. (2017). "Empires Versus States." Oxford Research Encyclopedia of Politics.
Davis, Norman. (1996). *Europe: A History*. Oxford: Oxford University Press.
Ferguson, Niall. (2003). *Empire: The Rise and Demise of the British World Order and the Lessons for Global Power*. London: Basic Books.
Gellner, Ernst. (2006). *Nations and Nationalism*. Oxford, UK: Wiley-Blackwell.
Goodfellow, Tom, and David Jackman. (2020). Control the Capital: Cities and Political Dominance. ESID Working Paper No. 135.
Gregory, Derek. (2011). "The Everywhere War." *The Geographical Journal*, 177: 238–250.
Grosfeld, Irena, and Ekaterina Zhuravskaya. (2014). "Cultural vs. Economic Legacies of Empires: Evidence from the Partition of Poland." *Journal of Comparative Economics*. https://ssrn.com/abstract=2216146 or http://dx.doi.org/10.2139/ssrn.2216146.
Hooghe, Liesbet, and Gary Marks. (2001). "Types of Multi-Level Governance. European Integration." *European Integration online Papers (EIoP)*, 5. http://ssrn.com/abstract=302786 or http://dx.doi.org/10.2139/ssrn.302786.
Hunt, Edwein, and James Murray. (1999). *A History of Business in Medieval Europe, 1200–1550*. Cambridge: Cambridge University Press.
Kaplan, Robert. (2013). *The Revenge of Geography. What the Map Tells Us about Coming Conflicts and the Battle against Fate*. New York: Random House.
Klinke, Ian. (2023). "Of Tanks and Tankies: What's 'Left' for Geography after the Invasion of Ukraine." *Transactions of the Institute of British Geographers*, 48(4): 671–834.
Marks, Gary. (1993). "Structural Policy and Multilevel Governance in the EC." *The State of the European Community*, 2.
Moisio, Sami. (2003). "Back to Baltoscandia? European Union and Geo-Conceptual Remaking of the European North." *Geopolitics*, 8(1): 72–100.
Motyl, Alexander. (2001). *Imperial Ends: The Decay, Collapse, and Revival of Empires*. New York: Columbia University Press.
Nizhnikau, Ryhor, and Arkady Moshes. (2024). "The War in Ukraine, the EU's Geopolitical Awakening and Implications for the 'Contested Neighborhood'." *Policy Studies*, 45(3–4): 489–506.
Percoco, Marco. (2013). "Geography, Institutions and Urban Development: Italian Cities, 1300–1861." *The Annals of Regional Science*, 50: 135–152.
Pounds, Norman. (1973). *A Historical Geography of Europe*. Cambridge: Cambridge University Press.
Radaelli, C. (2004). *Europeanization: Solution or Problem?* http://www.eiop.or.at/eiop/pdf/2004-016.pdf

Schimmelfenning, Frank, and Ulrich Sedelmeier. (2004). "Governance by Conditionality: EU Rule Transfer to the Candidate Countries of Central and Eastern Europe." *Journal of European Public Policy*, 11(4): 661–679.
Tilly, Charles. (1992). *Coercion, Capital and European States, AD 990–1992*. Oxford: Blackwell Publishing.
Tilly, Charles. (1994). "States and Nationalism in Europe." *Theory and Society*, 23(1): 131–145.
Zielonka, Jan. (2002). "Introduction: Boundary Making by the European Union." In *Europe Unbound: Enlarging and Reshaping the Boundaries of the European Union*, ed. by Jan Zielonka. London; New York: Routledge.

5 Asia

Together with Europe, Asia forms the continent of Eurasia, which occupies about 30% of the Earth's land mass. The borders of Asia are marked by nature itself: The Arctic Ocean in the north, the Pacific Ocean in the east, the Indian Ocean in the south. The western, European–Asian boundary cannot be drawn precisely. Officially, the border between Europe and Asia is considered a line that runs through the Aegean Sea, the Dardanelles, the Marmara Sea, the Bosporus, the Black Sea, along the watershed of the Greater Caucasus, along the northwestern part of the Caspian Sea and along the Ural River, then along the Ural Mountains to the Arctic Ocean. It is this boundary that is represented in most geographic atlases.

The hallmarks of modern Asia are the largest megalopolises (urbanized areas) in the world – Tokaido, uniting the cities of Tokyo and Yokohama; Chinese megalopolises "Pearl River Delta" (made up of adjacent cities of Hong Kong, Shenzhen, Dongguan, and some others); and Yangtze Delta, consisting of adjacent agglomerations of Shanghai, Suzhou, and Changzhou. Many experts argue that the twenty-first century is the "century of Eurasia" (or rather, Asia), and the evidence for this are the emergence of global cities in Asia, the implementation of infrastructure mega-projects on an unprecedented scale, such as the Chinese "One Belt and One Road," as well as the new role of China in the international arena.

A glance at the political map of Asia immediately gives an idea of the enormous vastness and complexity of this region. Asia is home to 48 independent states. The people of Asia speak more than 600 languages. The most ancient civilizations have emerged in Asia; world religions, such as Christianity, Buddhism, and Islam, are of Asian origin. The area of predominantly Muslim population stretches across the Malaysian Peninsula and the islands of Indonesia, the latter being the most populous Muslim country in the world.

Considering its territorial size, Asia, unlike Europe, is a region of exceptional geographic contrasts, which can be seen in many dimensions. For example, three countries, comparable to entire continents, Russia, China, and India, are disproportionally much larger in territorial size than the others; at the same time, there are very small states in Asia, for instance, Singapore, Bahrain, or the Republic of Maldives. The shape of the countries' territories varies, from relatively regular to quite peculiar, as in the case of Vietnam, whose shape can be compared to a beater.

DOI: 10.4324/9781003496731-8

The age of state formations also varies greatly: along with the oldest states in the world, such as China and Iran, there are new states in Asia – the United Arab Emirates or the youngest Asian state, East Timor, which appeared on the political map of Asia in 2002 and before that was under UN administration. There is an extraordinary gap between rich and poor countries in Asia. Measured in Gross National Income (GNI) per capita, the richest countries in Asia are Qatar, Singapore, Israel, United Arab Emirates, Japan, and South Korea. This group is largely composed of countries that are both small in size and either oil-rich or among the most business-friendly and technologically advanced economies.[1] At the same time, ongoing conflicts, poor governance, and corruption are three common factors contributing to poverty in nations like Afghanistan, North Korea, and Yemen which consistently rank among the poorest in Asia. Afghanistan, burdened by ongoing conflict, corruption, and inequality, consistently ranks as the poorest country in Asia by nearly any measure.[2]

A variety of political regimes are represented on the territory of the region – from democratic federal India to autocratic unitary Turkmenistan or totalitarian North Korea. Importantly, in Asia, democratic regimes are located, unlike in Europe, far from each other and do not form a cohesive group.

In Asian countries, inequalities of all kinds are among the most serious internal obstacles to development. The UN Economic and Social Council makes the distinction between three broad types of inequality: inequality of outcome, inequality of opportunity, and inequality of impact. Inequality of outcome refers to disparities among individuals in the material dimensions of human well-being, such as the level of income and wealth. Inequality of opportunity refers to unequal access to the fundamental rights and services required for individuals to sustain and improve their livelihoods, including education, health care, nutrition, water and sanitation, and energy. Finally, inequality of impact refers to the asymmetric impact of external factors or shocks, such air pollution, or a disaster, on different population groups. Inequality of impact is also called group-based inequality or horizontal inequality. In Asia the countries that stand out as particularly unequal are Afghanistan, Bangladesh, and India. On the other end of the spectrum are Maldives and Turkey (Subregional 2018).

Asian states also differ in their political weight in global politics: while China receives constant attention of the world community, and the "China factor" is extremely important for world politics, countries such as Bhutan and Laos are relatively little known and, as they say, "do not make the weather" for the global agenda.

In Asia, we find countries with both exceptionally favorable and exceptionally unfavorable geographical and geopolitical locations. Turkey, Singapore, Sri Lanka, Cyprus, and the small countries of Southwest Asia – Oman, Yemen, Jordan, and Bahrain – are examples of states with favorable geographic location. The favorability of the locations lies in their transit opportunities, or in its control over an important territorial object, or in its location "at the junction" (subregional or cultural). Turkey is one of the few states in the world, which is located in two parts of the world, Europe and Asia. The border between them passes through the

Bosporus and Dardanelles straits and the Sea of Marmara, and Turkey controls this important military–political and trade-economic route connecting the Black Sea and the Mediterranean Sea. The unusually advantageous position of Singapore, ideal for the organization of trade, was appreciated by British colonizers back in the early nineteenth century; later it was the position of Singapore that determined its transformation into a center of communications of global importance. Sri Lanka occupies a strategically important position on the sea routes from Europe to East Asia, Australia, and Oceania.

Empires fought each other over Cyprus's strategic position at the crossroads of trade routes from Europe to Asia. A favorable feature of Oman's geographic location is its control of the entrance to the Persian Gulf; Yemen is located at the exit from the Red Sea to the Gulf of Aden and the Indian Ocean; Jordan is the center of the Arab world of Asia (Mashreq); Bahrain is close to the Middle East oil basin and is at the crossroads of trade routes in the Persian Gulf.

However, Asia is rich with opposite examples – these are landlocked countries with no access to the sea. Armenia, Afghanistan (with the distance to the nearest seacoast is 500 km), the kingdom of Bhutan, which not so long ago was completely cut off from the outside world, Laos, Nepal, finally, Mongolia, the most remote from the ocean country in the world. With the collapse of the Soviet Union in 1991, the geographical position of the Central Asian countries has worsened considerably – they lost their access to the sea. For example, Tajikistan is one of the most remote countries of Asia from the world ocean (although the geographical location of Tajikistan has another important dimension: the border location between the Turkic world in the north and the Iranian-speaking world in the south; the disputes over these lands between the two great empires – the British and Russian – testified to the important geopolitical importance of this territory).

So Asia has it all: the farthest from the sea and the states surrounded by water. Such are Indonesia, the largest island state in the world; the Philippines, which is located on 11 large islands; and Japan, where the island location has formed a unique nation in terms of worldview and mentality.

Geography and institutions in the history of Asia

The great cultures in Asia owed their emergence to geography. In the ancient era (pre-fifth century AD), great cultures originated and developed in Asia along the great rivers. These were the Huang He and Yangtze, where the Chinese civilization grew; the basins of the Indus and Ganges, the birthplace of Indian (Vedic) culture; on the banks of the Tigris and Euphrates, the Assyria-Babylonian culture was born; finally, ancient Egypt was formed along the great Nile. These civilizations have got the name "hydraulic" – so important was their location by the water for their development (Butzer 1976).

In Mesopotamia (between the Tigris and Euphrates), the first political structures – city-states (e.g., Phoenicia), a chain of port city-states on the Syrian-Lebanese coast of the Mediterranean Sea) appeared from the middle of the fourth century BC. For many centuries, cities such as Byblos, Tire, and Sidon lived on active maritime trade; but from the first century BC, they came under the authority of the Roman Empire. In the third century, a large Sumerian kingdom emerged, the oldest of the Mesopotamian civilizations. It was located in the lower parts of the Tigris and Euphrates valleys. The alluvial soils of these territories were very fertile. The Sumerian city-states constantly competed; they were never part of a single centralized system. One of the peculiarities of the Mesopotamian civilizations was their connection with water – the organization of control over water consumption and the struggle against destructive floods.

The first large territorial polities of Asia were empires, but they were internally fragile. These empires collapsed, and new ones took their place, taking advantage of the inheritance of their predecessors. In the Middle East in the first millennium BC, huge empires were created, such as Midia, which consolidated the Persians, and Alexander the Great's empire, which absorbed the Persian Empire. At the same time, strong empires emerged in the Ganges valley (e.g., the Mauryan Empire). In the process of the unification of the ancient Chinese states, the Qin Empire was created. Despite the changing configuration, the Chinese empire was characterized by stability; originally its settlements also grew on the coastal alluvial soils, but the real growth began when the waters of the Huang He (Yellow River) began to be regularly delivered to the loess soils of the surrounding plains, that is, powerful irrigation systems were created (Dodgshon 1998: 63).

In the *Middle Ages*, large empires continued to play an important role. In Western Asia, the Arab Caliphate, established in the seventh century, was of great importance. The original nucleus of this state was the Muslim community (*umma*), established in Hijaz (Western Arabia); subsequently, because of Arab conquests, a larger structure began to form. The most important feature of the Caliphate, as well as of other Islamic states, was the fusion of religion (Islam) and political institutions. After the collapse of the Caliphate in the tenth–thirteenth centuries, the political map of the Middle East underwent constant changes, until the formation of the largest Ottoman Empire in the region. This was a geographically extended powerful empire that included almost all the lands of the former Arab Caliphate (Arabia, Iraq, Maghreb, part of Transcaucasia) and acquired new lands – the Balkans and the Crimea. The Ottoman Empire was a threat to both Europe and Russia. The Ottoman Empire lost its power by the end of the nineteenth century (Turkey, the heart of the empire was divided among the Entente countries after its defeat in World War I and gained its independence after the War of Liberation in 1919–1923, led by Kemal Ataturk).

In East Asia, the process of forming empires, their fall, and the emergence of new ones was also underway. Between the sixth and thirteenth centuries, the Chinese Confucian Empire flourished. The waves of territorial expansion of Chinese dynasties were accompanied by the cultural assimilation of neighbors caught in the field of Confucian influence. By the time of the Tang dynasty (618–907), China had exhausted its capacity for territorial incorporations, turning the Confucian area into a melting pot of ethnicities and peoples subjected to "Chineseization." The greatness of China was not that much military might but its dominating culture, which made it possible to harmonize interethnic relations in tense situations.

As noted here, the Chinese Empire belonged to the most stable ones; its growth and consolidation depended on how successfully the empire dealt with two major challenges – the integration of new territories and the control and protection of borders, which were constantly being pushed back. The more the empire expanded, the more acute was the problem of borders, especially in the north and northwest. The fact was that the less fertile soils of these territories were not suitable for the types of agriculture (intensive, with developed irrigation systems) that were widespread in the empire; local communities were predominantly pastoralists. The territorial solution found was the creation of wide internal and external frontier zones, which formed a buffer zone separating the empire and the tribes of the north and northwest (Dodgshon 1998: 64–65).

By the end of the thirteenth century, China was under Mongol rule; the Mongol khan received the title of Chinese emperor – that is, the periphery began to control the center. During this period, the campaigns of Genghis Khan and his descendants led to the conquest by the Mongols of many spaces of Siberia, Central Asia, Northern China, the Caucasus, Korea, East and Southeast Asia, and Eastern Europe. Peculiar multinational formations emerged in these places, where the Mongols themselves were in the minority. The most significant formation was the Golden Horde.

The European colonization

The formation of the political map of Asia was strongly influenced by European colonization, primarily by the formation of the most powerful British colonial empire. As early as in the seventeenth century, the British established a system of naval bases and stations – in North America, India, Indonesia, Australia, and on the west coast of Africa – which became the strongholds of British colonialism. The Portuguese expedition of Vasco da Gama in 1498, one of the most remarkable voyages of discovery, opened a sea route around Africa (from Europe to India) and marked the beginning of the colonial conquests in Asia.

In 1795, Britain seized the island of Ceylon, which had previously belonged to the Netherlands. However, the real "jewel" of the British Empire was India, where British possessions were constantly expanding, and by the mid-nineteenth century almost all of India and most of neighboring Burma became British colonies. India was undoubtedly the empire's most important possession. Its strongholds on the sea routes to India – several islands in the Indian Ocean, the Suez Canal area, and Aden in the south of the Arabian Peninsula – also became important components of the empire. At the same time, Singapore and the southern coast of the Malacca Peninsula were annexed to the British Empire. Later, British possessions in and around India further expanded at the expense of Afghanistan, thereby giving Britain control over the mountain passages linking India and Afghanistan. In the nineteenth century, the interests of the Russian and British empires clashed in Afghanistan; the latter regarded Afghanistan as a bridgehead to penetrate Central Asia (Bastin 1968).

However, Britain was not always the first to arrive in Asia; sometimes, there was a redistribution of colonial ownership. Thus, during the Age of Discovery, the Spanish came to the Philippines with Magellan's expedition in 1516. In the sixteenth century, Portuguese possessions appeared in the Malacca Peninsula and the Moluccas Islands. From the seventeenth to the twentieth century, control over most of what is now Indonesia was held by the Netherlands; Britain and France came to Southeast Asia later. It was not until the end of the nineteenth century that Southeast Asia was largely divided between Britain and France. France conquered the eastern part of the Indochina peninsula, then Cambodia and Laos became its protectorates. These territories constituted what was known as French Indochina. Great Britain took over Burma and most of Malacca. Siam (modern Thailand) was divided into spheres of influence between Britain and France.

Colonization of the islands of Indonesia began in the seventeenth century, and by the early twentieth century, the entire territory of what is now Indonesia became a Dutch colony. The large island of New Guinea was divided into three parts: the western part was part of Dutch India (modern Indonesia), the southeastern part belonged to Britain, and the northeastern part to Germany. As a result of the victory in the Spanish-American War of 1898, the United States occupied the former Spanish colony, the Philippines. In East Asia, the main territorial disputes of the late nineteenth to early twentieth centuries related to Chinese and Japanese expansion. The strongholds and spheres of influence of Great Britain, France, Russia, and Germany were created on the territory of China; the massive economic penetration of the European powers into China began.

In Japan, Europeans arrived in 1543; first, these were the Portuguese, then the Spanish, and then the British. However, Japan took a different path: it "closed off" from the outside world for almost 200 years, until 1854, when an American military squadron entered Japanese waters and then began a policy of territorial expansion. Between 1894 and 1895, Japan fought a war against China, which resulted in the acquisition of the island of Taiwan (Formosa). Victory in the Russo-Japanese War of 1904–1905 gave Japan the southern part of Sakhalin Island and the Liaodong Peninsula; in 1910, Japan annexed Korea. In 1931, Japan occupied Manchuria and created the "daughter" state of Manchukuo. Subsequently, during World War II, Japan occupied Myanmar.

Territories of Central Asia were joining the Russian Empire, beginning from the middle of the nineteenth century: first the territories of modern Kazakhstan, then Uzbekistan, Turkmenistan (as Transcaspian region), and Tajikistan. In the last case, Bukhara and Kokand khanates recognized the Russian Empire protectorate after long battles with Russian troops in 1868, although their accession to the empire allowed them to avoid another colonial dependence – from the British Empire. The emergence of Russian administration in the annexed and conquered territories was accompanied by the introduction of military, that is, strict, hierarchical, administration (as General Skobelev said, "Asia must be beaten not only in the scruff but also in the imagination!"). And yet after the seemingly easy conquest of Central Asia, the local ethno-cultural communities almost immediately developed a kind of "protective civilizational film," which allowed such different cultures to coexist without mixing (Zamyatin 2003: 240).

Let us consider the situation in Central Asia in more detail. By the mid-nineteenth century, Afghanistan was the node area, a kind of heartland, of this vast region: it was here that the borders – in strategic terms – of two empires, the Russian and the British, converged. Defining the northern Afghan border in 1870–1880, the boundary of the spheres of influence of the two empires was essentially the process of creating (or implanting) the European border on Asian territory. The significance of Russia's conquest of Central Asia was determined not only by the value of these territorial increments for the metropolis as such but also by their geopolitical position. Thus, Turkestan was not so much a Russian colony as a kind of operational base and/or geopolitical, the real (but not achieved) goal of the Russian Empire seemed to be India (Zamyatin 2003: 240). Russia's understanding of the importance of Central Asia as a self-valuable part of the Russian space developed only by the beginning of the twentieth century.

In the British Empire's sphere of influence, in India and Afghanistan, there was intensive cultural expansion, primarily in terms of material cultural achievements. In the Russian domains, such expansion was not effective due to Russia's technical and economic backwardness and a different mechanism of inter-civilizational contacts. On the contrary, Russia's cultural influence in Central Asia had always been quite weak, the economic development of these territories by the Russians was fragmentary and weakly expressed. Larissa Reisner, a journalist of the early Soviet times, who was traveling across Central Asia, wrote:

> Where Asia is touched by Russia, even where it penetrates it forcibly, in general, no visible trace remains. An ugly post-office among the joyful poverty of Bukhara bazaars, a Red Army man in an old overcoat and tattered boots on the border between Kushka and Childukhteran – and all the rest we have in common, after all. And this laziness, and insects, and poverty, and the melancholy disregard for one's time, for one's life. . . . England enters the borders of Afghan Asia in a very different way. Where the fields of our Turkestan are simply watered with the blood of nameless soldiers, Britain irrigates and dries, arranges artesian wells, puts mighty filters . . . A double row of highways connects India with Afghanistan . . . The telegraph and telephone are pushed to the very border.
>
> (Reisner 1925: 88–89)

In Central Asia, the Russians encountered a new phenomenon, or rather, the old term "border" took on a new meaning. Thus, in Central Asia there were both permanent borders of sedentary populations and constantly changing borders of nomadic tribes. The internal parts of the nuclei of Central Asian state formations (the nuclei of the Kokand, Khiva khanates etc.) had permanent borders, while the nomadic periphery of these formations made their borders very blurred – they acted as a kind of frontiers for the sedentary population. The border between Russia and the Central Asian states in the European sense did not exist. According to Zamyatin, the territory of Central Asia in the second half of the nineteenth century was unstable and "fluid," which began to change only with the invasion of Russian troops. Russia's advance into Turkmenistan, for example, led to the clarification and hardening of the Turkmen–Iranian border (unlike the European, the concept of the Asian border implies vague, indistinct contours and outlines) (Zamyatin 2003: 241, 253). In Central Asia, the strongest ethnic mosaic of this space, the pivots or cores of the territories were rivers – Syr Darya, Amu Darya, Zeravshan, Ili, Tedzhen, Murgab. Water – rivers, irrigation systems, artificial canals – held the landscapes together. The distribution of water and the location of irrigation systems determined both the economic geography of the territory and the political geography (administrative units were established along canals) and the social stratification of society, in which the quantity of water was the measure of wealth (Zamyatin 2003: 251).

The national–territorial demarcation in Central Asia, and in fact the split of the single civilization space took place in 1924–1925. Thus, in 1924, Turkmen and Uzbek SSRs were created (the latter included Tajik ASSR); in 1925, they were admitted to the Union of Soviet Socialist Republics as union republics. As part of the RSFSR, first the Kara-Kirghiz AO was formed and received the status of ASSR in 1925. The Tajik ASSR gained another status, the Union republic, and joined the USSR in that capacity in 1929, the same process passed Kirghiz and Kazakh ASSR, which joined the USSR as union republics in 1936.

Let us turn to the situation in Transcaucasia. In the sixteenth and eighteenth centuries, the territory of Azerbaijan was an object of struggle between Iran and Turkey; from the middle of the eighteenth century, there were more than 15 feudal states dependent on Iran. In 1813 and 1828, Northern Azerbaijan was annexed to the Russian Empire. Armenia in the sixteenth to eighteenth centuries was divided between Iran and Turkey, in the 20 years of the nineteenth century, Eastern Armenia was included into Russia, and Western Armenia remained in the Ottoman Empire.

In 1801, Eastern Georgia and, in 1803–1804, Western Georgia became parts of the Russian Empire (Tiflis and Kutaisi provinces were formed on their territories). Western Georgia became part of the Russian Empire (Tiflis and Kutaisi provinces were formed on their territories). In 1920–1921, Georgia, Armenia, and Azerbaijan became Soviet Socialist Republics, and in 1922, they formed a union, and then the Transcaucasian Socialist Federal Soviet Republic (SSFSR). In 1936, the SSFSR was abolished, and the three republics became part of the Union of Soviet Socialist Republics as separate Union republics.

In Southwest Asia, small territory-states fell under the protectorate of European countries, but the "island of Arabs" – Saudi Arabia – was ruled and collected by emirs (the Kingdom of Saudi Arabia was proclaimed in 1932). Iran in the late nineteenth century and early twentieth century became a semi-colony of Great Britain and Russia. Thus, Russia owned roads, railroads, banks, and many enterprises in Iran. After the revolution of 1905–1911 and adoption of the constitution, Iran gained independence. During World War II, Soviet and British troops were based on the territory of Iran, cargo flow from the countries of anti-Hitler coalition to the USSR passed through Iran.

With the occupation of Baghdad by Turkish troops in 1533, Iraq became part of the Ottoman Empire, but until the nineteenth century, the power of Istanbul on these territories was nominal and did not extend to the whole country, especially to its southern regions. The reason for that was primarily the geographical remoteness of Iraq from the center of Ottoman power, which was used by Iran, so that up to 1921, Iraq was an arena of struggle between the Ottoman Turkey and Iran. Istanbul's attempts to centralize the empire and establish tight control over the entire country met with resistance from the tribes, who constituted most of the population in Iraq; after that empire in the Middle East was divided between France and Great Britain, Iraq became a British Mandate Territory. Great Britain gave Iraq a special place in the geopolitical configuration of its part of the Ottoman inheritance because of its geopolitical and economic importance: even before World War I, oil reserves had been discovered here.

It is important to note that, in fact, not only European powers acted as colonizers in Asia; Asia also knew Eurasian colonizers, especially the Russian Empire and Japan. Asian territories show huge variations in the character of colonial legacy. This legacy has played very different roles for the developmental trajectories of Asian countries.

The collapse of the colonial system and the colonial legacy

The collapse of the world colonial system began with the decolonization of Asia, which unfolded almost simultaneously in all parts of the vast region. In 1945, Korea, Japan's largest colony, was liberated; Indonesia and Vietnam proclaimed their independence. In 1946, Jordan and the Philippines gained sovereignty, and the next year India was no longer a colony. It should be noted that the Independence Act provided for two dominions on its territory – the Union of India and Pakistan, and the division was based on the confessional principle: predominantly Muslim Pakistan and predominantly Hindu India. In turn, Pakistan consisted of two parts – the Western and the Eastern part, separated by Indian territory (the artificiality and geographical absurdity of such an entity were obvious, and in 1971, East Pakistan transformed into the sovereign Republic of Bangladesh).

The metropolis, Great Britain, gave India a single government, administrative and legislative structure; the country was constitutionalized on the principles of liberal democracy. The Indian elite still speaks English, and many Indian leaders studied in Western universities. However, despite its British heritage, India has maintained its distinctive character, "not assimilating foreigners (as China did), but rather isolating them from itself. Indian society . . . has survived by being impervious to outside cultures" (Kissinger 2001). Perhaps, it is to colonial domination that India owes its current territorial unity (the preservation of which is one of its greatest challenges, given its extremely diverse ethnic and religious composition and the socioeconomic disparities between regions and social groups); without it, it would most likely be a conglomeration of many independent states.

However, the interregional inequalities across India are stunning. A recent scholarship has found empirical support for the proposition that present-day regional inequality owes to two particular colonial institutional legacies: property right and indirect rule (Banerjee and Iyer 2005; Clark and Wolcott 2003; Roy 2002,

2014). Yes, British colonialism contributed to political integration, but it created its own divisions. A little over half of the territory in colonial India (1857–1947) was directly governed by the crown, the remainder being governed by the Indian princes and autonomous tribal councils. Although their affairs were observed by and sometimes supervised by British-appointed residents or commissioners, formally the freedom to rule was respected. This relationship between British India and the princely states is called indirect rule.

The princely states were the kingdoms, and many of them were former vassals of Maratha or Mughal empires, which British India did not annex. The political ground for not doing so was that these states were allies of the British, and those in northern India had demonstrated the loyalty during the great mutiny of 1857. However, nearly all these states suffered from bad geography: they were land-locked, arid or poorly irrigated, with forest cover, and, for these reasons, did not yield as much value as it might cost to acquire and maintain them. The states were required to maintain open borders to commercial traffic. They could have their own currency or legal systems, but the monetary autonomy existed only in name. Most had little incentive to insulate themselves from the pan-regional economic tendencies. No state was known to want to erect obstacles to market integration with British India.

At the same time, the directly ruled territory became differentiated in respect of rural property rights. Possibly the most important institutional innovation undertaken by the East India Company state (1793–1820) was the definition of the legal title of ownership of land and the creation of a system of courts and legal procedures to verify and uphold the right. This was in theory and in practice a departure from the past system where land ownership, with or without secure title, was tied to the performance of fiscal duties so that both a peasant and a tax collector could lay claims on a plot of land. The situation had stymied the land market, in the view of the colonial administrators. Their solution was to create an unencumbered ownership title. In practice, the title was delivered to former tax collectors (landlords or zamindars) in one part of India, individual peasants in southern and western India, and peasant collectives or extended kinship groups in parts of northern India (Roy 2014). Thus, in India, complex and persistent regional differences in economic conditions derived both from geographical diversity and from political-institutional diversity. They were both "natural" and "manmade."

When the British left India in 1947, not only was the subcontinent divided between the henceforth independent India and Pakistan, but also there were some 572 (!) principalities that were given the choice of joining India, joining Pakistan, or remaining independent. This prescription would have led to fragmentation, and the political map of South Asia would now look very different. In response to this challenge, the Indian constitution proclaimed the creation of a flexible federation that could annex both former British territories and principalities. Originally, the constitution divided the territories into three types, A, B, and C, but in 1956, India was reorganized into a federation of 15 states and six union territories (some of them, such as Goa, were subsequently granted statehood). A state is a full subject of the federation, with political autonomy guaranteed by the country's constitution;

a union territory is governed directly by the federal government. The geography of Indian federalism kept changing: new states were created so that at present India includes 28 states and six union territories. There are great contrasts between the states in terms of both population and territory size. For example, Uttar Pradesh has 166 million people, Sikkim (the smallest by population) has 697 thousand. The largest by land area is the desert state of Rajasthan; Goa is the smallest, with some union territories, such as the Andaman and Nicobar Islands, being even smaller. Each state represents a particular cultural integrity, with its own linguistic or socio-historical identity (Huma 2015; Singh 2014).

In addition to the aforementioned states, in the late 1940s, the former British possessions of Burma (present-day Myanmar) and Ceylon (Sri Lanka) gained independence; the State of Israel was created in accordance with a decision of the UN General Assembly.

In the early 1950s, French colonies in Laos and Cambodia, parts of French Indochina, were released. In the late 1950s to early 1970s, Malaya (Federation of Malaysia), Singapore, Cyprus, the Maldives, Kuwait, South Yemen, and several small states in the Persian Gulf received sovereignty. In most cases, the processes of decolonization were peaceful, but there were exceptions, such as Vietnam. Vietnam fought a long war of independence, first against the French colonialists, then against the US intervention. For a long time, the country was divided into northern and southern parts and united after the end of the war in 1976 to form the Socialist Republic of Vietnam. The series of wars that began in 1946 with hostilities between France and Vietnam and covered all of former French Indochina for almost 30 years still affect the politics and economy of the region.

Numerous studies have shown that variation in colonial institutions can explain the variation in contemporary economic and social outcomes (Acemoglu, Johnson and Robinson 2002, 2001; Mahoney 2010; Lee and Schultz 2011; Banerjee and Iyer 2005). Indeed, the colonization experience transformed the institutions in many Asian countries, and the colonial legacy had serious long-term effects, influencing the trajectories of states even until today. I have already mentioned India, where the British colonial legacy influenced the choice of administrative institutions after independence. Besides that, British rule gave the territories of India a common language English and contributed to the territorial consolidation of the country as a federation.

On the contrary, Central Asia received a very different legacy from the Soviet Union. After the collapse of the Soviet Empire, the five Central Asian republics immediately started to create national states, which meant creating not only independent institutions and policies but also national mythologies, rituals, and a pantheon of national heroes, rewriting school textbooks, etc. In other words, political elites have consistently put nation-building and national sovereignty to the top of their political agenda while the process of nation-building was accompanied by rapid re-traditionalization.

Criticism of the USSR was an important and unavoidable element in the nation-building in the region (the harshest version of criticism was observed in Uzbekistan). However, "Sovietness" has deeply penetrated the Central Asian societies and elites, indeed, the regions remained "post-Soviet" (the very existence and resilience of this term proves the importance of the Soviet legacy). This applied not only to the Russian language, which in these countries remains the official language (in Kazakhstan and Kyrgyzstan) or the language of interethnic communication (in Uzbekistan and Tajikistan)[3] but also to the existence of huge "presidential machines," to the great weight that was given to ideology and rituals (Abashin 2014: 92), and finally, the prevalence of informal institutions (Busygina and Filippov 2024).

Pakistan, Afghanistan, Tajikistan: geographic fragmentation, institutions, and development

Since Pakistan's independence from the British Empire, it was supposed to be the homeland of the Muslims of the Indian subcontinent, but geographically localized ethnic tensions have undermined and continue to undermine the country's stability. Pakistan was torn between Punjabis in the northeast, Sikhs in the southeast, Baloch in the southwest, and Pashtuns on the northwest frontier. At the same time, the state in Pakistan welcomed diversity to a much lesser extent than did, for example, the Indian state. Ironically, therefore, a monstrously ethnic and linguistically diverse India is more stable than a less diverse Pakistan. According to Kaplan (2013: 35), in terms of geographical expediency, Pakistan (as well as Iraq) is the most illogically constructed state between the Mediterranean Sea and the Indian subcontinent.

From the same point of view, *Afghanistan*, divided by high ridges into isolated parts, also does not constitute a "geographical whole." This country is essentially a geographical buffer between the Iranian Plateau, the Central Asian steppes, and the Indian subcontinent, populated by different tribes. In Afghanistan, geography itself – the nature of landscapes and lack of habitable territories – has conditioned the isolation of the ranges of the country's inhabitants. Moreover, the formation of Afghanistan's borders in the context of Russian and British Empire rivalry led to the separation of ethnic communities. Pashtuns were the titular ethnic group in Afghanistan (which, according to some estimates, no longer constitute the majority of the country's population), but the borders divided ethnic groups. This situation cannot but generate centrifugal tendencies in the country. Ethnic fragmentation is complemented by linguistic fragmentation: the inhabitants of Afghanistan speak 30 languages. Thus, modern Afghanistan has neither geographical integrity nor national unity; the national consciousness is not formed.

Geographic and ethnic fragmentation is reinforced by the political situation. After the Mujahedeen seized power in 1992, their government was unable to control the territory of the country, which broke up into several independent entities. With the emergence of the Taliban (predominantly Pashtun) on the political scene in 1994, the conflict gradually turned into a struggle between the Pashtun South and the non-Pashtun North. The Taliban sought to subjugate the northern territories but encountered stiff resistance. The Pashtun population was pushed out of the North.

As a result of the anti-terrorist operation conducted by US and British military forces, the Taliban regime was overthrown. At the end of 2001, power shifted to an interim administration headed by Hamid Karzai; key positions in the administration were given to representatives of the Northern Alliance, which naturally displeased the Pashtuns. So far, the country remains fragmented into a series of regions that exist autonomously from the center. The country is plagued by clan struggles to consolidate its influence. In addition, Afghanistan has turned into a "narcostate": opium was the main product of the east, south, and parts of the north. Along with East Timor and Nepal, Afghanistan is one of the three poorest states in Asia.

Another example is Tajikistan, which experiences problems with territorial integrity. Tajikistan was created from territories that for centuries were part of different, sometimes hostile, political entities. In fact, the territorial consolidation of the country has not yet fully occurred; its territory is split into at least four major parts: (1) the geographically isolated Leninabad region in the north of the country; (2) the Kulyab zone in the south of the country; (3) the Harm group of districts in the east; and (4) the Gorno-Badakhshan autonomous region in the mountains. Tajikistan politics very much remains clan politics based on neopatrimonial institutions. According to Goble (2015),

> Tajikistan's ethno-regional clans have played a key role in the political life of this Central Asian republic since 1991. These clans have their roots not so much in ancient and archaic forms of social organization but in the way in which Moscow's nationality policies intentionally and unintentionally promoted such divisions. In particular, the former Soviet central government created institutions that intensified or even created divisions that had been little in evidence earlier, the Bolsheviks, in most cases, did not take into consideration the main ethno-political, ethno-cultural and ethno-geographic factors.

Mongolia and Central Asia: geographic location, neighborhood, and the choice of institutions and policies

In Asia, we will find states whose geographic location imposes serious constraints on their institutions as well as on their foreign and domestic policies. As a rule, such a situation is manifested as "a (relatively) small state in close proximity to a giant state (or states)." Let us turn to the examples of Mongolia and post-Soviet countries. Smaller countries are forced to adapt their strategies to their geographic location.

The developments taking place in Mongolia's drive toward democratic reforms and economic restructuring came after the collapse of the Soviet Union that dramatically changed the external situation of Mongolia. In the post-Cold War period, the major changes occurred in Mongolia's two neighboring countries, Russia and China, which also had a direct impact on its external environment, particularly in terms of security. However, being located between two giants, Mongolia has limited (and rapidly shrinking) room for maneuver as it faces pressure from both Moscow and Beijing. "Mongolia, a robust democracy in a deeply authoritarian neighborhood, faces a difficult future as its two giant neighbors and former imperial overlords, China and Russia, seek to reorder Eurasia in their image."[4]

For Russia, leadership in post-Soviet Eurasia is an obvious priority. Its enormous territorial size and a long borderline with numerous neighbors imply that Russia (unlike most smaller countries) encounters a wide range of old and newly emerging foreign policy issues in the Eurasian region. Russia is incomparably more powerful militarily and stronger economically than its neighbors. For instance, the GDP of Kazakhstan represents around 10% of Russia's GDP, Belarus – less than 4%, while that of Armenia is less than 1%.

Since several years, relations between Russia and its Asian post-Soviet neighbors display a combination of formal signs of loyalty to Moscow and various forms of resistance to the growth of Russian influence in their political and public life. Leaders of these states have serious incentives not to challenge Russian domination openly. These incentives are different for different countries, including unfavorable geopolitical position (Armenia) and/or the presence of a significant Russian-speaking minority (Kazakhstan). Besides that, Russia is still a huge market for post-Soviet states, many of them greatly rely on supplies of Russian energy, and Russian investments are critical for their national economies (Busygina and Filippov 2021).

Smaller states located between giants have no other option but to rely on *hedging* that is mostly understood as an "insurance" method of strategically adopting counteracting policies designed to keep a state's options open. Hedging states do not clarify their ultimate patrons and do not take sides, hoping to benefit from competition for the influence and dominance among the global and regional powers. According to Koga (2018), "the hedging strategies are essentially combinations of the "balancing-bandwagoning" spectrum designed to reduce the risks and uncertainties" associated with full dependence only on one power. In the post-Soviet period, Russia's attempts to dominate in the neighborhood provoked various contestation strategies of other global and regional powers by supporting the hedging strategies of the ex-Soviet republics against Russia. The typical hedging strategies of the Russian neighbors are their "multi-vector" foreign policies. Vanderhill, Joireman, and Tulepbayeva (2020) posited that multivectorism in Central Asia is similar to the strategy of omni-enmeshment and complex balancing observed in Southeast Asia. Both strategies are effective for secondary powers to protect their sovereignty and to coexist with Great Powers without becoming their client states. The scholars see Kazakhstan's – located between Russia and China – foreign policy strategy as exemplar for secondary states. Indeed, considering Kazakhstan's geographic location, its strategy allowed it to protect its sovereignty. But was it good for the national development? Kazakhstan takes advantages of the economic opportunities its location presents, but at the same time, the proximity to two powerful autocracies limits opportunities for political reform and economic liberalization.

Uneasy geography of de facto states: relations with "parents" and "patrons"

De facto states – polities that appropriate trappings of statehood without securing the status of full states – have turned from an interesting anomaly in the international system of sovereign states to an almost routine element of the modern international order. No matter how successful and efficient de facto states are in the administration of their territories, they fail to achieve international recognition. The main priority is given to maintaining their existence and to an effort to convince domestic and international actors of their right to independence. Currently, most scholars consider only six entities as de facto states: Somaliland, Abkhazia, South Ossetia, Nagorno-Karabakh, Transnistria, and Northern Cyprus, five of them (all but Somaliland) are located in Asia. The main problem of de facto states is external sovereignty; however, serious problems arise also from their specific geographic location – direct proximity to the state from which de facto state has separated, these are potentially conflictual relationship. Equally important is the proximity to the patron country – a large country that for various reasons may formally recognize independence of a de facto state in exchange for dependency. De facto states have small size of the territory, small domestic market, as a rule, weak institutions, low quality of governance, and low level of development. All this puts considerable constraints on the choices of institutions and policies of the local elites.

Two de facto states that declared independence are located on the territory of Georgia. The leadership of South Ossetia, based on the results of a referendum in 1992, declared the independence of that region and raised the question of its secession from Georgia (and possible annexation to Russia). The results of the 2006 referendum confirmed the intention of the South Ossetian population to shape their own fate by seceding from Georgia.

In 1992–1994, an armed conflict between Georgia and the region led to the de facto secession of Abkhazia (the Autonomous Republic of Abkhazia) from Georgia. An extremely difficult problem arose in determining the political status of Abkhazia. The Abkhaz side made a demand for self-determination. The Georgian side was ready to grant autonomy to the region if the Georgian refugees (about 200,000 people) returned to Abkhazia. Until 2008, Abkhazia and South Ossetia had de facto independence from Georgia. Despite their small size, demographic problems, weak institutions, and geographic, political, and economic isolation, they managed to survive and even strengthen their desire to break away from Georgia. These territories are extremely poor: their economy, based largely on illegal operations, has allowed them to survive but not to develop. The feeling that the very existence of these ethnic groups was threatened formed the ideological context in which separatism was developing. The ineffectiveness of conflict resolution mechanisms also contributed to the strengthening of separatist sentiments.

After the war in South Ossetia in August 2008, the sovereign status of South Ossetia and Abkhazia was recognized by the Russian Federation, Venezuela, Nicaragua, and the Oceania states of Vanuatu and Nauru.

Today, both de facto states – South Ossetia and Abkhazia – are heavily dependent on neighboring Russia. Russia subsidizes these two economies and controls the choice and change in domestic institutions (executives, political parties, NGOs etc.). In fact, their geographical proximity to Russia allows these de facto states to survive.

Indonesia: governability in a fragmented state

Indonesia is a fragmented state consisting of more than 17,000 islands. The most widespread conflicts are between Muslims and Christians, but the main reasons for conflicts are not confessional or interethnic but have a socioeconomic background.

West Irian. Holland subjugated the western part of the island of New Guinea in the late nineteenth century. By the middle of that century, the territory was included in the colonial possession of Dutch India. However, after Indonesia's declaration of sovereignty (in 1945), the western part of New Guinea was not included in the new independent state and remained a colony of Holland. Indonesia began a struggle to incorporate West Irian (the Indonesian name for New Guinea). The further fate of this territory was submitted to the UN discussion. Since 1961, however, the Papuan population also joined the struggle for the liberation of the territory. In 1963, the western part of New Guinea was incorporated into Indonesia as the province of West Irian (later renamed Irian Jaya), but part of the Papuan population continued to fight for independence, now from Indonesia. The separatists demand the creation of an independent state; the main reasons for the population's discontent are social and economic: Irian Jaya remains the least developed and center-controlled region of the country. Another cause of discontent is the center-encouraged transmigration – the resettlement to West Irian of residents from other densely populated islands of Indonesia. In 1999, the Papuan elite issued a declaration of independence for Papua; Indonesian authorities proposed the idea of greater autonomy for the region. Since 2002, the region was granted the status of a special autonomy with its own anthem and flag, and the province should retain 80% of revenues from the exploitation of local mineral resources. However, the separatists have not stopped fighting. The situation in western New Guinea complicates Indonesia's relations with its neighbors, Papua New Guinea, and Australia, where refugees and separatists are streaming in.

Aceh. In the north of the island of Sumatra, the province of Aceh initially demanded more autonomy without seeking secession. In 1962, the central government granted Aceh status as a "special region" and autonomy in matters of culture, religion, and education. In the 1970s, the anti-centralization movement in the province revived, with separatists now demanding the establishment of an independent "Ace State" in northern Sumatra, with "Javanese colonialism" declared to be the main enemy. In the late 1990s, there was a new upsurge of separatism in Aceh, caused by the deteriorating economic situation in the region, the demonstration effect of the separation of East Timor from Indonesia as a result of the referendum in 1999, and the instability of the internal political situation in the country as a whole. In 1999, the country's parliament passed special laws on Aceh, under which local authorities were allowed to dispose of a large part of the income from the exploitation of the region's natural resources, the province's right to competence in the fields of education, religion, and culture was confirmed.

The fragmented character of the Indonesian state implied the choice for the institutions of decentralization because rigid, yet effective, management of communities scattered across multiple islands was simply almost impossible. The 1945

Constitution of the Republic of Indonesia structures the country as a unitary state, emphasizing the power of the executive institutions. But later, the national governments have embarked on sustained decentralization reforms (as an important part of democratization reforms) with the goal to enhance national development. Today, regional and village governments have democratic political structures and substantial financial resources (Siwage and Hutchinson 2021; Ferrazzi 2022). Indonesia's geography not only just favored building institutions of decentralization but made them imperative.

China: the problems of geographically localized inequalities and interregional disparities

To the non-specialist, China today may appear politically, culturally, and linguistically monolithic, since the Chinese became Chinese long ago. However, marked territorial differences do exist. For example, the inhabitants of the north and the south of the country differ greatly: the northerners resemble the Tibetans and Nepalis, and the southerners resemble the Vietnamese and the Filipinos. One look at the linguistic map of China will instantly dismiss the myth about the country being monolithic: apart from eight "big" languages spoken by 11–800 million people, there are more than 130 "small" ones. According to Russian historian and ethnologist Lev Gumilyov (2012), the very concept of "the Chinese" is equivalent not to "the French" or "the Germans" but rather to Western Europeans as a whole, since it is not an ethnicity but a system of ethnicities.

There are civilizational fault lines running through China: between the Chinese civilization and the Islamic civilization in the northwest, the Buddhist civilization in the southeast, and the Orthodox civilization in the northeast. In the terminology of Russian scholar Vadim Tsymbursky (2010), such territories as Xinjiang and Inner Mongolia were "limestones," that is, unstable margins of the corresponding civilizational platforms. These are transitional territories, within which the features of both the civilizational core to which the "limes" gravitated and the properties of the core of the neighboring civilization were manifested.

Interestingly, in technical inventions, China was once far ahead of Europe. Chinese inventions are well known: paper, printing, gunpowder, compass. Already in the eleventh century, coal was used in smelting of metals; 500 years earlier than in Europe paper banknotes were put into circulation. Even such innovations as horse harness, umbrella, wheelbarrow, and winnowing machine were invented in China. So why did the Chinese cede leadership to late-starting Europe? At least part of the explanation for this mystery lies in geography – political and physical. Europe was highly fragmented, disconnected, split into large and small political–territorial units; China, by contrast, was characterized by a rare territorial unity. Therefore, decisions (including those that were wrong) in China were centralized and rarely reviewed, while in Europe Columbus had the opportunity to ask different rulers to fund the expedition, and only his fifth attempt was successful. Chinese cohesion proved to be a disadvantage, not an advantage, in terms of diffusion of innovation; European fragmentation determined the existence of many competing centers of innovation. To this we add physical and geographical differences: the relative flatness of the Chinese coastline compared to the rugged coastlines of Europe with its five major peninsulas (Diamond 1999).

It should be noted that the non-Han (non-titular) ethnic groups in China lived mainly in the regions of Western and Central China, which occupy about 65% of the country. In China, deep ethno-regional cleavages began to manifest themselves after the Qin Empire was forcibly incorporated into the world system of international relations and itself became an object of Western expansion. Rebellions rose in the outskirts of the empire – in the south (Muslims), in the northwest (Dungans, descendants of Turkic tribes of Central Asia), and in East Turkestan (Uighurs, Kirghiz, Tajiks). The most acute problems today are those of Tibet and the Xinjiang Uygur Autonomous Region.

In 1912, the Chinese government declared Tibet, Mongolia, and Xinjiang as provinces. The Tibet issue was discussed at the Shimla Conference convened in 1913–1914, with the assistance of the British, which formally recognized the suzerainty (not sovereignty) of China over Tibet and forbade China to turn Tibet into its province. Lhasa, in turn, attempted to break its isolation and establish relations with other countries. Currently, the Dalai Lama's (i.e., Lhasa's) demands are reduced to cultural autonomy for "greater Tibet" (i.e., including adjacent areas in the south and east) within the PRC, but he does not recognize Tibet as an "integral part" of China. The PRC leadership continues its efforts to organically integrate the Tibet Autonomous Region into the sociopolitical and socioeconomic structure of China, and it has succeeded in stabilizing the situation in the region.

The situation in China's Xinjiang Uygur Autonomous Region (XUAR) is quite different. The region has a population of 18.9 million, including some eight million Sunni Muslim Uighurs. The mountains divide Xinjiang into two parts: the northern part, Dzungaria, adjacent to the Russian Altai and Kazakhstan, and the southern part, Kashgaria (or Eastern Turkestan), bordering Kyrgyzstan, Afghanistan, Tajikistan, and Pakistan. Since joining China, more than 15 major uprisings with religious overtones have occurred in XUAR.

The collapse of the USSR gave a new sharp impetus to Uyghur uprisings, because after the new Central Asian states gained sovereignty, the Uyghurs remained the only major Turkic people without a state of their own. In 1996, the World Uyghur Kurultai, held in Istanbul, officially recognized the armed way of fighting for independence, as nonviolent means of struggle proved ineffective. For example, in 2014, there was a terrorist attack in the capital of XUAR that killed 31 people. The Uyghur problem is one of the rifts undermining the integrity of Chinese statehood. For years, this ethnic group has been discriminated against by the communist government of the PRC, economically, politically, and culturally. Chinese authorities have harshly suppressed protests and accused Uyghur groups of separatism, religious extremism, and terrorism. At the end of 2016, Beijing increased pressure on the Uyghurs by installing surveillance systems throughout the region and establishing mass detention centers (Roberts 2020).

In China, institutions of decentralization, by stimulating interregional competition, act as a significant source of national development; its regions compete for investment and skilled labor (Libman and Rochlitz 2019). That said, however, China's geography determines that coastal regions have much greater competitive advantage over inland regions and are growing and developing much faster. In many ways, these are worlds apart. Regional economic development in China is unbalanced and polarized with Shanghai and Beijing as the center, the eastern coast as the secondary center, the central and western regions occupying subordinate positions (Yang, Huang and Li 2024).

Korean "experiment": divided nations and institutions but the same geography

Throughout the twentieth century, Korea was repeatedly at the epicenter of Asian crises. In 1945, Japan's defeat led to the loss of all its colonies. The surrender of the Japanese army on the Korean Peninsula to the north of the 38th parallel was accepted by Soviet troops and to the south by American troops. In the future, general elections were supposed to be held. However, under conditions of the Cold War, in 1948, Korea was divided along the 38th parallel (this division was a de facto reflection of the division of spheres of interests between the USSR and the United States). In the US zone of occupation, the establishment of the Republic of Korea was proclaimed. In North Korea, the Democratic People's Republic of Korea (DPRK), Kim Jong Il was brought to power with the Soviet Union's help and built one of the most repressive communist regimes in the world (the so-called barracks socialism system). In 1950, this regime unleashed a war against South Korea, but its takeover was averted. Since then, the 38th parallel marks one of the most absolute, "total" dividing lines in the world – in terms of ideology, economics, and politics. According to the constitution, the DPRK is a "sovereign socialist state" that is guided in its activities by the ideas of "chuchhe" (the basis of these ideas is self-reliant development).

South Korea, a parliamentary republic, builds its economy on the principles of openness and deep involvement in globalization; it sees in its alliance with the United States both a condition for maintaining its own independence and a "key" to reunification with North Korea. North Korea is a "rogue state" with totalitarian political regime that is developing nuclear weapons and long-range missiles. Thus, the trajectories of the North and South Koreas after the separation were strikingly different.

Acemoglu, Johnson, and Robinson (2005: 404–407) proposed to think of the splitting of the Koreas 50 years ago as a natural experiment. Indeed, at the time of the separation, the two states were very similar in terms of income per capita, they shared the same historic legacy and culture, and the same geographic possibilities in terms of access to markets and the cost of transportation. What was different in two countries? The institutions. As Acemoglu, Johnson, and Robinson (2005) argued,

> [T]hese two independent countries organized themselves in very different ways and adopted completely different sets of institutions. The North followed the model of Soviet socialism and the Chinese Revolution in abolishing private property of land and capital. Economic decisions were not

mediated by the market, but by the communist state. The South instead maintained a system of private property and the government, especially after the rise to power of Park Chung He in 1961, attempted to use markets and private incentives to develop the economy . . . By the late 1960's South Korea was transformed into one of the Asian "miracle" economies, experiencing one of the most rapid surges of economic prosperity in history while North Korea stagnated. Already by 2000 the South had become a member of the Organization of Economic Cooperation and Development, the rich nations club, while the North had a level of per-capita income about the same as a typical sub-Saharan African country. There is only one plausible explanation for the radically different economic experiences on the two Koreas after 1950: their very different institutions led to divergent economic outcomes.

What's around the corner?

They say the dawn of the Asian century is coming. "History has turned a corner," – says Kishore Mahbubani, a prominent Asian scholar. The era of Western domination is ending. The resurgence of Asia in world affairs and the global economy, which was happening before the emergence of COVID-19, will be cemented in a new world order after the crisis. The deference to Western societies, which was the norm in the nineteenth and twentieth centuries, will be replaced by a growing respect and admiration for East Asian ones. The phrase has been bandied around for a while, but the pandemic could mark the real start of an Asian century. The pandemic crisis highlights the contrast between the competent responses of East Asian governments (notably China, Singapore, South Korea, and Taiwan) and the incompetent responses of Western governments (such as America, Britain, France, and Spain). "The far lower death rates suffered by East Asian countries offer a lesson to all. They reflect not just medical capabilities, but also the quality of governance and the cultural confidence of their societies."[5] It is nothing more than wishful thinking, say others.

In my sense, ambitious statements of this kind are vulnerable already because they make claims about the rise of *all* of Asia, which is principally impossible. From the perspective of this book, Asia is interesting not just because of its "rise" but because it demonstrates the myriads of relationships between geography, institutions, and development. Asia shows both remarkable examples of good institutions and successful development relying on favorable geographical factors and examples of bad institutions reinforced by bad geography (unfavorable geographical location and internal territorial cleavages). The factor of geographical neighborhood plays a huge role; just think of the countries of Central Asia for which the neighborhood with revisionist aggressive Russia significantly limits their development prospects.

Notes

1 Richest Asian Countries 2024 (worldpopulationreview.com).
2 Poorest Asian Countries 2024 (worldpopulationreview.com).

3 Russian is the least used language in Turkmenistan: in the capital city of Ashkhabad, there is only one school with instruction in Russian.
4 https://foreignpolicy.com/2020/06/26/russia-putin-mnb-wants-to-keep-mongolia-in-its-place/
5 https://www.economist.com/the-world-ahead/2020/11/17/kishore-mahbubani-says-this-is-the-dawn-of-the-asian-century

References

Abashin, Sergei. (2014). "Nations and Post-Colonialism in Central Asia: Twenty Years Later." In *Development in Central Asia and the Caucasus: Migration, Democratization, and Inequality in the Post-Soviet Era*, ed. by S. Hohmann, C. Mouradian, S. Serrano, and J. Thorez. London, UK: I.B. Tauris.

Acemoglu, Daron, Simon Johnson, and James Robinson. (2001). "The Colonial Origins of Comparative Development." *American Economic Review*, 91(5): 1369–1401.

Acemoglu, Daron, Simon Johnson, and James Robinson. (2002). "Reversal of Fortune." *The Quarterly Journal of Economics*, 117(4): 1231–1294.

Acemoglu, Daron, Simon Johnson, and James Robinson. (2005). "Institutions as a Fundamental Cause of Long-Term Growth." In *Handbook of Economic Growth*, Vol. IA, ed. by Philippe Aghion and Steven N. Durlauf. Amsterdam, Holland: Elsevier B.V.

Banerjee, Abhijit, and Lakshmi Iyer. (2005). "History, Institutions and Economic Performance." *American Economic Review*, 95(4): 1190–1213.

Bastin, John. (1968). *A History of Modern Southeast Asia: Colonialism, Nationalism, and Decolonization*. Englewood Cliffs, NJ: Prentice-Hall.

Busygina, Irina, and Mikhail Filippov. (2024). *Non-Democratic Federalism and Decentralization: Lessons from the Post-Soviet States*. London, UK: Routledge.

Busygina, Irina, and Mikhail Filippov. (2021). "Trade-Offs and Inconsistencies of the Russian Foreign Policy: The Case of Eurasia." *Journal of Eurasian Studies*, 12(1).

Butzer, Karl. (1976). *Early Hydraulic Civilization in Egypt: A Study in Cultural Ecology*. Chicago: The University of Chicago Press.

Clark, Gregory, and Susan Wolcott. (2003). "One Polity, Many Countries: Economic Growth in India 1873–2000." In *In Search of Prosperity: Analytic Narratives on Economic Growth*, ed. by Dani Rodrik. Princeton, NJ: Princeton University Press.

Diamond, Jared. (1999). *Guns, Germs, and Steel: The Fates of Human Societies*. New York; London: W. W. Norton.

Dodgshon, Robert. (1998). *Society in Time and Space: A Geographical Perspective on Change*. Cambridge: Cambridge University Press.

Ferrazzi, Gabriele. (2022). "Decentralization, Local Governance, and Localizing the Sustainable Development Goals in Indonesia." In *Decentralization, Local Governance, and Localizing the Sustainable Development Goals in Asia and the Pacific*, ed. by Bruno Carrasco, Hanif A. Rahemtulla, and Rainer Rohdewohld. London: Routledge.

Goble, Paul. (2015). "Today's Ethno-Regional Clans in Tajikistan Are Products of Soviet Nationality Policy." *Eurasia Daily Monitor*, 12(136).

Gumilyov, Lev. (2012). *Three Chinese Kingdoms*. Moscow: Algorithm.

Huma, Baby. (2015). "Understanding Indian Federalism." *The Indian Journal of Political Science*, 76(4): 792–795.

Kaplan, Robert. (2013). *The Revenge of Geography*. New York: Random House Publishing Group.

Kissinger, Henry. (2001). *Does America Need a Foreign Policy? Toward Diplomacy for the 21st Century*. New York: Simon & Shuster.

Koga, Kei. (2018). "The Concept of 'Hedging' Revisited: The Case of Japan's Foreign Policy Strategy in East Asia's Power Shift." *International Studies Review*, 20(4): 633–660.

Lee, Alexander, and Kenneth Schultz. (2011). Comparing British and French Colonial Legacies: A Discontinuity Analysis of Cameroon. APSA 2011 Annual Meeting Paper.
Libman, Alexander, and Michael Rochlitz. (2019). *Federalism in China and Russia*. Cheltenham, UK: Edward Elgar.
Mahoney, James. (2010). *Colonialism and Postcolonial Development*. Cambridge: Cambridge University Press.
Reisner, Larissa. (1925). *Afghanistan*. Moscow: Gosudarstvennoe izdatel'stvo.
Roberts, Sean. (2020). *The War on the Uyghurs: China's Internal Campaign against a Muslim Minority*. Princeton Studies in Muslim Politics, 76. Princeton, NJ: Princeton University Press.
Roy, Tirthankar. (2002). "Economic History and Modern India: Redefining the Link." *Journal of Economic Perspectives*, 16(3).
Roy, Tirthankar. (2014). "Geography or Politics? Regional Inequality in Colonial India." *European Review of Economic History*, 18(3): 324–348.
Siwage, Dharma Negara, and Francis E. Hutchinson. (2021). "The Impact of Indonesia's Decentralization Reforms Two Decades On." *Journal of Southeast Asian Economies*, 38(3): 289–295.
Subregional Perspectives on Inequality in Asia and the Pacific and Update on Subregional Activities for Development. (2018). UN Economic and Social Council, ESCAP/74/30.
Surander, Singh. (2014). "Restructuring Indian Federalism: A New Perspective." *The Indian Journal of Political Science*, 75(2): 359–368.
Tsymbursky, Vadim. (2010). *Russia – the Land Beyond the Great Limit of Civilization and Its Geopolitics*. Moscow: Editorial URSS.
Vanderhill, Rachel, Sandra F. Joireman, and Roza Tulepbayeva. (2020). "Between the Bear and the Dragon: Multivectorism in Kazakhstan as a Model Strategy for Secondary Powers." *International Affairs*, 96(4): 975–993.
Yang, Wanping, Ruoying Huang, and Dong Li. (2024). "China's High-Quality Economic Development: A Study of Regional Variations and Spatial Evolution." *Economic Change and Restructuring*, 57(86).
Zamyatin, Dmitry. (2003). *Human Geography: The Space and the Language of Geographical Images*. Saint Petersburg: Aleteiya. [Zamyatin, Dmitry. (2003). Gumanitarnaya Geographiya: Prostranstvo i Yazyk Geographicheslikh Obrazov. Saint Petersburg: Aleteiya].

6 Africa

Africa is the second largest of the world's continents, second only to Asia, and is currently home to 57 independent nations. Africa is the only continent that stretches from the northern temperate zone to the southern zone and contains the world's most waterless deserts and the largest tropical rainforests.

Africa is home to the largest desert in the world Sahara (from the Arabic *al-Sahra*, "desert"), which occupies about one-third of the African continent and is located in its northern part. The word "Sahara" itself evokes associations with endless sands and a lack of water. But the desert was not always so dry; between the ninth and fourth centuries BC these areas had a wetter climate, many lakes and lush pastures, and the local population was predominantly herders. Perhaps no other desert in the world has caused as much controversy over its borders as the Sahara. The boundaries have been defined according to different geographical indications, based on which the Sahara ranges from 6.2 million square kilometers to 11 million square kilometers. The northern boundary of the desert is drawn along the southern tip of the Sahara Atlas Mountains, while the southern boundary moves along the entire front to the south every year if the year is dry and shifts to the north in wet years.

Africa is the poorest region of the world, home to most of the least developed countries; nine out of ten poorest nations are located in sub-Saharan Africa. To cite Bloom and Sachs,

> [T]he poverty of sub-Saharan Africa is one of the most obdurate features of the world economy. Since the industrial revolution, this has been the world's poorest and also its most slowly growing region . . . Africa's poor economic growth has been chronic rather than episodic.
>
> (Bloom and Sachs 1998: 207–208)

Indeed, the problems of the African continent pose a challenge to the whole world. The pace of economic growth and modernization is too low, and the scale of corruption is enormous. Interethnic and interclan wars are tearing apart vast territories. Epidemics are wiping out the population: 70% of adults and 80% of children with AIDS worldwide live in Africa.

Forty-four countries in the world do not have direct access to the sea, as they are "locked." Sixteen from these 44 are in Africa. Besides that, an acute problem

DOI: 10.4324/9781003496731-9

of the continent is that of the connectivity of territories by road networks. This is not even a question of reaching remote hard-to-reach areas but of intercountry contacts: for example, the road from the Congo to Cameroon exists but is accessible only to pedestrians. All said above relates mainly to sub-Saharan Africa – vast tropical lands located between the Tropic of Cancer and the Tropic of Capricorn. As Fernand Braudel argued: "In understanding Black Africa, geography is more important than history. The geographical context is not all that matters, but it is the most significant" (Braudel 1995: 120). Sowell (1998) had also emphasized the role of geography, especially regarding making cultural interaction more difficult both between Africa and the rest of the world and also within the continent.

Africa is full of geographical mysteries, one of them was mentioned by Diamond (1999: 380–381). Only 250 miles separate the large island of Madagascar from the coast of East Africa, so the island is much closer to Africa than to any other continent. The people who inhabit the island are a mixture of two elements. One, not surprisingly, is African. The other element, however, consists of inhabitants who are recognizable as inhabitants of the islands of southeast Asia. The language spoken in Madagascar is very similar to that of the inhabitants of the Indonesian island of Borneo (only 4,000 miles from Madagascar). These Indonesian-like people lived on the island as early as 1500, when it was first visited by Europeans. How could the prehistoric inhabitants of Borneo, who traveled by boat, without maps and compass, have reached Madagascar? This is an astonishing mystery, comparable to, say, Columbus reaching Cuba and discovering that the island was inhabited by blue-eyed blondes of Scandinavian appearance, speaking a language resembling Swedish.

The first political communities in Africa

During the ancient period, the most powerful center of civilization in North Africa was the "gift of the Nile" – ancient Egypt. Egypt was geographically tied to the great river, so from the very beginning this state formation was characterized by a certain insularity. The first proto states emerged in Egypt around temples (such communities later became known by the Greek term "nom"); several dozens of settlements gravitated to each temple. Subsequently, at the turn of the fourth to third centuries BC, the nomes of Upper and Lower Egypt were gradually united under the power of pharaohs – rulers of Upper Egypt. Ancient Egypt in the era of the so-called New Kingdom was a powerful state, an empire. During the period of the Late Kingdom (the first millennium BC), Egypt came under the power of foreign rulers (including those from Midia, the Achaemenid power).

Carthage (located in the territory of modern Tunisia) should also be added to the hotbeds of ancient civilization in North Africa. The city was founded in 825 BC by the Phoenicians and by the beginning of the third century BC, when the territories of North Africa, Sicily, Sardinia, and the south of Spain were conquered, it became a great power in the Mediterranean. The city was made famous by a Roman senator Cato the Elder. During the Punic Wars between Rome and Carthage, no matter what was discussed in Senate sessions – the prices of vegetables in Roman markets or the collection of taxes – Cato invariably ended his speeches with the same phrase: "And besides, I think that Carthage should be destroyed!" Cato saw the very existence of a city so rich and powerful as a threat to Rome. And Carthage was destroyed: at the end of the Third Punic War, the city was wiped out, and even the place where it stood was plowed away by Roman plows. In addition to Carthage, there were factories set up by Phoenicians on the shores of North Africa. Thus, in the ancient age, there were only isolated pockets of (proto)statehood on the African continent, mainly in North Africa (on the shores of the Mediterranean Sea and along the Nile).

At the beginning of the medieval period (fifth to fifteenth centuries), the Arabs tried to conquer North Africa – Arab influence extended as far as the Congo region. The Arabs attempted not only to conquer these lands but also to explore them. They knew Madagascar well but penetrated Inner Africa later, moving from northwest to southeast. The Arabs established Islamic kingdoms in place of the proto states in Middle Niger and Lake Chad.

During this long period, the process of establishing state-like entities also spread to other regions of Africa. Thus, in the first centuries AD, the kingdom of Aksum was formed in the territory of Northern Ethiopia. In the fourth and fifth centuries, it extended its influence to Nubia (a historical area in the Nile valley, in the territory of modern Egypt and Sudan), the Ethiopian Plateau and the north of the Horn of Africa. After the collapse of the kingdom of Axum, several states were formed on its territory at the end of the eleventh century, and later – the Christian Ethiopian Empire, which reached its heyday in the fifteenth and sixteenth centuries. The formation of states on the territories of Western and Central Sudan is actively going on. In Western Sudan, during the fourth to fourteenth centuries, the leading role was played by the states of Ghana, Mali, and Songai (Gao Empire). In Central Sudan, two centers of statehood developed in parallel – the Sudanese proper and the one south of Lake Chad. In South Africa, we should mention the center of statehood on the territory of modern Zimbabwe between the Zambezi and Limpopo rivers. On the territory of modern Nigeria, a city-state of the Yoruba people has been formed.

Colonial partition of Africa

European exploration of Africa began with expeditions by southern European explorers, who initially turned their attention to the west coast of the continent – as early as 1291 and 1346 expeditions were sent there, albeit unsuccessfully. In 1383, the vigorous King John I ascended the throne in Portugal – the Portuguese era of African conquest began. In 1487, Bartolomeo Dias managed to sail around the southern tip of the continent – the Cape of Storms, renamed by the king as the promising Cape of Good Hope. Vasco da Gama then managed to establish a link between the Cape of Good Hope and the trading factories along the eastern coast; a northern direction was taken from the eastern shore, and a shore was sighted, which was named Christmas Land and still retains that name (Natal). Near the Bay of Mozambique, the expedition encountered Arabian merchant ships. The general outlines of Africa were now known to Europeans. In the following centuries, however, Africa receded into the background, the attention of European seafarers was directed to the Americas and to India, while the exploration of Africa, which was considered unattractive, progressed slowly.

The period between 1550s and 1750s was a time of slow and uncoordinated penetration into the interior of the continent. For the most part, these campaigns were undertaken by merchants and missionaries, rarely by explorers. In the seventeenth century, missionaries actively contributed to the exploration of many countries in Africa, and we owe them valuable information, many myths, and just plain mistakes. Missionary journeys and attempts at colonization continued into the eighteenth century (the most important were travels and explorations of the Nile, Senegambia, and the Cape), and mapping of Africa was well underway.

Thus, the Arabs were the first explorers of Africa, followed by Europeans, who explored "on the edges" of the continent before entering the interior areas. The great explorer of southern Africa was David Livingstone (1813–1873), who walked north from the southern tip of the continent through the Kalahari Desert. Livingstone wrote about the need to promote the values of Christianity in Africa and believed that relations with African tribes should be based on the idea of equitable trade, which was impossible without progress and prosperity of the peoples. Livingstone discovered a waterfall and named it after Queen Victoria, and numerous lakes in volcanic rifts (Nyasa, Kivu, Edward etc.). The failure of Livingstone's expedition was due to miscalculations on the navigability and possible commercial navigation of the Zambezi River – it turned out to be unsuitable for this purpose (and remains so to this day) (Ferguson 2003). Livingstone was followed to Africa by Henry Stanley, specially sent on his quest by the "New York Herald" (Stanley greeted Livingstone with what would later become world-famous: "Dr. Livingstone, I presume?"). Livingstone believed in the word of God, Stanley in calculation and strength. The time for romantics in Africa was over.

Few things in modern African politics have been as significant as European colonization. Beginning in the 1870s, Africa became the main arena of territorial expansion of European states that were looking for resources and new markets and sought to strengthen their geopolitical position on the Black Continent. As Hahn (2005: 23) wrote (his work on the study of Africa was first published in the very beginning of the twentieth century), "now comes the time when the vague boundaries of Arab-African kingdoms must be replaced by properly delineated borders of spheres of influence, as European diplomats outline them, paying little attention to the areas of former states."

We know this from school: Africa was colonized by European powers. It's a fact, so the question of why Europeans colonized Africa, rather than the other way around, Africans colonizing Europe, simply doesn't come to mind. Diamond not only posed such a question but also formulated an answer that claimed to explain not only African colonization by Europeans but also the general developmental differences between societies. Diamond (1999: 406–407) wrote that continents differ from one another in a wide variety of physical and geographic characteristics, and these characteristics affect the trajectories of societies. According to Diamond, four groups of geographic characteristics were the most significant:

(1) the presence of wild animals and plants on the continent, which can serve as "starter material" for domestication; (2) the rate of spread of cultivated and domesticated species to other areas of the continent (this rate was greatest in Eurasia); (3) the rate of species spread between continents; (4) differences between continents in area and population. Greater area and population size mean more innovations, more competing communities, and, most importantly, more need to assimilate innovations, since communities that are unable to assimilate innovations will lose out to others. "Geographic destiny" has overtaken Africa, and the fact that Europeans colonized Africa rather than vice versa has nothing to do with the differences between the people of Europe and Africa. This course of history, according to Diamond, can be explained by the randomness of geography and biogeography.

In 1879, more than 90% of African territories were ruled by local rulers; by 1900, the entire continent, except for extremely small areas, was under European colonization: Africa was colonized with unprecedented speed. By the 1870s, European traders began to penetrate deeper into the continent: the French moved along the Senegal River valley, and the British traded along the lower Niger; by this time, French and British trading companies had already divided West Africa into "spheres of influence." Somewhat later, two other European states, Belgium and Germany, entered the "game." King Leopold II of Belgium, a passionate believer in the riches of Africa, claimed control of the Congo Basin. He carefully prepared international recognition of his territorial claims: he persuaded the French government and German Chancellor Bismarck to support him, and he enticed British trading companies with the promise of lucrative contracts in the future. For the newly unified German empire, participation in the colonization of Africa was a confirmation of its new high status in world politics.

The major European powers of the time, France and Great Britain, were the most successful in expanding their colonial possessions. The ideologist of British expansion in Africa Cecil John Rhodes, in his 1877 work *The Creed*, anticipating even Friedrich Ratzel's "Political Geography," wrote about the lack of living space for the British, which caused the British people not to produce the population growth they were capable of. As a result, instead of being populated by Englishmen, vast areas were populated by "the most despicable specimens of the human race." The way out, according to Rhodes, was to expand the British Empire in every way possible (Verschoyle 2018).

As early as the late eighteenth century and the first decades of the nineteenth century, Britain captured important positions in West Africa (the colonies of Sierra Leone and Gambia), on the routes to East Africa (via Cape Town) and in the Indian Ocean (Mauritius). However, the empire's plans were much more ambitious and envisaged the creation of an unbroken chain of possessions between South and North Africa along the line of Cape Town to Cairo ("all British from Cape to Cairo"). In implementing this territorial strategy, in 1887–1890, Britain colonized Zanzibar, the territory on which Northern and Southern Rhodesia (named after Cecil Rhodes) as well as Uganda were formed. In 1895, the territory of Kenya was declared an East African protectorate of Great Britain, followed by the formation of the Anglo-Egyptian Sudan, which was formally declared a condominium of Great Britain and Egypt but in fact was governed by Britain. By 1904, after defeating the resistance of local rulers, Britain had gained control of most of the territory of Nigeria.

The major war of this period, which had an international resonance, was the Anglo-Boer War of 1899–1902, a war in southern Africa between the "second wave" British colonizers and the Boers, the first colonizers, the descendants of the Dutch colonists. The war ended in favor of Great Britain, which seized the Boer republics of Transvaal and Orange. The result was the creation of the British dominion of the Union of South Africa.

France's geopolitical goals included the creation of a continuous chain of possessions from Senegal to Somalia, and it managed to capture vast (but sparsely populated) territories in West and Equatorial Africa (French West Africa – 1896, French Equatorial Africa – 1916). In the same 1896, France declared a protectorate over the island of Madagascar.

Obviously, the process of colonization of Africa could not proceed without disputes and conflicts. They were resolved, as a rule, by bilateral and multilateral agreements. The Berlin Conference of 1884–1885 was important for the elimination of conflicts. The Conference was attended by 13 European countries and the United States. The purpose of the conference was to establish the "rules and principles" of colonization; it was actually a matter of not giving any power an advantage in colonization and defining spheres of influence. The conference also stipulated that any claims to establish colonies or protectorates on the coasts of Africa must be notified to the other powers, and such claims must be confirmed by the establishment of effective authority in the territories in question. In fact, the conference put an end to the British idea of an "informal empire" in Africa. Finally, the conference established freedom of navigation in Niger and Congo (Oliver and Atmore 2005: 126). Great Britain remained extremely dissatisfied with the results of the conference: only Egypt and the colonies in the very south of the continent remained virtually untouched.

After the conference, negotiations began to establish borders between the colonies; treaties decided the fate of vast territories (e.g., the 1890 treaty between Great Britain and Germany on East Africa). During negotiations, territorial exchanges between colonizers were not uncommon: for example, in 1911 a treaty between France and Germany gave the latter a part of the Congo (joining it to German Cameroon) in exchange for France's establishment of a protectorate over Morocco (Wesseling 1996).

In addition to Great Britain and France, Belgium, since 1908 in Equatorial Africa, owned the colony of the Belgian Congo, many times the size of the metropolis. Portugal, by the beginning of the twentieth century, owned the large colonies of Angola and Mozambique, as well as Portuguese Guinea and the Cape Verde Islands. Spain owned part of Morocco (Spanish Morocco) and the western coast of the Sahara (Spanish Sahara). Somewhat later, united Germany and Italy also got involved in the process of the division of Africa. Germany succeeded in capturing the territories of Togo and Cameroon. Italy's colony was Libya, but its main target was Ethiopia. After colonizing Eritrea in 1890, Italy went to war against Ethiopia in 1894 but lost the war, and Ethiopia remained an independent state.

In general, by the beginning of the twentieth century, only Ethiopia and the Republic of Liberia in West Africa (which, however, was economically dependent on the United States) remained independent states on the African continent.

Let us now consider the intrigues of the geographic and political divisions of Africa in a little more detail.

The first groups of Europeans penetrating Africa were small, and Africa itself was vast, so they rarely had contact with each other. Initially, the policy of the Europeans was negotiation, aimed at organizing trade contacts but not conquest. The Europeans "infiltrated" local political life, supporting some groups and trying to isolate others. Gradually, more and more Europeans came to talk about the practical demarcation of the African territories.

In the 1880–1990s, Lord Salisbury played a huge role in the revival of the British colonial initiatives. Prime Minister of Great Britain during 1885–1892, Salisbury made a series of truly ingenious deals. His first move was to declare a protectorate over Bechuanaland (present-day Botswana); his second action was aimed at East Africa (territories left over from the German annexations of 1884). In 1886, Salisbury negotiated with Bismarck the division of East Africa into "spheres of influence," according to the present boundary between Kenya and Tanzania. In 1890, after giving Germany the island of Helgoland in the North Sea, he persuaded Bismarck to sign a series of boundary agreements under which Germany recognized British possessions in Zanzibar, Kenya, Uganda, Northern Rhodesia (Zambia), Bechuanaland (Botswana), and Eastern Nigeria. In the same year, Salisbury concluded a treaty with France recognizing the western border of Nigeria in return for the recognition of the French protectorate over Madagascar. In 1891, Salisbury concluded an agreement with Portugal concerning Nyasaland (Malawi) and both Rhodesias. The cornerstone of Salisbury's African policy remained the British occupation of Egypt. Thus, by the end of Lord Sainsbury's tenure in 1892, the general lines of the division of Africa were already outlined. It should be noted, however, that the division of Africa was initially on paper, but it took time to implement it "on the ground" (Oliver and Atmore 2005: 128–129). Later, the British effectively strengthened their presence in Sierra Leone, the Gold Coast and, most importantly, Nigeria. In East Africa and the Congo Basin, the Arabs became their main rivals (as well as those of Belgium and Germany, who also claimed these territories). They eventually lost to the British Empire.

The French made significant efforts to consolidate their holdings in West Africa: by 1893, the colonies of Ivory Coast and French Guinea were officially proclaimed. The same year the French entered Dahomey (Benin). However, the main French expansion unfolded in the Senegal Basin. In addition to West Africa, the French occupied Gabon, entered areas of Central Sudan but had to yield to the British (it is noteworthy that the local Tuareg tribes living in the Sahara felt the presence of the colonizers only after World War II). France and Spain divided Morocco. In 1894, France sent a large military expedition to Madagascar, which in a short time provoked bloody local conflicts – between religions and clans. In the end, the French were forced to declare the island their colony to "pacify" and "reconcile" the local warring factions.

The only East African country that successfully resisted the colonizers was Ethiopia. Italy captured the Eritrean coast of the Red Sea in 1883 and claimed the coast of Eastern Somalia. In 1896, however, the Italian army was defeated by Ethiopian troops: it was one of the first battles in which a non-European army defeated an army led and partly manned by Europeans.

The last years of colonial rule and the decolonization of Africa

World War II dramatically broadened the "political horizon" of Africans: African soldiers drafted by Britain and France fought in Ethiopia, North Africa, Italy, and against the Japanese in Burma. And even before the war, the first generations of young men educated in the metropolises appeared in the African states. Although Britain and France nominally continued to control vast empires after the war, it was clear that political, economic, and military leadership has shifted from the European states to the two superpowers, the United States and the Soviet Union.

In the postwar years, the European powers began to roll out massive development programs in Africa. These programs were aimed at expanding production and diversifying agriculture, building hydropower plants for industrialization, and increasing the level of education. Another important task was the development of local self-government in the colonies, and here the only possible way was to follow Western models: soon almost every local chief found himself surrounded by an elected council (Oliver and Atmore 2005: 220–222). Central institutions also became more representative. By 1955, the European powers (except for Belgium and Portugal) that ruled the African territories from the Sahara to the Zambezi realized that they had entered the last phase of European colonization of Africa. But nevertheless, as Oliver and Atmore (2005: 224) stated, "the French and British colonial governments played their roles in the last act of the colonial drama with unprecedented courage and enthusiasm."

First, the process of decolonization began to unfold in the countries of North Africa: Libya was proclaimed an independent state in 1951, the French protectorate over Morocco and Tunisia was terminated in 1956, Algeria gained its independence after a long confrontation with France (1954–1962). During the same period (1950s), Sudan, Ghana, and Guinea gained sovereignty. Since then, the process of decolonization in Africa has taken an avalanche character: in 1960, which was the "Year of Africa," 17 new independent states, former British and French colonies, appeared on the political map of the African continent. In total, 34 African countries gained sovereignty between 1956 and 1966. In the 1970s, the process of decolonization continued, albeit less actively. The collapse of the Portuguese colonial empire led to the independence of Angola, Mozambique, and Guinea-Bissau (mid-1970s).

In South Africa, the process of forming a new political map was complicated: in the 1960s, the British-controlled territorial structure – the Federation of Rhodesia and Nyasaland – collapsed, the latter proclaimed its independence as the state of Malawi, and Northern Rhodesia became the sovereign Zambia. Then Lesotho (former Basutoland), Botswana (former Bechuanaland), and Swaziland achieved independence. In 1980, Southern Rhodesia became independent Zimbabwe, thus effectively completing the decolonization of the African continent.

How were the borders between the new sovereign states drawn? Importantly, – and this is a peculiarity of Africa – the borders between African states not only followed the demarcation lines between the spheres of influence of the European colonial powers, but they also reflected the administrative boundaries – within each colonial sphere. In East and West Africa, for example, Britain and France owned colonies with long coastlines, so it proved productive to divide these colonies into smaller administrative units so that each had access to the sea. In the postcolonial era, each of these units became a sovereign state with a capital on the coast. In contrast, in Central Africa, small Belgium possessed a vast territory but did not control a long coastline (there was only a small outlet to the sea at the mouth of the Congo River). This vast territory was ruled by Belgium as a single entity and later became an independent state with many internal conflict lines. It is also important to note that administrative boundaries in the colonies were drawn without regard to ethnic and/or tribal identity; moreover, colonial authorities often found it useful to separate ethnic and tribal groups to prevent opposition to colonizers. Borders, those "geographical institutions," which were in the hands of the colonizers and served as an important tool of colonization, became, after decolonization, an obstacle to the independent development of African states; they undermined their legitimacy. These borders were not embedded in the geographies of African countries.

Since independence, several African states have attempted to apply the institutions of federalism in the process of state-building. The idea was to give autonomy to ethnic communities within states and thus prevent violence and conflict by disaffected groups. However, in most cases, interstate unions either collapsed, or federal states were subsequently constitutionalized as unitary states. Thus, the federation of Ethiopia and Eritrea (the latter seceded from Ethiopia in 1993), the Federation of Mali in Mali (former French Sudan), Sudan and Senegal (established in 1959, dissolved in 1960), the Federation of Rhodesia and Nyasaland (existed from 1953 to 1963, now Malawi, Zambia, and Zimbabwe), Senegambia (1981–1989, former Confederation of Gambia and Senegal) turned out not to be viable. The weak state capacity of the new independent states has caused these countries to fail in federalism.

Congo (former Belgian colony) gained independence in 1960. Two years later, a law on the new administrative-territorial structure of the country was passed according to which any region with a population over 700,000 people could obtain the status of a federal subject – a province. According to the constitution, the Congo was a federation of 21 provinces, but in 1967, under the new constitution (adopted after the coup), it became a unitary state. The United Kingdom of Libya was a constitutional federal monarchy from 1951 to 1963, but federalism did not "take root" in this country either. Since 1961, Cameroon was a federal republic, and since 1972, according to a referendum, it has been a unitary state. In fact, federalism is preserved only in Nigeria and Tanzania, which is in association with the island of Zanzibar.

Independent African states were born in a climate of political euphoria. The colonial powers left them with many of the problems I discussed earlier, but they also left them with (potentially) working administrative and financial systems, basic economic and transport infrastructures. The first postcolonial leaders of African states put a lot of effort into developing foreign policy: they had to establish good relations with neighboring countries to secure their borders, as well as to find new trading partners in the world. In the 1960s, many thousands of young enthusiasts from Europe and the United States went to Africa to teach and heal. And yet, African political systems very quickly showed their incapacity for sustainable development: a series of military coups (Ghana, Sudan, Togo . . .) began as early as the second half of the 1960s. The coups were followed by periods of civil wars (although there were, of course, exceptions: civil leaders in Morocco, Tunisia, Senegal, Tanzania, Malawi, Zambia, and Madagascar managed to keep the military under control).

The case of Liberia was interesting – as a failed attempt at institutional transfer from one continent to another. In 1816, the American Colonization Society, initially the Society for the Colonization of Free People of Color of America, was founded by Robert Finley to encourage and support the repatriation of freeborn people of color and emancipated slaves to the continent of Africa. Indeed, the goal of the organization was ambitious – to find a new home in Africa for former slaves. In 1822, local rulers granted the society's representatives a territory on Cape Mesurado (later called Monrovia, after US President James Monroe) in West Africa, and the first African Americans began to settle there. In 1847, with the expansion of settlements, the Republic of Liberia (meaning free state) was created. Most Americans today are unaware of Liberia's origins, although its flag resembles the US flag – "stars and stripes" (Liberia has only one star). Liberia is an extremely poor country; more than half the population is illiterate. Today, only about 5% of the population are descendants of immigrants from the United States (Magstadt 2002: 549).

To resolve interethnic contradictions, consolidate society, overcome interregional and social imbalances, and as a symbol of the beginning of the country's independent history "from a clean slate," two states, Côte d'Ivoire and Nigeria, built new capitals located in the interior, Yamoussoukro and Abuja. The former capitals of Abidjan and Lagos were located on the coast; they continued to play a major role in the life of these states. However, this has not led to accelerated development in these countries.

Violence remained routine practice in many African states.

Colonial legacy

Colonial legacy had an enormous impact on modern statehood in Africa and the perspectives of development. Colonialism brought new institutions and administrative practices to Africa, the implementation of those disrupted the previous political dynamics in the conquered territories. African rulers were displaced and subordinated to European administrations (often corrupt and incompetent). Traditional relations of trade and exchange were replaced by institutions brought up by the European trading companies. Trade unions and voluntary associations developed vigorously in colonial cities and regions considered "useful" by the colonizers while their development was severely controlled in "useless" territories. Thus, Africa inherited its current territorial asymmetries from colonial times. After independence, African leaders also focused mainly on urban centers – "useful" in terms of supporting the political regime as the rulers redistributed the rent to those groups. As a rule, the policy of colonial administrations was to manipulate social groups living in the territories that they controlled: they involved some local groups in governing while excluded others. The latter became permanently ignored minorities, unable to influence the nature and outcome of the decision-making process. Institutions that structured this process were predominantly informal. This legacy of informality proved to be enduring: informal institutions "have penetrated into the heart of modern economic and political organization" of African countries (Meagher 2007: 405).

Formally, African countries have opted for democracy after decolonization. However, that was rather the imitation of the Western democratic institutions, and authoritarian backsliding began almost simultaneously with the building of new states. One reason for the shift of African states toward authoritarianism in the postcolonial period also lay in the colonial legacy. European powers conquered territories, drew borders, established administrations, collected taxes, and imposed currencies and identities. After decolonization, most African countries lacked institutional legacy on which they could build a system of new (democratic) norms and rules. In addition, the colonial authorities appointed only a very narrow circle of the local establishment to administrative positions. Similarly, postcolonial leaders restricted electoral competition and freedom, prevented the recruitment of new personnel, and selectively distributed public goods. Power was concentrated: neo-patrimonial deals and agreements tended to reflect the preferences of a single leader who controlled access to power and wealth.

Colonialism was responsible, at least in part, for making violence in Africa a routine practice. As Heilbrunn argued,

> the central feature of colonialism was violence. Groups "excluded" from the colonial state developed informal networks to pursue their political and economic interests. After independence, these networks continued to operate as a response to the policies of new leaders who ignored the inhabitants of peripheral regions. The emergence of non-state actors prone to violence was a logical result of attempts to control the center, also based on violence. In countries rich in natural resources, leaders captured and consumed the proceeds of resource exports. Colonialism in Africa created neither a national identity nor (for the most part) viable administrative structures that could legitimize the new states.
>
> (Heilbrunn 2006: 140)

At the same time, colonialism set some benchmarks and frameworks for postcolonial architects of states. For example, in Francophone Africa, ministries were built on French "tracing devices," while the British administrative practices were used in many former colonies of the British Empire. But generally, this did not bear fruit. After decolonization, many new sovereign states became "lazy": they did not invest in bureaucracy, the army, or tax collection. States did not develop foreign policy: decisions were made by the United Nations and Western powers (Herbst 2000).

Nowadays, most African states are presidential republics, but in fact determining the regime of government in some cases is quite difficult: informal institutions rule, or most of the country's territory is outside the control of the central government. Western democratic principles have been poorly instilled on the continent, in most cases it is an imitation of institutions, while the real political process develops outside formal institutions, it boils down to a struggle for domination, where the result is achieved through coups and/or intertribal and interclan conflicts and wars. Civil wars are transformed into conflicts between states (this was the scenario in the DRC, i.e., the former Zaire). Some African countries are still characterized by brutal forms of despotic personal power.

Explaining African statehood

African continent contains more states than any other continent of the world. But these states are so different to the European. In Europe, a community – a nation – appeared first, and then a state emerged combining nation and territory together and surrounding it by borders; in Africa, the state preceded the nation. No nation means no nationalism that proved extremely useful for national consolidation. On the contrary, national sentiments and feelings of belonging to the state in Africa were generally suppressed by populist leaders who ruled on the basis of nepotism and violence.

The mechanistic creation of states, whose citizens were brought together in an almost random fashion, contributed to their inherent instability and conflict. There are also more specific arguments. Acemoglu and Robinson (2010) explained African states by the late and incomplete political consolidation of states based on the seizure and sale of slaves. Collier (2008) saw the explanation in objectively existing "traps" in which most African states have fallen. These are the traps of conflict, natural resources, poor governance and, most importantly for us, the trap of being "trapped" (landlocked) and surrounded by "bad" neighbors (conflict-ridden states with weak and inefficient institutions which export their conflicts abroad). Indeed, more than 30% of Africa's population live in resource-poor, landlocked states with problematic neighbors.

Thus, Africa's main sociopolitical problem hindering development (in both a narrow economic and broader social sense) is an "imperfect," weak statehood. Africa has a dysfunctional system of states, which is unable to provide citizens with the political space to represent their interests (Herbst 2000). The reasonable question then arises: is European-like state a viable form on the African continent, at least in most of the African territories?

This question proves even more reasonable when to remember that Africa also has examples of the so-called stateless societies that are tribal groups headed by tribal leaders. The leader and his entourage form and determine the rules of the organization of group life (institutions) and resolve conflicts. The "stateless" retains a high degree of political autonomy. The decision-making process in traditional African societies is proto-democratic rather than authoritarian. The leader in this system is not a dictator but a central figure for the preservation of peace and justice and the maintenance of social order. The institutional systems of traditional African societies were characterized by equilibrium and a considerable degree of stability. At the same time, they were in a state of conflict with the institutions imposed on these societies by the colonizers.

New forms of social organization (institutions of a modern centralized state) came into sharp conflict with traditional social structures in Africa. For instance, pastoralist conflicts have both geographic and institutional dimensions and are important development outcomes in Africa.[1] According to Penu and Paalo (2021), pastoralist conflicts are competitions over land and land-based resources between pastoralists or between them and crop farmers. Herders of livestock, keen to identify pastures for their flock, sometimes lead the flock to graze on farmers' crops, pollute water bodies, degrade cultivable lands, or overgraze fertile lands. This expectedly creates frustration among crop farmers and eventually results in clashes (sometimes violent) between these farmers and herders. On the other hand, the pastoralists fault crop farmers and other groups for animal rustling and mistreatment. Generally, the institutional discourse around pastoralist conflicts in Africa has been framed around the interaction between state-led policies and community-led traditions about the use of grazelands, especially in relation to the engagements between pastoralists (Penu and Paalo 2021: 227).

The main task of a state (in Africa as in other parts of the world) is to provide its citizens with public goods, the most basic of those is security. In exchange for security, citizens pay taxes to the state, obey laws, participate in political life, etc. Not surprisingly, the concepts of failed states and collapsed states have emerged not somewhere else but in Africa. A "failed state" provides poor services to its citizens; to achieve security and prevent conflict, citizens are forced to act outside formal institutions. In a "collapsed state," conflict resolution mechanisms do not work, and social services are unavailable to citizens. Moreover, a state cannot operate if it inadequately distributes services across the territory and is unable to ensure representation of group interests; a "collapsed" state collapses if its administration does not function, services are unavailable to the population, security is absent, and violence becomes routine (Heilbrunn 2006: 135–150).

Digression is appropriate here. How do we determine whether a state is weak or strong? A strong state guarantees law enforcement, protects property rights, and provides security for its citizens. A weak state makes inadequate use of administrative institutions outside the central cities. Thus, the strength of the state is a function of its "ability to penetrate society, regulate social relations, extract resources, and use them in a certain way" (Migdal 1988). We judge the strength of a state by the extent to which it can provide security for its citizens, provide services for them, establish a system of regulatory institutions, and ultimately promote the well-being of its citizens.

Heilbrunn (2006: 138) identified the reasons for the "failure" of states on the African continent:

- The effects of "partial statehood" because of colonial practices;
- The practice of violence, which had become routine in colonial times and was continued after independence;
- Incomplete control over the country's territory (parts of it remained outside the control of the colonial administration).

The quality of states that have emerged in Africa is now subject to quite harsh criticism. Despite the collapse of many African states, after a period of crisis or even chaos, state forms are being rebuilt "from the ashes of wars."

Borders and border conflicts in Africa

The African continent is shaped by interstate and intrastate conflicts, as well as mass migrations of refugees. Africa has often been called a "continent of conflicts" and "the most conflict-prone region in the world." "Geographic" conflicts – over disputed territories and ownership of rivers and other water resources – are extremely characteristic of the African continent. For example, in East Africa alone there are conflicts between Sudan and Kenya, Kenya and South Sudan, Kenya and Uganda, Eritrea and Ethiopia, and Sudan and South Sudan. Namibia and South Africa are in conflict over the Orange River (a very old conflict), Botswana and Namibia over the Okavango River, and the Republic of Congo and the DRC over the Congo River. Lake Malawi cannot be divided between Tanzania and Malawi. Ethnic conflicts are particularly brutal; in Africa they border on genocide, for example, in Rwanda, Sudan, and Sierra Leone. The difficulty is, among other things, that these conflicts develop according to their own internal logic, incomprehensible to the outside observer. Needless to say, these conflicts are destructive to the development of the countries involved.

The political map of the African continent is relatively recent; it is the result of the dissolution of colonial European empires. On no other continent were the interstate borders so directly reflective of the particularities of the division of the spheres of control of the imperialist powers. The arbitrary colonial division of African borders contributed a lot for the contemporary African problems. The blind partition of African borders caused the disintegration of same ethnic groups into different countries and the merging together of different ethnic groups into same countries. This, in turn, resulted in intrastate and interstate conflicts (Bayeh 2015).

As in Asia, postcolonial states emerged within colonial boundaries (thanks to British colonization, India was governed as a single entity; in Indonesia, Dutch colonial rule served as a major unifying principle – otherwise, the territories of these two states would most likely have been fragmented). Thus, in Asia, colonialism consolidated territories: India, Malaysia, and Indonesia are larger today than they were before colonization. Postcolonial Africa, by contrast, shows a tendency toward fragmentation. No country in Africa, except for Nigeria and South Africa, can play a significant role even on a continental scale.

Territorial conflicts in Africa

The struggle for territory and its natural riches is an important component of intrastate conflicts in Africa, and border conflicts also arise. Separatists see in the armed struggle for separation from the main part of the state an opportunity for their ethnic group to obtain the resources of "their" territory. The problem of borders and their correspondence to the real ethnic settlement is extremely acute.

The following are some examples. One of the most violent and protracted conflicts that has been resolved with the help of the United Nations was the conflict in Angola. The situation is complicated by the so-called Cabinda problem, the northern exclave of Angola, which is extremely rich in oil. Angola's exclave of Cabinda, on the west coast of Central Africa, is separated from it by a thin strip of land that gives the DRC access to the Atlantic Ocean. Angola received this territory from Portugal along with independence. There is a pro-independence movement in Cabinda, the FLEC (Front for the Liberation of the Cabinda Enclave). Angola regards Cabinda as an integral part of its territory and is fighting against the FLEC. The situation is complicated by the presence of American and French oil companies on the territory of Cabinda and their attempts to intervene in the conflict.

Democratic Republic of Congo (DRC): The conflict in this country is sometimes referred to as the first inter-African war, since virtually all central and southern African states were directly or indirectly involved in it. Like most conflicts, it has its roots in the colonial past. According to scholars studying the impact of the colonial legacy on the nature of postcolonial development of states, the failure of Zaire's political and economic system is not least related to the factor of Belgian colonization: King Leopold of Belgium used methods very similar to those later used by Mobutu in exploiting the country's wealth (Bayeh 2015). The country's enormous mineral wealth became, in fact, the curse for its development.

Sudan and South Sudan

Sudan, a former British colony, and Africa's largest country by area, gained independence in 1956. Sudan is home to at least 19 ethnic groups, and more than 100 languages are spoken. Several territorial conflicts are present and intertwined in Sudan: the dominant north–south conflict (between Sudanese Muslim Arabs and the Negro Christian and animist populations of the south); local conflicts in the regions; and center–periphery conflicts – between the center and the regions – the west (Darfur region), the east, and the north. The main cause of the conflicts is the weakness of central institutions and the inability of the state to control the country's territory. The project of "Arabization and Islamization" of the country proposed by the ruling regime was clearly not suitable for such a fragmented society. This project was built on the exclusion of huge groups of Sudanese from nation-building.

In fact, until 2011, Sudan consisted of two regions with different identities: the African south and the Arab north. The political elites in the south have for years insisted on independence or broad autonomy for the region; an insurgency in the south began as early as the 1950s. The situation was exacerbated by the presence of large oil reserves in the south. By the mid-2000s, the conflicting parties (in fact, two authoritarian political regimes) agreed to hold a referendum on the independence of South Sudan and the creation of an independent state. That referendum was held in South Sudan in early 2011, with 98.8% of participants voting in favor of independence. In July 2011, South Sudan's sovereign status came into effect; the new state immediately became a member of the United Nations. South Sudan is a landlocked state.

In Sudan, the Darfur region in the west of the country remains an acute problem. In Darfur itself, several conflicts are intertwined: the struggle of the region's political elite against the marginalization of the region by the center; the conflict over land use between the tribes of nomadic herders and peasant agriculturalists; and the ethnic conflict between Arabs and non-Arab population groups.

Rwanda

After independence in 1962, Rwanda formed a government composed mainly of the Hutu ethnic group (the Hutu constitute about 85% of the population). The Tutsis (15% of the population), who had held key positions in the precolonial and colonial periods, were gradually ousted from power. Tensions swelled, with the Tutsi genocide beginning in 1990 and culminating in 1994.

Burundi

The conflict in Burundi followed much the same pattern as in Rwanda, with a Tutsi minority and a Hutu majority. Massacres and coups d'état have been repeated in Burundi since its independence in 1962.

Somalia

For several years, Somalia has been without a central authority. Since the early 1990s, there has been an ongoing struggle for power in the country; the central government has not been able to control the territory of the country, in fact, only the capital, and not all of it. The country has disintegrated into regions controlled by armed clan groups. In the north of the country emerged the Republic of Somaliland (formerly British Somalia), not recognized by the international community. Shortly after, the Italian and British colonial territories in Somalia gained independence in 1960, they voluntarily united to form the Republic of Somalia. The colonial era "inherited" Somalia with the structures of a modern centralized state that did not "dovetail" with traditional social structures.

Nevertheless, in the early years after independence, Somalia was considered almost a model for democracy in Africa. There were numerous political parties, formed mainly on a clan basis. From 1961 to 1969, elected governments succeeded each other. Unlike most other African states, the Somali population spoke mostly one language and practiced one religion. However, Somalis also lived in the territories of neighboring countries – Djibouti, Ethiopia, and Kenya, which gave rise to the idea of uniting all territories inhabited by Somalis into "Greater Somalia" and, naturally, led to conflict with neighboring states.

In 1969, because of a military coup, General Barre came to power in Somalia, and his government declared a policy of establishing a modern nation-state based on the socialist model. In pursuit of this policy, a single-party system and a centralized authoritarian political regime were established, which made extensive use of repressive measures to assert total control over citizens. However, the results of such a rule proved counterproductive; the population became increasingly oriented toward a clan identity to survive.

General Barre's military dictatorship collapsed in 1991, thereby formally ending the period of a state in Somalia that had long been unable to provide security or services to the population. However, the period of dictatorship was followed by a period of chaos. An external intervention in the form of the UN mission (UNOSOM) proved ineffective and ended after three years. The UN humanitarian intervention can be seen as a natural response of the international community to the existence of "black holes" on the political map, but if one considers that the crisis in Somalia was a reflection of the state's inability to exercise internal sovereignty (i.e., to provide a minimum level of security for its citizens), then one cannot expect an external intervention to be a constructive substitute for the lack of sovereignty (Doornbos 2006: 185).

Somaliland, an unrecognized state[2] in the Horn of Africa, is also a product of colonial rule. Somaliland is home to about a third of Somalia's population (approximately three million people). In 2003, the territory held a referendum in which about 99% of those who participated voted for independence and adoption of a new constitution for Somaliland. In 1960, the two former colonies of Italian Somalia and British Somalia were united, but these two territories never became a single country. Many "appanage principalities" were formed on the territory of Italian Somalia, and British Somalia is trying to build its own, separate statehood. So far, Somaliland has not been recognized by the international community. According to Hippler, Somaliland meets the criteria of a sovereign state (although it is not recognized as such by anyone). Thus, this state (let's call it by that name) was established in 1993 by a referendum, so that the state and its institutions are legitimized by the decision of two million people. The established state guarantees a relatively high level of security to its citizens. The two houses of parliament are formed through direct elections, and the government and the opposition develop constructive political competition. Somaliland has an independent judiciary, a vibrant civil society, free media, and security agencies that are under public scrutiny. The state has its own currency, a central bank, an international airport, and port, and finally a growing economy. And yet the international community refuses to recognize Somaliland as a sovereign state on the grounds of the principle of inviolability of colonial borders and the need to preserve and protect the "national unity" of Somalia (Hippler 2005: 65).

A paradoxical situation has emerged in Somalia: "mainland" Somalia has external sovereignty as a recognized sovereign state but clearly lacks internal sovereignty; on the other hand, Somaliland, with all the attributes of internal sovereignty, is not recognized by the international community as a sovereign state.

Ethiopia and Eritrea

The armed conflict between Ethiopia and Eritrea was one of the largest wars of the last decade of the twentieth century. Eritrean independence was proclaimed in 1993, but the signed treaty did not define the interstate borders. Thus, both ports on the Red Sea, Massawa and Assab, became the property of Eritrea, which alone received about 18% of its budget revenues in the form of duties and fees on Ethiopian goods passing through Assab. Conflict also arose over the Badame region, about 100 miles east of Sudan. In 2000, war broke out between Ethiopia and Eritrea. After the war, the states signed a peace agreement, but the fate of the disputed territories has not been completely resolved.

As for the beginning of 2020s, 58 territories in 29 African countries were pursuing an active policy of secession, trying to break away from the "mother" territory of the country, thus undermining its territorial integrity and generating deep conflicts.

Nigeria: the "mirror" of Africa's problems

Nigeria is Africa's largest state by population. Many of the continent's problems are reflected in this country as a kind of "mirror." Nigeria emerged as a result of the 1914 colonial amalgamation (Othman, Osman and Mohammed 2021: 187). The country is one of the largest hydrocarbon producers; it is one of the top ten oil exporters in the world (at the turn of the third millennium, its proven oil reserves were about 3% of the world). Nigeria is also rich in iron ore. The country's economy is resource-based, and modernization is slow and uneven, so such notions as "growth without development" and "enclave industrialization" are quite appropriate when describing Nigeria's economic evolution in recent decades (this type of economic development is also typical of other African countries) (Onyimadu 2015).

The country has a population of 218.5 million (as of 2022). The population density (about 100 people per square kilometer) is one of the highest on the continent. In recent decades, urbanization in Nigeria has been explosive, with the urban population growing at a rate of 6–8% per annum, accounting for more than 40% of the population. With more than 60 major cities (with more than 100,000 inhabitants), Nigeria is far ahead of any other country in Africa. Nigeria is home to about 250 ethnic groups, among which the largest are the Hausa-Fulani (29% of the country's population), the Yoruba (21%), the Igbo (18%), and the Ijo (10%). The country's inhabitants speak 400 languages. The most populous are the northern and coastal states of Nigeria, each having 3–5 million people. Between the densely populated south and north of the country is a so-called zone of demographic depression, which was formed when the Europeans penetrated these territories. The central regions were most depopulated because of the enslavement of their inhabitants. Subsequently, this pattern of settlement was, if not reinforced, at least perpetuated by the faster economic development of the southern and northern parts of Nigeria, compared to the central parts of the country.

Europeans came to the territory of modern Nigeria in the sixteenth century, and the coast became the largest center of the slave trade and was called the "Slave Coast." In 1914, there was a single formation of the Colony and Protectorate of Nigeria in the modern borders (except the northern part of British Cameroon, which was annexed to Nigeria in 1961). The formation was artificial and served the interests of the British metropolis. Note that even after unification, the north and south of the country were governed by separate administrations. The British used the so-called system of indirect administration, preserving the formal rights of the traditional power structures. Under the 1947 constitution, Nigeria was divided into three regions, becoming a federation comprising the Northern, Eastern, and Western regions. Each region was dominated by one of the major ethnic groups, the Hausa-Fulani, Igbo, and Yoruba, respectively. The country's leading political parties had a regional character.

Nigeria's independence was declared in 1960, when the country became a Federation of Nigeria within the British Commonwealth (Nigeria became a republic in 1963). However, ethnic federalism did not resolve ethno-regional conflicts: in 1967, the independent Republic of Biafra was proclaimed on the territory of the Eastern Region. The government immediately adopted a decree on the new administrative division of the country into 12 states, but this did not prevent a civil war in which, according to various estimates, from 500,000 to two million people died. The war ended with the surrender of Biafra troops.

In the late 1960s and early 1970s, there was an "oil boom," which was associated with the rise of the Nigerian economy. In the mid-1970s, a new administrative reform was carried out: the country, while maintaining its federal character, was divided into 19 states. A federal metropolitan area was created in the geographical center of the country, "free" from the conflicting past and designed to serve as a symbol of the country's unity.

Interethnic regional contradictions escalated in the country in the early 2000s: Hausa-Fulani Muslims in the northern states drive out Yoruba Christians, and nine northern states officially introduce Sharia law, which contradicts Nigeria's secular constitution. Tensions between the north, on the one hand, and the west and the east, on the other, are growing. In addition, ethnic tensions are growing in the Niger Delta, which is extremely rich in oil.

Federal solution seemed to create additional problems. Almost 70 years have passed since federalism was introduced in the country, but the performance of the Nigerian federal system is still considered poor, with adverse consequences of "tragic policy failure" (Friedman 2018). The foundations of federalism in Nigeria were laid during colonial times; a process called "creeping federalism" became widespread. The 1946 constitution provided for three regions that corresponded to the administrative colonial division. The 1963 constitution already provided for four strong regions with their own constitutions and institutions. In 1967, the four regions were replaced by 12 states, and seven more states were added in 1976. The process of fragmentation continued until 2005, when there were 36 states in Nigeria (Osieke 2006: 201–202).

One of the problems seems to be that Nigeria has not been able to reconcile the institutions of federalism with a suitable territorial structure that responds to the geographical, ethnic, and religious specificities of the country, with the boundaries of these communities cutting across each other. The history of federalism in Nigeria is a history of constant changes in the composition and boundaries of regions – the partitioning of the Middle Belt/Central Nigeria from the Northern Region; the Biafra from the Southeast, Niger Delta from the South-South, and secession threats by the Yoruba nation and Igbo-dominated Southeast Nigeria under the umbrella of the Indigenous People of Biafra (IPOB), to the Movement for the actualization of the Sovereign State of Biafra (MASSOB) (Othman, Osman and Shehu 2021: 186).

Geography and/or institutions and development in Africa

There are several sets of factors that have frequently been invoked to explain African states' chronically poor economic performance and lagging development: (1) colonial legacy, in particular, long period of slave trading and practices of violence; (2) heavy dependence on a small number of primary exports (oil, diamonds, copper, gold, coffee, tea, cocoa, palm oil, and rubber); (3) bad domestic politics and policies: nepotism and clientelism, corruption, and political instability; (4) ineffective economic policies, in particular, protectionism; (5) rapid population growth; and (6) unfavorable social conditions like deep ethnic divisions, indicated by high levels of ethnolinguistic and religious diversity and low levels of "social capital."

There is no point in arguing with this long and sad list. Two other factors make this list longer – these are institutions and geography. In terms of institutions, it is not only modern institutions but also those that existed in Africa before European colonization. Acemoglu and Robinson (2012) called these institutions extractive: such institutions are formed when the state does not provide services to the population but instead tries to extract as much as possible from its population. In the fifteenth and sixteenth centuries, the Portuguese and the Dutch noted in the Congo poverty reaching the point of begging. Technology was in its infancy: the Congolese knew neither the wheel nor the plow and had no written language. The reasons for this were the "extractive" nature of the country's economic institutions. Thus, to develop, it was necessary to use new, more advanced technologies, but it was not profitable, because any profit made with their help was immediately expropriated by the king and his entourage. As a result, the Congolese "escaped" from the state by settling as far away from roads, markets, and slave traders as possible. The state did not provide services to the population (e.g., with the help of the Portuguese, the Congolese elite quickly became literate but made no attempt to promote literacy in the masses) but tried to extract as much as possible from its population. Poverty was ubiquitous, but political elites were extremely, obscenely wealthy.

Bloom and Sachs (1998: 212–213) saw the root of Africa's long-term growth crisis in its extraordinary geography. Researchers explained their focus on geography with three reasons:

> First, there is little to be gained from, yet another recitation of the damage caused by statism, protectionism, and corruption to African economic performance. Second, most economists are woefully neglectful of the role of forces of nature in shaping economic performance in general, and in Africa in particular. They treat economies as blank slates onto which another region's technologies and economic history may be grafted. . . . Third, and perhaps most important, good policies must be tailored to geographical realities. If agricultural productivity is very low in Africa for climatological reasons, perhaps the real lesson is that growth should be led much more by outward-oriented industry and services, rather than blindly making yet another attempt to transplant "integrated rural development" strategies from other parts of the world without customizing them to Africa's unique conditions.

Thus, this was also the geographic location and its consequences – climate, soils, topography, and disease ecology – that predetermined Africa's suffering from chronically low agricultural productivity (especially food production) and high disease burdens.[3] (Indeed, in the African continent, the small temperate zones at the north and south have significantly higher incomes than the tropical core).

Unfavorable neighborhood is another geographical factor that complicates national development in Africa. State failures can destabilize an entire region. Instability, unrest, and civil wars increasing the risk for state collapse are not limited to the failed or collapsed state; its neighbors – or those located within close distance of a failing state – are also likely to experience subsequently higher levels of political instability, wars, and interstate conflicts. The processes associated with state failure diffuse to the neighbors (Iqbal and Starr 2008). This is very much the case in sub-Saharan Africa. According to the 2019 Fragile States Index (FSI), 21 of the 30 most fragile countries are to be found on the African continent.[4] There are exceptions, of course. Mauritius about which Mark Twain in 1896 said that it "was made first and then heaven . . . and heaven was copied after Mauritius" has become the first African nation to break through to the Very Stable category of the Fragile States Index (FSI), a reflection of its political stability, economic development, and social cohesion between cultures. But Mauritius is an island, it does have land neighbors. And its sea neighbors – Seychelles and Botswana – have also ranked in the Stable category of the FSI.

Notes

1 Pastoralist conflicts are also quite typical in countries outside Africa, for instance, India and China.

2 Internationally Somaliland is recognized as *de jure* part of Somali.

3 Hall and Jones (1997) have also found empirical evidence that a country's distance from the equator is strongly positively associated with income per capita.
4 Africa's Islands of Stability | Fragile States Index.

References

Acemoglu, Daron, and James Robinson. (2010). "Why Is Africa Poor?" *Economic History of Developing Regions*, 25(1): 21–50.

Acemoglu, Daron, and James Robinson. (2012). *Why Nations Fail: The Origins of Power, Prosperity, and Poverty*. New York: Crown Publishers.

Bayeh, Endalcachew. (2015). "The Legacy of Colonialism in the Contemporary Africa: A Cause for Intrastate and Interstate Conflicts." *International Journal of Innovative and Applied Research*, 3(2): 23–29.

Bloom, David, and Jeffrey Sachs. (1998). "Geography, Demography, and Economic Growth in Africa." *Brookings Papers on Economic Activity*, 2.

Braudel, Fernand. (1995). *A History of Civilizations*. New York: Penguin Books.

Collier, Paul. (2008). *The Bottom Billion*. Oxford: Oxford University Press.

Diamond, Jared. (1999). *Guns, Germs, and Steel: The Fates of Human Societies*. New York; London: W. W. Norton.

Doornbos, Martin. (2006). *Global Forces and State Restructuring: Dynamics of State Formation and Collapse*. London: Palgrave Macmillan.

Ferguson, Neill. (2003). *Empire: The Rise and Demise of the British World Order and the Lessons for Global Power*. London: Basic Books.

Friedman, Andrew. (2018). "States, Countries, and Peoples: A Comparative Look at Bicameralism in African Federal States." *Fletcher F World Affairs*, 42(2): 165–178.

Hahn, Friedrich. (2005). *Africa*. Saint Petersburg: Prosveshenie.

Hall, Robert E., and Charles I. Jones. (1997). "Levels of Economic Activity across Countries." *American Economic Review*, 87(2): 173–177.

Heilbrunn, John. (2006). "Paying the Price of Failure: Reconstructing Failed and Collapsed States in Africa and Central Asia." *Perspectives on Politics*, 4(1).

Herbst, Jeffrey. (2000). "States and Power in Africa: Comparative Lessons in Authority and Control." *Princeton Studies in International History and Politics*, 85.

Hippler, Jochen. (2005). *Nation-Building: A Key Concept for Peaceful Conflict Transformation*. London: Pluto Press.

Iqbal, Zaryab, and Harvey Starr. (2008). "Bad Neighbors: Failed States and Their Consequences." *Conflict Management and Peace Science*, 25(4): 315–331.

Magstadt, Thomas. (2002). *Nations and Governments: Comparative Politics in Regional Perspective*. Boston; New York: Bedford/St. Martin's.

Meagher, Kate. (2007). "Introduction: Special Issue on 'Informal Institutions and Development in Africa'." *Africa Spectrum*, 42(3): 405–418.

Migdal, Joel. (1988). *Strong Societies and Weak States: State – Society Relations and State Capabilities in the Third World*. Princeton: Princeton University Press.

Oliver, Roland, and Anthony Atmore. (2005). *Africa since 1800*. Cambridge: Cambridge University Press.

Onyimadu, Chukwuemeka. (2015). A Case of Growth Without Development: A Comparative Study Between Nigeria and Malaysia. MPRA Paper No. 77202.

Osieke, Ebere. (2006). "Federal Republic of Nigeria." In *Legislative, Executive, and Judicial Governance in Federal States*, ed. by K. Le Roy and Ch. Saunders. *A Global Dialogue on Federalism*, Vol. 3. Montreal, Canada: McGill-Queen's University Press.

Othman, Muhammad, Nazariah Osman, and Isah Shehu. (2021). "Nigerian Federalism: An Overview of Its Imperatives and Impediments." *Journal of International Studies*, 17: 183–209.

Penu, Dennis, and Sebastian Paalo. (2021). "Institutions and Pastoralist Conflicts in Africa: A Conceptual Framework." *Journal of Peacebuilding & Development*, 16(2): 224–241.
Sowell, Thomas. (1998). *Conquests and Cultures: An International History*. New York: Basic Books.
Verschoyle, Frederick. (2018). *Cecil Rhodes: His Political Life and Speeches, 1881–1900*. Merton, UK: Forgotten Books.
Wesseling, H. L. (1996). *Divide and Rule: The Partition of Africa, 1880–1914*. Westport, CT: Praeger.

7 Latin America

Latin America is the common name for a group of countries located in the southern part of the North American continent (south of the Rio Grande River), in the West Indies (it includes the Atlantic Ocean islands of the Bahamas, the Greater Antilles, and the Lesser Antilles), and on the South American mainland. It is the only region in the world that occupies an entire continent, South America, and a large part of another continent – North America. The region has an extremely advantageous political, economic, and geographic location. It includes 33 sovereign states, as well as possessions of Great Britain, France, the United States, and the Netherlands. The contrasts between the countries of the region in terms of area are extremely large, for example, between the island states of the West Indies and Brazil, which is comparable in area to the continent. Two states, Paraguay and Bolivia are landlocked. The latter is currently the poorest country in Latin America, though it has shown significant progress in recent years, reducing its extreme poverty rate from 38.2% in 2006 to 15.2% in 2019.[1] Countries of Caribbean region also belong to the group of the poor countries, while the other countries of Latin America belong to the middle-income group.

Latin America is an area of frequent natural disasters. Almost every year one or another country in the region (and often several) suffers from a variety of natural disasters. In Peru, Chile, Ecuador, Colombia, Nicaragua, and Guatemala, these are earthquakes; in Honduras, the Dominican Republic and Mexico – destructive hurricanes; and Argentina and Peru suffer from floods; Brazil suffers from periodic droughts.

There are few regions in the world that can match Latin America in terms of inequality. As of 2023, of the 20 "champions" of income inequality in the world (as measured by the Gini coefficient), eight were in Latin America (and the rest in sub-Saharan Africa). In addition to income inequality, the levels of socioeconomic development of different Latin American territories vary enormously. There are areas where income levels and the provision of social services are comparable to the poorest African countries, but there are also cities where these indicators are closer to those of the European countries. Do such scales of inequalities and disparities relate to geography?

Geographic conditions in Latin America are very different at the level of individual countries. For example, the territories of Uruguay and El Salvador belong

DOI: 10.4324/9781003496731-10

to the same natural zone, while Bolivia, Brazil, Ecuador, Colombia, and Peru show remarkable geographic diversity, few countries on other continents can match them in this respect. This geographic diversity causes a high level of geographic fragmentation, which is reflected in population distribution and has serious political implications.

Population fragmentation is usually defined as the possibility that two individuals taken at random sampling do not belong to the same group. Geographic fragmentation can be defined as the probability that two individuals taken at random do not belong to the same natural area. The level of fragmentation is defined from 0 (which corresponds to the entire population living in the same natural zone) to 1 (each of the individuals living in a different natural zone). Political and economic studies tend to ignore the level of geographic fragmentation, which is surprising, since political and economic divisions are often explained by geographic factors. Geographic fragmentation is an important dimension of social and political conflicts, and it is worth considering in institution building and decision-making (Gallup, Gaviria and Lora 2003: 11–12). Geographic fragmentation alone does not create conflict, but it does contribute to its duration and make it more difficult to resolve.

The name of the region, Latin America, reflects the "Latin" type of colonization carried out by the Spanish and Portuguese, people of the Latin (Romance) language group. In Latin America, about 63% of the population speaks Spanish, and about 34% speaks Portuguese. Although language is the "common denominator" for most of the region, Latin America is a mix of cultures and traditions. The nations in Latin America are extremely distinctive, resulting from a long mix of descendants of immigrants from Europe, indigenous Indian populations, and African slaves brought in during colonization. The most homogeneous in national composition are the settler countries of Argentina, Uruguay, and Chile. The region as a whole shares a common heritage rooted in historical ties with Spain and Portugal.

At the end of the fifteenth century, Christopher Columbus, who in fact ushered in the remarkable period in world history known as the Age of Discovery, led an expedition mounted by the Spanish crown in search of the shortest route to India. But as a result, he discovered a new part of the world (he made a total of four expeditions to the New World). October 12, 1492, the day the expedition reached one of the Bahamas (it was San Salvador or Guanahani; now Watling Island), is considered the officially recognized date of European discovery of America.

Columbus was not the first European to reach the New World, but he was the first to go back and bring the news to Europe – and thousands went across the ocean. If the members of the Lisbon Academy of Astronomy and Mathematics were able to make correct predictions, they would not have rejected the project that Columbus presented back in 1485, would not have declared his calculations fantastic, and the glory of "sponsorship" of the discovery of America would not have gone to the Spanish but to the Portuguese crown. However, Portuguese scientists failed to consider all the previous unsuccessful attempts of travelers and see that, by all indications, the breaking point in the search for new lands was about to be reached (Bronner 1996).

The conquest of lands across the ocean gave an extremely powerful impetus to seafaring and trade; numerous expeditions of conquering conquistadors rushed after easy riches, colonizing new lands, and destroying pockets of early American civilizations. The belief in the wealth of the discovered lands is evident even in the names the travelers gave them: "rich coast" (Costa Rica), "rich port" (Puerto Rico). So most of today's Latin American states are former colonies of Spain, and Brazil is a former colony of Portugal, which gained independence in the early nineteenth century (as a result of the wars of liberation in 1810–1825 or even earlier, like Haiti and Ecuador).

Geographical factors have often acted as an obstacle to economic development in the region and to national consolidation – the establishment of administrative and political institutions, the legitimization of power, and the entrenchment of a sense of citizenship. The spread of national identity (as opposed to local and regional identity) was blocked by physical barriers – mountain systems, jungles, and sparsely populated plains. In Bolivia, Peru, and Guatemala, for example, most inhabitants still identify themselves not with the country (as Bolivians, Peruvians etc.), but with their tribe, village, or locality (Magstadt 2002: 370).

Anthropological heterogeneity in the region is combined with a relative monolithic population in religious and linguistic terms. Spanish is the official language in most of the region's sovereign states; Portuguese is the official language in Brazil. The region's population has been growing very slowly for centuries, with a dramatic change occurring only in the 1950s and 1960s. Latin America is characterized by significant disparities in population distribution: the highest population densities are found in the West Indies and Central America, the lowest – in Suriname, Guyana, and Bolivia.

An important dimension of inequalities is spatial inequalities manifested in many Latin America countries as "agglomeration without growth." The institutional framework is generally biased to promote the concentration of people and economic activity in the capital, and the excess of agglomeration constraints economic growth while reducing, at the same time, potential opportunities in the peripheral cities. This situation has exacerbated since the mid-twentieth century with the acceleration of the urbanization process. The largest agglomerations are Mexico City in Mexico (that is one of the most populous cities globally), São Paulo (Brazil), Buenos Aires (Argentina), Rio de Janeiro (Brazil), Lima (Peru), and Bogota (Colombia). Furthermore, Latin American institutional frameworks have been historically marked by favoritism in support of the main cities and the predominance of spatially "blind" policies that contributed to the increase of spatial inequalities (Aroca and Atienza 2016).

After World War II, for three decades Latin America was a region of authoritarian, often military regimes (the exceptions were, to some extent, Costa Rica and Colombia). Since the 1980s, the political and economic transformations in Latin America have been no less radical than those that later affected Eastern Europe and the Soviet Union. Military leaders were replaced by civilians elected by the population, and even the fact that in some places this movement went backwards (not to mention Cuba) does not detract from the overall striking process: throughout

Latin America, the democratic alternative was chosen. In addition to the political choice in favor of democracy, the economic choice was also made in favor of market relations. In recent years, however, opinion polls have shown that support for democracy has declined considerably – citizens have realized that democracy itself (and even more so the idea of democracy) does not guarantee them prosperity or equality. Throughout the Western Hemisphere people are losing faith in democratic institutions.[2] But today, the split in the debate around the famous question "What to do?," is between those experts who believe that the transformation of the states in Latin America has not been completed, hence there is the need to "build up" democratic and market reforms, and those who oppose reforms, attributing today's situation precisely to their effects.

It should be reiterated that after the wave of democratization in Latin America, almost all countries in the region followed common principles and approaches in reforming their states. However, some countries have managed to maintain stable reform courses and have demonstrated sufficient flexibility in adapting to changing economic conditions, while others have either been prone to change course whenever the political landscape has changed or proved highly inflexible and have maintained ineffective rules, thus failing to give political courses stability and credibility (Scartascini, Stein and Tommasi 2010). As Latin America shows, there are no universal recipes for democratization. There is also no universal set of "right" policies.

Today, the possibility of war between Latin American countries was considered low: interstate disagreements were resolved at the negotiating table (border clashes, such as the one between Peru and Ecuador in the 1980s, were rather a recurrence of the past). However, in 2023, Venezuela has been laying claim to the mineral-rich Essequibo region, which covered about two-thirds of neighboring Guyana's surface area. Guyana condemned Venezuela for not abiding with the agreements, in which the two countries agreed not to use force or to threaten each other. Besides that, guerrilla groups and guerrilla warfare against the central government are an important part of the political life of many Latin American states. In recent decades, Nicaragua, Ecuador, El Salvador, Guatemala, Colombia, Chile, and Peru have faced guerrilla warfare.

At the same time, these conflicts do not present Latin American countries as showing remarkable will for building common institutions. Latin American countries have been actively creating supranational institutions and are involved in regional integration through the UNASUR (Union of South American Nations) group; Mexico has joined NAFTA – the North American Free Trade Association. The West Indies and Central America also have their own regional groups.

It is said that Latin America has missed its opportunities and hopelessly lost the "competition" with North America. In the mid-eighteenth century, the two continents were roughly equal in per capita income, but since then the gap between them has steadily widened and is now about 1:5. This can be explained by two "bad" periods in Latin American history: the long and conflicting decolonization (1810–1870) and poor economic policies since the 1970s. The book of Beatriz Armendáriz and Felipe Larraín (2017) highlighted five explanations of why Latin

America has lagged behind, four of those are directly related to geography and institutions.

Geography is the *first* one. Over 70% of Latin America is in the tropics, which makes everything more difficult. The region is more exposed to diseases – like malaria, yellow fever, dengue, cholera, and others – and is geographically far from key markets. *Second* is large-scale agricultural plantations in Latin America. In the North America, there was more mixed farming centered on grains and livestock, and smaller units, which led to more democratic and decentralized political institutions, a more robust protection of property rights, and a larger middle class. *Third,* the region's institutional legacy plays a role because institutional arrangements in the South were weaker as opposed to the North. And finally, ethno-linguistic and cultural fragmentation in Latin America, which goes back to the colonial periods, have also held back the region, although the influence of this factor is much less important than in Africa, for example.

According to Larraín, Latin America has also lost competition with many Asian countries. In the early 1960s, its per capita income was more than double that of East Asia. Today, the region lags significantly behind. Several Asian countries that started from low levels of income 50 years ago – such as South Korea, Singapore, Taiwan, and Hong Kong – have become developed nations. No country in Latin America can be named developed, although a few are higher-middle income. The only country in Latin America that has been able to diversify away from commodities is Mexico. In Mexico, about 25% of exports come from natural resources. That figure is about 60% or higher for the rest of the region. In cases of extreme dependence, like Venezuela, that figure is over 90%. Latin America has been able to significantly reduce poverty, but it has been less successful in reducing inequality. The key to fighting against poverty and reducing inequality is having adequate institutions.[3]

Pre-Columbian civilizations

Existing hypotheses tell us that the indigenous populations of Latin America belonged to the great Mongoloid race. They migrated 12,000 to 15,000 years ago across the Bering Strait to the north of America and gradually moved south as far as Tierra del Fuego. Another hypothesis considers the possibility of indigenous migration in the direction of Asia–Oceania–America. In any case, already many centuries ago in Latin America Indian civilizations, the first layer of civilizational stratification of this region of the Earth, began to form.

When Spaniards came to Latin America they established a new system of government there after destroying, adapting, or assimilating preexisting cultures and civilizations. Researchers know quite a lot about ancient American civilizations, and yet the rapid destruction and assimilation led to the fact that these truly unique great kingdoms of ancient America carried with them many mysteries that will never be solved again.

Between the third and sixteenth centuries three major civilizations existed in Latin America. The Maya civilization reached its peak in the seventh century; the

Maya inhabited the Yucatan Peninsula (Mexico), Guatemala, and Western Honduras. The territorial structure of the Maya state consisted of virtually independent city-states (for this reason the Maya were called "Greeks of the New World"), the most famous of which were Tikal, Palenque, and Copan. Anthropologists discovered the Maya may have been in the Yucatan as far back as 500 BCE. This new evidence indicated the Maya had a very complex social structure, distinctive religious practices, and unique technological innovations that made civilization possible in the harsh jungle of the Yucatan.[4]

The Aztecs occupied the whole north of Mexico (and called themselves "Mexica"). In 1325, they founded the city of Tenochtitlan (modern-day Mexico City), which later became the capital of the Aztec Empire. The centralized Inca Empire, with its capital in Cuzco, extended from the south of modern Colombia to the north of Chile. At its height, the Inca Empire had a population of 10–30 million people, most of whom belonged to the Inca-conquered tribes (Barton 1997: 34). Each of the pre-Columbian civilizations had a large geographical extent.

The Aztecs and Incas were bellicose: as they expanded their empires, they joined new tribes, which had to be fully integrated into their political systems. The empires had excellent transportation systems (road networks). In contrast, the Maya were not a warlike civilization; they (like the Incas, for that matter) were architects and scientists. The Maya invented the calendar and had their own writing system (which the Incas did not have). Religion was such an important part of Maya life that their political system was a kind of theocracy.

Geographical factors played an important role in the settlement of pre-Columbian civilizations. The Aztec and Inca empires were located on the tropical plateaus, areas better suited for agriculture. As it is known that they did not conduct maritime trade (and did not even know the wheel), the proximity to the sea did not give them any economic benefits (Gallup, Gaviria and Lora 2003: 14).

Spanish–Portuguese colonization

After the discovery by Columbus, the Spanish and Portuguese conquest of the New World proceeded at a rapid pace. In 1500, a Portuguese expedition led by Pedro Cabral discovered Brazil; in 1501–1502, an expedition of Gonzalo Cuella and Amerigo Vespucci set sail for Brazil. Ten years later, the Spanish detachment of Vasco Nuñez Balboa crossed the Isthmus of Panama and reached the "South Sea," that is, the Pacific Ocean. In 1519–1539, the Spaniards subjugated Mexico (in 1519–1521, in bloody battles, the troops of Hernán Cortés conquered Aztec lands, and he was appointed Spanish proconsul in Mexico City, a city built on the ruins of Tenochtitlan, the great Aztec capital) (Rinke 2023). Oswald Spengler described the death of the Aztec civilization (these words describe the fate of other pre-Columbian civilizations as well) as the only example of the violent death of a civilization that did not die of its own accord but received a fatal blow and died like a sunflower whose head was torn off by a random passerby (Spengler 1926).

In 1523–1524, Pedro de Alvarado's army defeated the Maya. Almost at the same time (from 1524 to 1553), the Spaniards discovered Peru, Chile, and the

Amazon River (in the 1920s Francisco Pizarro reached the Inca Empire and, having obtained permission from the Spanish court, conquered and colonized it); in the early 1540s, the Spanish (an expedition led by Francisco de Orellana) crossed the continent from West to East – from ocean to ocean.

The Spanish Conquest posed a challenge to historians. How could a handful of adventurers defeat civilizations? According to Hennessy,

> [I]t is difficult to comprehend just how original an enterprise the Conquest was. No European power has attempted to establish an empire at such a distance. The logistical problems were daunting, flora and fauna overturned every established conception. It is scarcely surprising that Spanish historiography have concentrated on that golden heroic age.
>
> (Hennessy 1993: 6)

While we understand the brutality of the colonization process and the ambiguity of conquistadors, we cannot but pay tribute to their courage, powers of endurance, their military and organizational skills. In Spanish America, conquistador was a culture hero.

The routes of the expeditions were not accidental and were largely determined by the so-called first partition of the world – between Spain and Portugal. This division was in fact produced by Pope Alexander VI Borgia, who in 1493 issued his bull "Inter cetera." The bull (and another that appeared the next day) became the basis of the Spanish–Portuguese negotiations, which ended in 1494 with a treaty. The boundary between the two countries' spheres of influence in the Atlantic Ocean was henceforth drawn further westward from the Cape Verde Islands in favor of Portugal (until then Portugal had operated within the rights granted by the popes in 1452–1456). Under the new partition, Brazil was included in Portugal's sphere.

The metropolis itself – Spain – had only recently become a single state under Ferdinand and Isabella, after a long war with the Arabs. Therefore, generations of Spaniards knew nothing but war, so they easily became "soldiers of fortune" and went to the New World for adventure and easy riches.

The first Spanish settlements were established in the Caribbean islands, where the colonists crushed local resistance and established a system based on slave labor. Much later, the geographic factors of one of the islands, Haiti, have destroyed two armies.

In the 1890s, Britain and Spain, at war with republican France, decided to divide the French colony of Santo Domingo (now Haiti) between themselves. Spanish troops came in from the north, the British from the south. The natives revolted against the colonizers. But yellow fever and malaria proved far more frightening to the colonizers than to the natives. A typical case: a unit of 700 soldiers lost 500 of them in one month; only seven were killed in action, the rest fell victim to disease. It was the first European defeat. Later, as Napoleon consolidated his power in France after 1799, he directed his efforts toward Santo Domingo, which he intended to use as a staging post to strengthen French control of the Louisiana territory. But he, too, suffered a setback. French troops were not only unable to fight; they were unable to survive in Haiti's "morbid" climate. In 1802, the troops quickly occupied almost all the island – only to lose 80% of the available troops to yellow fever just as quickly. The Haitian uprising was one of the very few historical examples of successful slave revolts; but the real winners were the tropical diseases (Gallup, Gaviria and Lora 2003: 16).

Colonial institutions

Spanish possessions in the Americas were divided into four territorially huge viceroys:

- New Spain, which included Mexico, Florida, Oregon (the latter two were sold to the United States in 1819), Texas (annexed to the United States in 1848), and the territories of California, Arizona, New Mexico, Nevada, and Utah, which were transferred to the United States in 1848.
- New Granada – the territories of present-day Colombia, Ecuador, Panama, and Venezuela.
- La Plata – the territories of present-day Argentina, Paraguay, Uruguay, and Bolivia.
- Peru – present-day Chile and Peru.

Spanish America also included Cuba and the eastern part of San Domingo, and this colonial empire occupied an area of more than ten million square kilometers.

The consolidation of the institutional system in the Spanish colonies took place in stages, from the late fifteenth century until the 1770s. In the early "Caribbean phase" of the Spanish conquests, colonial policy in the West Indies was carried out by a subcommittee of the Castille Council, to which individual governors of the islands were subordinated. After the conquest of Mexico, in 1524, a special Council for the West Indies was established. In the colonies themselves the main administrative-territorial unit was a province governed by a governor. A governor was usually one of the conquistadors. Later, when the territory was fully annexed to the crown, one of the officials of the royal court became governor. By the end of the sixteenth century, the process of conquest had ended, and the period of colonization begun.

Spanish and Portuguese colonists began developing the territory with small maritime trade settlements and mining camps. Gradually, however, urban networks emerged in the empires, which became the drivers of further colonization process. In the 1680s, there were already 250 urban centers in the colonies. Urban networks grew from north to south, from Central America, Venezuela, and Colombia to Peru, Ecuador, Bolivia, and on to La Plata (Barton 1997: 41–42).

In the process of colonization, the relative importance of certain regions of Latin America has been changing. Thus, in the early stage of colonization, the Andean mines were the most important and expensive for the Spanish crown (the silver mines of Potosí became a symbol of New World wealth, and in 1600, Potosí was the most populous city in Latin America). Later, in the eighteenth century, Lima became the most important center, a powerful trading port for exporting goods to Spain. Then, after the depletion of the mines, Venezuela and the territories of the La Plata basin as centers of agricultural production became key.

In the second half of the sixteenth century, the Spanish state began to attempt to "rearrange" the Indian world to achieve greater control over it. Many Indian territories suffered from depopulation; the Indian population lived in tiny settlements, far apart from each other and also exhausted by hunger and diseases. The Spanish administration started to relocate the Indians, concentrating them in cities and large Spanish rural settlements. The first resettlements emerged in Peru, and there was an economic reason for that; gold and silver deposits had been discovered in Peru, and their exploitation required a steady inflow of labor (Williamson 1992: 90).

Importantly, Spanish colonization was fundamentally different from the British colonization of North America. In North America, the colonists, having established the first 13 colonies on its east coast, slowly and gradually moved into the interior of the continent, building a new nation and new state institutions. The Spanish, on the contrary, very quickly and forcibly destroyed previous civilizations and seized vast spaces for the Spanish crown. However, it proved to be much easier to conquer territories than to systematically colonize (organize) them. Spanish imperial rule – centralized and hierarchical – proved highly ineffective, although it was the common colonial experience that later contributed to the emergence of a common identity in the region (Grafe and Irigoin 2008).

The main problem of Spanish rule was that the crown sought direct control over parts of the colonial empire, but local rulers had to make decisions without waiting for the reaction of the crown (maritime communication between the colonies and the metropolis took months). The problem was to be solved by the viceroys of the crown, who issued laws, collected taxes, spread Christianity, and commanded the Spanish troops. The Spanish administration, inefficient in structure, was corrupt from the beginning: every position had a price. Even taking into account that standards of political behavior in the seventeenth and eighteenth centuries are difficult to assess from a twenty-first-century perspective, it can nevertheless be argued that corruption was universal and, in most cases, went unpunished. High-ranking officials were not happy with those below them:

> [V]iceroys and royal inspectors frequently charged colonial officials were too stupid, lazy, and unexperienced to carry out their duties efficiently.
>
> (Andrien 1984: 1)

The Catholic Church played an extremely important role – its representatives not only registered births and deaths but also built and managed schools, hospitals, and had its own court system. Gradually, the state started to perceive the Church as a threat and powerful competitor; the schism between them lasted long after the end of the period of Spanish rule and took particularly acute forms in Mexico, Central America, Colombia, and Ecuador (Magstadt 2002: 379).

In addition to religion, the instrument of Spanish imperial rule was severe mercantilism – the siphoning of natural resources (above all gold and silver) from the colonies. Spain not only did not contribute to the economic development of the colonies but imposed severe restrictions on their trade. Only two Spanish ports – Seville and Cadiz – were allowed to receive colonial goods, and all imports into the colonies went through New Spain (Mexico) or Peru. Trade between the colonies was also tightly controlled.

It is remarkable that one of the important political instruments during the colonization period was the map, or rather maps of the new territories, claiming to "correctly" reflect the world built by the conquistadors. Maps were meant to legitimize brutal conquest and brutal colonization, expressing the spirit of Spain's "discovery" and "civilizing missions."

Let's add that geographic factors in the colonization period were fundamentally changing societies. As Angeles and Elizande wrote,

> [S]uffering the consequences of a new disease environment, the aboriginal population of the Americas (Amerindians) was decimated over the hundred years following first contact with Europeans. In its place, a society of "whites" (European descendants), mestizos (people with mixed Amerindian and European ancestry), Amerindians and Africans, these last ones brought to the continent as slave labor, took over. Amerindians have always occupied the lower ranks of the new social hierarchy established with the colonial conquest, while European descendants, and later mestizos, have dominated political and economic affairs ever since.
>
> (Angeles and Elizalde 2017: 26)

Decolonization

The preconditions for the decolonization of Latin America were created by events in Europe. Napoleon's conquest of Spain undermined the power of the proconsuls in the colonies. In Latin America independence movement had much to do with the chaos that prevailed in the colonies after Spain's defeat in Europe (in Brazil, the situation was quite different, it was a relatively peaceful transition to an independent existence). Another factor influencing the rise of the anti-colonial movement was the example of the Northern neighbor – the formation of the United States of America. Simon Bolivar (The Liberator), the most famous fighter for independence, rebelled against the Spanish crown in 1811. In 1813, he captured Caracas, the capital of Venezuela. After Napoleon's defeat in Europe, however, Spanish troops were sent to Latin America, and the revolt (as well as several earlier ones) was crushed. But the war was not only between the colonies and the metropolis, but the colonies also fought each other in civil wars – there was a struggle between local royalists and supporters of independence.

Spain and Portugal lost their colonies in a relatively short period – during 1810–1825. (except for Cuba and Puerto Rico, which Spain lost later). The first documents adopted by the newly independent states were the constitutions of Venezuela (1811), the Union of the Peoples of Colombia (1819), and Argentina (1819). The large viceroydoms were divided into several independent states (United States of Mexico, Peru, Great Colombia, Argentine Confederation, Uruguay, etc.), politically and economically unstable, plagued by internal conflicts and claims against each other. It turned out that the departure of the metropolis was not accompanied by a solution to the problems that arose during its rule: the first decades after independence were marked by violent battles between the caudillos (local/regional rulers). The civil war was particularly brutal in Argentina, Mexico, Colombia, and Venezuela.

The caudillos, unlike Bolivar, were not charismatic leaders, they were usually very pragmatic military men who were not interested in ideas and ideals but rather in resources and power. Constitutions were adopted to legitimize the seizure of power (e.g., in 1811, Venezuela was the first to adopt a constitution and has had at least 20 more since). So historically the law was subordinate to order, and order was established by the military, not civilian leadership. The important role of the military in domestic affairs, even under civilian rule, became a hallmark of Latin American political regimes.

Another distinctive feature of Latin American politics is localism, that is, a strong attachment to a "small motherland," a particular geographic area. Militarism and localism were deeply rooted in the political culture of Latin American states and even in their geography, which isolated certain regions/places and made communication difficult (e.g., the Andes are rarely crossed even today, the tropical forests also impede communication in South and Central America). Geographic isolation fed tendencies toward local particularism and hindered the political integration of states – so geography explains to some extent why civil wars and guerrilla wars have been so frequent in Latin American history.

The political map of Latin America continued to change. After gaining independence, states struggled to achieve territorial consolidation and also engaged in internecine wars, seeking to expand territory and seize lands rich in natural resources. For example, in the territory of modern Argentina, for ten years two state formations have existed – the Confederation of Provinces and the Province of Buenos Aires. The regions and the capital could not agree on the degree of political autonomy of the provinces within a single state. The crisis was not resolved until 1862. Paraguay confronted an alliance of Argentina, Brazil, and Uruguay, resulting in Paraguay's near-total destruction. In 1879, the so-called Saltpeter War began (which lasted until 1883), which Chile fought against Peru and Bolivia and won. As a result, Bolivia lost its access to the sea.

Some of the large states formed during decolonization later broke up: the Great Colombia was divided into Colombia, Ecuador, and Venezuela (the state proved extremely unstable due to competing regional and local interests); the United Provinces of Central America broke up into five independent states. Provinces, states, federations, and confederations became the building blocks of postcolonial reorganization, but it proved extremely difficult to establish stable administrative-territorial units that would meet the interests of regional elite groups.

Unlike the Spanish colonies, the decolonization of Brazil was peaceful due to the peculiarities of the political process both in the metropolis itself and in Western Europe as a whole; being geographically extremely remote, they nevertheless determined the fate of the colony. In 1807, King Juan VI of Portugal, fleeing from Napoleon, moved his court to Rio de Janeiro. When, after Napoleon's defeat, the king returned to Lisbon, he gave power over Brazil to his son Pedro, who in 1822 proclaimed an independent empire and himself emperor. In 1889, the monarchy in Brazil was abolished, and the country became a federal republic.

The "departure" of the former metropolises, Spain and Portugal, from Latin America was accompanied by a growing US role in the region. In 1836, the Americans forced Mexico to abandon Texas, and as a result of the American-Mexican War of 1846–1848, Mexico lost the entire Southwest – the territories of California, Nevada, Utah, and most of New Mexico and Arizona. The United States took over the Spanish possessions of Puerto Rico and Cuba, and in 1898, it annexed a group of Hawaiian Islands, which had been an independent native state in the past. This accession allowed the United States to occupy an extremely important position in the central Pacific.

Geopolitically interesting was the case of Panama, which remained part of Colombia after decolonization. The United States, realizing the strategic importance of Panama's geographic location (the Central American isthmus), supported the independence movement. In 1903, the country obtained independence, and 15 (!!!) days later a treaty was signed with the United States, which gave them "in perpetuity" a part of Panama for the construction of an inter-oceanic canal and its subsequent operation. The canal, cutting the country into two parts, began operation (during its construction so much money was stolen that the word "Panama" has become synonymous with a grand fraud) in 1914, and the communication through it was officially opened in 1920. Till now, the canal is the "supporting pillar" of the country's budget: its maintenance provides about a third of Panama's GDP.

Importantly, the break with Spain and Portugal did not bring with it any immediate changes in the existing social and economic structures. Political and economic institutions in Latin American countries were redefined through a lengthy and painful process, and disorder after independence increased transaction costs. Trade became critical. Release from the colonial trade burden produced net gains for the economies of Latin America. As De La Escosura (2007: 502) argued, "trade did not have the strength to pull the rest of the economy, but whenever geographic and institutional barriers did not impede it, trade represented a handmaiden of growth." At the same time, the opening of the Latin American countries to the international economy was associated with a deepening of income inequalities within and across nations. This was a trend that Latin America has never been able to overcome.

Changing "geographical institutions": border conflicts and territorial disputes

After the independence, "New World strongmen exploited the vacuum and seized the power . . . anarchic negativism invited macho warlordism" (Landes 1998: 313). In the words of De La Escosura, the consequences of independence were "the fragmentation of political power, the militarization of society, and the mobilization of resources and men for war. Political turmoil did not end with independence. Disputes over national borders and civil wars continued for decades" (De La Escosura 2006: 464).

To avoid territorial disputes and conflicts between Latin American states, as early as 1819 at the Angostura Congress Simon Bolivar, President of the Congress, announced that the new states would be constitutionalized within the borders corresponding to the colonial administrative-territorial division of 1810. However, this solution did not work. For instance, the territorial conflict between Paraguay and the combined forces of Brazil, Argentina, and Uruguay lasted from 1864 to 1870 and is considered the bloodiest in Latin American history (Paterson and Flynn 2023).

Access to the sea is an important factor for the political and economic development of a country. Bolivia and Paraguay, the two "locked in" states of the Latin American continent, demonstrate how important access to the sea is for stimulating economic activity; the lack of access to the sea is one of the explanations of low socioeconomic indicators in these countries (per capita income, poverty rate etc.). Bolivia has long struggled to gain direct access to the ocean with Chile and Peru, but so far it has no sovereign rights to territorial access to the ocean. (Common misfortune of having no access to the sea is, of course, not a guarantee against bilateral conflicts. For example, in 1928, there was a military conflict between Bolivia and Paraguay over the oil-rich Chaco region. In 1935, Paraguay won the war, severely damaging its economy).

In the southern cone of the continent, tense diplomatic relations between Chile and Argentina are related to long-standing conflicts over borders along the Andes and in southern Patagonia. In 1979, the two states, then controlled by military regimes, almost began hostilities, and only the intervention of the Pope as mediator in the conflict defused the situation.

The border between Peru and Ecuador was a constant hotbed of conflict. The beginning of the conflict dates to the early- to mid-nineteenth century, the period of decolonization. In 1842, Ecuador claimed two Peruvian border territories. In response to Ecuador's claims, the Peruvian government asserted its own claims, and Ecuador meanwhile asserted claims for a new delimitation of the border with Colombia. Ecuador and Colombia are currently in conflict over the Oriente region (in the Amazon), an underdeveloped area sparsely populated by Amerindian tribes and very poorly connected to other regions. For both states, its value lies in its significant resource potential, especially oil reserves (Barton 1997: 68–79).

There are also many so-called dormant conflicts on the continent, which, under the influence of the exploration of new resource deposits, migration flows, and simply nationalist rhetoric, could turn from latent to active. Territorial and border conflicts in Latin America have relatively rarely led to armed clashes, but their very existence is an important factor in the development of relations between the states of the continent, even despite the involvement of states in economic integration processes.

In the following, I look at certain cases to show specific examples of how geography influences national development, either through institutions or directly.

Mexico–US: the benefits and the burdens of neighborhood

Mexico is a large federal republic with 31 states and a federal district (Mexico City, the capital). Mexico is one of the most developed states in the region. The state has an exceptional geopolitical position, located between two oceans and two continents – North and South America. Oil and natural gas are Mexico's greatest natural assets. The discovery of large oil fields in the states of Chiapas and Tabasco and the offshore area in the Gulf of Campeche in the 1970s made Mexico one of the leading oil reserves and production countries in the world. A characteristic feature of Mexico's urbanization, like that of many other Latin American countries, is the hypertrophied development of the national capital, Mexico City, at the expense of peripheries.

Mexico is the largest trading partner of the United States and enjoys all the benefits of a special relationship with it. *No country with such a large population has such a long border with such a rich neighbor!* Mexico is strongly connected to the United States through geography, commerce, and family ties. The factor of geographical neighborhood with the United States determines a lot for Mexico's development.

The Mexican constitution of 1824 was influenced by the US constitution of 1787, especially regarding federalism. It is not that Mexican politicians believed in the philosophy of the US system; rather, they simply saw in their neighborhood an example of a system that worked (Smith 1962) and that was able to create capable central institutions without infringing on regional autonomy. However, the "good" institutions were not embedded in the national context (including geographical conditions) and therefore could not be effective enough for development purposes. In the 1920s, the central Mexican government waged an intense struggle against the most powerful and independent regional rulers, the caudillos, attracting members of local political clans, the caciques, to its side. The caciques were in effect viceroys of the central government, supporting its political decisions. By the end of this period, some caudillos had been killed while others surrendered to the central government.

The country's political and geographic heterogeneity repeatedly contributed to political instability in Mexico (e.g., there were repeated rebellions against the central government in the south and north of the country). In the mid-1990s, the government twice sent troops into the southeastern state of Chiapas to fight insurgents; in 1996, a guerrilla uprising began in the Pacific state of Guerrero.

An extremely important task for Mexico is the completion of the process of national consolidation, that is, the integration of different parts of the country. Integration is complicated by economic, ethnic, and regional disparities. The latter are related to the presence of five regions on the territory of Mexico, which have the strongest differences in terms of socioeconomic development. These are Metromex – the capital and its surroundings (Mexico City yields more than one-third of Mexico's GNP); New Spain – the old colonial Heartland; Mexamerica – a dynamic region in the north, along the border with the United States; Southern Mexico – an underdeveloped poor region located between the capital and the border with Guatemala; and Club Mex – wealthy coastal resort regions (Magstadt 2002: 434).

Today, thanks to its neighborhood with the United States, Mexico can take advantage of globalization: the attributes of the new globalized economy are entering Mexico almost simultaneously with the developed countries. The interchange between Mexico and the United States is reinforced by the implementation of the United States–Mexico–Canada Agreement, which is fed by enormous US investment. The country has potential for becoming a more important player in the international arena (if it can effectively address its many problems). And the country's problems are very serious social polarization, an inefficient budget system, and the drug trade.

At the same time, Mexico has caused many problems for its northern neighbor, as what happens in Mexico directly affects the security and prosperity of the United States. 1.5 million US citizens live in Mexico. The most dangerous activities in Mexico relate to illegal drugs – ranging from the movement of cocaine to the production of opioids and synthetics to the distribution of fentanyl. At the same time, Mexicans are victimized by weapons illegally smuggled into the country from the United States. The United States depends substantially on the efforts by and cooperation with the Mexican military and law enforcement to help combat narcotraffickers and organized crime.

Mexico's cooperation has further been instrumental in helping the United States manage the challenge of immigrants seeking to enter the United States. In the context of global challenges from terrorism to pandemics, Mexico's cooperation and the quality of Mexico's governance are fundamental to US security. In addition, as Ellis (2020) argued, "as China increasingly poses a geopolitical challenge to the United States in Latin America and elsewhere throughout the globe, having a friendly, stable Mexico next door is a strategic necessity."

Interestingly, despite Mexico's obvious structural problems, there are predictions for a great future for Mexico in the second half of the twenty-first century. George Friedman argued that as the European countries withdraw from the world stage (!), Mexico will strengthen its position and become one of the world's leading economic powers at the end of the century. At the same time, the confrontation between Mexico and the United States will be the culmination of the twenty-first century (Friedman 2009).

Colombia: the problems of territorial control

Another problem that hinders national development and relates to geography is state's control over territory. In Colombia, the central government has de facto given control of several territories to the guerrillas. In fact, the authorities control the situation in Bogotá and the big cities while the rest of the country is divided into zones of influence between the ultra-left forces – the Revolutionary Armed Forces of Colombia and the National Liberation Army – and far-right groups – The United Self-Defense Forces of Colombia.

Columbia, on the one hand, has a history of democratic government, but on the other, it has a tradition of extreme violence and civil wars. The latter is due to the extreme territorial heterogeneity of the country. Different cultures in different parts of the country produced different societies: the uplands, inhabited mainly by the descendants of European settlers; the coastal valleys, inhabited mainly by the descendants of slaves brought into the country in the nineteenth century; and the forest areas, where the culture of Indian tribes is preserved. Civil wars are closely connected to the production of drugs (most of which enter the United States and are consumed there). Drug traffickers subsidize the guerrillas, who in exchange for weapons provide security for drug production. All this makes Colombia not only unsafe for its own population but also makes it a dangerous foreign policy problem.

Peruvian central government is also unable to secure sovereignty over certain territories. In Peru, the Maoist guerrilla movement, the *Shining Path* (Sendero Luminoso) terrorized the country in the 1980s and early 1990s. Like Bolivia, Peru's territory is extremely fragmented; few countries are in 28 climate zones! In the most general division, the territory of the country includes the following zones: costa (coast and coastal plains), sierra (Andean ranges), and selva (Amazon jungle). The coastal area of Peru (11% of the total area of the country, where about 50% of the population lives) is one of the driest areas on the planet. The exceptional diversity of geographic conditions, combined with enormous interregional disparities, makes Peru an intriguing case to study the nature of the relationship between geographic factors and economic growth.

Let me emphasize again that the weakness of the central government and its inability to secure sovereignty over certain territories of the country have resulted in permanent legitimacy crises. And such crises practically rule out the plans to accelerate development.

Argentina: the geopolitics of the Falkland Islands/Malvinas

For most of its history, Argentina has not been oriented toward its neighbors but toward Europe, maintaining close ties with it and welcoming many immigrants. But in the words of Henry Kissinger, sophisticated elite has been unable to prevent odious governments from ruining the country's beautiful prospects (Kissinger 2001).

The Falkland Islands (Malvinas) was a disputed territory between Argentina and Great Britain. The islands came under Argentine control in the 1920s. In 1833, they were captured by a British landing and became a British colony in 1892.

In terms of natural resources, the islands are characterized by poor soil, they are suitable only for sheep and fish farming. They are sparsely populated. Thus, the chronic conflict over the islands between Britain and Argentina was not a conflict over resources, its cause was the important geopolitical location of the islands in relation to the South Atlantic, Antarctica, and the connection of the Atlantic and Pacific Oceans through the Strait of Magellan. The Strait, the "Gibraltar of the South Atlantic," was considered during the heyday of the British Empire to be the "key" to the Pacific Ocean, and islands lying so close naturally attracted increased British attention.

The question of ownership of the islands was considered at several sessions of the UN General Assembly, which urged the two governments to solve the problem through negotiations. However, negotiations were unsuccessful, and in 1982 Argentina landed troops on the islands. Great Britain responded with military action and defeated the Argentine forces. The islands came under British rule, governed by a governor appointed by the British Queen. However, the position of the Argentine leadership remains unchanged: the islands are original Argentine territory and belong to Argentina. (The famous Argentine writer and philosopher Jorge Luis Borges wittily called the Falkland War between Britain and Argentina "a fight between two bald men over a comb").

Brazil: the giant of Latin America

Of contemporary Latin American states, only Brazil, the fifth largest country in the world in terms of both territory (8.5 million square kilometers) and population (217.6 million people in 2024), is considered a "giant" country. Indeed, the country is comparable in size to an entire continent. When Brazilians want to emphasize the length of their country, they say "from Chui to Oyapoka" (as Americans would say "from Alaska to Florida," and Russians – "from Kaliningrad to Vladivostok"). The Chui Stream on the border with Uruguay is the extreme south; the Oyapoka River on the border with French Guiana is almost the extreme north (although, in fact, the extreme northern point of Brazil is Mount Monte Caburai on the border with Guyana).

Brazil is home to about one-third of the population of Latin America and produces about 40% of its GNP. The country has a developed industrial economy. Brazil has no major religious conflicts, and the last armed confrontation between the center and the region dates to 1932, when the rich state of Sao Paulo refused to submit to the central government.

At the same time, Brazil is typical example of a "giant" suffering from the problems of geographic inequalities and asymmetries and imbalances in economic development. These domestic problems are to blame for the fact that Brazil's comparative advantages – its large domestic market, abundance of natural resources, and young population – remain mere potency, and fail to move Brazil from a regional power to a global power (Busygina 2017).

Brazil remains a country of contrasts, including geographic. The modern cities and rural areas of the southern and central regions of the country are comparable to those of southern Europe, but the entire northeast remains poor and underdeveloped. Thus, on the scale of social and interregional disparities, Brazil belongs to the most unevenly developed countries in a region already known for its uneven development (Magstadt 2002: 438). Journalists have figuratively called Brazil "Belinda" (from Belgium–India), referring to the fact that the megalopolises on the coast are already close to developed Belgium while the interior of the country is closer to developing India.

Nearly half of the population inhabit only 7% of the country, a narrow strip of Atlantic coastline. Up until the second half of the nineteenth century, Brazilians did not seek to develop inland territories as settlers in North America did; they clung to the narrow coast as if trying to maintain contact with the Old World. Perhaps, this was because before independence Brazil was not so much a colony as the largest part of the unified Portuguese kingdom. It was in 1960 that President Kubitschek initiated an ambitious territorial project to build a new capital, the city of Brasilia, in the interior of the country, on "empty space." Moving the capital from Rio de Janeiro to Brasilia was one of the initiatives aimed at developing and settling the country's interior. However, this did not happen.

The number of millionaire cities reaches 15, the two largest agglomerations continue to grow – Sao Paulo (about 20 million residents) and Rio de Janeiro (about 14 million). A specific feature of Brazil is the extremely widespread proliferation of unauthorized slum settlements on the outskirts of the city – favelas; in the state of São Paulo alone more than three million people live in favelas.

The equatorial forest plains of the Amazon, the Amazonian jungle, can safely be called a miracle, and this wonder belongs to Brazil. Amazon forests are called "green hell" – and "the lungs of the planet." Lungs – for the whole planet, hell – for travelers. There are over 4,000 species of trees in the Amazon (every fourth tree in the world grows in the Amazon area), a realm of bloodthirsty insects, poisonous snakes, predatory fish (piranhas!), and debilitating diseases. The area of the Amazon forests decreases every year. Forests are burned for plantations or cattle factories ("turning the jungle into a pampa"). The most valuable timber from deforestation is exported, while less valuable timber is used for mass production of pulp and paper.

The first settlement of Portuguese colonists appeared on the Brazilian coast in 1530, but for more than 100 years (until 1654), the territory of Brazil was also claimed by the Dutch, with whom the Portuguese colonists had constant conflicts. The Portuguese crown's interest in Brazil was more than obvious: gold was discovered in 1695 and diamonds in 1729.

When Napoleon conquered Portugal in 1807, the royal family found refuge in Brazil. Under the direct rule of the Portuguese monarch, Rio de Janeiro became the capital of the Portuguese empire, and colonial culture flourished – schools, libraries, theaters, newspapers, and banks were opened. (Note that the church in Brazil was poor and, unlike in the Spanish colonies, had little political influence.) In 1821, the king returned to Portugal, but his son, Prince Pedro, stayed in Brazil and in 1822, with a cry of "Independence or death!" proclaimed himself emperor. The decolonization of Brazil was bloodless and relatively painless, but it is noteworthy that traces of colonization persist at the micro level, including in the geography of political culture. Thus, in places where large sugarcane plantations were prevalent, where communities consisted of a small rich elite and disenfranchised slave, localism prevailed, a desire to distance oneself from the colonizers. In contrast, in places where the mines dominated, communities were composed mainly of free, poor whites. In these places, the empire tightly controlled all aspects of community life (Naritomi, Soares and Assunção 2009).

In 1889, the monarchy became a republic, and the US constitution was adopted as a model. The first years were characterized by sharp conflicts for power between the rulers of the different states. Under the slogan "order and progress" (this motto is still reproduced on the Brazilian flag), the military factions wanted to replace the empire with a strong centralized state, but by 1891 the civil elites of the largest and most economically powerful states managed to gain control of the new state. They favored a decentralized federation. The constitution gave the states even more political autonomy than the US states had (it was the American experience that inspired the Brazilian creators of the basic law). The "Old Republic," as it was called, was dominated by the regional oligarchs of the strongest states – São Paulo and Minas Gerais. The political regime of the "Old Republic" fell after the revolution of 1930 (interregional conflicts were one of the factors of its internal instability), the regime of the new president Vargas, the "New State," envisaged a greater role for the central government.

Thus, after decolonization, Brazil has emerged as conglomerate of territories by "coming together" model. Stepan has called Brazil the most "demos constraining" federation in the world (Stepan 2004), where the state governors play central role in political process and control the access to resources and key positions, and the senators are not national politicians but rather ambassadors of their states. Even during the years of military dictatorship, the center had to make compromise with the states looking for their political support (Samuels and Abrucio 2000). Federalism – how it is exercised in Brazil – is the main explanation for the crises of governability in the country. Besides that, there exists a serious problem of overrepresentation: the "weight" of one vote for a senator in the state of Roraima is 144 more than of one vote in the state of Sao Paolo. The region's political priorities principally differ – weaker regions prefer to have stronger and patronizing national center, while strong ones support more autonomy and decentralization.

Conclusion

Historians studying economies and political institutions in Latin America generally agree that the income gap between Latin America and Anglo-Saxon America was not a product of the twentieth century and that Latin American underdevelopment observed today arose during the colonial era and in the aftermath of independence. As Victor Bulmer-Thomas noted, "the economic development of Latin America since independence is a story of unfulfilled promise." He stressed that "the gap between living standards in Latin America and those in the developed countries has steadily widened since the early nineteenth century" (Bulmer-Thomas 2003: 392). Independence has brought to Latin America fragmentation of political power and militarization of societies and economies. Disputes over national borders and civil wars continued for decades. Geographic fragmentation, huge distance to world markets, and expressed inequalities were (and are) serious problems and challenges to breakthroughs in development.

Still there is no need to fall into a fatalist trap; Latin America is well-known for its ups and downs in the speed of development. Modernization of institutions and their adaptation to the region's difficult geography would be the means to speed up development. Difficult, expensive, time-consuming, and generally not favorable to incumbent politicians, it's nonetheless necessary.

Notes

1 "Poorest Countries in South America 2024." World Population Review. Accessed May 9, 2024. https://worldpopulationreview.com/country-rankings/poorest-countries-in-south-america[^1].
2 "Support for Democracy Is Waning across the Americas." The Conversation. Accessed May 9, 2024. https://theconversation.com/support-for-democracy-is-waning-across-the-americas-174992[^5].
3 "Missed Opportunities: The Economic History of Latin America." IMF. Accessed May 9, 2024. https://www.imf.org/en/News/Articles/2017/10/05/NA100517-Missed-Opportunities-The-Economic-History-of-Latin-America[^8].
4 "Modern-Day Maya." National Geographic. Accessed May 9, 2024. https://media.nationalgeographic.org/assets/reference/assets/modern-day-maya-4.pdf[^9].

References

Andrien, Kenneth. (1984). "Corruption, Inefficiency, and Imperial Decline in the Seventeenth-Century Viceroyalty of Peru." *The Americas*, 41(1): 1–20.
Angeles, Luis, and Aldo Elizalde. (2017). "Pre-Colonial Institutions and Socioeconomic Development: The Case of Latin America." *Journal of Development Economics*, 124: 22–40.
Armendáriz, Beatriz, and Felipe Larraín. (2017). *The Economics of Contemporary Latin America*. Cambridge, MA: The MIT Press.
Aroca, Patricio, and Miguel Atienza. (2016). "Spatial Concentration in Latin America and the Role of Institutions." *Journal of Regional Research*, 36: 233–253.
Barton, Jonathan. (1997). *A Political Geography of Latin America*. London; New York: Routledge.
Bronner, Fred. (1996). "Portugal and Columbus: Old Drives in New Discoveries." *Mediterranean Studies*, 6: 51–66.
Bulmer-Thomas, Victor. (2003). *The Economic History of Latin America since Independence*, 2nd ed. Cambridge: Cambridge University Press.
Busygina, Irina. (2017). "Rising Powers in the Contemporary World: Sources of Sustainability." In *Vocabularies of International Relations after the Crisis in Ukraine*, ed. by Andrey Makarychev and Alexandra Yatsyk. London: Routledge.
De La Escosura, Leandro Prados. (2006). "The Economic Consequences of Independence in Latin America." In *The Cambridge Economic History of Latin America*, ed. by Victor Bulmer-Thomas, John H. Coatsworth, and Roberto Cortés Conde, pp. 463–504. Cambridge: Cambridge University Press.
De La Escosura, Leandro Prados. (2007). "When Did Latin America Fall Behind?" In *The Decline of Latin American Economies: Growth, Institutions, and Crises*, ed. by Sebastian Edwards, Gerardo Esquivel, and Graciela Márquez. Chicago: University of Chicago Press.
Ellis, Evan. (2020). "Neighbor at Risk: Mexico's Deepening Crisis." CSIS, Accessed September4,2020.https://www.csis.org/analysis/neighbor-risk-mexicos-deepening-crisis.
Friedman, George. (2009). *The Next 100 Years: A Forecast for the 21st Century*. New York: Doubleday.
Gallup, John, Alejandro Gaviria, and Eduardo Lora. (2003). *Is Geography Destiny? Lessons from Latin America*. Stanford: Stanford University Press.
Grafe, Regina, and Alejandra Irigoin. (2008). A Stakeholder Empire: The Political Economy of Spanish Imperial Rule In America. LSE Working Papers No. 111/08, London School of Economics.
Hennessy, Alistair. (1993). "The Nature of the Conquest and Conquistadors." *Proceedings of the British Academy*, 81: 6.

Kissinger, Henry. (2001). *Does America Need a Foreign Policy?* New York: Simon & Schuster.

Landes, David S. (1998). *The Wealth and Poverty of Nations: Why Some Are So Rich and Some So Poor*. New York: W. W. Norton.

Magstadt, Thomas. (2002). *Nations and Governments: Comparative Politics in Regional Perspective*. Boston; New York: Bedford/St. Martin's.

Naritomi, Joana, Rodrigo Reis Soares, and Juliano J. Assunção. (2009). "Institutional Development and Colonial Heritage within Brazil." IZA Discussion Papers No. 4276, Institute for the Study of Labor (IZA), Bonn.

Paterson, Pat, and Rory Flynn. (2023). "Border Disputes in Latin America." *Regional Insights*, 2.

Rinke, Stefan. (2023). *Conquistadors and Aztecs: A History of the Fall of Tenochtitlan*. Oxford: Oxford University Press.

Samuels, David, and Fernando Luiz Abrucio. (2000). "Federalism and Democratic Transitions: The 'New' Politics of the Governors in Brazil." *Publius: The Journal of Federalism*, 30(2): 43–61.

Scartascini, Carlos, Ernesto Stein, and Mariano Tommasi. (2010). *How Democracy Works: Political Institutions, Actors, and Arenas in Latin American Policymaking*. Cambridge, MA: Harvard University, David Rockefeller Center for Latin American Studies.

Smith, Watson. (1962). "Influences from the United States on the Mexican Constitution of 1824." *Arizona and the West*, 4(2): 113–126.

Spengler, Oswald. (1926). *The Decline of the West*. Translated by Charles Francis Atkinson. New York: Alfred A. Knopf.

Stepan, Alfred. (2004). "Toward a New Comparative Politics of Federalism, Multinationalism, and Democracy: Beyond Rikerian Federalism." In *Federalism and Democracy in Latin America*, ed. by Edward L. Gibson, pp. 46–49. Baltimore: Johns Hopkins University Press.

Williamson, Edwin. (1992). *The Penguin History of Latin America*. London: The Penguin Press.

8 North America

America, or the New World, consists of two continents, North America and South America (therefore it is sometimes referred to as the Americas in the plural). North America includes the United States, Canada, and the Atlantic Ocean islands of Bermuda, Saint-Pierre-et-Miquelon, and Greenland, the largest island on the globe.

Unlike other continents, there are only two countries in North America. But what nations they are! As for 2023, the United States with the population of 341.8 million people (the third place among the countries of the world after China and India) had the largest economy in the world by GDP (26.95 trillion) and one of the highest GDP per capita ($78.843). Canada with the population of 39.1 million, had 2.12 Tn GDP and the GDP per capita $54.2. Together these countries make 27.86% of the world GDP.[1] Accessing political rights and civil liberties in 210 countries, Freedom House scores Canada 98 and the US 83 (out of 100).[2] These are both "giant countries": Canadian territorial size is the second largest in the world (after Russia), and the United States occupies the fourth place.

What strategic advantages for development did these countries have? What was the role of geography and institutions? It is important to emphasize that while both neighboring countries have successfully met the challenges of development, they have made both similar and very different choices embedded in their different geographies.

The United States is a country of one nation. But it has 52 states. More specifically, the territory of the United States consists of the territories of the 48 contiguous states ("the United States proper") located in the middle part of the North American continent and bordering Canada and Mexico, as well as the states of Alaska and Hawaii. Alaska is located on the northeastern edge of North America and the adjacent islands (Alaska became a state in 1958). The Hawaiian Islands (24 islands) in the central Pacific were annexed to the United States in 1898, declared a "United States territory" in 1904, and in 1959 designated the fiftieth state.

The United States is a federal republic consisting of 50 states; the US constitution went into effect in 1789. Interestingly, the capital, the federal District of Columbia, is an independent territorial unit and was separated from Maryland in 1791 specifically as location for the future capital, Washington, DC. The District of Columbia is under the jurisdiction of the US Congress, and its residents do not vote in elections to that body.

DOI: 10.4324/9781003496731-11

The area of Canada is considerably larger than that of continental United States, and the countries look somewhat alike on the map – if no transportation routes or cities and towns are marked on it. If these are shown, they indicate that the level of connectivity is much higher in the US constitution in comparison to Canada, and distribution of population in two countries is also very different. Canada, the northern neighbor of the United States, is a member of the Commonwealth, led by Great Britain, so that nominally the head of Canada is the King of Great Britain, represented "provisionally" by the governor-general. Canada consists of ten provinces and three territories – the Northwest, Yukon, and Nunavut.

Both the United States and Canada have "grown" from European colonies. Both countries went through similar stages of socioeconomic development – immigration and the construction of railroads to achieve connectivity of territories, the development of vast tracts of land in the steppes and prairies, the colonization of the Mountain West, and accelerated industrialization. However, the pace of economic and political development has not been the same. The continental United States being located farther south than Canada was more attractive to settlers from Europe. Having separated from the metropolis, the United States devoted the energy of the nation to the creation of a new state, while Canada continued to develop mainly by importing British capital and under control of Britain.

Few countries in the world can boast such stunning natural conditions as the United States. In addition to the remarkable climate of its vast coastal areas (in some areas they can grow two crops a year), other regions of the United States (such as the Midwest) are endowed by nature with excellent conditions for agriculture – fat soils, flat terrain, and a humid climate. But these beautiful natural conditions mean nothing for development if there are no people to utilize them. And a large territory requires a lot of people. They could only be found abroad, so immigrants became the most important source of the country's development.

The United States has been called "the land of immigrants," with about 55 million people arriving since the first census in 1790. Until the 1920s, immigration was a major factor in population growth; since the beginning of colonization, the number of immigrants from England and other Western European countries and as well as the importation of slaves from Africa has grown steadily. Immigration reached its peak at the beginning of the twentieth century, when it grew at the rate of about one million people a year.

The driving forces in the process of national development were large cities: there are eight of them with a population of more than one million people (the largest US cities are New York, Los Angeles, and Chicago). However, if we count not cities, but urban agglomerations (i.e., areas of cities with suburbs and satellite cities), there are about 40 "millionaire" agglomerations in the United States, located both on the East Coast (New York, Washington, and Baltimore) and on the West Coast (Los Angeles, San Francisco). The urban agglomerations, in turn, combine to form urbanized areas (megalopolises); the largest (about 40 million people) stretches for nearly 1,000 kilometers along the East Coast, from Boston to Washington, DC (the so-called BosWash). Megalopolises are also emerging in the Lakes Region (from Milwaukee to Pittsburgh), in California (from San Francisco to San Diego), and in Florida.

Importantly, urban agglomerations are located on both ocean coasts, thus making the territorial structure of the country balanced (compare this with Russia with its relatively developed western part and structurally and economically weak Far East).

Very broadly, the idea of the American state was to create something new, better, and different from Europe. From below, this state should have been supported by the energy of the nation and its basic values – individual freedom; mobility and a propensity for change – "America is a process" (Zelinsky 1973: 40–41). Individualism was expressed in many forms, in particular, were the "the frontier spirit," the Protestant labor ethic brought by the first settlers to New England (ideas migrated with the people!), and the culture of success. The propensity for self-improvement, the persistent hope for a better future, is evident in the names Americans gave to their towns. On the map of Pennsylvania alone, we find Concord, East Freedom, Edenville, Effort, Enterprise, Freedom, Frugality, Harmony, Independence, Industry, Liberty, New Hope, New Jerusalem, Paradise, Philadelphia, Pleasant Unity, Progress, Prosperity, Unityville, and Zion.

Canada outnumbers the United States in territorial size, but mother-nature had not been so favorably disposed to her. Canada is a northern country, and much of it is Arctic and tundra areas. Canada is a one of the most sparsely populated countries in the world with an average population density of three people per square kilometer. Most of the population (about 90%) is concentrated in a narrow border region in the south of Canada, which is called the "Canadian province." Population distribution is very uneven, with the largest concentration of people in the two provinces of Ontario and Quebec, which together account for about 61% of the total population. Canada is a highly urbanized country, with about a third of its urban population living in the three largest metropolitan centers of Toronto, Montreal, and Vancouver.

The United States: the beginning

Imagine, such a huge country started from a dot on the map! The history of the English settlement of North America began on an April morning in 1607, when three ships under the command of Captain Christopher Newport docked off the coast of Chesapeake Bay. The birth of a new nation and the building of new institutions were not easy, but the favorable geography, which the Americans skillfully exploited, played a very significant role in facilitating and accelerating the colonization process.

The first permanent English settlement in America was the fort and settlement of Jamestown in Virginia, founded in 1607. The initial population growth was slow: by 1619 no more than 2,000 people lived in Virginia. It was a special year. *First*, a ship arrived from England carrying 90 "young girls," who became the wives of those colonists who could pay for their "delivery" of 120 pounds of tobacco. *Second*, the first ship carrying African slaves arrived. Finally, *third*, at Jamestown Church, where a few years earlier John Rolfe had made peace with the Indians by taking Pocahontas as his wife, a Legislative (representative) Assembly, consisting of a governor, six councilors, and two representatives from each of the ten planter colonists, met for the first time in the continent's history. Representative bodies were subsequently established in all the states. *The 13 colonies, territorially covering a narrow strip along the Atlantic Ocean, became the place where new political institutions were acquired, which were later extended to the entire vast territory of the gradually expanding country and "incorporated" into its geography.*

Look at the map: the ruggedness of the Atlantic coast, the many bays and inlets encouraged the emergence of several small colonies rather than one large one – 15 colonies, including Nova Scotia and Quebec, emerged rather quickly, and this predetermined the diversity of political institutions. Beyond the coastal plains rose the Appalachian Mountains, which were difficult to cross. So the coastal colonies took a long time to "gather strength" and build roads before penetrating the uncharted world beyond the mountains. Beyond them a gigantic, fertile plain with numerous waterways (the Mississippi-Missouri River System) was discovered, and settlers developed these territories at an enviable rate. Further west the climate became drier, the system of the Rocky Mountains making development difficult, so Americans came from the west, developing the Pacific coast: California was a populated state back when a wide unpopulated belt separated it and Oregon from the "older" parts of the country. But it did not remain unpopulated for long: ranchers went into the territories, the areas were covered by a network of roads, and the number of farms was growing rapidly. By the 1890s, the frontier had all but disappeared, as had the Wild West itself. It should be added that, fortunately for the colonists, the Indian tribes were too few to pose a serious obstacle to colonization. This is a dark page of the American history, indeed.

But that was later. First, the 13 colonies, territorially covering a long strip along the Atlantic Ocean, became the place where new political institutions were acquired, which were later extended to the entire vast territory of the country being gradually created.

The history of the founding of each of the first 13 colonies is special. In 1620, a community of English Calvinists, sailing from Plymouth on the famous "Mayflower," reached the Massachusetts coast and established their colony. In 1634, the colony of Maryland was founded and became the home of religious liberty. The famous Quaker William Penn is associated with the founding of Pennsylvania and the "city of brotherly love," Philadelphia. The history of the rich New York colony developed very differently: Dutch colonists were the first to come to the island of Manhattan and founded the colony of New Amsterdam. But the English could not allow the existence of an "alien" element in the heart of British America. In 1664, English warships laid siege to the colony, but the military confrontation was not lasting. Although old Peter Stuyvesant[3] declared that he would "rather be carried out dead" than forced to surrender, most Dutch did not mind the change of sovereignty, and the English flag was hoisted over the city, renamed New York (note that Dutch architecture is still intact, and Dutch families belonged to the elite and played an important role in the history of the state) (Klein 1972).

A great role as instruments of colonization was played by private interest – trading companies, which founded by many coastal cities and even states, as well as by the so-called proprietary grants, under which the British crown granted large tracts of land in the New World to members of the British aristocracy: Lord Baltimore received Maryland; William Penn, son of an admiral, received Pennsylvania; the favorites of the royal family received both Carolinas. These "recipients" had great power over the way the colonies were governed. William Penn, for example, convened an assembly as early as 1682, all whose members were elected by the colonists, and the assembly adopted the Pennsylvania constitution (the so-called Great Charter).

The first colonies were self-supporting societies with their own access to the sea, each of them becoming a separate, independent entity. Nevertheless, many problems transcended the individual colonies and required a joint resolution. The 13 colonies that later formed the United States were New Hampshire, Massachusetts, Rhode Island, Connecticut, New York, New Jersey, Pennsylvania, Delaware, Maryland, Virginia, North and South Carolina, and, founded last, Georgia.

Two major factors contributed to the emergence of a distinctive "American" people already during the colonial period – new people (a kind of amalgam of European nations) and a vast, rich, and almost unpopulated territory. Colonization was facilitated by the fact that the English language and English institutions were immediately established as dominant; neither the German or Swedish communities nor the French Huguenots founded separate colonies. This at once gave the new country a certain unity, although the commonality of language and basic institutions coexisted with a remarkable diversity among the colonists (Conway 2020).

The establishment of the colonies triggered "great waves" of migration from Europe to Massachusetts and Virginia. Boston became one of the most important seaports in the world, and Harvard College was founded. Among the migrants who came to the New World were the ancestors of Franklin, Adams, and Lincoln. The new settlers were no longer only farmers and merchants but also doctors, lawyers, and teachers. New England became a microcosm of "old" England.

The first settlers were inexperienced: some pilgrims expected to encounter numerous wild beasts; the dandies, on the other hand, believed that they could live in the New World just as they did in London. Gradually, however, the settlers adapted to the new conditions, gaining experience of their new environment, so that they looked less and less like their former neighbors left behind in England and even less like their children. Every settler came to America with a sense of hope and new freedom, and while initially they identified themselves primarily with England and the empire and only later with Virginians and New Yorkers, gradually the old system of identification eroded.

The colonies grew economically and culturally and gradually accumulated experience of self-government. The colonists saw the colonies more as self-governing communities with little connection to London. Initially, they lived under English law and order – with legislative assemblies, a system of representation, and customary guarantees of individual liberties. But lawmaking became increasingly adapted to American conditions, and conflicts between assemblies elected by the people and governors appointed by the king became more frequent. The colonists were even able to deprive the governors of their duties, for the latter generally received funds for their subsistence only from the assemblies.

Inventing political institutions

Importantly, political institutions were invented and tested initially on a small scale, first in the 13 colonies and then gradually spread over the territory of the vast country. At the same time, the colonies were located in a group (more precisely, a zone along the Atlantic coast, respectively, they had access to the ocean).

Already by the beginning of the eighteenth century, a system of quite sophisticated democratic-like institutions had developed in all the colonies (attempts to establish theocratic regimes in a number of states were an obstacle to the establishment of these institutions. The most famous example is that of Massachusetts, where the Puritans tried to introduce strict centralized control of the church over society. The rules imposed provided for compulsory church attendance and voting rights only for members of the church congregation. This regime was in effect in the state until 1691, when the new constitution made it a royal province). Rhode Island and Connecticut were fully self-governing communities (they were small republics within the British Empire), but the systems of institutions were similar. The governor was appointed either by the crown or by the owner of the colony, and the members of the governor's council were also appointed (if the governor was an Englishman, the council members were usually Americans). Initially, the council had administrative functions, but later it was increasingly transformed into the upper house of the state legislature (parliament). Each colony also had a representative body (the lower house of the legislature).

Three main features distinguished the political system of the American states:

(1) Written constitutions acted as guarantors of the states' liberties (note that England had no written constitution);
(2) The constant conflict of interest between appointed governors and elected members of the Legislature – in fact, it was a conflict between imperial interests and those of the colonies;
(3) The constant struggle of the legislatures to expand their powers (Aguilera-Barchet 2015; Olson 1992; Lokken 1959; Tully 1994).

By 1750, the population of the 13 colonies was about a million and a half. Geographically, the colonies were divided into New England, the Mid-Atlantic colonies, and the southern colonies.

New England was a land of farmers and sailors, a land of great "power of expansion," in whose communities, church, school, and city life proper played a special role, and crime and pauperism were less pronounced than in the other colonies. The Mid-Atlantic colonies were more diverse, both in terms of population composition (while the New England population was almost entirely "white") and in terms of economic specialization. The southern colonies, dominated by slavery on vast plantations (each one functioning almost entirely as a subsistence farm), produced cotton, rice, and tobacco. Thus, these were agrarian colonies (only the cities of Charleston and Baltimore were of some importance) with rigid class stratification. (As we can see, the North (New England) and the South were fundamentally different, and the Mid-Atlantic colonies had features of both.) Finally, further west, from Maine to Georgia, stretched the *frontier*, a fluid boundary between developed and undeveloped lands, where trade with the Indians was active.

The frontier was an important concept in the US geography and politics, and the frontier movement became one of defining factors in American history. "Washington [D.C.] is not a place to live in. The rents are high, the food is bad, the dust is disgusting, and the morals are deplorable. Go West, young man, go West and grow up with the country" – this appeal of 1865 was often attributed to the American author and newspaper editor Horace Greeley.[4] "Going West" was considered not just a task for Americans but as their destiny. American politicians saw it as a process of global significance: in the late nineteenth century, future US President Theodore Roosevelt wrote that the spread of English-speaking peoples over vast areas was a striking phenomenon in world history. For Americans, the road to the West had a sacred significance as a movement of faith and piety from East to West. Domestically, the frontier strengthened the culture of individualism, independence, and self-reliance (Bazzi and Fiszbein 2017). Geopolitically, the American frontier was an extension of the continental strategic presence and the American West's entry onto the world stage.

The problem of empire

The British victory in North America was not initially indisputable; they had to face the Spanish and the French, the "prize" in this struggle being control of the continent. The Spaniards were the first to arrive on the continent: in 1565, they established the first settlement in Florida; by the end of the sixteenth century, they had established themselves in New Mexico, later in California. The Spanish did not invest in developing representative institutions or a middle class; the Spanish settler was more of a soldier or missionary than an artisan or industrialist.

From the north came the French in 1608. Samuel de Champlain founded Quebec, the first permanent French settlement in New France, but it was not until 1661 under Louis XIV that the French monarchy began to provide permanent support for colonists in Canada. By establishing relatively weak factories, the French advanced along waterways – the St. Lawrence River, the Great Lakes, the Illinois, Wisconsin, and Wabash rivers. Conflicts between the British and the French over North American territory were inevitable, and it would seem that the victory should be on the side of centralized and more militarized New France. In the end, however, the British won the conflict – they were better prepared to fight, their commanders were more experienced, and finally the colonies were better situated strategically. Under the peace treaty of 1763, England received Canada (from France) and Florida from Spain, which also went to war with Britain. Thus, from the Atlantic to the Mississippi, North America became British (except for New Orleans). At the same time, Louisiana was ceded from France to Spain. The triumphant Seven Years' War put the 13 colonies in a whole new position relative to the empire – it showed their maturity and gave the colonists military experience.

At the same time, the British Empire itself faced a major problem in North America – the problem of governing such vast territories so distant from the metropolis. In the middle of the eighteenth century, the empire was in fact semi-federal in nature (the separation of powers between the central and local governments was envisaged), but it was, by law, a centralized structure. Thus, the preservation of territorial integrity for the empire was possible only through flexible accommodation and decentralization, but the empire failed in this task. The colonies (especially New England) increasingly resented the metropolis, which they felt was "robbing" them by levying exorbitant fees and duties (Nevins and Commager 1992: 32).

In addition, another line of conflict between the metropolis and the colonies arose and deepened. The colonists of Pennsylvania, Virginia, South Carolina, and North Carolina were experiencing a growing "hunger" for land. They wanted to go west, but the British government was pursuing a harsh policy toward the new lands. To ensure peace with the Indian tribes and to keep the colonists under English control, it announced in 1763 that the settlement line should stop at Appalachia and that lands west of that line were deemed to belong to the crown (Nevins and Commager 1992: 38).

Problems heated up and the level of mutual misunderstanding grew steadily. What London saw as just and necessary, whether dealing with the Indian problem or levying high taxes on the colonies to ensure their own security, was seen by the colonies as a policy of violence and pressure, an obstacle to their self-development. The revolution became irreversible when new revolutionary legislatures, the so-called provincial congresses, began to emerge in the colonies (the former representative institutions could not be used because they were largely composed of conservatives dependent on the governors of the crown). The first Congress was convened in Boston in 1774. In 1775, the Continental Congress, convened in Philadelphia, organized the colonists' troops into the American Continental Army and appointed George Washington as its commander. The War of Independence lasted more than six years and was fought in every colony. On the side of the Americans was the genius of Washington and the fact that they were fighting on their own soil. On July 4, 1776, Congress adopted the Declaration of Independence, but this document was still a formality because the main battles were ahead (one of the most important was the Battle of Saratoga in early 1777). The Congress proclaimed the creation of a new independent state, the United States of America. The state was created on federal principles, so that while broad powers were given to the head of state, the president, the colonies (states) also retained political autonomy (LaCroix 2010).

Overall, the colonial legacy has proven to be more of a positive factor for the country's further development. The colonial legacy of the United States can be regarded as:

- English as the language of communication and a prerequisite for the creation of a nation;
- Tradition of representative institutions and, as a consequence, high civic engagement of the population;

- (Relative) religious tolerance in the colonies;
- The spread of the idea of a "special destiny," a mission of the American people that, among other things, helped them to advance to the West.

We can see that this is a fundamentally different colonial legacy compared to Asia, Africa, and Latin America. In Africa, colonialism left a legacy of violent conflicts and routine practices of violence to the states; in Latin America, these were poor economic and political institutions. All these were bad preconditions for later development. This was different for the United States and Canada. The United States and Canada were different because former British colonies were considerably more democratic than other countries immediately following independence (Lee and Paine 2016).

Combining territorial size and democracy

With independence, Americans began to think about their territory – its size, topography, resources, and population. Studies on American geography, written not by Europeans but by Americans, began to appear. Geographical writings were composed by such significant political figures as Thomas Jefferson and David Ramsey. One geographer even suggested that the country be given a new poetical name, Fredonia (and its inhabitants would be called Fredonians), which would reflect the residents' joy at gaining independence.[5] In fact, the "geographic fever" reflected Americans' growing interest to the geographic size and diversity of their country. Realizing that it was precisely because of this scale that they could not visit all parts of their huge country physically, Americans turned to maps and geography itself, the latter thereby becoming a means of reducing the distances between people.

For Americans at the time, the size of the territory was also a political problem. The new geography served as a means of reflecting a new idea: vast territory was not at all a threat to the republican form of government but, on the contrary, could accelerate its entrenchment. Thus, federalists believed that a larger territory was a factor for increasing its political stability. Moreover, if the system of representation is fair and its quality high, the size of the territory is not decisive. This idea was extremely important in practical terms: residents of states with small territories and relatively low populations believed that representation should be based on the territorial (spatial) principle, that geography was the most important variable for the formation of representative institutions. An expression of this approach was, in particular, the placement of state capitals based on purely geographical considerations.

On the other hand, citizens of states with vast unpopulated territories and abundant populations faced very different challenges. They did not think in terms of geography but in terms of demography, locating state capitals in aggregate population centers, using proportional representation in the lower houses of legislatures, arguing for proportional congressional representation, and supporting the principle of electorate representation. Their situation forced them to understand that population, not territory, is the most important variable in structuring representative institutions. Thus, we can speak of a clash of two approaches to representation – spatial (on the part of small states) and demographic (on the part of large states).

The victory of the demographic approach was a kind of revolution in the understanding of representation. Of course, representative systems contain a territorial component; after all, some territorial unit will always be at the core of representation. The underlying factor, however, is population, that is, in fact, the number of voters. Americans have changed the basis of representation from territory to population and introduced the district as a unit – as a new unit of the political community – whose boundaries can be reconsidered. Deputies thereby represent not a territory, but a certain number of citizens and an equal number of citizens should have the same representation in the lower houses (Zagarri 1987).

By the mid-nineteenth century, demographic representation had spread across the United States. This concept was adopted by states with large territories and significant populations. In 1842, Congress made proportional representation (based on electoral districts) in its own elections, mandatory for all states. Thus ended a decades-long dispute between large and small states (Zagarri 1987).

Thus, in 1783, the metropolis recognized the independence of the new state, and the United States gained its independence. The separation from the metropolis, on the one hand, meant the development of democracy: in the colonies, governors were now elected, not appointed by the crown. On the other hand, however, the central institutions of the new state were not yet built up. In 1781, the Articles of Confederation, establishing the "League of Friendship," were adopted, but there was in fact no national executive power. The single-chamber Continental Congress, in which each state had one vote, was not an effective institution, it could not collect taxes and had no leverage over the states: the new state had to solve the problem of federalism, and this problem had to be solved urgently, since conflicts between individual states (especially conflicts over borders, e.g., between Pennsylvania and Vermont) were growing, and relations with the Indian tribes were in disarray.

Note that, despite its obvious weakness, the Confederate government took at least one important and wise step. This was Northwest Ordinance. The government decided to open the lands west of the Allegheny Mountains to permanent and progressive settlement and thereby create new states equal in rights to the original 13. The Ordinance of 1787 was directed to lands north of the Ohio; three to five states were to be created in three stages: (1) the creation of a "territory" with an appointed governor and judges who could make laws, but Congress had veto power; (2) when the population reached 5,000, a bicameral legislature was created; (3) when the population reached the 60,000 mark, the "territory" received state rights. Thus, the United States solved the so-called colonies problem, and the algorithm created by the Ordinance made it possible to subsequently create a state consisting of 50 states. In all other respects the Confederacy was extremely weak; Washington wrote of the states being bound by a "rope of sand"; civil war between them was quite possible (Nevins and Commager 1992: 103). The Northwest Ordinance created the original legislative basis for territorial expansion, but just as importantly, the constitution continued this policy: Article IV, Section 3 stated: "Congress shall have power to dispose of the territory . . . belonging to the United States."

To build effective national institutions a convention was called (remarkably, each state had the right to send to the convention as many representatives as it wished; the size of the delegation was of little importance since the states voted with one vote. For reasons of economy, states did not send large delegations, so a total of 55 representatives came together) (Nevins and Commager 1992: 106). The purpose of the Convention was to create a system in which an effective central government would be established while preserving the political autonomy of the states. It should be noted that American legislators could not rely on historical experience: the federations created by that time were either very small in area (like Switzerland), or they were weak collapsing unions. The members of the convention decided to follow the following principle: clearly define the powers of the central government and consider the rest to belong to the members of the federation. To resolve the conflict between large and small states (the latter feared that their representation would be too insignificant), it was decided to create a bicameral parliament: in the Senate (upper house) all states were given equal representation (two senators from each state), and in the House of Representatives (lower house) the number of seats allocated to a state was proportional to the number of its population. A special institution was created for the election of the president of the United States.

When Americans vote in the presidential election, they are not actually voting for the next president. Instead, they are voting for their state's representatives in the Electoral College, who will then vote for the president. Jesse Wegman, a member of *the New York Times* editorial board and author of the book *Let the People Pick the President: The Case for Abolishing the Electoral College*, explained that

> American democracy isn't just quirky – it's also unfair. Five times in our history, presidential candidates who have won more votes than their opponent have still lost the election. Why? Our 230-year-old jerry-built system for picking the president, known as the Electoral College.[6]

Indeed, the United States is the only democratic country in the world where a presidential candidate can lose an election by winning a majority of the national vote.

How did such a bizarre institution, which has no direct analogues in the world, as the "electoral college," which, having been developed in the late eighteenth century by the founding fathers of the United States, survive to this day in little changed form? At the dawn of American independence, the question of how the country's president should be elected was decided in a fierce debate (the only clarity, perhaps, was that George Washington should be the first president). The states began to demand that they be given a decisive role in electing a president, as a guarantee that the central government would not deny them the autonomy for which their citizens had shed blood in the War of Independence. The founding fathers, on the other hand, were convinced that such an important choice could not be left to the people, but that the direct election of the president must be entrusted to a select group of the most worthy and informed individuals who could be guided by the national interest in the highest sense of the word. The result of the debate was the approval of the concept of "electors" – it embodied both the ideas of the founding fathers about indirect democracy through "the best citizens" and the idea of the rights of the American federation entities – the states. The question of how to "elect electors" was decided independently by the states: in some states it was the right of all citizens allowed to vote, in others it was done by the state legislatures. The number of electors from each state had to be equal to the number of legislators who represented that state in both houses of Congress.

No other institute of the American constitution has perhaps attracted as much criticism as the institution of the "electoral college" of the president, but look – it's still there. It persisted, reflecting the history of the formation of American federalism.

The Congress has created a state with a strong national executive. But the states retained strong political autonomy. The first President of the United States was George Washington.

The institutional system was established, and the constitution was written. The next question was how to ratify it. The Congress ruled that the document was valid when nine states out of the 13 voted to ratify it. By the end of 1789, the constitution had been adopted in Pennsylvania, Delaware, and New Jersey. At this point the ratification process reflected a serious line of conflict: a split between Federalists and Anti-Federalists, that is, those who wanted a strong national government and those who insisted on maintaining a confederation, a "league" of states. The ratification struggle resulted in the classic texts of which America is still proud today, The Federalist, 95 articles written by Alexander Hamilton, James Madison, and John Jay, in defense of the constitution. The constitution of a federal state was adopted. The Americans succeeded in combining the territorial size with democracy using federal solution.

Crossing the Appalachian Mountains and heading further West

In 1789, there were about four million people living in the United States and 3.5 million of them were white. This was a predominantly rural population; the largest cities were Philadelphia (42,000) and New York City (33,000). In third place by a wide margin was Boston (18,000). The communications system was still underdeveloped though the immigrants were arriving at a rapid pace – immigration from Europe was on a monstrous scale. The country had been created, and its energy was now directed forward to the West!

In the vast area west of the coast, new state formations were springing up as pioneers crossed the Appalachian Mountains and headed further west. The United States faced the so-called problem of empire – the need to establish a way to settle and govern the new lands. A limited self-government was imposed in the Northwest Territory, regulated by the Ordinance of 1787. Initially, it was a single district governed by a governor and judges appointed by Congress. It was envisaged, however, that when the number of adult men living in the district reached 5,000, a legislature of its own would be established. In addition, one non-voting representative would represent the district in Congress.

In the Northwest Territory, three to five states were to be formed. As soon as any of them reached a free population of 60,000, it was allowed to enter the union on the same basis as the original states. This was a new policy of colonization, based on the principle of equal rights; it recognized that colonization was only an extension of national boundaries and that the colonies enjoyed not privileges but rights equal to those of the metropolis. This provision of the ordinance formed the basis of American policy on public lands, and on these principles, there was a consistent expansion of American territory to the Pacific (Nevins and Commager 1992: 154).

The development of domestic trade united the nation. The construction of railroads helped to link the various parts of the rapidly expanding country. Industry boomed in the East, and agriculture grew in the Midwest and South. It should be noted, however, that the process of replenishing the federation with new members was rather difficult. For example, there was serious opposition to the admission of new members to the United States. Anti-Federalists still believed that the republican form of government was incompatible with a large territory; democracy could function successfully only within a relatively compact territory. Federalists challenged these arguments by insisting that a small territory does not guarantee domestic political stability. On the contrary, the larger the territory, the greater the opportunity to avoid the imposition of narrow interests by one or another elite group on the local community. However, even those in favor of expanding the US territory were often against giving the newcomers the same status as the founding states of American statehood. They argued security concerns: the inclusion of new states might weaken national security, and the costs would fall precisely on the eastern states. Nevertheless, in the end, the issue was resolved in favor of the inclusion of the new states on the principle of equal rights (Nevins and Commager 1992: 170).

The presence of a moving frontier of settlement in the West had a tremendous impact on all American society. By 1800, the Mississippi and Ohio River basins had become the great frontier region. The outflow of population to the West led to new frontiers: the territory of the state was expanding to the south and west. In 1803, the United States bought vast Louisiana (more than 2.5 million square kilometers) from France; in 1819, Spain ceded Florida to the United States for next to nothing; in 1840–1850, the Americans conquered the northern parts of Mexico; in 1846, the United States annexed the northwestern territory of Oregon between the Rocky Mountains and the Pacific Ocean. Let us not forget the purchase of so-called Russian America – Alaska and the Aleutian Islands – from the Russian Empire in 1867. The United States also distinguished itself northward from British possessions (future Canada): here the border was set at 49°N.

Institutional compromises, the war, and the strategies of territorial expansion

One of President Jefferson's moves nearly doubled the new state's territory. Spain long held territories west of the Mississippi with the crucial port of New Orleans. Napoleon then forced the transfer of Louisiana to France, but his plans for a vast colonial empire west of the United States, thereby curbing Anglo-Saxon domination of North America, threatened the trade and security of the American states. Napoleon, however, did not want another war. He decided to fill the treasury, to make Louisiana out of British reach, and at the same time to gain US support; so, for $15 million the vast territory of Louisiana went to the United States (note that Jefferson thereby violated the constitution, which did not provide for the purchase of foreign territory; moreover, he acted without the consent of Congress). Nevertheless, this acquisition further strengthened support for the president, and in 1804, he was reelected for a second term.

On the wave of success, the Americans attempted to push back the British in the north by capturing Canada. But the attempt ended in great failure; the War of 1812 is considered one of the most unsuccessful events in American history. In addition, the war sharply divided the states, with the South and West in favor of military action and New York and New England against the war (Nevins and Commager 1992: 140). In addition, the War of 1812 led to conflict between the northeast and the central government: during the war, the government's economic policies damaged the commercial interests of the northeast, and, in 1814, representatives of that region convened a conference in Hartford on the question of secession. Although this did not happen (the war came to an end soon after the conference), the conference itself reflected Northeastern dissatisfaction with the legitimacy of political decisions made at the national level.

Soon after the new states were admitted to the union, a political map of the lands east of the Mississippi River emerged. Within five years, six states emerged: in 1816, Indiana; 1817, Mississippi; 1818, Illinois; 1819, Alabama; 1820, Maine; and 1821, Missouri. The original settlement boundary had Europe as its "rear," next to the Atlantic coast, but the population of the Mississippi Valley looked more to the West than to the East.

One of the most serious conflicts that called into question the territorial integrity of the new state was the conflict between the free states and the slave states. This conflict became the center of the country's political life and permanently shaped its political agenda. For some time, the crisis was resolved through the application of the equilibrium rule.

In 1818, federal lawmakers were considering admitting Missouri to the federation. Northerners, who feared a Southern preponderance in the national government, proposed that Missouri be given state rights and admitted to the union on condition that slavery be abolished there. The proposal passed the House of Representatives but was defeated in the Senate, where Southerners had equal representation and vetoed the Northerners' proposal. However, a compromise was eventually reached. Missouri was accepted as a slave state, but at the same time Maine was separated from Massachusetts and given statehood (naturally, free, not slave); and Congress decreed that slavery should be permanently excluded from the territory north of 36° 30′ – along Missouri's southern border. As the future showed, the crisis was not resolved but postponed; the war between the North and the South was ahead. In addition, the Missouri Compromise produced an "equilibrium rule," which granted state rights based on equal representation in the Senate of the North and the South. Not only did the "equilibrium rule" grant each region a veto over policies that were not in its interest, but it also became a basic principle of national political life in the years subsequently leading up to the Civil War.

Meanwhile, the frontier continued to move westward. As I mentioned earlier, the American frontier was not just a line on a map or even just a border, it was a social process – the development of the West. The frontier was moving: the first was the Atlantic coast; the second was the Appalachian Mountains; the third great frontier region was, by 1800, the Mississippi and Ohio River valleys ("Hi-o, away we go, floating down the river on the O-hi-o," the settlers sang). By 1796, Kentucky and Tennessee were full-fledged states, Ohio was about to follow; by 1820, Indiana and Illinois in the northwest, Louisiana, Alabama, and Mississippi in the southwest all became states. The first frontier was closely related to Europe, the second to the coast, but the Mississippi Valley people were no longer looking backward, they were looking forward – to the West (read Fenimore Cooper!), and wars with Indians (with the Creek tribe in the South, the Seminole in Florida, and the Tecumseh in Indiana) could not stop the pioneers.

The construction of roads has begun: the first important route to the West becomes the Cumberland Road from Maryland to Illinois (started in 1811). But the real breakthrough in transportation was the construction of the Erie Canal, which connected the Hudson River and the ocean to the Great Lakes, that is, it created a waterway into the heart of the continent. Cities sprang up and grew along the canal, and the canal established New York as a leader in commerce and finance. Note that later, during the Civil War, the canal helped save the Union (North) by connecting the Mississippi Valley with the northern Atlantic states in time. Migrants moved predominantly in a latitudinal direction – along the parallels. Alabama and Mississippi were settled by Southerners and Michigan and Wisconsin by Northerners. In Ohio, Indiana, and Illinois, the two streams joined.

The vast lands west of the Mississippi were explored in 1803 by the Lewis and Clark expedition sent by Jefferson; the travelers produced detailed maps and descriptions of the lands. On their return, Clark established the Missouri Fur Company, John Astor – the American Fur Company; and in 1822, William Ashley organized the Rocky Mountain Fur Company. It was not only enterprising traders who developed the land; missionaries played an active role.

Texas became one of the important acquisitions of the American nation. Texas was originally a sparsely populated part of Mexico, whose government was ineffective and corrupt. In 1835, American settlers in Texas rebelled against Mexico and achieved independence. The Texas republic prospered, attracting many new colonists. For the United States, Texas with its cheap cotton and new lands was extremely attractive, and, in addition, there were fears that Britain would try to create its protectorate in Texas. In 1845, Texas was annexed to the United States. Even today, it belongs to the most powerful cultural and geographical areas of the United States, the influence of Texas culture is felt not only in Texas but also to the west and southwest of the state: Meinig called the state "imperial" (Meinig 1969: 93).

In 1845, California, like Texas before it, was very sparsely populated. The territories nominally belonged to Mexico, but there was little or no administration: there were no courts, no police, no post office, and no schools. Communication between Mexico City and California was sparse; meanwhile, the American "element" in the region was steadily increasing. Many in the United States expected California to fall like a "ripe peach into the outstretched hand" of the United States. Perhaps this would have happened had it not been for the US war with Mexico, which began in 1846. The immediate cause of the conflict was a dispute over the Texas border, but the Americans used the occasion to enter Mexican territory and seize the capital. Under the peace treaty of 1848, the United States annexed not only California but also the vast territory between it and Texas. After that California developed very fast, even by the American standards, and in 1850 it received the status of the state. Having established itself on the Pacific coast, the United States turned the frontier back toward the central, still underdeveloped parts of the continent.

Meanwhile, the conflict between the free and slave states was escalating, and the new state had to endure another major test: The Civil War (1861–1865). It was a struggle between the bourgeois North and the slaveholding South. With the admission of new states to the union, the Missouri Compromise was hampered, and in 1850 a new, even more difficult compromise was proposed to contain the conflict. In 1854, the conflict escalated again (on October 16, 1854, President Lincoln gave a famous speech in Peoria against slavery as an institution that should be limited and later completely abolished). But things were moving toward war and not only because of sharp differences in attitudes toward the institution of slavery. The North and the South developed according to different models. The South was almost entirely rural (except for large New Orleans), while the North saw the growth of large, urbanized areas, with New York City approaching one million inhabitants. In the South, industry was extremely underdeveloped, while in the North it was the motor of development.

The secession of the Southern states from the Union and consequently the outbreak of hostilities were prompted by Lincoln's election to a second term as president. But Lincoln, as his first term showed, could not (and did not even intend to) abolish slavery in the South at once; he advocated gradual abolition, so that Southerners seemed to have nothing to fear. However, in 1861, delegates from eight Southern states met in Montgomery, Alabama, and proclaimed the creation of a Confederacy of American States. A little later three more states joined them, increasing the Confederacy to 11 members.

South Carolina set the example for secession. In December 1860, the state legislature passed a secession ordinance stating that "the union existing between South Carolina and the other states is dissolved." A month later seven more slave states seceded: Mississippi, Florida, Alabama, Georgia, Louisiana, Texas, Tennessee. A little later, three more: Arkansas, Virginia, and North Carolina. The separated territories accounted for about 40% of the area of the formerly united country. In February, the creation of the Confederacy of the Southern States of North America, which consisted of sovereign independent states, was proclaimed. The Constitution of the Confederacy recognized slavery as a legal institution not only in its territory but also in all territories that would join the Confederacy (Nevins and Commager 1992: 181–203).

The 23 Star-Spangled States (the North) outnumbered the Southerners in population and level of development. But the Southerners also had an advantage: they would not have to win the conflict with the North by conquering territories directly; they would not have to advance but only to hold their territories. The war between the North and the South had its great heroes: the Northerner Abraham Lincoln and the Southerner Robert E. Lee. The Confederacy lost the war with the North, but the hatred between the two parts of the country lasted for decades. The order of reconstruction of the postwar South provided for military administration and the division of Confederate states into five military districts. Gradually, however, the Southern states regained their rights.[7] The consequences of the war were the creation of secret societies of a radical persuasion, such as the infamous Ku Klux Klan. Still, the victory of the North led to the abolition of slavery and contributed to the rapid development of a country with a vast territory, a rapidly growing population, and abundant natural resources.

It is important to reiterate that the central conflict leading to the war was the dispute over *institution* – the slavery. The question was whether slavery would be permitted to expand into the Western territories, leading to more slave states, or be prevented from expanding, that would place slavery on a course of ultimate extinction. The importance of this conflict was, among other things, that it was a conflict of two fundamentally different modes of development which could not peacefully coexist with each other – politically, economically, and socially.

After the defeat in the Civil War, the South was no longer able to rely on the previous model of development based on slavery; the transition to another model was long, painful, and accompanied by resistance and violence. Processes of transition developed at different rates in different Southern states. Territorial differences between North and South proved to be very persistent. Regional gaps in income dating back to the pre-Civil War era still persist in the United States. The economies of the pre-1940s southern states, along with their climate and geography, could be compared to that of contemporary developing countries. However, provision of federal policies and aid contributed to the gradual transformation of the southern states (Khawar 2017).

After the war, the United States had only one territory left to develop: the Great Plains (present-day Nevada, Colorado, Montana, Wyoming, North and South Dakota). These lands became "kingdoms" of coal mining and cattle ranching, and a great many cities, mostly small ones, were established. Some of them flourished, others fell into disrepair and became "ghost towns"; in Kansas alone some 2,000 of the names of towns created in the course of development have now disappeared from the map. By 1900 over 800,000 people were living on the new lands. The last American frontier had disappeared.

In the last quarter of the nineteenth century, nearly the entire country was divided into states and territories. The settlement of the West was greatly accelerated by the Homestead Act of 1862 (a homestead is land for building a farm, which requires a fee of $10), which gave free land lots of 64 hectares to citizens if they occupied and worked it. By 1880, 22.4 million hectares of land had gone to private owners. The settlement boundary had all but disappeared by 1890.

The success in building a great nation has boosted the American geographical imagination that was associated with the idea of an expanding frontier. The idea has crossed the borders of the country and started to serve as a major metaphor for describing American initiatives outside the United States. American geographers spoke of the duality of this imagination: on the one hand, it was the idea of a vast national continental space, mastered by people with a civilizing mission, and on the other, it was the idea of a national project beyond geographical borders, based on projecting into the world values derived from the nation's frontier experience. Presidents McKinley and Theodore Roosevelt were the first to perceive the United States as a powerful agent of a global order based on the American experience of mastering and governing their own country. The American experience of frontier development and its projection onto the world was embodied in two important principles: that market expansion was necessary for political and socioeconomic well-being and that economic freedom is a derivative of freedom in general (Agnew and Sharp 2002: 79).

The United States: geographic and institutional differences

The American nation has developed in a specific geographic environment. American culture (including political culture) is characterized by a strong regional identity of its citizens, by virtue of which they clearly associate themselves with a certain area of the country, addressing to it their patriotism and contrasting themselves, sometimes quite rigidly, with other areas of the country and their inhabitants. As Leonid Smirnyagin concluded,

> [T]he special role of the geographical factor is one of the main specific features of the American people. Modern Americans have quite convex mental maps of the USA in their heads; the regional identity is not dying out – this form of identity cuts across the borders of ethnic communities and unites people of different generations.
>
> (Smirnyagin 1989: 335)

A geographic region is a territory and a climate; it is a certain type of relations between social groups; it is a type of economy and relations with the federal government; finally, it is a set of institutions and specific cultural norms. Coexisting and complementing each other on the map of the country, regions unite people, their roots lie in the relationship of the human community and a particular territory. Thinking in a regional perspective seems best suited to the understanding of American geographic and institutional diversity.

From the earliest steps of colonization, areas with sharp differences among them began to emerge across the United States. The northern part of the country was settled mainly by small farmers, the southern part by planters. Therefore, a conflict (which later developed into the Civil War) between the bourgeois capitalist North and the slaveholding South immediately arose. The border between the two officially ran along the boundary between Pennsylvania and Maryland

(37°N). In addition, a major new region, the West, began to emerge behind the line of solid development. By the early twentieth century, three major regions of the country had been formed, and their images are meaningful to Americans. For example, the North is a powerful industry and large cities, enterprising, democratic, and peculiar (Protestant) work ethic. At one time the North was far ahead of other areas in terms of development, but now the pace of economic development is much higher in the South and the West. The South is not only and not so much the heat but also the stereotypes of the slavery era, the high proportion of blacks in the population, and the rigid class stratification of society. The West represents vast horizons and almost limitless human possibilities and simplified rules of life and living. The districts of the country defined themselves through each other, so the North defined its identity primarily as fundamentally different from the South, and vice versa. (It should be noted that the North–South division is characteristic of almost any large country, it is enough to mention such European countries as Germany, France, and Italy).

Daniel Elazar explained the geographic distributions of political subcultures in the United States. He asserted that the American political culture can be viewed as a hybrid of three identifiable subcultures, which were derived from cultural streams of immigration to the country. Because of the basically westward pattern of migration across the continent, the various subcultures have become dominant in different geographic areas. According to Elazar, the individualistic subculture emphasized the centrality of private concerns and views politics as a means of personal advancement. There was no obligation to participate in politics, but one was free to do so if political activity was seen as beneficial to the individual. By contrast, the moralistic political subculture viewed the political order as a commonwealth in which everyone had a responsibility to participate – not for private, but for the public good. Then, the traditionalistic subculture was essentially elitist. Politics is viewed as properly left to the "better people" who act as custodians of the traditional structures and norms (Elazar 1970, 1972; Schiltz and Lee 1978). Later, in the 1990s, Lieske presented his own classification of the United States's regional subcultures (Lieske 1993).

American regional subcultures still retain their importance. However, a new "spatial geometry" was gradually taking shape in the United States. The principle of dividing the territory into "pieces" (areas adjacent to each other, as in a puzzle) is replaced by the so-called hyperspace, which is a kind of multilayered "sandwich," in which each layer, having a different thickness, nevertheless hugs the entire territory of the country (Zelinsky 1973: 74).

The picture of American political landscape would be, certainly, incomplete without mentioning Native American lands that span state borders and are often rich in natural and cultural resources. But paradoxically, these lands are often the poorest parts of the United States. Native Americans own private businesses at a much lower rate per capita compared to other Americans, and the businesses they own produce less income on average than the businesses owned by all other racial groups. Almost 30% of American Indians and Alaska Natives are below the official poverty line (compared to 15.3% for the nation as a whole). Roughly 22%

of Native Americans live on federally recognized reservations or other specially designated areas. According to Lofthouse,

> [N]ative Americans live under *fundamentally different institutions* than other Americans. The federal land trust shapes Native American economic life through bureaucratic control of land and other resources. The complex property-rights regime of the federal land trust stifles mutually beneficial exchange hampers the market process and allows government officials to intervene heavily in economic affairs. In addition, the dual bureaucracy of federal and tribal officials increases transaction costs in general because of the broad authority and discretion that these officials must make public policy. Under those unique institutions, the federal government has created an environment of uncertainty and high costs that pose significant barriers to entrepreneurial action, thus limiting economic development at large.
>
> (Lofthouse 2019: 242)

However, Native American societies demonstrate phenomenal resilience. Cornell and Kalt conclude that

> in the last several centuries, they have faced winds of economic, political, and cultural change that have blown as fiercely over them as over any people in history. These winds have brought military violence and subjugation, epidemics of disease, seizures of land and property, vicious racism, and economic deprivation. Yet, hundreds of distinct Native American societies built upon dozens of cultural lineages still persevere and grow, variously bound together by ties of family, language, history, and culture. The lesson from Indian Country is a lesson of strength.
>
> (Cornell and Kalt 1994: 3)

The territorial development of Canada

The contours of the Canadian Confederation were drawn by the struggle between the two great powers of England and France. In 1497, the first English ship with Captain John Cabot reached Newfoundland; in 1534, the first Frenchman Jacques Cartier entered the Gulf of St. Lawrence. In 1663, Canada became an official French colony, but English colonization was also expanding, largely due to the establishment of the English Hudson Bay Fur Trading Company. After the Seven Years' War, the treaty made Canada a colony of England, and the French formed the core of the French-Canadian province of Quebec. (The Anglo-Franco-Canadian relationship has since then become the country's main political–geographical "intrigue"). Immigrants from England settled in the Atlantic coast and the central part of the country (the Great Plains). The development of the middle Steppe provinces in Canada was greatly aided by the Homestead Act of 1872, like that passed in the United States.

France's colonial policy in the sixteenth and eighteenth centuries is characterized by two main stages: the ascending stage, which lasted until the beginning of the eighteenth century and corresponded to the period of the rise and flowering of French absolutism, and the descending stage, corresponding to the period of the growing crisis of the Old Order. If during the first stage an active colonial policy was pursued, although not always consistent, the second stage saw a decline in colonial activity and a purely utilitarian approach to the exploitation of already existing colonies – the eighteenth century was the time of the fall of the first French colonial empire.

The nature of French colonial expansion differed fundamentally from England's colonial policy. The scale of territorial expansion of the English was small, they mastered only a relatively small strip of the Atlantic coast of North America, but the English colonies outnumbered the French many times over in terms of population. In the English colonies, bourgeois relations developed intensively, colonization was carried out by people who came to America in search of religious and political freedom. A very harsh policy was pursued against the native Indian population.

The French colonial empire had a very different character: its territory was vast and its population negligible; feudal orders prevailed. French colonization was distinctly state driven, with the Catholic Church playing a major role in it.

The main role in the colonization and development of Canada belonged to the absolutist state, which had purely political objectives, but at the same time the state never gave priority to the colonization of Canada. This explains the specific structure of the French colonial empire. Territorial expansion always came first; as a result, thanks to the efforts of a handful of enthusiasts, the French were able to incorporate half the North American continent into their dominions. However, since the expansion was not supported by economic interests (the fur trade, the logic of which required the constant inclusion of new territories, could not "digest" the entire territory), and the support of the French government was completely insufficient, the empire was largely ephemeral.

As a result, New France was a small settler colony in the St. Lawrence Valley, surrounded by vast, sparsely populated spaces formally considered French possessions, where individual French forts, missions, and trading posts were scattered and where Indian tribes roamed freely. In Canada, where the fur trade played an important part in the system of colonial exploitation, the Indian was a "compulsory element" of the system, without which the fur business could not exist. However, later, with the settlement of the Canadian western territories, the colonial authorities implemented a particularly ruthless policy against the Indians.

The first half of the eighteenth century was characterized by the rivalry between France and England to assert their dominance in North America. After the formation of the Hudson Bay Company in 1670, New France was squeezed between the English possessions, and the rivalry between them intensified on the grounds of trade competition.

In 1791, the British Parliament approved a bill for Canada called the Constitutional Act. All the remaining British colonies on the continent were declared a single possession called British North America, headed by a governor-general with his residence in Quebec. The term "Canada" has since been used frequently in reference to the entire territory. The former colony of Quebec was divided into two provinces: Upper (English) Canada and Lower (French) Canada. British North America consisted of Upper and Lower Canada, Nova Scotia, and New Brunswick. The British crown possessed a huge landholding in Canada.

In 1840, the English Parliament passed the Act of Union, which united Upper and Lower Canada into one colony called the "Province of Canada."

The interests of the economic development of British North America required a closer connection of its territories and the removal of internal tariff barriers. The expansion and unification of the domestic market required the formation of a new political structure in place of the fragmented colonial provinces. The union of the colonies began to take shape only in the 1850s. In 1862, an interprovincial conference in Quebec decided on the introduction of freedom of trade in manufactured goods. The discovery of new lands and the development of the North American continent continued. Vast areas as far away as the Pacific Ocean were discovered, but there were almost no settlers there. To prevent British possessions in the Far West from being annexed to the United States, the British government bought Vancouver Island from the Hudson Bay Company in 1858 and established the colony of British Columbia. By this time, the boundary between Canada and the United States had been extended to the Pacific coast by the Oregon Treaty of 1846 along the 49th parallel. British Columbia's incorporation into the Canadian federation as a province in 1871 marked the far western frontier of the new state as well as the southern one. In the center of the continent lay a "dead space."

The federal union in Canada was initiated by the Atlantic provinces: in 1867, the House of Commons in Westminster passed the British North America Act. The provinces of Canada – French-speaking Quebec and English-speaking Ontario, Nova Scotia, and New Brunswick – were united under a single federal dominion under the British crown. In 1870, the Hudson Bay Company ceded vast territories from the Great Lakes to the Rocky Mountains to the Dominion of Canada. In the same year, the province of Manitoba and later Saskatchewan and Alberta were formed there. In 1871, Canada included British Columbia and in 1873 Prince Edward Island.

Canada was in fact a semi-sovereign, semi-autonomous federation of former colonial provinces. The formation of a dominion of four provinces initiated the formation of a single pan-Canadian state with the original territory of the dominion at its core, primarily the provinces of Ontario and Quebec, the axis of the territorial structure of modern Canada.

The problem of regional separatism in Quebec, which has the potential to deprive the country of territorial integrity, is widely known. The main intrigue is the unification of the two nations, Anglo and French Canadians, in a single state, with many of the latter, compactly settled in the province of Quebec, wanting to secede from the "rest" of Canada.

Let's return to history: when the British came, Canada was just one of the provinces that made up the French Kingdom. Interestingly, despite its small population, New France astonished researchers with its high level of cultural and spiritual life. The situation changed radically when Britain took control of Canada: after the Treaty of Paris in 1763 the French elite left Canada and was replaced by a new, British elite. Gradually, however, a special, Franco-Canadian elite developed, which was a group with no political control over its territory. The British used political, legal, and administrative institutions to achieve and subsequently reproduce control over Canadian territory; its French-speaking population became a minority by the mid-nineteenth century. Only the St. Lawrence Valley remained predominantly French-speaking and became the political "core" of Quebec. At the same time, however, not all French-speaking Canadians lived in Quebec: the diaspora extended into the prairies, into northern and eastern Ontario, and into New England (US territory). In fact, the preservation of Quebec's autonomy in one form or another became a matter of survival for a French-Canadian culture without statehood.

With the secession of Quebec, the country would have lost 25.3% of its citizens and 15.5% of its territory. In addition, secession would have other serious consequences, in particular the long-established equilibrium of the territorial structure: the province of Ontario, which is home to about half the population of the country, would become a "super-giant," completely dominating the new federation. This, in turn, could lead to attempts at secession on the part of both British Columbia and the smaller Atlantic provinces (they would be completely isolated from the rest of the country), and the country would become a classic confederation. The leaders of the Quebec Party, the "motor" of separatism, claimed that their goal was to eliminate the economic and cultural injustices to Quebec. Indeed, the federal government did much to appease the separatists: Quebec had a "special status" in federal programs since 1964, and in 1989, under Prime Minister Mulroney's initiative, a constitutional agreement was drafted that recognized Quebec as a "distinct society." In fact, an *asymmetrical devolution* process was launched by the federal center, but it has not yet been successful.

In 1980 and 1995, there were two referendums on the question of Quebec's independence. In the first, 59.56% of the participants were opposed to secession, and 40.44% were in favor of secession. The second referendum had a greater number of supporters of independence in Quebec, 49.42%, compared to 50.58% who opposed secession. Both referendums did not lead to the sovereignty of the province, although the second time the difference was very small and was contested by the losing side.

There is no other country in the world where separatists are treated as tolerantly as in Canada. On the one hand, the consequences of Quebec's secession would be, if not disastrous, at least quite severe for the rest of Canada. But the principles of democracy are unshakeable, and the country's political elite shares the conviction that Canada will remain united only if its citizens wish to live together *voluntarily*. The country must not and cannot be built on force; this idea is essential, and Canadians will pursue it, perhaps at the cost of the territorial integrity of their country.

The process of settling the country went very quickly. In only ten years, between 1872 and 1882, 42,000 homesteads were distributed in the province of Manitoba and in the future provinces of Saskatchewan and Alberta. Much land was also distributed in the provinces of Ontario and Quebec.

Is Canada disunited by its geography?

The question of the relationship between the characteristics of territory and the political unity of the Canadian state is intriguing. Some Canadian geographers believe that the physical and geographical environment itself contributed to the unity of the country, or rather the hydrographic system – the St. Lawrence River, the Great Lakes, the Saskatchewan, Mackenzie, and Fraser Rivers. Once the fur trade began to develop, merchants used these natural communications to develop the territory and unify the country. Other scholars believe that geography played against the unification of the country, in which three major regions – British Columbia, the Western Plains, and the more fragmented East – developed autonomously, almost in isolation and, indeed, experienced a constant attraction not to each other but to the United States. Only one region escaped the magic of the powerful southern neighbor's attraction – the Laurentian region proper, the land of the Franco-Canadians.

Most of the Canadians live along the southern border of their country. Why is this? Climate is not the only answer; it is also geology. More than half the Dominion is covered by a rocky formation that has dominated the development of Canada almost from the very beginning. This Pre-Cambrian or Laurentian shield, as it is called, lies like a gigantic collar around Hudson Bay. This formation is made up of the stumps of ancient mountains that have been ground down by the action of glaciers in ages past. It is a wilderness of rocks, lakes, and evergreen trees. Long ago it blocked the advance of settlement. It has been of economic use for only three purposes – at first for the furs it produced and more recently for its wealth of forest and mineral resources. The Pre-Cambrian shield is to blame for crowding the population of eastern Canada in a narrow belt of territories along the south. It has also cut Canada in two, separating the East from the West by a huge, almost uninhabited area. So, there is no "Middle West" in the Dominion of Canada.[8]

Geography divides Canada into four quite separate sections: the first comprising the three little Maritime Provinces; the second the two big provinces of Central Canada, Quebec, and Ontario; the third the three large Prairie Provinces; and the fourth is the province of British Columbia. Few countries in the world are so disjointed physically. The inhabited portions of the Dominion, instead of forming a compact block, are separated from each other and stretched out from ocean to ocean. Railways, therefore, mean more to Canada than to any other country. The natural result of geography is a strong tendency toward sectionalism, much more so than in the United States. The inherent sectionalism in the Dominion is one of the major problems of the country.

Conclusion

Both the United States and Canada have managed to successfully combine their institutions with geographic factors in a way that they became strategic sources of their development while the territories of these countries were expanding. While an important role was played by the frontier movement, the federal solution was crucial for the simultaneous maintenance of democratic institutions and territorial integrity. Both countries are advanced liberal democracies, though the United States is a federal republic, Canada is the federal parliamentary democracy. Both belong to the world's longest-lived federations and share a continent and a long border (Simeon and Radiny 2010: 357). Both are territorially highly diverse countries in terms of geography, culture, linguistics, and historic legacies, so they had to accommodate this diversity in different ways, through different institutions of federalism and decentralization.

According to Simeon and Radiny (2010: 360),

> [I]n Canada, the federalism debate is primarily about language, region, and managing difference. National unity versus difference, "province-building" versus "nation-building," "national standards" and common social citizenship versus provincial autonomy and valuing diversity are the fundamental preoccupations that shape the Canadian federalism discourse. In the United States, the discourse at the founding was much more about federalism as a device for sharing power, limited government and checks and balances.

American federal model is symmetric, while Canada is an asymmetric federation. Though Quebec does not have any special legal status in the Canadian federation, it is recognized that "the Quebecois form a nation within a united Canada" (Hogg and Wright 2022). Besides provinces, Canada has territories located in the northern parts of the country. What explains the choice of the asymmetric federal solution considering that it is generally more difficult to manage an asymmetric system than a symmetric one? It is historic legacy, but Canadian geography plays an equally important role. Canadians had to focus on unity and the management of diversity much more than the Americans had to do so.

Notes

1 GDP Ranked by Country 2024 (worldpopulationreview.com).
2 Countries and Territories | Freedom House.
3 Peter Stuyvesant the last of the Dutch governors in New Amsterdam (historyofholland.com).
4 No one has yet proven who first used this phrase in print.
5 The United States of Fredonia? | The New York Public Library (nypl.org).
6 Is the Electoral College a Problem? Does It Need to Be Fixed? – The New York Times (nytimes.com).
7 Rebuilding the South After the War | American Experience | Official Site | PBS.
8 https://www.historians.org/about-aha-and-membership/aha-history-and-archives/gi-roundtable-series/pamphlets/em-47-canada-our-oldest-good-neighbor-(1946)/is-canada-disunited-by-its-geography

References

Agnew, Jonh, and Joanne P. Sharp. (2002). "America, Frontier Nation: From Abstract Space to Worldly Place." In *American Space/American Place. Geographies of the Contemporary*

United States, ed. by J. Agnew and J. Smith, pp. 79–107. Edinburgh, UK: Edinburgh University Press.
Aguilera-Barchet, Bruno. (2015). "From Monarchy to Representative Government: The American 'Revolution'." In *A History of Western Public Law*. Cham: Springer.
Bazzi, Samuel, and Martin Fiszbein. (2017). Frontier Culture: The Roots and Persistence of "Rugged Individualism" in the United States. Frontier-Culture-The-Roots-and-Persistence-of-"Rugged-Individualism"-in-the-United-States-2.pdf (bu.edu).
Conway, Stephen. (2020). "Colonial Politics." In *The Oxford Handbook of American Political History*, ed. by Paula Baker and Donald T. Critchlow. Oxford: Oxford Handbooks.
Cornell, Stephen, and Joseph P. Kalt. (1994). "Reloading the Dice: Improving the Changes for Economic Development on American Indian Reservations." In *What Can Tribes Do? Strategies and Institutions in American Indian Economic Development*, ed. by Stephen Cornell and Joseph P. Kalt. American Indian Studies Center, Oakland, CA: University of California Press.
Elazar, Daniel. (1970). *Cities of the Prairie: The Metropolitan Frontier and American Politics*. New York: Basic Books.
Elazar, Daniel. (1972). *American Federalism: A View from the States*, 2nd ed. New York: Crowell.
Hogg, Peter, and Wade Wright. (2022). *Constitutional Law of Canada*, 5th ed. Toronto: Thomson Reuters Canada.
Khawar, Mariam. (2017). "Did Geography Influence the United States?" In *The Geography of Underdevelopment*. New York: Palgrave Macmillan.
Klein, Milton. (1972). "New York in the American Colonies: A New Look." *New York History*, 53(2): 132–156.
LaCroix, Alison. (2010). *The Ideological Origins of American Federalism*. Cambridge, MA: Harvard University Press.
Lee, Alexander, and Jack Paine. (2016). "Did British Colonialism Promote Democracy? Divergent Inheritances and Diminishing Legacies." Lee-and-Paine-Britain-and-democracy.pdf (rochester.edu).
Lieske, Joel. (1993). "Regional Subcultures of the United States." *The Journal of Politics*, 55(4): 888–913.
Lofthouse, Jordan. (2019). "Institutions and Economic Development on Native American Lands." *The Independent Review*, 24(2): 227–248.
Lokken, Roy. (1959). "The Concept of Democracy in Colonial Political Thought." *The William and Mary Quarterly*, 16(4): 568–580.
Meinig, Donald. (1969). *Imperial Texas*. Austin: University of Texas Press.
Nevins, Alan, and Henry Commager. (1992). *A History of the United States*. New York; London.
Olson, Alison. (1992). "Eighteenth-Century Colonial Legislatures and Their Constituents." *The Journal of American History*, 79(2): 543–567.
Schiltz, Timothy, and Rainey Lee. (1978). "The Geographical Distribution of Elazar's Political Subcultures among the Mass Population: A Research Note." *The Western Political Quarterly*, 31(3): 410–415.
Simeon, Richard, and Beryl A. Radiny. (2010). "Reflections on Comparing Federalisms: Canada and the United States." *Publius: The Journal of Federalism*, 40(3): 357–365.
Smirnyagin, Leonid. (1989). *The US Regions: The Portrait of Modern America*. Moscow: Mysl'. [Raiony SShA: Portret sovremennoi Ameriki].
Tully, Alan. (1994). *Forming American Politics: Ideals, Interests, and Institutions in Colonial New York and Pennsylvania*. Baltimore: John Hopkins University Press.
Zagarri, Rosemarie. (1987). *The Politics of Size: Representation in the United States, 1776–1850*. Ithaca, NY: Cornwell University Press.
Zelinsky, Wilbur. (1973). *The Cultural Geography of the United States*. Hoboken, NJ: Prentice-Hall.

9 Oceania

Oceania is a region made up of thousands of islands throughout the Central and South Pacific. It includes Australia, the smallest continent in terms of total land area. Most of Oceania, including Australia, is under the Pacific, a vast body of water that is larger than all Earth's continental landmasses and islands combined. Australia is the largest country in Oceania incomparable in the size of territory with other Oceanian states. The other two major landmasses of Oceania are the microcontinent of Zealandia, which includes the country of New Zealand, and the eastern half of the island of New Guinea, made up of the nation of Papua New Guinea. Oceania also includes three island regions: Melanesia, Micronesia, and Polynesia (including the US state of Hawaii).[1] Apparently, *nowhere in the world geographical factors were so important for development.* Its history and economic development are deeply intertwined with the ocean. In the poetic words of Laughlin,

> to belong to an island is to look outwards, understanding that the horizon is not simply a boundary between what is visible and what is invisible, what is known and unknown, but a challenge: to imagine, to yearn, to leave, to search, to return.
>
> (Laughlin 2017: 10)

Australia is the largest economy in Oceania, followed by New Zealand and Papua New Guinea. These three together hold a huge 99.4% share of the Oceanian economy. Tuvalu is the smallest economy in Oceania.[2] Australia has one of the highest Human Development Indexes (HDI) in the world, it is the only giant country that is in the top ten, coming in fifth from the top. Most small Oceanian states have middle HDI.[3] Importantly, for many of those who study (and love) Oceania, Western concepts of development are not applicable to it.[4] Oceania has its own "sense" of what development is (I will turn to it later in this chapter).

Australia

The island continent of Australia is about the same size as Europe (excluding Russia) and the United States (excluding Alaska and Hawaii), but it is inhabited by only 24.5 million people (2023). Australia is

DOI: 10.4324/9781003496731-12

> a country of great climatic, bio, and physical diversity, ranging from the tropical and monsoonal north to temperate and Mediterranean climatic zones in the south; from great inland deserts to the small alpine region and the densely forested mountains of the southeast; and from the high rainfall areas of the northeast and the island State of Tasmania to the vast areas in which rain seldom falls. It is a land almost continuously subject to natural disasters – droughts, cyclones, floods, bushfires and even earthquakes-but it also has great mineral, pastoral and agricultural wealth. Distance is a factor which has great social and economic significance for all Australians, not only because of the problems it creates for internal transport and communications but also because of its effect in isolating Australia from the rest of the world.
> (Mathews 1981: 1)

This description points to two critical geographical factors for Australia – diversity and distance.

Australia has a developed economy and high standards of living. As of 2023, Australia was ranked thirteenth in the world in both GDP and GDP per capita.[5] Since the 1960s, Australia's urbanization rate has consistently been above 80%, and in 2022 it has reached its highest ever rate at 86.49%. Historically, Australia has been one of the most urbanized countries in the world, due to high rates of immigration since the twentieth century; immigration flows headed generally to coastal, urban areas. Australia belongs to the group of giant countries (in territorial size), but its population density is among the lowest in the world.[6]

In his book *The Tyranny of Distance: How Distance Shaped Australia's History* (1966) Geoffrey Blainey described how distance and isolation have been central to Australia's history, shaping its national identity and also its developmental trajectory. Even today, in our globalized world, Australia is geographically distant from many important cities, regions and countries. On the other hand, isolation has its advantages, providing a kind of comfort and sense of security, as Australia is geographically far from wars and conflicts.

Almost a third of the country's territory, mostly inland areas, is desert or semi-desert, not occupied by agricultural land. Sixty percent of the land is drainless, with only one major river system, the Murray-Darling in the southeast, used for navigation and irrigation. The main natural wealth of Australia is minerals. The continent ranks first in the world in reserves of bauxite (one-third of the world's reserves), zirconium; it is one of the first in reserves of iron ore, nickel, gold, and tin. On the shelf and in the state of Queensland oil deposits have been discovered; in the state of Western Australia – gas deposits. Australia also owns not less than one-third of the world reserves of uranium (in the Northern Territory, South and Western Australia).

By the time of the appearance of Europeans, Australia was inhabited by Aboriginal tribes, whose ancestors came from South Asia, presumably in the late Paleolithic period. The first Europeans to reach Australia were the Dutch Willem Jansson (1606) and Abel Tasman (1642), so Australia was originally named New Holland, but it was the British who began more systematic colonization. The road to colonization was paved by a British navigator James Cook. Cook, on his first circumnavigation expedition, discovered the east coast (1770) of Australia, named it New South Wales, and declared it the property of British King George III.[7] The first British colony was established in what is now Sydney in 1788.

Australia is a resettlement country: originally, its territories served as a place of exile for criminals from the metropolis: in total, about 150,000 people were exiled to Australia until 1868, the date when the continent's use as a place of exile ended. (Nowadays, in Australia, it is a kind of "chic" to be descended from convicts, proof of a long connection with the continent. It's almost like in the United States being a descendant of those who sailed on the "Mayflower" from Britain to the New World.) The discovery of remarkable wealth in the late nineteenth century (primarily gold) and the accompanying "gold rush" (1851–1861) led to a dramatic increase in the flow of migrants. By the mid-1880s, most of the population living in Australia had been born on the continent, so the initial sense of exile, of being disconnected from their roots, had somewhat diminished. Indigenous people were driven off their territories and moved to reserves.

It is noteworthy that the metropolis – London – was poorly informed about the natural conditions, the nature of development, and the peculiarities of the population of its distant colony. The materials of parliamentary (Westminster) hearings of the nineteenth century showed that England was going to create in Australia "little England," inhabited by "enlightened yeomen." Until the end of the nineteenth century, Australia was a continent but not a nation. Its six colonies developed as a distant periphery of the British Empire, supplying the metropolis with raw materials and receiving from it a "surplus" population. In 1901, the six British colonies were united into the Commonwealth of Australia (the British Dominion), and in 1911, two new entities appeared in the federal structure of the country: the Northern Territory (taken over from South Australia) and the Capital Territory: the latter was acquired by the federal government from the state of New South Wales. For the Capital Territory to have access to the sea, in 1915 the government acquired the territory of Jervis Bay from the State of New South Wales (it was separated from the Capital Territory in 1988 and is administered by the Department of Transport).

Political elites of the colonies – the future Australian states – understood the need for unification, primarily because of the economic advantages of a single market, but the creation of the Commonwealth of Australia was a difficult task and was accomplished in several stages. The continent's vast territory and low population density meant that before the formation of the federal union, the six states that formed it were poorly connected, both economically and politically. As the *New York Times* wrote in 1889, the colonies looked as if they

> constituted separate independent states . . . there was more jealousy and grievance among them toward each other than among the old American colonies. They had different tax policies and were in a constant state of tariff warfare among themselves; they had no common ground on security matters, and their coins and postage stamps were also different.

In addition, the colonies saw their place within the future union differently. For example, the political elites of New South Wales, the most developed colony, were willing to accept only a union in which New South Wales would dominate.

The first two attempts to negotiate unification were unsuccessful. A third attempt began in 1890 with a proposal to draft a federal constitution. In 1891, a conference attended by delegates appointed by the colonies adopted the first constitutional draft, but it was not until 1897, six years later, that a second convention, already composed of citizen-elected deputies, adopted a version of the constitution that incorporated all the amendments. This document was sent to the state parliaments for a vote. The parliament of New South Wales voted against it. The constitution is not adopted until 1899, after a specially convened Congress of Colonial Prime Ministers adopted another amended version of the constitution, which increased the political role of New South Wales, including, in particular, the provision that the capital of the new state – a federal union – should be located in the territory of this state (Filippov, Ordeshook and Shvetsova 2004: 199–200).

The union was granted full sovereignty in 1931. Weakening ties with Great Britain, especially after World War II, strengthened Australia's national identity and led to a reorientation in foreign relations. Today, the major trading partners of Australia are the United States, Japan, the United Kingdom, New Zealand, Korea, and Germany. External factors contributed to the unification of the colonies and their transformation into a stable political entity – these were the intensification of France's colonial policy in Oceania and Japan's increased military presence in Asia.

Australia is characterized by sharp interregional disparities in population distribution. More than 60% of the population lives in or near the five major urban centers. More than three-fourths of the population is concentrated on the east coast, in New South Wales, Victoria, and Queensland. About 85% of Australians live within 80 kilometers of the sea, and major cities are in this band. Every two in five Australians live in either Sydney or Melbourne; every three in five live in state capitals.

British legacy, geographic constraints, and institutional development

Democratic institutions were imported by Australians from the metropolis. This was quite a successful import strategy. Ville (2007) identified phases of institutional development and change in Australia since British settlement. For much of the nineteenth century, Australian institutions were those of the British Empire, imported into Australia though insufficiently adapted to local conditions. These institutions have rather served the specific needs of a British penal colony than the market economy of an emerging state. Due to geographic distance from London, communication delays, misunderstandings, and asymmetries of information were routine (Ville 2007: 7). At the same time, many convicts sent to Australia from the metropolis brought with them business experience, entrepreneurial values, and trade skills (Oxley 1996).

British migrants carried with them to the colonies large stocks of social capital, which helped to form a European-style civil society (Greene 2001).

However, as Ville (2007: 9) wrote,

> [F]or most of the XIX century, economic growth remained largely under the custodianship of British institutions: Australian wool and other commodities were largely sold in London; "colonial capital" was raised on the London Stock Exchange and managed by British boards of directors; economic policy, such as the Navigation Laws, was British; and technological innovation focused upon the needs of the industrializing British economy with a very different climate and set of factor costs from primary-producing Australia. The dominant groups ("elites") driving institutional change were British or "Anglo-Australian," that is settlers in Australia who still considered Britain their home.

British institutions were placed in the "soil" for which they were not designed. The differences between British and Australian "soils" centered around geography (location and climate) and factor costs. Australia's location in the south Pacific was the antipodes of Britain and remote from the regions of major human settlement and modern economic progress. Australian hot and dry climate contrasted with Britain's mild and wet one. Australia's land abundancy, but labor deficiency, was similarly the converse of the much smaller but populous British Isles (Ville 2007: 9–10).

Over the years, emerging self-determination, the economic crisis in the 1890s, and the move to federated nationhood in 1901 invoked the development of distinctive national institutions, which increasingly replaced those of the British Empire. However, there were still two objective constraints to enhanced development – the geographical distance and the small population size of the nation. Distance and poor communication between the former colonies – now states – have cultivated the sense of independence and the development of separate and distinctive institutional structures. The legacy of this has been fragmented and less efficient institutions (Ville 2007: 12).

Federal solution was most probably the only one that matched Australian "soil." The Australian federation was established as composed of six states – New South Wales, Victoria, Queensland, South Australia, Western Australia, Tasmania, and two territories – the Northern Territory and the Capital Territory – the city of Canberra. Federation in Australia was formed "from below," as a union of colonies. The states and territories had their legislative power – parliaments, executive power – governments, and considerable political autonomy. The states have representation in the upper house of the federal parliament, the Senate, which has 76 deputies – 12 from each state and two from the two territories. Senators from the territories are elected every three years; senators from the states are elected for six years, with half of them reelected every three years. The states are headed by governors appointed by the British monarch on the proposal of the state governments. The preservation of the institution of governor in the "old" form is determined by the fact that the states, even after the establishment of the Commonwealth of Australia, sought to maintain a link with the British crown independent of the federation.

Australia is often compared to Canada. These two countries are sometimes even called "brotherly." Indeed, both Australia and Canada are territorially extended settler countries, colonial federations. Both states are characterized by sharp disparities in the distribution of population and economic activity, although geographically these disparities look different: while Canada is characterized by a shift of population and economic activity to the south, to the border with the United States, in Australia a band of increased population density stretches along the east coast. Finally, both states have so-called problem regions prone to secession. In Canada, it is the province of Quebec; in Australia, it is the state of Western Australia, which in 1933 attempted to secede from the union. After a referendum in which the state's citizens supported secession, the state government asked the king and the British Parliament to recognize the act. However, the British Parliament refused to approve Western Australia's secession from the Commonwealth of Australia.

The geographic fragmentation of the territory made it difficult to create a single federal state in Canada, but this problem was even more acute in Australia. When Australia had a national telegraph network connecting it to the rest of the world, it still did not have a national, uniform-gauge rail network because of railways being deployed independently by colonial governments (De Percy 2008: 132). Conversely, Canadian federalism was concerned with connecting communities which formed predominantly along the overland northern border of the United States and focused on "railway-building and the expansion of Canadian territory" (Burgess 1990: 43).

Federal solution though necessary could bring only fragmented federalism in the country, where differences existed between the individual state constitutions, thus adding considerably to the complexity of federal–state government relations (Costar 1999). The incomplete constitutional transformation was also explained by Olson (1984) as allowing institutional sclerosis to take hold in Australia and with it the capture of government policy by interest groups. As Ville (2007: 29) argued, the continuing patterns of Australian development included geographical distance, small population size, and fragmented institutions.

Immigration and the Aboriginal problem

Initially, Australia's population was sharply dominated by immigrants from Britain and Ireland. Immigration from Asian countries, particularly Vietnam and China, has grown rapidly since Australia abolished its white immigration policy in 1973. In addition, there are already well-established Greek and Italian communities in the cities. Thus, multiculturalism is the imminent feature of Australian society.

Mass postwar immigration was an unprecedented phenomenon for Australia. It was a real revolution for Australians of English descent. A particular curiosity were the people from Lebanon, Vietnam, and Sri Lanka, who changed the very nature of Australian society. Today, Australia's immigration policy is based on attracting highly skilled migrants, primarily in the fields of information technology, financial services, and medicine. In recent years, an average of 120,000–180,000 people has entered the country annually, and it is this immigration (rather than internal sources) that has determined the country's population growth (De Blij 2010: 585).

The share of Aboriginal people in the Australian population is 3.2% (or about 812,000 people[8]), and all social indicators of this group differ from those of other social groups for the worse – Aboriginal people have lower life expectancy, higher unemployment, much lower education levels, but higher incarceration rates. Most Aboriginal people live in the states of Queensland, Western Australia, and the Northern Territory (Ghosh 2018). Europeans pushed Aboriginal people out of all areas they considered suitable for development. Only in the northern and western parts of the continent were relatively intact communities left. One hundred years of European colonization almost destroyed 40,000 years of Aboriginal traditions. Until 1967, Aboriginal people were not even counted in the census (Diamond 1999: 320).

In the 1990s, the Supreme Court of Australia, answering the question: "Do Aboriginal people have the right to demand the return of lands that fed them for thousands of years and then were taken away by European colonizers?" gave a positive answer. The Court's ruling stated that Aboriginal organizations and tribal unions can judicially challenge ownership of lands they have traditionally considered their own. The challenge now was to reconcile the right of local tribes to own land with the country's mining and agriculture laws. This will not be easy, as Aboriginal claims cover about 40% of the country's territory. In doing so, the Supreme Court overturned the well-known position that when Captain Cook declared British sovereignty over Eastern Australia in 1770, this territory belonged to no one (it was so-called *terra nullius*).

As Diamond argued, Australia is the only continent where some Aboriginal communities now live with almost no "signs of civilization" – no institutional structures, no settled occupations, no written language, not even iron tools. They still use stone tools. Meanwhile, unlike the Australian Aborigines, the Papuans of New Guinea are engaged in the cultivation of various crops and pig breeding. Diamond formulated a reasonable question: Why didn't the New Guineans migrate to Australia when these territories are separated from each other only by the 90-mile-wide Torres Strait? Another reasonable question of him related to New Guinea. When Europeans began to colonize it in the late nineteenth century, its inhabitants were illiterate, used stone tools, and, with a few exceptions, were not politically organized even into tribal unions. So if the Papuans of New Guinea were considered "more advanced" than the Aborigines of Australia, why were they significantly less advanced than many Asian, African, and Amerindian communities?

Jared Diamond answered his own questions. The shortest answer: it's geography. As he argued, the traditional societies of Australia and New Guinea developed in isolation from the Asian societies that once gave birth to them (these are primarily the island societies of Indonesia). However, the societies of Australia and New Guinea – both isolated – subsequently took different paths, and natural geographical factors largely determined these paths. First, New Guinea lies close to the equator, while Australia is far out in the temperate zone. Second, New Guinea is a mountainous country, while Australia is predominantly flat. Third, New Guinea is one of the wettest places on earth, while Australia is one of the driest (unpredictable droughts can last for years). Finally, New Guinea's soils are young, fertile volcanic soils, while Australia is covered with old, leached, and infertile soils. As a result, New Guinea produces high yields of sweet yams, taro, bananas, yams, while in Australia agriculture is unproductive, Australian wild flora has the only "usable" species (though very tasty) – macadamia nut. This is why New Guineans are sedentary, and Australians are accustomed to unpredictability and change: when local natural conditions deteriorated, they simply moved to where conditions seemed better. It was the geographical conditions that have determined that Australian Aborigines remained hunter-gatherers. However, Australia is also heterogeneous: within it, the island of Tasmania is a unicum region, the quintessence of the "simplicity" of material culture. The Australian mainland is more populated and less isolated than Tasmania, which represents the smallest group of the most isolated populations of any continent.

The advantages of New Guinea over Australia were clear; but what about its disadvantages in comparison with other societies? The development of New Guinea was limited by such factors as the low protein content of traditional foods and the limited areas suitable for habitation (due to the mountainous terrain). The territory of New Guinea is highly fragmented: a thousand different languages are spoken there, about half of them with no more than 500 users. Neighboring villagers do not understand each other, and the country's population is fragmented into a huge number of microcommunities.

Unlike Australia, both Americas and South Africa, the European population of New Guinea is small, and the country was populated predominantly by indigenous people. The main obstacle to European settlement of New Guinea before 1880 was malaria (the country had a terrible reputation in this regard) and other tropical diseases. In addition, European crops and breeds of livestock did not adapt well to the nature and climate of New Guinea (Diamond 1999: 295–311). These cases are beautiful, classic illustrations of the impact of geographical factors on development.

Oceania or the Pacific region

Oceania is the largest in the world in terms of spatial extent, covering almost half of the globe and stretching from the Bering Sea to the Southern Ocean[9] and from Ecuador to Indonesia.[10] The geographical quality that unites the Pacific islands as a region is their insularity. The islands have an array of physical landforms. Low-lying atolls with vast central lagoons are typical in Polynesia and Micronesia. Nauru and Niue are raised atolls with no lagoons. There are high volcanic islands in Polynesia and Melanesia, and continental islands in Melanesia include Papua New Guinea with its snow-capped mountains.

The Pacific islands include some of the world's smallest countries (Table 9.1). Indeed, the number of microstates – states with resident populations of fewer than half a million – is one of the region's main identifying geopolitical characteristics. There is no greater concentration of microstates on the planet. The region also remains the one last bastion of unresolved nineteenth-century colonialism since a third of its polities remain dependencies of the United States, France, Great Britain,

Table 9.1 Pacific island countries

Country	*Capital*	*Land (sq. km)*	*EEZ (sq. km)*	*Population [year]*	*GDP (US$) [year]*	*Political status*
American Samoa	Pago Pago	199	404,391	67,242 [2011]	462.2 million [2005]	Dependent territory
Cook Islands	Rarotonga	236	1.8 million	13,200 [2009]	206.5 million [2009]	Freely associated state
Federated States of Micronesia	Pohnpei	702	2.9 million	110,000 [2010]	269.7 million [2009]	Freely associated state
Fiji	Suva	18,300	1.3 million	900,000 [2010]	3.3 billion [2011]	Independent republic
French Polynesia	Papeete	4,000	4.8 million	267,000 [2009]	5.6 billion	An overseas country within the French Republic
Guam	Agaña	544	221,504	183,286 [2011]	Data not available	Dependent territory
Kiribati	Tarawa	811	3.6 million	100,000 [2010]	163 million [2011]	Independent republic
Nauru	Yaren	21	320,000	9,771 [2009]	55 million [2009]	Independent republic
New Caledonia	Noumea	18,600	1.4 million	245, 580	8.9 billion [2010]	"Special collectivity"
Niue	Alofi	260	390,000	1,536 [2009]	15.8 million [2009]	Freely associated state
Northern Mariana Islands	Saipan	464	758,121	40,050	633.4 million [2000]	Dependent territory
Palau	Koror	458	600,900	20,397 [2009]	179.6 million [2009]	Freely associated state
Papua New Guinea	Port Moresby	463,000	3.1 million	6.5 million [2010]	11 billion [2011]	Constitutional monarchy
Pitcairn Islands	Adamstown	47	842,000	48 [2011]	Data not available	Dependent territory
Republic of Marshall Islands	Majuro	181	2.1 million	54,000 [2009]	161.7 million [2008]	Freely associated state
Samoa	Apia	2,944	120,000	187,000 [2010]	606 million	Independent republic
Solomon Islands	Honiara	28,900	1.6 million	500,000 [2010]	770 million [2011]	Constitutional monarchy

Source: Department of Foreign Affairs and Trade country and region fact sheets (http://www.dfat.gov.au/geo/fs/index.html); CIA 2011, The World Fact Book, (https://www.cia.gov/library/publications/the-world-factbook/).

Australia, New Zealand, and Chile (Herr and Bergin 2011: 8). Interestingly, Oceania's dependent communities do not always aspire to independence. For example, New Caledonia held referendums on secession from France and independence in 2018 and 2020. Both times, most of the population voted against secession.

The largest state in Oceania is New Zealand (seventy-fifth place in the world by the size of territory), which is part of the British Commonwealth. The state is located on two large islands, the North and South Islands, and several small islands. Since 1840, New Zealand was a colony of Great Britain; in 1907, it received the status of a dominion; in 1931, it gained sovereignty.

The autochthonous population of New Zealand is called Māori and belongs to the Polynesian group. Most Māori live on the North Island; the colder South Island has never had more than 5% of the population. After the first contact with Europeans, the Māori population began to decline catastrophically due to the influenza viruses and venereal diseases brought by Europeans and due to internal intertribal warfare (with the guns the Māori received from Europeans causing a much higher number of casualties), and finally due to psychological demoralization. The mortality rate among Māori was so high that the very existence of this people was in question, but the crisis was gradually overcome, and now Māori (unlike the aborigines of Australia) have a stable population. Today, most Māori have both Polynesian and European ancestry; many New Zealanders who identify themselves as Māori look more like Europeans than Polynesians.

Māori adaptation to European culture has been far from easy; they have accepted some aspects and rejected others. For example, the Māori accepted Christianity as their faith but categorically rejected some rituals, such as the Christian funeral rite. In general, it seems impossible to call Māori culture a "conquered" or "suppressed" culture; this distinctive culture was no more "conquered" by European culture than Japanese (the difference would be that for most Māori the language of communication is English, and they do not know their native language well, while the Japanese are not strong in English and communicate in their native language). Fate was more merciful to Māori than to Aboriginal Australians: the Treaty of Waitangi of 1840 between the Māori and the British guaranteed them possession of their lands and preservation of their cultural traditions (Yoon 1994: 295–296).

No other macro-region in the world has a similar territorial structure as Oceania; Oceania's geopolitical situation is unique: for centuries, small communities have survived on thousands of islands surrounded by ocean. Oceania is the most remote and inaccessible part of the world, and its isolation has greatly influenced the process of statehood formation. It should be noted that there is an uneven distribution of islands on the territory of Oceania, with the concentration of their location and size decreasing from west to east. Thus, Melanesia has the smallest number of states compared to other parts of Oceania. At the same time, not every island is a separate state: as a rule, a state consists of several islands (Marshall Islands, Solomon Islands, Mariana Islands).

The Federated States of Micronesia, located northeast of New Guinea and east of the Philippines, comprise some 600 islands and have a population of just over 104,000 people. While small in land mass, Micronesia stretches over 2,700 kilometers in length and covers an area of 2.6 million square kilometers, making it the tenth-largest country (after Kazakhstan) in terms of surface. Occupied by Spain from the sixteenth century, they were sold to Germany (1899) and were then occupied by Japan (1914). Post-World War II, they were administered by the United States. The example of Micronesia illustrates the region's many paradoxes and its often-contested nature. The Pacific region is also characterized by far-reaching linkages and diversity. For example, the Northern Mariana Islands and American Samoa represent the western and southern extremes of the United States. The islands of Wallis and Futuna are part of France while Tokelau is the northernmost part of New Zealand.

The region represents contradictions of scale. While the Pacific is the planet's largest entity, accounting for nearly one-third of the Earth's surface, most of the countries in the region are island states that are tiny in terms of both size and population. Yet many of the region's inhabitants take a different view. They do not see themselves as citizens of small island nations but as custodians of vast ocean environments. Kiribati's ocean area is larger than the land surface of all but six countries in the world.[11]

History and territorial structure

In the second half of the nineteenth century, the "pirates" of global capitalism – sandalwood, coffee, copra traders, planters, recruiters, guano miners, and settlers – began arriving on the islands of Oceania, driven by the task of finding a livelihood outside the legal systems of their countries. The overall effect of the arrival of colonial powers in the Pacific was to bring the island territories into the world economy on terms that suited the colonial powers. European colonists tried to grow everything – tobacco, rubber, coffee, vanilla, and cocoa. But plant diseases and labor shortages meant that, with a few exceptions such as rubber in Papua and coffee in New Caledonia, only one thing was the most profitable: copra.

The colonial partition of Oceania was completed relatively late, by the end of the nineteenth century. Importantly, when Europeans arrived on the islands of Oceania, they established colonial rule over them, though they did not settle there *en masse*. Only New Zealand, New Caledonia, and Hawaii, the largest and most remote islands lying farthest from the equator and thus having the most temperate (European-like) climates, had large European settler populations. So, unlike Australia and both Americas, Oceania was populated predominantly by East Asians and local nationalities (Diamond 1999: 353).

The decolonization process began in the 1960s. In 1962, Western Samoa (previously under the administration of New Zealand) gained independence; in 1968 – the island of Nauru (was under the joint administration of Great Britain, Australia, and New Zealand), in 1970 – the Kingdom of Tonga (former British protectorate) and the Fiji Islands (former British colony). Then, in the 1980s, the status of the Caroline Islands, Marshall Islands, and Mariana Islands changed; they became "associated states" with the United States. To date, of the 21 territories of Oceania, only 11 have achieved full sovereignty. These include Samoa (in 1962), Nauru (in 1968), Tonga (in 1970), Fiji (in 1970), Solomon Islands (in 1978), Tuvalu (in 1978),

Kiribati (in 1979), Vanuatu (in 1980), Micronesia (in 1986), Marshall Islands (in 1986), and Palau (in 1994).

Oceania is traditionally divided into three historical and geographical areas: Melanesia, Micronesia, and Polynesia.

Melanesia is located in the western part of Oceania, most of it in New Guinea, a kind of "micro-mainland" of Melanesia. The "micro mainland" is divided into two parts: the western part is part of Indonesia, and the eastern part is occupied by the state of Papua New Guinea, a member of the British-led Commonwealth. The Commonwealth also includes the Solomon Islands, Nauru, Samoa, Tuvalu, Tonga, Kiribati, and Vanuatu. To the east of Micronesia lies the Republic of Fiji, which became independent in 1970 and has an amazing relationship with the British Commonwealth. The republic joined the Commonwealth at the same time as independence but was expelled from the Commonwealth in 1987 due to coups and the abrogation of the constitution. Fiji rejoined the Commonwealth in 1997, withdrew in 2000, rejoined in 2001, and withdrew again in 2006.

Micronesia occupies the northwestern part of Oceania and includes three main archipelagos – the Caroline, Mariana, and Marshall Islands, as well as the Gilbert Islands. The following states are located here: the Commonwealth of the Northern Mariana Islands, the Federated States of Micronesia, the Republic of the Marshall Islands, and the Republic of Palau. Of special importance is the island of Guam in the group of Mariana Islands – the largest military-strategic base of the United States.

Polynesia stretches from the southwest of Oceania to its eastern limits. It includes the islands of New Zealand, Tonga, Samoa, Wallis, Tuvalu, Tokelau, Cook, Society, Tuamotu, Marquesas, Hawaii, Easter Island, and others. In the second half of the twentieth century, independent states were formed in Polynesia – Western Samoa, Kiribati (it is noteworthy that the islands comprising this state are located in four hemispheres – Northern and Southern, Western and Eastern!), Nauru, the Kingdom of Tonga, and Tuvalu.

In studying the identity formation of Oceania's islanders, Ron Crocombe categorized the islands into three major groups, depending on the degree of influence of the metropolis on the identity formation of the islanders:

(1) Highest: free access of islanders to the metropolitan state (all islands north of the equator and Eastern Samoa to the United States; Cook Islands, Niue, Tokelau, and Norfolk Islands to New Zealand and Australia; New Caledonia, French Polynesia, Wallis, and Futuna Islands to France; Pitcairn Island to Great Britain and New Zealand; Easter Island (Rapanui) to Chile).
(2) Middle: islands with significant access to one or more metropolitan states (Western Samoa has special access to New Zealand and to Australia; through Eastern Samoa, many residents obtain a green card or US citizenship; Tonga has access to Australia, New Zealand, and the United States; Tuvalu and Kiribati have special limited access to New Zealand; Fiji island populations migrate to Canada, the United States, Australia, New Zealand, as well as India and Europe).
(3) Extremely limited access to the outside world: Central Melanesian States – Papua New Guinea, Solomon Islands, and Vanuatu (Crocombe 1994).

Islanders in Oceania are characterized by multiple identities, a phenomenon that is becoming increasingly widespread. For example, islanders north of the equator have some degree of American identification: through their status as an associated state with the United States, they have free access to the United States – the right to enter, work, and reside. Residents of the Cook Islands, Niue, and Tokelau have the same rights in New Zealand. Many residents of Samoa, Tonga, and Fiji have dual citizenship and, accordingly, two (and sometimes three) passports.

On average, each of the languages of Oceania is spoken by about 5,000 people. The main language for communication is English, which is studied in schools in all countries of Oceania. As for religions on the islands: in the late 1940s, American missionaries replaced Spanish missionaries, and many missions from Great Britain were also preserved. So there are many Christian movements on the islands. In addition, Tuvalu, Tonga, and Kiribati have the fastest growing numbers of adherents of Islam.

I mentioned earlier that the most important geographical features of Australia that have influenced its development are diversity and distance. In Oceania, these two features are also present, but a third one is added – *islandness*. According to Stratford,

> [I]slandness is a complex expression of identity that attaches to places smaller than continents and surrounded entirely by water. These identifications include, but are not confined to, strong perceptions of island-self and mainland-other, as well as potent connections to island communities and environments. They embrace water, sky and land, flows and boundaries, edges and interiors, isolation and access.
>
> (Stratford 2008: 160)

Islandness could be converted to a key ontological resource for those who govern islands (Stratford 2008). This explicitly implies that Oceania needs special approaches to development, different from those developed for other countries. I will now turn to these approaches.

Specific approaches to development

With a general – at least, formal – orientation toward democratic development based on Western models, the countries of Oceania strive to preserve their identity, even to the point of isolationism. Often, Oceanians are portrayed as "latecomers" in a global grand narrative of anti-colonial struggle (Robie 1989: 23). In many countries of Oceania, political life traditionally continues to develop at the local level, and the establishment of centralized and effective state power faces objective difficulties due to geographic factors.

Importantly, there is an assumption among researchers that Oceania being a very distinctive kind of society requires a special approach to conceptualizing "development." Oceanians, they argue, have everything – they had enough resources to survive, to grow populations, to have enough resources left over to plan for weddings, festivals, etc. They had enough extra time after taking care of those necessities that they could engage in cultural events and activities. The only thing was that they didn't have much money. So Oceania

> went against the very assumption of development as defined by Westerners. Oceania had little income, so according to mainstream development ideas, life should be bad, people should have a really hard time just trying to survive, there shouldn't be enough food and other necessities, and people should be stuck working long hours for low pay just to survive. Oceania broke those so-called definitions. There was very little income, but people seemed to be doing fine! To be clear, they didn't have much stuff: TVs, cars, smartphones, video games, or the ability to buy the latest fashion trends, or spend money on travel, etc. However, they also didn't have hunger, starvation, homelessness, or mental illnesses associated with isolation. They had their own built-in safety net.
>
> (Watters 2008)

Watters described the Village Mode of Production to explain why mainstream development couldn't figure out Oceania (Watters 2008). This differed from the Capitalist Mode of Production, which relied on two things: private property and market economies. The Village Mode of Production has also been called the traditional economy or the *kastom* economy. Why was this fundamentally different from a capitalist economy? There was no private property in Oceania in "Western" sense, and no market economies, which are two fundamental components of capitalist economies. Instead, land was held by kin groups and couldn't be bought or sold. Work and production were based on reciprocity does not profit; production was done to meet social goals and not profit accumulation (Firth 2000).

At the same time, Oceania's governments have an interest in emphasizing the specialness of their communities to receive benefits. As Firth (2000: 191) argued, the Pacific Islands continue to claim that they are special and should be treated specially in terms of development classifications. To be classified by international organizations as a least developed country brings benefits and concessions in a globalizing world. The South Pacific Forum pushed again for the completion of a comprehensive vulnerability index – a measure of the exposure of economies to forces beyond government control, such as natural disasters, smallness, and isolation – which could then be included among the criteria for determining Least Developed Country status. Thus, "so bad" geography could be converted into special developmental status that brings benefits.

"Pacific paradox" and "Polynesian experiment"

Toatu (2002) posed a reasonable question regarding relatively poor performance of the Pacific Islands countries. What explains this poor performance when countries elsewhere of the same size and characteristics have registered impressive growth performance during the same period? The answer was that it was not the lack of capital or good policies or even bad geography that constrained the economic growth and development of these island economies but rather the lack of appropriate institutions and incentives to accumulate and acquire human and physical capital and to make policies effective. Ineffective institutions, as well as corrupt practices and bureaucratic ineffectiveness, led to large reductions in the average rate of growth of national income in these countries.

According to Toatu, geographical factors such as size, location, and climate are "facts of life.

> they are the "pot" in which alterable ingredients of growth (i.e., physical capital, good policy, human capital, and institutions) are mixed. The Oceanian countries must make the absolute best of these facts of life and not resign themselves to poor economic performance because of them. The success stories of other small states, notably Hongkong and Singapore, and some small island countries such as the Maldives in the Indian Ocean, have demonstrated that small countries are more adept at surviving economically and performing more successfully provided they get the fundamentals right.
>
> (Toatu 2002)

Toatu called it "paradox." In my view, this is not a paradox, it's geography. This is hardly possible to compare Oceanian countries with Singapore or Hong Kong as their geographic location is so much different.

Jared Diamond arguing that geography was power, and that it was geography that shaped how history unfolded across the world,[12] suggested that Oceania (or more precisely, Polynesia) could be viewed as a unique natural laboratory for studying the impact of geographic factors on human society and development trajectories. Polynesia is a cluster of islands that vary greatly in area, degree of isolation, altitude, climate, land cover, and biological resources. At the same time, the ancestors of Polynesian peoples were similar in culture and language.

What do we observe? The same people inhabited different islands, nevertheless the types of societies were radically different. In the cold climate of the Chatham Islands, the inhabitants had no alternative but to remain hunters and gatherers. This society simply could not afford to support those who gave nothing to the common pot – military, officials, chiefs . . . Besides, the Chatham Islands are relatively small and remote territories, which can feed no more than 2,000 hunter-gatherers. The result was a small peaceful community with primitive technology and weak social hierarchy. A completely different example would be the North (warmer) Island of New Zealand. It is the largest island in Polynesia and is quite suitable for agriculture. Before the arrival of Europeans, the population of the aborigines of the North Island (Māori) was constantly increasing, surplus crops allowed to feed the soldiers, so that Māori tribes were constantly fighting with each other, and the tribes were characterized by a rigid hierarchical structure.

Thus, Polynesian societies were very diverse: here we find both egalitarian village societies and complex, clearly stratified hierarchical societies, where each stratum is impenetrable to the others. From the point of view of political organization,

Polynesian societies are also diverse: from small, independent units (uniting one tribe or one village) to proto-empires covering many islands and expanding by making wars and seizures of territories. Thus, by the time of the arrival of Europeans in the eighteenth century, Tonga was a maritime pro-empire covering an entire archipelago. This archipelago consisted of several large islands with undivided surfaces, each having its own chief. Then the chief of the largest and most powerful island, Tongatapu, united all the islands: this is how the proto-empire came into being. Like Tonga, Hawaii became a political community of several inhabited islands. By the time the islands were discovered by Europeans in 1778, each major island was already internally united, and the first attempts at inter-island unification were underway.

Diamond identified six geographic variables that explained the diversity of Polynesian societies: climate (from tropical to temperate to sub-Antarctic), island geological type (volcanic origin, coral atoll, continental fragment), availability of marine resources, island area (from the tiny island of Anuta to the huge islands of New Zealand), fragmentation (divided into valleys) of the island surface, and degree of isolation. To this list should be added the productivity of agriculture: the most efficient on the islands of Polynesia is taro in irrigation fields, in addition to yams, breadfruit, sweet yams, bananas, coconuts. As a result of all these factors, the population density on the islands varied most dramatically: from five people per square kilometer on the Chatham Islands to 210–250 people per square kilometer in Tonga, Samoa, the Society Islands, and 300 on Hawaii. The economy is most primitive on small islands with low population density, while specialization of the economy is developed on more populated islands, such as Samoa, Tonga, and Hawaii (Diamond 1999: 53–66).

Notes

1 Australia and Oceania: Physical Geography (nationalgeographic.org).
2 GDP of Oceanian countries 2023 – StatisticsTimes.com.
3 Human Development Index (HDI) by Country 2024 (worldpopulationreview.com).
4 Development in Oceania (arcgis.com).
5 Australia Economy Ranking: by GDP and 60 other indicators (georank.org).
6 Australia: degree of urbanization 1960–2022 | Statista.
7 Cook was certainly a man of exceptional character. He led three around-the-world expeditions, during which he made several geographical discoveries: he surveyed and mapped parts of Newfoundland and the east coast of Canada, Australia, New Zealand, the west coast of North America, and the Pacific, Indian, and Atlantic Oceans. Many of his maps were unrivaled in their accuracy and precision for many decades.
8 Australia: Aboriginal and Torres Strait Islander population summary | Australian Bureau of Statistics (abs.gov.au).
9 The Southern Ocean is the conventional name for the waters of the three oceans (Pacific, Atlantic, and Indian) surrounding Antarctica, sometimes informally referred to as the "fifth ocean." The Southern Ocean does not have a clearly delineated northern boundary of islands and continents.
10 The name "Oceania" is attributed to Danish cartographer Conrad Malte-Brun (1755–1826), who referred to a supercontinent in the southern Pacific that included Australia and the South Pacific islands.

11 Letter from the Editors: Engaging with Oceania: Some Background about the Region – and Why It Matters for IB Research | Published in AIB Insights.
12 'Guns, Germs and Steel': Jared Diamond on Geography as Power (nationalgeographic.com).

References

Blainey, G. (1966). *The Tyranny of Distance: How Distance Shaped Australia's History*. Melbourne: Macmillan.
Burgess, Michael. (1990). *Canadian Federalism: Past, Present and Future*. Leicester: Leicester University Press.
Costar, Brian. (1999). "State Government." In *Institutions in Australian Society*, ed. by J. Henningham, 2nd ed., pp. 34–52. Melbourne: Oxford University Press.
Crocombe, Ron. (1994). "The Continuing Creation of Identities in the Pacific Islands: Blood, Behavior, Boundaries and Belief." In *Geography and National Identity*, ed. by D. Hooson, pp. 311–331. Oxford: Blackwell.
De Blij, Harm, and Peter Mueller. (2010). *Geography: Realms, Regions, and Concepts*. Hoboken, NJ: John Wiley & Sons.
De Percy, Michael. (2008). "Broadbanding the Nation: Lessons from Canada or Shortcomings in Australian Federalism?" In *Australia Under Construction: Nation-Building – Past, Present, and Future*, ed. by J. Butcher, pp. 127–147. Canberra: ANU E Press.
Diamond, Jared. (1999). *Guns, Germs, and Steel: The Fates of Human Societies*. New York: W. W. Norton & Company.
Filippov, Mikhail, Peter Ordeshook, and Olga Shvetsova. (2004). *Designing Federalism: A Theory of Self-Sustainable Federal Institutions*. Cambridge: Cambridge University Press.
Firth, Stewart. (2000). "The Pacific Islands and the Globalization Agenda." *The Contemporary Pacific*, 12(1): 177–192.
Ghosh, Ratna. (2018). "Multiculturalism in a Comparative Perspective: Australia, Canada and India." *Canadian Ethnic Studies*, 50(1): 15–36.
Greene, Jack. (2001). "Social and Cultural Capital in Colonial British America: A Case Study." In *Patterns of Social Capital: Stability and Change in Historical Perspective*, ed. by R. I. Rotberg, pp. 491–509. Cambridge: Cambridge University Press.
Herr, Richard, and Anthony Bergin. (2011). *Our Near Abroad: Australia and Pacific Islands Regionalism*. Canberra: Australian Strategic Policy Institute.
Laughlin, Nicholas. (2017). "Foreword." In *So Many Islands: Stories from the Caribbean, Mediterranean, Indian, and Pacific Oceans*, ed. by N. Laughlin and N. Folami Imoja, pp. 9–12. London: Little Island Press.
Mathews, Ronald. (1981). "Regional Disparities in Australia." In *Studies in Comparative Federalism: Australia*. Canberra: Advisory Commission on Intergovernmental Relations.
Olson, Mancur. (1984). *Australia in the Perspective of the Rise and Decline of Nations* (Discussion Paper No. 109). Canberra: Centre for Economic Policy Research, Australian National University.
Oxley, Deborah. (1996). *Convict Maids: The Forced Migration of Women to Australia*. Cambridge: Cambridge University Press.
Robie, David. (1989). *Blood on Their Banner: Nationalist Struggles in the South Pacific*. London: Zed Books.
Stratford, Elaine. (2008). "Islandness and Struggle over Development: A Tasmanian Case Study." *Political Geography*, 27(2): 160–175.
Toatu, Teuea. (2002). Unravelling the Pacific Paradox.
Ville, Simon. (2007). "The Institutional Legacy and the Development of an Australian National Innovation System." In *Institutions and Market Economies: The Political Economy of Growth and Development*, ed. by W. R. Garside, pp. 112–136. Houndmills: Palgrave Macmillan.

Watters, Ray. (2008). *Journeys Towards Progress: Essays of a Geographer on Development and Change in Oceania*. Wellington: Victoria University Press.
Yoon, H.-K. (1994). "Māori Identity and Māori Geomentality." In *Geography and National Identity*, ed. by D. Hooson, pp. 295–320. Oxford: Blackwell.

10 Russia

This book devotes a separate chapter to Russia, the last one; and there is a reason for that. Russia is a country of exceptional territorial size and diversity. It can be called a kind of laboratory for studying how geographical factors influenced the choice of political and economic institutions, and what this meant for the trajectory of national development. It is not that Russia is not a developed country, it is a middle-income country. The mystery for the researchers was not the level of the country's development but the pronounced asymmetry between economic and social indicators (like the level of education) and indices of the level of corruption, openness of the political regime, human rights, and so on. In other words, Russia is too "developed" to have such poor institutions and to launch a bloody war against a neighboring country.

For many Russian philosophers, Russia was rather a geographic concept than a "normal country." Vast territory and borders "stretching to infinity" were traditionally perceived in Russia as something sacred, destined for Russia either by God or by fate itself. Russia, according to the philosopher Leontiev, "was doomed by history to grow, even despite itself" (cited in Trenin 2002: 29). So the role of the "geographical factor" in Russian history was enormous – and the conquest of space has long remained its key idea. There is one fact, wrote the Russian philosopher Chaadaev,

> which dominates our historical movement, which runs through our entire history, which contains, so to speak, its entire philosophy, which appears in all epochs of our social life and determines their character, which is at the same time both an essential element of our political greatness, and the real cause of our mental impotence: this is a fact of geography.
>
> (Chaadaev 1992: 48)

While other nations might regret that they existed without "sufficient" space, for Russia it was the opposite: space without people; vast tracts of steppes and forests in Siberia, endless silent tundra . . . Imperial (in essence, spatial) imperative opened ever more distant spaces. Famous historian Klyuchevsky argued that colonization was the "basic fact" of Russian history: "The history of Russia is the history of the country, which is colonized" (Klyuchevsky 1956: 31). Indeed, without

DOI: 10.4324/9781003496731-13

understanding the specifics of Russian colonization, it would not be possible to understand neither the history of the country nor the nature and origin of political power and the country's developmental trajectory.

In 2004, at the end of President Putin's first term, Andrei Shleifer and Daniel Treisman published an optimistic article in *Foreign Affairs* summarizing the results of the post-Soviet reforms. Arguing that Russia became "a normal middle-income country," the authors acknowledged that Russia's economic and political systems remained far from perfect, but those deficiencies, in their opinion, were typical for countries at a similar level of economic and political development. The article concluded:

> That Russia is only normal may be a disappointment to those who had hoped for more. ... But for a country that was an "evil empire" as little as 15 years ago-threatening people at home and abroad – it is a remarkable and admirable achievement.
>
> (Treisman and Shleifer 2004: 38)

Hardly anyone would call Russia normal now, at the beginning of Putin's firth term.

The territorial size

Russia's exceptional territorial size gave rise to theories explaining Russia's uniqueness and greatness, as well as those that believed that territorial size was the main obstacle to the country's development. Ivan Ilyin, Russian philosopher, political thinker, and publicist was convinced that Russia was not the mechanical sum of its territories and peoples but an organic whole, with its geography itself being an important and primary component of that organic unity. The unity of Russia was first

> geographically prescribed and imposed on us by the land. From the very first centuries of its existence the Russian nation found itself on an open and only conventionally divided plain. . . . Russia could not and should not become a traveling, cultural and commercial barricade; her world vocation was primarily creative and mediating between peoples and cultures, and not locking and separating . . . Russia should not be transformed, like Western Europe, into . . . a system of small states with their outposts, customs, and eternal wars.
>
> (Ilyin 1992: 431–432)

But back in 1831 Russian historian and poet Pyotr Vyazemsky made the opposite point:

> I am so fed up with our geographical fanfarons: from Perm to Tavrida and so on. What good is there to be glad about, and what is there to boast of, that we lie stretched out, that we have five thousand versts from thought to thought.
>
> (cited in Treivish 2010: 25)

According to Russian geographer Kagansky, Russia's vastness is extensive but fictitious: developed parts of the country are isolated and distant from each other. In fact, the "Archipelago of Russia" is a set of cells connected with each other through distant centers (Kagansky 2010: 87). There's no doubt about one thing: the size of Russia's territory is of such outstanding magnitude that it is itself an explanation for many processes and phenomena of a political, economic, and cultural nature.

The vastness of Russia's spaces, Pushkin's "immense plains" and Gogol's "immense expanse," and most importantly, the geographic location of Russia between West and East, gave rise to the division of Russian public thought in the nineteenth century into two intellectual camps – the Slavophiles and the Westerners. Both wanted their homeland to develop and prosper, but they saw the development in different ways. While Slavophiles laid emphasis on Russia's specific national identity and the role of traditional institutions (commune – *obshina* and absolute monarchy), Westernizers, on the contrary, denied that Russia had a "special way" and stressed the importance of modernization through borrowing the European institutions and social patterns – division of power, social and political rights, pluralism, and urbanism. Russia, in their views, was not special, it was just large and lagging Europe. In the early 1920s, the Eurasianists joined the discussion. Eurasianism was originally a Russian philosophical and political current of public thought that emerged in exile (emigration after the October putsch of 1917). Eurasianists viewed Russia as "Eurasia," a "separate world," endowed with the features inherent in a special cultural type. The bearers of the Eurasian views of the time were deeply disappointed in the achievements of Western civilization, primarily its "spiritual impotence." One of the central ideas in Eurasianism was the idea of "place-development" – the conviction that the very territory (place) on which Russia is located makes the integration of the lands around it inevitable. In the 1990s, after the collapse of the Soviet Union, Eurasianist ideas regained popularity. Today, the central idea of neo-Eurasianism is the unification of the post-Soviet space around Russia.

I emphasize once again that for Russia, both for elites and for the citizens, the exceptional territorial size of the country has been and remains an explanation for the fundamental difference of Russia from other countries and at the same time an explanation for the particular moves of its foreign and domestic policies.

Territorial contrasts and centralization as a pattern in Russian history

The intercontinental border between Europe and Asia, which runs through the Ural Mountains and descends to the Caspian Sea, divides Russia in two parts – European and Asian. This so-called West-East gradient arose as a product of historical asymmetry in the development of the territory. In fact, it is about the "mismatch" of the location of area, population, and resources. For example, the European part of the country accounts for about 80% of the population, but only a quarter of the country's area. The main deposits of natural resources are in the eastern part of the country.

There are also differences of ethnic nature: between the Russian nucleus of settlement (Eastern European, Orthodox cultural circle by genesis) and ethnic regions, that is, fragments of other local civilizations integrated into Russia. Thus, the main Great Russian core is the densely populated area of Central Russia with the Moscow megalopolis. The second core is the Russian regions of the Urals and Western Siberia. Smaller cores are in Eastern Siberia and the south of the Far East. Ethnocultural regions include the Mountain Caucasus, the Ural–Volga region (both belong to the Islamic cultural circle), the South Siberian Turkic-Mongol belt and the areas inhabited by the small indigenous peoples of the North, Siberia, and the Far East, and finally the enclaves inside the Russian population (the Republics of Yakutia, Komi, and Karelia).

Russia is a country of sharp contrasts and amazing territorial diversity and – at the same time – of rigid centralization of political, economic, social, and spiritual life. Ironically, the words of the Russian philosopher Nikolai Berdyaev, written by him in 1917, quite describe Russia today, a hundred years later:

> Russia is a country of great contrasts . . . All countries combine many ages. But the immense size of Russia and the peculiarities of its history have given rise to unprecedented contrasts and opposites. . . . The immaturity of the deaf province and the rottenness of the state center are the poles of Russian life. And Russian public life is pushed to these poles. Life of the advanced circles of Petrograd and Moscow and life in the remote corners of the Russian provinces belong to different historical eras. Historical system of Russian statehood has centralized the state and public life, poisoned the bureaucracy and crushed the provincial social and cultural life. In Russia there was a centralization of culture, dangerous for such a vast country. Russian cultural energy doesn't want to spread over the vast expanses of Russia; it is afraid to sink into the darkness of the remote provinces and tries to keep itself in the centers. There is a kind of fear of the dark and absorbing depths of Russia. This phenomenon is painful and threatening. Russia is not France. And in France, the exclusive concentration of culture in Paris gives rise to an exorbitant difference in the age of Paris and the French province... In Russia, this centralization is quite painful and keeps Russia on the lower stages of development. Spiritual and cultural decentralization is essentially necessary in Russia.
>
> (Berdyaev 1990: 73)

The giant role of Moscow is the most vivid expression of the centralization of Russian space. Moscow has no competing cities, but at least seven cities claim to be the "second capital of Russia": Yekaterinburg, Kazan, Nizhny Novgorod, Novosibirsk, Perm, Samara, and St. Petersburg.

Perhaps, the perennial Russian centralization of space would be overcome by moving the nation's capital to a city that is closer to the geographic center of the country? Indeed, the hypercentralization of Russian space, the outstanding role of the capital in every respect, is the reason for periodically escalating discussions about the need to move the capital to a new place, closer to the geographical center of the country. However, as the experience of a number of large countries (the United

States, Argentina, and China) shows, the capital can also lie "on the edge" of the country. Moving the capital from Moscow would hardly be economically efficient: no other city in Russia has such a high degree of contact with other cities as Moscow. It is better equipped to perform the functions of the capital than any other city.

Another option would be to "unload" Moscow from functions that are not proper to a capital city, in particular, from a part of industry, and to strengthen genuinely metropolitan activities. In addition, other alternative urban centers should be developed: Russia requires two to three dozen major cities to form a "supercity framework" of the country.

Back in 2010, the Russian government announced the concept of territorial reorganization of Russia, assuming the division of the country into 20 highly urbanized territories (agglomerations). The "agglomeration solution" may indeed contribute to accelerated economic development of Russia and increase its level of competitiveness in the global world. However, this path is extremely complex. It is fundamentally important to distinguish between agglomerations as an "aggregation of everything" – a mechanistic approach, which, alas, is widespread in Russia, and an approach based on agglomeration economy, where agglomerations give increased growth and development due to clustering of innovative businesses and accumulation of "creative capital." The second approach is much more complicated, it is honest about risks, a lot of losers (not every big city can become an agglomeration!) and a high degree of uncertainty of the outcome. The role of the central state in this approach is limited and does not guarantee success, while the role of regional and city authorities, on the contrary, is critically important. Why does the process of geographical concentration in Russia continue? Because it is favorable to Moscow and its elites.

Peculiarities of the geographic location

Russia ranks first in the world in terms of area (17.1 million square kilometers) and eighth in terms of population (146.7 million in 2023). The second largest country in the world, Canada, has a territory of ten million square kilometers. The territory of Russia is about 11.4% of the Earth's land area. The European part of Russia is 42% of Europe and the Asian part is 19% of Asia. The length of Russia's borders is more than 60,900 thousand kilometers.

The country is located in the north of the Eurasian continent, in the northwest it borders on Norway and Finland, in the west – on Estonia, Latvia, and Belarus (the exclave of Russia – the Kaliningrad region – has a common border with Lithuania and Poland). In the southwest, Russia borders Ukraine, Georgia, and Azerbaijan; its southeast and east neighbors are Kazakhstan, Mongolia, China, and South Korea. Russia has access to the Baltic, Azov, Black and Caspian Seas. In the Far East, Russia has access to the seas of the Pacific Ocean. Russia is a northern country: the northern zone (permafrost) covers about 11 million square kilometers and has ecological significance on a planetary scale.

The peculiarities of Russia's geographical position are related to the length of its territory from west to east by almost 10,000 square kilometers and from north to south by 4,000 square kilometers. Inland areas of the country are located at a great distance from sea areas. The size of the territory generates the inevitable problem of "overcoming space," which is manifested in the complexity of territorial management and high transport costs. One of the main problems for Russia is the connectivity of the territory. Another problem is the production and diffusion of innovations throughout the country. As Hosking argued, in Russia's harsh climatic and geographic milieu, novelty and experimentation could genuinely be hazardous, even disastrous (Hosking 2011).

Russia has considerable and diverse resource potential. Fuel and energy resources are of global importance: the country has about 13% of the world's oil reserves, 35% of natural gas, and 12% of coal. Russia also has 20–25% of the world's timber reserves. Of great importance are the reserves of uranium ores, gold, iron and copper ores, nickel, tungsten, molybdenum, and other metals. An extremely important feature of the distribution of resources across the country is that most of the resource potential is in the eastern (Asian) part of the country, while industrial production and the population are concentrated mainly in the western (European) part.

One of the explanations for the weakness of institutions in Russia and the lack of incentives for modernization has to do with the abundance of resources. The term "resource curse"[1] was first coined by British economists in 1993. It means that, oddly enough, more resource-rich countries often grow more slowly than those less endowed with resources. This is because natural resources reduce the dependence of the state authorities on the population: the authorities do not need the taxes paid by the voters as much. The oil rent helps the authorities (1) to more actively fund the power structures to suppress the opposition; (2) to bribe discontented social groups by redistributing part of the rent; (3) to reduce incentives to increase political freedoms (resource-rich countries can do without innovation and high technology). For instance, Fish has found significant negative correlation between openness and raw material abundance, which he linked to Russia's endemic corruption (Fish 2005). Until recently, the existence of the resource curse was considered fully proven, but new research raised doubts about the universality of this mechanism. The reality showed that not all resource-rich countries were subject to the resource curse; Malaysia, Norway, the United States, and Chile are not on this list. Recent empirical literature pointed to a "conditional resource curse" dependent on existing political structures, primarily on the quality of economic and political institutions. If a country has weak institutions and a personalistic and non-patrimonial political system, then oil does make it easier for elites to concentrate power (Haber and Menaldo 2011). On the contrary, in a country where strong institutions and diversified power are already present, interested parties will not allow rent-seeking elites to monopolize natural resources.

The population is extremely unevenly distributed throughout the country. The vast majority of the population (93%) lives in the so-called main settlement belt, which covers about a third of the country. Its borders are a wedge with peaks in St. Petersburg in the north, Novorossiysk in the south, and Krasnoyarsk in the east, and a strip further to Primorsky Krai. This is also where all the major Russian cities are concentrated.

There is a general rule in Russia: the larger the city, the closer it is to the historical core of the country, that is, generally more westward. Such asymmetry of the inhabited space is not uncommon, but in Russia, unlike the United States, Canada, and Brazil, this asymmetry is complemented by the depth of the location of the main centers and their remoteness from the coast. One of the most striking pieces of evidence of this is the fact that Russia, unlike Canada and especially the United States, has not managed to create powerful urban poles on the Pacific coast.

"Collecting of lands" and the beginning of colonization

Feudal fragmentation of Kievan Rus in the second half of the eleventh century led to the formation of several large independent principalities on its territory. It was possible to overcome this fragmentation by the appanage Principality of Moscow, which was separated from the Vladimir-Suzdal Grand Duchy. By the time of the defeat of the Golden Horde by Grand Prince of All Russia Dmitry (1380), this principality was the largest and strongest in Russia; later it was joined by Novgorod, Tver, Pskov, and Ryazan. The population of the Muscovite state was formed as a result of the decline of Kievan Rus, which caused people to move from the middle Dnieper to the southwest and northeast, that is, from the center of Kievan Rus to its outskirts. The state "moved both behind the settlers and ahead of them, trying to settle the occupied territories" (Achiezer 2002: 72–73).

At the turn of the fifteenth and sixteenth centuries, a unified Russian state was formed. Initially, the territorial expansion of the state was aimed at the European North and the Volga region, but the creation of a unified state and the strengthening of its centralization contributed to the socioeconomic and political consolidation of the territory and allowed an active foreign policy. The capture of Kazan and accession of the Astrakhan Khanate put under Russian control the most important trade route along the Volga River and opened opportunities for further territorial expansion in the eastern direction.

The rapid expansion of the state's territory to the northeast in the sixteenth and seventeenth centuries was associated with the campaigns of Russian pioneers.

> Russians had been marching to the Northeast for centuries. The Slavic wave rolled across the Eurasian continent until it reached America. . . . Each new stage (of development) exacerbated the sense of the North in Russian history and geography. The Pomeranian lands, the Urals, finally Siberia.
>
> (Vail and Genis 1996: 80)

Territorial expansion or "territorial imperative" is the logic of the development of empires; with the development and colonization of new territories, Russia was gradually turning into a kind of universe, a self-sufficient world. In the historical and geographical context of Russian space, one can distinguish a primary Russian Orthodox nucleus, formed in the northern and northeastern lands of ancient Russia in the fifteenth and sixteenth centuries, and the frontiers of exploration, the most important of which were the northern (going back to Novgorod colonization), eastern (beyond the Volga and Urals, to Siberia), and southern (beyond the Wild Field, to Novorossiya, to the steppe Caucasus). The southern and eastern borders of the empire were, in the full sense of the word, frontiers whose purpose was to prevent the invasion of other peoples into the empire.

As Achiezer showed, the history of land colonization in Russia allowed to look at Russian space as a way of revealing the specificity of society and institutions. Thus, people's decisions were motivated by the possibility of engaging an increasing mass, an "infinite abundance" in a potentially endless territory of extensively absorbed resources. In other words, colonization opened possibilities for the development of territories through already established methods, through extensive forms of activity, and thus constituted a mechanism that *paralyzed development.* In addition, the history of colonization showed that the constant pursuit of undeveloped territories came at the expense of the degradation of the "rear," that is, of territories that had already been developed.

The possession of gigantic spaces hindered the development of integration mechanisms (economic, interregional, cultural) but increased the importance of administrative mechanisms. Thus, unlike in Western Europe, trade in Russia did not become the basis of economic activity or a way of life; it did not become a motor for further economic development. The resources necessary for the integration of the state in an ever-expanding territory were constantly insufficient. Ultimately, the possession of gigantic territories proved ineffective in terms of societal development because people were not forced to develop the ability to intensify their activities. In fact, those who colonized territories for Russia left descendants with increasingly complex problems; colonization came at the expense of the future (Achiezer 2002: 74–78).

The reunification of Ukraine and Russia took place in 1654. In the eighteenth and nineteenth centuries, the Russian Empire incorporated part of the Commonwealth of Poland and Finland in the west; Transcaucasia, Crimea, Kazakhstan, and Central Asia became southern "increments"; in the east, the empire incorporated Priamurye and Primorye and Sakhalin. By the end of the nineteenth century, Russia had become a multinational empire with the total area of 22.4 million square kilometers and 128.2 million inhabitants (according to the results of the first all-Russian census of 1897). Russia was predominantly an agrarian country: the share of the urban population was no more than 13%.

The peculiarities of the Russian Empire in terms of its territorial composition were:

(1) Russia's colonies were a de facto continuation of its territory (unlike, e.g., the British Empire, which made its territorial acquisitions "beyond the seas," far from the metropolis).
(2) The empire's territories lying to the west of the "core" (Poland, Finland) were more developed economically and politically than the empire's "core" itself.
(3) Territorial unity of the vast empire was based on a large army and state bureaucracy and not on trade and exchanges.

(4) The loyalty of the empire was maintained, among other things, by the fact that local colonial elites were co-opted into the elite of the "core" – the metropolis and could occupy high positions in the government; non-Russian population was assimilated.

In essence, the Russian Empire had more similarities to the traditional Austro-Hungarian and Ottoman empires than to the maritime British or French empires.

Dmitri Trenin distinguished three models of territorial expansion in Russian history:

(1) The model of "collecting of lands" (according to this model, lands were gathered around Moscow in the fourteenth and early sixteenth centuries; during numerous wars with the Polish state in the seventeenth century territories of Ukraine and Belorussia were annexed under the slogan "liberation of the Slavic brothers from the Polish Catholic yoke."
(2) The model of "border movement" (colonization) – this model was used from the sixteenth to the nineteenth century during the annexation of the territories of Siberia, the Far East, Northern Kazakhstan, and the Don and Kuban regions to Russia.
(3) The model of "strategic boundaries" – during all periods of history, Russia annexed territories for purely strategic reasons, beginning with the Kazan and Astrakhan Khanates (1552 and 1556 respectively) and the Crimea (1783). Russia created so-called buffer states, some of which were later incorporated into the empire (Finland, Transcaucasia, and Central Asian territories), while others, like Afghanistan, became a zone delimiting the spheres of influence of the empires – Russian and British (Trenin 2002: 36–51).

Interesting and specific was the fate of the Novgorod Republic. Novgorod was first mentioned in chronicles in 859 as a major political and trade center. In 860, the Slavs, tired of endless strife, invited the Varangian princes Rurik, Sineus, and Truvor to reign. After their death Rurik became the sole ruler of Novgorod. After Rurik's death, Prince Oleg seized Kiev, and in 882, transferred there the capital of the Old Russian state, and since that time there has been a rivalry between the three cities of Novgorod, Kiev, and Polotsk. The formation of the city-state in Novgorod was accompanied by a long struggle of the Novgorodians for independence from Kiev. The independent Novgorod Republic lasted from 1136 to 1478. Novgorod intensively colonized the present-day Northwest of Russia establishing trading settlements and converting Finno-Ugric tribes to Christianity. Novgorod had close trade ties with the cities of the Hanseatic League.

By the middle of the fifteenth century, Moscow had subjugated most of the principalities of northeastern Russia. Novgorod's independence was in clear contradiction to the process of unification of the lands around Moscow. Novgorod's institutions by this time could not withstand competition from the young, aggressive centralized state with its better management and resource mobilization mechanisms. In 1471, Moscow's troops invaded Novgorod's lands, and after a seven-year war, Novgorod lost its independence; Moscow, fearing a rebirth of the republic, was resolutely destroying the city-state's identity.

Prior to the seventeenth century, Russian lands enjoyed considerable autonomy, there was no unified system of administrative-territorial division; lands (principalities) were formed from a system of vassal possessions. New territories were conquered from the Golden Horde and its successors. As a result, the principalities differed sharply in the size of territory and population and had bizarre, inconvenient borders.

The most important feature of Russian colonization was *the central role of the state* in the administration, development, and even settlement of territories. The constant expansion of the empire's territory was a large-scale historical and geographic process. For 400 years, from the sixteenth century till the beginning of the twentieth century, the state territory increased 36 times! Russia was a territorially extended continental empire, a complex polity where the metropolis dominated the periphery through relationship of inequality and subordination. The imperial ideology, based on the rhetoric of conquest and Divine Providence, was the most important factor in legitimizing the empire. Note that the imperial elites' strategy for the annexation and further incorporation of territories was highly diverse, there was no unified system of peripheral administration, and the methods depended on specific regions.

Siberia joins Russia. Russian frontier

Lomonosov's famous statement that Russia's power would be added by Siberia was about territorial expansion: the power of the Russian state could be increased only by new, colonized territories. Initially, the main incentive to move east was rather practical – this was fur-trading. From the end of the sixteenth century, hundreds of enterprising people went beyond the Stone Belt (the Urals). Most of them were Pomors, the people who lived along the White Sea coast ("Pomor" means a person who lives "by the sea" – po moru) and did not know serfdom (they accounted for more than 80% of Russian settlers) (Ageev 2005: 92). The first Russian expedition that reached the Pacific Ocean was led by Ivan Moskvitin, a Tomsk Cossack: in 1639, Cossacks reached the Sea of Okhotsk, and in 1640, they reached the mouth of the Amur River. The incorporation of Siberia was undoubtedly an outstanding event in the process of creating the empire.

The nature of the Russians' relations with the local peoples was important in advancing eastward. There was plenty of free territory in Siberia, so Russian pioneers did not seek to displace the local population from their land. From them they received help, traded, received tribute – *yasak* and valuable information about the new rich lands. Conflicts happened, but they could not prevent the Russians from moving eastward. In fact, the annexation of the "frontier" peoples was set by the logic of "gathering lands," the logic which followed from the task of building a centralized state with well-guarded borders. Thus, the annexation of (Western) Siberia was similar to the annexation of the Volga and other territories.

The vast expanse of Siberia was traversed by Russian explorers in an incredibly short period of time. In the seventeenth century, pioneers passed all of Siberia but settled only in the forest-steppe edge of the taiga and river banks, that is, landscapes similar to the places where their ancestors lived. And in Russia as a whole, and to an even greater extent in Siberia, the nature of life and development of the territory was determined by the natural, primarily climatic situation. Siberia is a part of Northern Asia, very far from warm seas and under the influence of the Arctic Ocean. The scarcity of soils and the short duration of the cycle of farming required extreme exertion to obtain a minimum surplus product.

Farmers went where the soils were more fertile, where the climate was warmer, and where there was an abundance of water. Just as the Americans willingly settled the Mississippi River basin and the banks of its tributaries, so the Russians settled the basins of the Volga, Don, Yaik, and Kuban rivers. The settlers went further – to the relatively fertile forest-steppes of Western Siberia, but very reluctantly settled further east – in regions with a sharply continental climate, where the soil was poor and the annual temperature amplitude reached 100 degrees Celsius. The difference in natural and climatic conditions between the American West and Siberia is enormous. According to Ageyev, Siberia did not become an object of competition between the colonial powers and in a few decades was "conquered" by Russia precisely because of extremely unfavorable natural and climatic conditions. The discovery of Siberia coincided with the time period of the Great Geographical Discoveries. There turned out to be so many fertile, warm, and rich places on Earth. Cold and lacking in riches, Siberia did not attract the attention of the European colonial powers.

Let's note the role of the Cossacks in the development of Siberia. Cossack formations were the attribute of the empire, which ensured its security. It was a regular, professional, and mobile mounted army. Until the sixteenth century, the Cossacks were not allowed to engage in farming; their task was not only to defend the borders of the empire but also to move them forward. The Cossack formations that marched through Siberia stood at the very beginning of its history as part of the Russian state, so if we talk about frontier in relation to Siberia, we should add Cossack – this was "Cossack frontier" (Ageev 2005: 95–96).

In addition to nature and climate, the slow pace of development (not of annexation!) in Siberia was determined by the enormous distances separating its territories from the European centers of the country and the ultra-long transport and economic ties. In such circumstances, the problem of transport and road construction became a key issue. However, the plans of building the Great Northern Route to settle and develop Siberia and the Far East, as well as to strengthen the military and strategic positions of Russia, which had been discussed since the early 1870s, did not materialize. After the Trans-Siberian railway was built, small settlements and short branches to the north appeared on it, but the road did not have a decisive influence for the development of large territories: in the south, there was the state border, and in the north, there was permafrost. So, the "Russian frontier" looked, unlike the American one, like a narrow long column squeezed by the border from the south and the harsh climate from the north.

Thus, unlike the American West, which was deeply integrated into the system of world economic relations, Siberia at the end of the colonization process remained, in accordance with Wallerstein's scheme, "the far periphery of a semi-peripheral country," that is, Russia.

Was there a deliberate state policy toward Siberia? The decisive importance of Russia's external orientation – westward – has found symbolic expression in the transfer of the empire's capital to the far northwest, to Saint Petersburg, where it remained for more than 200 years. The colonization of Siberia was directed and strictly regulated by the state, but the real policy of development began late and was not consistent. Instead of policy, the Russian state predatorily exploited vast territories of Siberia. The most famous move in the policy of the development of Siberia was "Stolypin resettlements." It was an attempt to repeat the experience of the British settler colonies. However, these attempts were unsuccessful because, for the Russian state and Russian capitalism, the task of settling Siberia could not compare with the importance that North America had for England and all of Europe. In contrast to the United States, in the case of Siberia, political expansion was not based on economic expansion. The main industry of Siberia in the nineteenth century was gold mining. Gold did not need to find markets; it settled in the treasury. This industry also did not contribute much to the development of the territories.

The exploitation of Siberia could not but bring to life a local movement to expand its autonomy or even separate Siberia from Russia. This movement was called "Siberian regionalism" and emerged in the second half of the nineteenth century and early twentieth century. In 1917, the Siberian regionalists developed active efforts to create a "Siberian state" under the slogan "Siberia for the Siberians." The Provisional Siberian Regional Council was created, followed by the Provisional Government of Autonomous Siberia. In the following years, many such "governments" were created in Siberia and the Far East. All of them were associated with the interventionists, and these regionalist initiatives were brutally suppressed by the Bolsheviks (Ageev 2005: 286–287).

During the Soviet era, Siberia continued to be a semi-colony. The systematic colonization of Siberia, the Far East, and the Far North by the state was built on coercion: through the system of camps, organized recruitment, and forced evictions after collectivization. In the 1920s and 1930s in the Soviet Union, there was a division of labor in which Siberia economically occupied the place of a resource appendage. To this day, Siberia retains the colonial features that are already entrenched in the territorial division of labor in the country.

This also applies largely to the Far East. The Far Eastern region is the largest in terms of area and the least populated. It is the most distant from the developed centers of the European part; the distance from Moscow to Vladivostok is 9,300 kilometers. The Russian government's first steps to develop the Far East (1850–1860) – the establishment of a new Cossack army, an attempt to plant agriculture on the left bank of the Amur River, and the establishment of some benefits for settlers from the old-developed areas – were largely ineffective. Further efforts were directed toward developing a new, more detailed administrative division of the Far East, considering the geopolitical aspect of Russia's presence in the Far

East, founding the city of Vladivostok, establishing a major Pacific naval base, and developing political and economic ties between the Far East and the European part of Russia. Nevertheless, the Far East remained a distant periphery of the empire. In a sense, the fate of the Far East was more favorable than that of Siberia: although extremely distant, the Far East was a geopolitical frontier and, as such, required attention while Siberia was rather a "dead space" in the center of Eurasia.

The problem of "overcoming space" is particularly acute for the Russian Far East. Huge transportation costs limited participation of the Far East in the all-Russian division of labor. The problems of the Far East are rooted not only in the ultimate remoteness of these territories from the center but also in the fact that for many years the state policy was motivated not by economic but by geopolitical considerations. This approach has led not only to population migrations outside the region (a trend that cannot be changed overnight!) but also to a gradual deterioration in the quality of economic infrastructure, primarily in the energy sector. This is compounded by the extremely high cost of transport services.

By the end of the nineteenth century, Russia's geopolitical space had acquired the parameters that still determine its dynamics today. The huge geographical size of the Russian Empire led, on the one hand, to the sparse Russian space (weak infrastructural connectivity), and on the other, contributed to its sharply polarized structure.

Institutions for governing of huge territory: administrative-territorial divisions and federalism in the Russian Empire and the Soviet Union

The Russian Empire

Before Peter the Great's rule, Russian state consisted of fragmented spaces with little impact of the national capital on peripheries: the channels of communication between them remained extremely narrow. The continuously growing space was poorly and unreliably mapped, for example, until the beginning of the eighteenth century, the Siberian administration did not have a map of Siberia! The situation with the management of the territories was ambiguous: on the one hand, Moscow wanted to concentrate all the administration in the central office (*Prikaz*), but on the other hand, due to the weak connection between the territories, nothing prevented the managers on the periphery to engage in self-management.

The way to centralize governance was the creation of a so-called military framework. Thus, in 1719, Peter the Great based the territorial division on the military disposition among civilians: the lowest unit became a district (the place of a regiment's dispersion, which corresponded to 50,600 souls of the civilian population), districts were merged into provinces. The military hierarchy embraced local government officials, and the post of governor, established as early as 1708, also had a military character. With the expansion of the empire, military expansion moved deeper inland, enveloping in circles all the settled space of the empire. The purpose of the reform was the centralization of state administration and concentration of power in the hands of the monarch. In 1708, eight huge general-governorates were formed, in 1719, their number was increased to 11, and they themselves were divided into provinces (first – 47, later – 50).

A huge influence on the formation of Russian regions, especially in the European part of the country, were the reforms of Catherine II, which lasted until 1785. At that time, clear criteria for dividing the country into provinces (*gubernii*) and districts were developed (thus, the population of the provinces was set at 300,000–400,000 men's souls). The provinces, established back in the eighteenth century, existed until the transformations after the Bolshevik revolution of 1917. Moreover, the current borders between Russian regions often follow the boundaries drawn more than 200 years ago. Fifty-four percent of the boundaries of the Central region repeat the old, Catherine-time boundaries. By 1785, in the Russian Empire there were 41 provinces (as the new provinces were called at first), three provinces, and one province on the rights of a vicegerency. By 1796, the number of provinces had increased to 51.

In the nineteenth century, the territory of the empire continued to expand almost continuously; administrative regions were formed on the new territories: provinces, territories, governor-generalships, and provinces that were divided into regions, while the territorial structure of the central part remained generally stable.

Catherine II's idea regarding the organization of the country's expanding territory was similar to the American principle: to use a symmetrical institutional solution based on a single territorial unit – a province (like a state in the United States). However, the symmetrical solution failed. The Russian system of territorial organization became increasingly asymmetric, reflecting not a federal (as in the United States) but an imperial principle. The bizarre boundaries between territorial units in the Russian Empire in no way resembled the linear boundaries between many American states.

By 1913, there were 77 provinces in the Russian Empire, including 49 governed by the General Institution, four governed by the Siberian Province, ten governed by the Kingdom of Poland, seven governed by the Caucasus, and eight governed by the Finnish Province; 18 regions, including five Caucasian, three Turkestan, five steppe, four Siberian, Transcaspian region and the Don Army's region; one district in the Caucasus region and Sakhalin Island; and four cities set up as city councils – Petersburg, Odessa, Sevastopol, Kerch-Yenikale. At the same time, the system of administrative-territorial division in the empire deliberately disregarded ethnic boundaries, cutting the areas of compact residence of ethnic groups. For example, the compactly settled region of the Tatars in the Middle Volga was divided between five provinces.

It is commonly believed that, throughout its history, Russia has had a tightly centralized unitary form of government. This is an exaggeration. The origin of Kievan Rus was confederal – it was a loose union of tribes, held largely on the unity of the blood of their princes (Russian historian Khomyakov (1992: 61) has described this polity as "a federation of regions independent, covered by a single chain of guards"). It was this confederacy that prevented the Horde from conquering Russia; polycentricity helped its survival.

In the Russian Empire, ultimate centralization was rather an idea, a principle, an intention but not a reality. The outskirts of the empire had real autonomy. In the seventeenth or eighteenth century, the journey from St. Petersburg or Moscow to Yakutsk took more than one month, so it was virtually impossible to govern Siberia rigidly from the European center. Autonomy was the inevitable price for the unprecedented expansion of the state's borders, a way of maintaining the stability and loyalty of the new parts of the country. Autocracy reproduced itself in all the administrative-territorial cells of the state. At the same time, the governor, appointed from the capital, was in a dual position: being loyal to the monarch, he always had to consider local interests. In the Russian Empire, the highest level of autonomy was granted to the Grand Duchy of Finland and the Kingdom of Poland. The Grand Duchy of Finland had its own police, education system, currency, and official language; the revenues from duties and taxes were used entirely in the territory of the Duchy. As an empire, Russia also had "proto-federal" elements, which provided the necessary flexibility of the state system.

The Soviet Union

The defeat in World War I, revolutionary events of 1917, and overthrow of the monarchy led to the dissolution of the Russian Empire. In December 1922, a treaty was concluded between Russia, Belarus, Ukraine, and the Transcaucasian Federation on the establishment of the Union of Soviet Socialist Republics (USSR). Subsequently, other republics joined the union (15 union republics in total). Thus, a centralized vertically integrated state with a rigid system of administrative and party management was gradually created. The first decades of Soviet power were a period of almost continuous experimentation with the territorial structure – it was a time of alternating waves of enlargement and new fragmentation of regions. The territorial structure of the Russian Soviet Socialist Federative Republic (RSFSR) stabilized only after the 1950s.

Importantly, for the founders of the Soviet state, federalism was an unwanted but unavoidable solution and a way to pacify the "national outskirts." From the very beginning, Soviet federalism was a way of solving the national (ethnic) question. The imperial model ignored interethnic boundaries; the Soviet model of federalism, on the contrary, revived them and made the ethnic principle fundamental. As early as November 2 (15), 1917, the Council of People's Commissars in Petrograd adopted the Declaration of the Rights of the Peoples of Russia. This document proclaimed the principles of equality and sovereignty of peoples, their right to self-determination up to separation and formation of an independent state. III All-Russian Congress of Soviets of Workers' and Soldiers' Deputies adopted the Declaration of Rights of Working and Exploited People, which was included in the Constitution of the RSFSR of 1918. According to the declaration, the Soviet Russian Republic was established "on the basis of a free union of free nations as a federation of Soviet national republics."

The RSFSR was formally a federation (the only one out of 15 union republics). However, in reality it was rather an anti-federation. The most significant feature of the Soviet administration was the Communist Party's aspiration to merge politics and administration in all spheres. The system was built on the democratic centralism principle which, according to Hedin (2021), meant that regional and local administrations were part of the vertically integrated state-party system. For regional administration, the principle of democratic centralism was reinforced by the Soviet doctrine of double subordination. It meant that each unit was sorted under two parallel chains of command. First, each administrative unit at the regional and local levels was sorted hierarchically under the relevant ministry, which in turn received instructions from the relevant secretariat of the Central Committee apparatus. Second, regional administrations answered also to the party's regional leadership, which was part of a parallel chain of command – which also started in the Central Committee.

The Soviet Union had an extremely complex territorial structure: on the eve of disintegration, it included 15 union republics, 20 autonomous republics, eight autonomous regions, ten autonomous okrugs, six territories, and 123 oblasts. The Soviet state was a federation according to some formal attributes (presence of quasi-state institutions in the regions, a bicameral parliament), but in reality, it was characterized by an extremely high level of centralization of powers and a rigidly hierarchical governing structure.

The collapse of the Soviet Union was caused by a whole complex of reasons: economic stagnation and general limitations of the economic model, the crisis of the Communist Party management system and communist ideology, the fiasco of Soviet foreign policy, and others. In 1990, Latvia, Lithuania, and Estonia seceded from the Soviet Union and formed sovereign states. In 1991, the Belovezh Accords led to the collapse of the Union. On June 12, 1990, the Declaration on State Sovereignty of the Russian Federation was adopted. A sovereign state – the Russian Federation – has emerged.

All this allows us to highlight specific features of the organization of spaces in Russia:

(1) In the course of its history, Russia was trying to develop huge and diverse spaces as "Russia bordered on one side with civilization, and on the other – with infinity" (Vail and Genis 1996: 80).
(2) The statuses of regions/territories were originally diverse (there was no principle of equality, as in the United States). The system of ATD in Russia was characterized by flexibility, but at the same time by extreme complexity, asymmetries, and confusion.
(3) The Soviet period was characterized by constant experimentation with the ATD grid: waves of enlargement were replaced by waves of fragmentation of regions.
(4) The Russian territorial structure combined the "old" (mostly regions of the European part of the country) and the "young" regions formed in the Soviet period in the 1940–1950s.

The institutions of federalism and national development in the 1990s

Federalism fixes the relationship between the central and regional (or group) governments and authorities based on the separation of powers and the existence of the right of self-government for territories (regions) and/or social groups within the framework of a unified political system. The essence of federalism as a normative principle is the combination of unity and diversity (Watts 1999). As Daniel Elazar stressed, "federalism is more than just a structural construction; it is also a particular way of political and social behavior, including a commitment to partnership and active cooperation on the part of individuals and institutions" (Elazar 1987: 479). Federalism is the most "geographic" set of institutions for structuring and organizing power. Federalism can stimulate economic development as it is a governance solution of the state to credibly preserving market incentives. Market incentives are preserved if the state is credibly prevented from compromising on future economic success and from bailing out future failures. The salient features of federalism – decentralization of information and authority and interjurisdictional competition – help provide credible commitment for these purposes (Qian and Weingast 1997; Weingast 1995). However, the institutions of federalism and decentralization can be also used by authoritarian incumbents to secure their political survival as it happened in Russia under Putin (Busygina and Filippov 2024).

After the collapse of the Soviet Union and Russia's independence, the new Russian state was extremely weak, and Moscow was torn by political contradictions. President Boris Yeltsin badly needed the support of regional elites. At this time, the so-called parade of sovereignties began in the regions. Shortly after the Declaration on Sovereignty was adopted in Russia, speaking in Tatarstan, President Yeltsin uttered the most famous phrase: "Take as much sovereignty as you can swallow." Ethnic regions began to adopt their own declarations of sovereignty. The declarations often violated the principle of the supremacy of federal law. For example, some republics declared the possibility of seceding from Russia (Komi, Tatarstan) or declared themselves sovereign states (Udmurtia, Kalmykia). In fact, many republics formalized not a federative but a confederal type of relationship with the Russian Federation. Thus, at the beginning of the 1990s, the slogans of federalism served as a cover and justification for spontaneous decentralization, that is, mass appropriation by the regions of the functions and powers of the federal center.

It should be noted that the choice of a federal institutional form of government in Russia was motivated by three main reasons:

- The need to prevent the territorial disintegration of the country on the model of the Soviet Union;
- the need to reform ethnic relations;
- the need to institutionalize the expanding process of spontaneous economic decentralization.

On March 31, 1992, the Federative Treaty was signed between Moscow and the regions. The Federative Treaty of 1992 legitimized the asymmetrical nature of Russian federalism, dividing the subjects of the federation into "classes" in terms of the volume of political and economic rights – the republics received the greatest number of rights. The Treaty was signed by the heads of 87 subjects of the Russian Federation; the heads of the Republic of Tatarstan and the Chechen Republic did not sign the document. The Chechen case was the most dramatic. The history of relations between Russian state and Chechens is extremely tense, it includes both the colonial conquest of Chechnya in the nineteenth century and the Chechen deportation in 1944. In post-Soviet history of Russia, the republic became the only example of a de facto separation of the region from Russia. The aim of the "restoration of constitutional order" resulted in the invasion of Russian forces in late 1994 and a war that lasted 18 months. A ceasefire was signed in 1996, but it failed to stabilize the situation. In 1999, under the banner of the fight against terrorism, a second war broke out. Capitalizing on Chechen society's divisions, the Kremlin established a loyalist government under Akhmad Kadyrov in June 2000; he was assassinated in May 2004. Akhmad's son, Ramzan Kadyrov, was elected president and till now is the main guarantor of political stability in the republic. During Vladimir Putin's reign, Chechnya has turned from the worst troublemaker to the most loyal to Putin reign.

An objective obstacle to the development of federative relations in Russia was the acute struggle for supreme power that broke out between the President and the Supreme Soviet of the Russian Federation in the Fall 1992–Summer 1993; at that time, there was in effect no center in the country. In autumn 1993, after the anti-constitutional resolution of the dual power situation the main political actor (the President) sharply increased his influence. On December 12, 1993, a referendum adopted a new Constitution of Russia, which laid the basis for the federal relations, although it failed to resolve several existing problems. The constitution defined the foundations of Russian federalism. The Russian Federation consisted of 89 subjects: 21 republics, six territories, 49 regions, one autonomous region, ten autonomous districts, and two cities of federal importance (Moscow and St. Petersburg).

Federalism of the 1990s gave the regional elites an experience of the search for independent ways of survival and growth in the new political and economic conditions. In the 1990s, contractual relations – a new practice for Russia – began to take shape; there was a search for compromises between the interests of the center and the regions, which was precisely in keeping with the essence of the federative process. However, federal institutions of the 1990s were unable to stimulate national economic development. By the end of the 1990s, Moscow had almost completely exhausted its ability to influence the situation in the regions. There were no mechanisms for federal intervention – it was a typical concession by a weakened and fragmented federal government to regional elites.

The development of federal relations was characterized by President Yeltsin's reliance on a system of exclusive relations with the regions and the development of political favoritism when informal institutions and rules of the game began either to replace new formal institutions or to fill the existing institutional vacuum. The dominance of informal institutions has become the main structural characteristic of Russian federalism.

In most regions, the consolidation of political regimes took place not on a democratic basis but on authoritarian principles. Political science literature has coined the term "feudalization," referring to the emergence of regional "feudal lords," whose aim was to monopolize administrative and financial resources. Thus, federalism in Russia did not increase the openness of society or the permeability of the political system, but, on the contrary, led to regional power becoming fenced off from federal power, fencing off the system of local self-government from the latter as well.

Putin's federalism

The reform of federal relations carried out in 2000 under the leadership and at the initiative of President Putin was multicomponent and included several dimensions. The reforms were intended to weaken the regional elites and concentrate resources (administrative and financial) in the hands of the federal bureaucracy. The federal bureaucracy was to become the locomotive that would ensure economic growth and development. Putin subsequently solidified a personalist regime, essentially bestowing unlimited and unaccountable powers upon the presidency. In 2021, during his third term, Putin ratified legislation that could potentially extend his rule until 2036. Bertelsmann Transformation Index (2022) placed Russia (scoring 4.4) in the "Hard-line Autocracies" group.

After the consolidation of political regime in the 2000s, center–regional relations in Russia have become important integrated parts of the institutional system supporting the legitimacy and stability of the political regime. Elements of federalism and decentralization helped to maintain the stability of their entire nondemocratic institutional systems and helped the regimes to deal with the political and economic challenges – for example, from mass protests and the coronavirus pandemic to military mobilization.

In Russia, the territorial stability and resilience of center–regional relations have been achieved primarily by imposing ever-increasing limitations on political competition. Russia has gradually built models of center–regional relations, including federalism and decentralization, based on undemocratic principles of their entire political systems. This model works and is stable because the nondemocratic system persists at national, regional, and local levels. Most likely, serious attempts of democratic reforms will threaten to destroy the key conditions for the sustainability of center–regional relations and, in many ways, will return Russia to the situation of the early 1990s.

In essence, Russia has restored modifications of the Soviet model of center–regional relations, including Soviet practices of controlling the institutions of federalism and decentralization. In the Soviet model and its modern modification, the central authorities control subnational and local elites by nondemocratic means. The main difference between the modern models of center–regional relations and the Soviet model is in the role of a dominant party. The Soviet model of center–regional relations was part of an authoritarian regime with a dominant party (the Communist Party of the Soviet Union), while the nondemocratic system of Russia is a personalist regime (Busygina and Filippov 2024).

Imperial legacy: center–periphery relations and the role of Moscow

Constitutionally, Russia is a federation, though center–regional relations in the country are imperial rather than federal. In this respect, today's Russia draws on a powerful legacy. This is the centuries-long tradition of state centrism and the dominant role of capital cities Moscow and St. Petersburg that have cemented the dichotomy of center–periphery pattern in Russia. For centuries, Russia has demonstrated patterns of economic and social development that implied that the center extracted resources from the provinces and initiated state modernization, sought to impose modernization requirements on the peripheral provinces despite their latent resistance, and preserved the dominant position and continued to extract resources from the provinces (Busygina and Filippov 2023).

A characteristic of empire is the role of the capital city. It's no surprise that the capital city (especially if it is also the largest city in a country) develops faster, and its population lives better thanks to the agglomeration effects (Fujita and Thisse 2002). This is happening in many countries (if not most). In Russia, however, Moscow is an imperial center that plays an exceptional economic, social, cultural, and political role (Bater 2004). In Russia's urban settlement structure, Moscow has no competing cities. As O'Loughlin and Kolossov rightly stressed, it is almost paradoxical that the democratization, federalization, and market reforms of the 1990s did not lead to any reduction in the role of Moscow within Russian space (O'Loughlin and Kolossov 2002).

Before the war against Ukraine started in 2022, Moscow has effectively "monopolized" the functions of a mediator between the country and the world economy and thus has become by far the most important national node of financial flows (Busygina and Filippov 2018). As Brade and Rudolph have argued,

> [T]he development of Moscow is characterized by an increasing separation from the national urban system and a growing international orientation. . . . measured against the relevant economic indicators, the Russian capital is a long way ahead of the remaining Russian cities, which are primarily integrated into national and regional economic flows and participate in the global economy only to a limited degree. Moscow, in contrast, is increasingly striving to integrate itself into transnational and international economic structures.
>
> (Brade and Rudolph 2004: 69)

After the outbreak of the war and the imposition of unprecedented Western sanctions against Russia, partial de-globalization predetermined that Moscow lost much of its mediator functions, at least in terms of ties with the West. However, because of the war, it has increased its role domestically as well as in some parts of the world as a main center for confronting the West.

The empire is predominantly built on vertical ties at the expense of horizontal ties, which the empire tries to suppress, seeing such ties as a potential channel for coordinating resistance to the empire. In Russia, perhaps the most prominent feature of center–regional relations has been the extreme weakness of interregional horizontal ties. By the end of the twentieth century, a prominent Russian geographer Leonid Smirnyagin observed that contacts between neighboring regions were limited at best; the citizens, as a rule, are mostly interested in what's going on in Moscow and are quite poorly informed about the events taking place nearby. Administrative borders between the regions were often

> overgrown with woods; highways terminated at them, making them easy to distinguish even from satellite photographs. Nothing similar exists in any other developed country. It is because of this that the territorial fabric of Russia, woven only from vertical communications, is thin and precarious.
>
> (Smirnyagin 1998, 3–4)

Since 2000, the situation has hardly improved. Now, there are no institutions in the Russian Federation that could serve as a platform promoting interregional cooperation and coordination without Moscow's control. The war did not contribute to the strengthening of ties between regions. There is no practical evidence that the regions' interest in cooperation with each other increased after the outbreak of war.

The empire is flexible; it allows for special relations with some individual peripheries. These relations may go far beyond formal institutions and be based on personal ties between the rulers of the empire and the periphery. In Russia, such a special case is the Chechen Republic and the relationship between Russian President Putin and the head of Chechnya Ramzan Kadyrov. By many measures, the Chechen leader Ramzan Kadyrov is an outlier among regional heads in Russia. During Putin's rule, Chechnya has gone from a main "troublemaker" to the most Putin-loyal region. Back in October 2010, in an interview with *Newsweek* magazine, Kadyrov explained that he considered Putin his idol. "My idol," he said,

> is Vladimir Putin. I would like him to remain president for the rest of his life. I love him as much as only a man can love a man…Those who criticize Putin are not people, and they are my personal enemies. As long as Putin has my back, I can do anything – Allahu Akbar![2]

For years Kadyrov had carte blanche for everything that happened in "his" republics and to the Chechens wherever they were in Chechnya, in Russia proper, or outside Russia.

Twenty-five years ago, at the very end of the twentieth century, Alexander Motyl, a brilliant expert on empires, argued that the reestablishment of the imperial relations between post-Soviet Russia and some of its neighbors was highly probable (Motyl 1999). He was right; this is what happened in Russia: under Vladimir Putin, imperial relations were reestablished. These relations between Moscow and Russia's regions were crafted before the Russia's war against Ukraine. So far, the war has not brought any major changes to it. On the contrary, it can be said that these relations serve as one of the main pillars of Russia's resilience in times of war.

Conclusion: territorial expansion, militarization, and development

Russia does have exceptional geographical characteristics; these include the territorial size of the country, abundance of natural resources, and its huge neighborhood (Russia shares a common border with 14 states by land and with two by sea). Throughout Russian history, these features have played a major role in terms of the nature of the Russian state and its institutions. The Russian foundational narrative – the basis of the legitimacy of the state – has been linked precisely to the vastness and exclusivity of the country's territory. With the beginning of Vladimir Putin's rule, the annexation of Crimea in 2014, and especially after Russia's invasion of Ukraine in 2022, this narrative has been powerfully reinforced through state propaganda.

The "territorial factor" is important not only to Russian state authorities but also to the population. During Soviet times, school children already from the first grade proudly repeated in chorus: "The Soviet Union is the largest state in the world, occupying one-sixth of the world's land mass." Remaining the largest country in the world, post-Soviet Russia has inherited this Soviet pride. A direct consequence of this is that the increase in the country's territory in the eyes of Russians is the indisputable, ultimate evidence of the country's success, the only true confirmation of its greatness. Russia cannot shrink territorially; it can only grow in size. Russia's ongoing war against Ukraine is a war for territory, it is precisely for the primitive physical expansion and physical possession of new territories. The slogan of 2014 – "Crimea is ours!" – is precisely the formula for possession. For years, the Russian leadership has been educating its citizens in this very spirit while also educating itself in this spirit. And now Putin can no longer offer the Russians another measure of success.

The consequences Russia's fascination with territorial size and the possibility of its expansion are Russia's blatant threats to territorial integrity of other neighboring countries (for instance, Kazakhstan) and distinct disregard for the smaller countries in Europe or elsewhere. From the Russian perspective, their insurmountable disadvantage is that they are incapable of territorial expansion. And it is not only the occupation of new territories that is important to the Russian leadership; the final chord is the official inclusion of new lands into Russia. This is how Crimea and Sevastopol were hastily incorporated into Russia in early 2014 (Russia added two regions). In September 2022, due to quasi-referendums in Ukraine's occupied territories, Russia formed four more new constitutional entities with unrecorded borders against the backdrop of the war. For the majority of Russians, the success of the war is measured precisely by an increase in the country's territory ("ours!"). Let it be destroyed, depopulated territories, at the cost of enormous losses and incredible human suffering. To possess more territory – this is the only proof of victory – and the only way for Putin to justify the war in the eyes of Russians.[3]

Neither the outcome nor the duration of Russian aggression is known. What is clear, however, is that this is a long-term trend; even after the "hot war" is over, the unprecedented Western sanctions against Russia will not be lifted. Realizing this, the Russian leadership has begun a large-scale territorial restructuring of the economy. After the 2014 sanctions, this was Moscow's declared "turn to the East" aimed at rapprochement with China by investing in the accelerated development of Far Eastern regions. After 2022, the "turn to the East" was reinforced with additional funding, but the main thing was the expansion of the military presence in the country's border regions and the beginning of the militarization of the Russian economy. A significant military build-up is noticeable in the high North: Russia has continued recent and rapid militarization in the Arctic region[4] and the Kyril islands[5] (which Japan claims as its "Northern Territories"). The enterprises of the military-industrial complex in central Russia, the Volga region, and the Urals work around the clock. All this is done by the state in its uncontrolled expansion and for the glory of the state. Unlike the United States, Canada, and Australia, where the institutions of federalism helped maintain diversity, Russian authoritarian federalism maintains uniformity thus helping Moscow control territories.

What does this mean for national development prospects? Russia will need huge investments in military infrastructure and ever larger defense budget, as it cannot count on transfer of technology from the West due to sanctions and Russia's doctrine of "technological sovereignty." In spheres other than the military, the technological lag will grow. In addition, there will be inevitable losses and problems in social development, which will also accumulate. To combat social discontent, the state will intensify repression and increasingly close off Russian society from the rest of the world. Economist Sergei Guriev warned that Russia could become like "North Korea on steroids."[6] But North Korea is territorially small, while Russia is the largest nation in the world. Militarization is very likely to increase interregional disparities and inequalities.

But can we expect fragmentation of the Russian territory? So far, there is no evidence of this. Russian geographical factors (of course, in combination with other factors such as the Soviet legacy) have contributed to the formation of a state in Russia whose main characteristic is not its strength but its unlimited character.

Notes

1 The idea is also known as the "paradox of plenty."
2 https://www.vedomosti.ru/opinion/articles/2010/10/26/putin_moj_idol
3 The Desire to Possess: Russia's War for Territory – PONARS Eurasia.
4 Russia's militarization of the Arctic shows no sign of slowing down | CNN.
5 Russia's Militarization of the Kuril Islands | New Perspectives on Asia | CSIS.
6 Russia could be like "North Korea on steroids" when Putin is replaced (cnbc.com).

References

Achiezer, Alexander. (2002). "Russian Space as a Subject of Comprehension." *Otechestvennye Zapiski*, 6. [Rossiiskoe prostranstvo kak predmet osmysleniya].

Ageev, Alexander. (2005). *Siberia and American West: The Movement of Frontiers*. Moscow: Aspect Press. [Sibir' and Amerikanskij Zapad: Dvizhenie Frontirov].

Bater, James. (2004). "Moscow's Changing Fortunes under Three Regimes." In *World Cities Beyond the West: Globalization, Development, and Inequality*, ed. by J. Gugler, pp. 191–211. Cambridge: Cambridge University Press.

Berdyaev, Nikolai. (1990). *Fate of Russia*. Moscow: Sovetskij pisatel'. [Sud'ba Rossii].

Brade, Isolde, and Robert Rudolph. (2004). "Moscow, the Global City? The Position of the Russian Capital within the European System of Metropolitan Areas." *Area*, 36(1): 69–80.

Busygina, Irina, and Mikhail Filippov. (2018). "The Low Quality of National Governance and Unevenness in the Economic Competitiveness of Regions: The Case of Russia." *Russian Politics*, 3(2): 196–215.

Busygina, Irina, and Mikhail Filippov. (2023). "Center-Regional Relations in Russia." In *Routledge Handbook of Russian Politics and Society*, ed. by Graeme Gill. London: Routledge.

Busygina, Irina, and Mikhail Filippov. (2024). *Non-Democratic Federalism and Decentralization: Lessons from Post-Soviet States*. London, UK: Routledge.

Chaadaev, Petr. (1992). *Apologia of Madman*. Moscow: Respublika. [Apologiya Sumasshedshego].

Elazar, Daniel. (1987). *Exploring Federalism*. Tuscaloosa, AL: University of Alabama Press.

Fish, Steven. (2005). *Democracy Derailed in Russia: The Failure of Open Politics*. Cambridge: Cambridge University Press.

Fujita, Masachisa, and Jacque-Francois Thisse. (2002). *Economics of Agglomeration*. Oxford: Oxford University Press.

Haber, Stephen, and Victor Menaldo. (2011). "Do Natural Resources Fuel Authoritarianism? A Reappraisal of the Resource Curse." *American Political Science Review*, 105(1): 1–26.

Hedin, Astrid. (2021). Communist State Administrative Structures. http://dx.doi.org/10.1093/acrefore/9780190228637.013.1411. Published online: 31 August 2021 Communist State Administrative Structures | Oxford Research Encyclopedia of Politics.

Hosking, Geoffrey. (2011). *Russia and the Russians: A History*. 2nd ed. Cambridge: Harvard University Press.

Ilyin, Ivan. (1992). *Russia Is a Living Organism*. Moscow: Republic. [Rossiya est' zhivoi organism. Moskva: Respublika].

Kagansky, Vladimir. (2010). "Russia as a Large Country: Problematization." In *Giant Countries: The Problems of Territorial Stability*. ed. by Irina Busygina, Leonid Smirnyagin, and Mikhail Filippov. Moscow: MGIMO University. [Rossiya kak bol'shaya strana: problematizatsiya. V Strany-Giganty: Problemy Territorial'noi Stabil'nosti. Pod red. Iriny Busyginoi, Leonida Smirnyagina i Mikhaila Filippova. Moskva: MGIMO-Universitet].

Khomyakov, Alexey. (1992). "About the Old and the New." In *Russian Idea: Anthology*, ed. by Mikhail Maslin, pp. 52–64. Moscow: Respublika. [O starom i novom].

Klyuchevsky, Vassily. (1956). *History of Russia*. Vol. 1. Moscow: Alpha-Kniga. [Istoriya Rossii].

Motyl, Alexander. (1999). "Why Empires Reemerge: Imperial Collapse and Imperial Revival in Comparative Perspective." *Comparative Politics*, 31(2): 127–145.

O'Loughlin, John, and Vladimir Kolossov. (2002). "Moscow: Post-Soviet Developments and Challenges." *Eurasian Geography and Economics*, 43(3): 161–169.

Qian, Yingyi, and Barry R. Weingast. (1997). "Federalism as a Commitment to Reserving Market Incentives." *Journal of Economic Perspectives*, 11(4): 83–92.

Smirnyagin, Leonid. (1998). *Russian Federalism: Paradoxes, Contradictions, Prejudices*. Moscow: MONF. [Rossiiskii Federalizm: Paradoksy, Protivorechiya, Predrassudki].

Treisman, Daniel, and Andrei Shleifer. (2004). "A Normal Country." *Foreign Affairs*, 83(2): 20–38.

Treivish, Andrei. (2010). "What Are Giant States and How to 'fight' Them." In *Giant Countries: The Problems of Territorial Stability*, ed. by Irina Busygina, Leonid Smirnyagin, and Mikhail Filippov. Moscow: MGIMO University. [Chto takoe gosudarsva-giganty i kak s nimi "borot'sya. V Strany-Giganty: Problemy Territorial'noi Stabil'nosti].

Trenin, Dmitry. (2002). *The End of Eurasia: Russia on the Border between Geopolitics and Globalization*. Moscow: Carnegie Endowment for International Peace.

Vail, Petr, and Aleksandr Genis. (1996). "60s." In *The World of a Soviet Man*. Moscow: NLO. [60s. Mir Sovetskogo Cheloveka].

Watts, Ronald. (1999). *Comparing Federal Systems*. 2nd ed. Montreal; Ithaca: Published for the School of Policy Studies, Queen's University by McGill-Queen's University Press.
Weingast, Barry. (1995). "The Economic Role of Political Institutions: Market-Preserving Federalism and Economic Development." *Journal of Law, Economics, & Organization*, 11(1): 1–31.

11 Conclusion

More than 20 years ago, Dani Rodrik (2002), Harvard University Professor of International Political Economy, called the gap in incomes between the world's rich and poor nations "the central economic fact of our time." He concluded that the world is split sharply between countries that have managed to sustain economic growth over long periods of time and those that have not. This is still true today, and while maintaining centrality, this fact goes far beyond economics; it is a fact or trait that has become immanent to human development. Jeffrey Sachs enthusiastically argued that a "wonderful thing that I think we can do is to bring an end to extreme poverty on the planet and it can be accomplished by the year 2025" (Sachs 2008: 17). In his book *The End of Poverty: Economic Possibilities for Our Time* (2005), he proposed several "simple and inexpensive" tools and strategies to achieve this goal. Now, in two decades, the world is as far from realizing that goal as it was in 2005.

Moreover, this gap between the richest and poorest nations (as well as the gap between subnational regions within the countries, both rich and poor) has grown over the past five years. Several poorest countries are now worse off than they were before the COVID-19 pandemic, their developmental perspectives for the coming years are bleak. Ayhan Kose, Deputy Chief Economist of the World Bank, talks about "very serious structural regression, a reversal in the world" and calls for ringing the alarm bells."[1] The poorest countries are spatially clustered (as well as the rich ones) while middle-income countries are scattered all over the world. This spatial pattern has not changed for many decades.

Of course, international institutions and individual countries are not at all indifferent to these issues. Every year, billions and billions of dollars are sent in as foreign aid and development assistance to poorest nations with more than worthy goals to alleviate hunger, end poverty, and foster economic development and good governance. International institutions are full of good intentions: they develop numerous programs, initiatives, prescriptions and advice on how and what reforms should be taken to accelerate development. International aid is certainly important, however, it is more a way of putting out the fire than a real and effective contribution to changing the development patterns of poor countries. Reform prescriptions work imperfectly, or, at least, very unevenly. The poorest countries are clustered in Africa, and Africa remains the poorest continent in the world according to the Human Development Index (HDI) (Tang and Bundhoo 2017).

DOI: 10.4324/9781003496731-14

James Wolfensohn, the former World Bank President, listed the most commonly cited reasons for the ineffectiveness of international aid "corruption, bad policies and weak governance" (Wolfensohn 2002). These reasons migrate from one official speech to the other. Is this list of causes, first, exhaustive, and second, are they actual causes or, rather, the effects of workings of some other factors? Perhaps, aid and good prescriptions are ineffective because they are not "produced" in isolation from the discussion of *long-term* determinants of economic development?

A major topic in this book has been the role of the so-called fundamental (long-term) determinants of development of nations. I was looking at two of them – geographical factors and institutions. The various roles of these determinants were of major importance and had a great variety in past and contemporary development experiences. However, there was no consensus among scholars and experts about which of these determinants is more important than the other and, accordingly, should be at the center of discussions on reform programs and projects to accelerate development of nations. Two rivaling schools of thought emerged emphasizing the role of institutions or geographic factors, respectively, as the main determinant of comparative development (Auer 2013: 180). Behind these schools of thought were two hypotheses, "institutional hypothesis" and "geographical hypothesis" opposed to each other.

The correlation between institutions and development (conceptualized in different ways, as economic concept or as freedom) is well-established, but with geographic factors the situation is less certain. *First*, the set of these factors itself is not entirely clear. *Second* is a long-standing debate on the precise channels through which geography affected development either directly or through the choice and operation of institutions.

In the book, I present three groups of geographic factors: (1) "first-nature geography like climate, soils, altitude, spread of diseases (it is the influence of these factors on development that has been the focus of research); (2) "second-nature geography" – these are geographical factors that relate to state territory – its size, shape, and location (neighbors, access to the sea, distance from strategic objects); (3) "geographical institutions" – these are borders and federalism or territorial autonomy. Importantly, these factors affect, directly or indirectly, the development of states and societies simultaneously in a system, so that the positive action of one factor can be offset by the other. Then I look at direct and indirect channels through which geography and institutions influence development. A wide variety of cases and situations on different continents and in different historical periods illustrates these influences.

The book looks at states as complicated multidimensional entities where various systems work together in combination. The institutional system defines rules and expectations and constrains the choices. The book contends that the geographical system – a set of geographical factors mentioned earlier – is another important system of states. Like the systems of institutions, geography creates its own opportunities and constraints for development. The geographical system interacts with the institutional one setting a corridor of choices for political and economic actors that can accelerate or hinder a country's development. In addition, it is important that institutional and geographical systems intersect with the formation of "geographical institutes."

The main conclusions of the book can be summarized as follows.

First, searching for an answer to the question of which determinant of economic development is the deepest, is unproductive (Ros 2013); it is essentially useless. Such search does not provide theoretical advancement and also makes it difficult to adequately frame practical discussions and design effective development programs and projects. In some cases and situations, "bad" institutional choices may be the major factor hampering development. North Korea would be a "classical" example here. It is much poorer than South Korea. As the example of landlocked Western European countries demonstrates, good supranational institutions can overplay unfavorable geography. On the other side, in a certain period geographical disadvantages may be of much more importance than institutions. This is the case of Mexico that lagged the United States and Western Europe before the advent of the railways in the late nineteenth century, but afterwards the significance of geographical disadvantages was much less important (Ros 2013: 411–412).

The unproductive search for the deepest determinant of economic development makes it equally unproductive to oppose the two hypotheses – the institutional and the geographic ones. Both institutions and geography *always play some role in development*. The development of nations and societies is inconceivable without institutions, but it is also inconceivable without geography, since all nations and societies live in a particular geography.

Second, both hypotheses are valid. But they are the "product" of different disciplines, that is political science and geography. This difference between disciplines roots in more basic difference between nomothetic and ideographic sciences. As approach to knowledge, nomothetic is generally based on generalization and describes the effort to derive laws that explain types or categories of objective phenomena, in general. Idiographic is based on a tendency to specify; it is the effort to understand the meaning of unique, specific. While political science (and economics) is nomothetic, geography (and history) is idiographic science. In the words of Hartshorne, "geography deals with the spatial differentiation of phenomenon. Since geography deals with particular phenomenon, generalization in the form of laws is useless and any prediction in geography is of insignificant value."[2] For the topics discussed in this book, this means that while the "institutional hypothesis" generally supports "universality" (and therefore gives sense to institutional borrowing), the "geographical hypothesis" supports the uniqueness and particularities of a particular situation and a particular place. Institutions can be borrowed but geography cannot. Combining the "institutional" and "geographical" hypotheses, that is, universality and uniqueness, can be very productive for the elaboration of developmental plans and projects.

An important distinction for us between geography and institutions is also that geography, unlike institutions, brings considerations of scale to discussions of development. This is an immanent feature of geographic discipline. The scale – continental, regional, national, subnational, local – helps determine the level of detail and the extent of an area and allows for a more accurate and comprehensive understanding of spatial phenomena. Diamond (1997: 405) pointed to the striking differences between the long-term histories of peoples of the different continents due to the differences in their environments. But there are also a myriad of not less striking differences between places at the smaller scale, be it the geographic isolation of Pitcairn Island or the geographic location of Singapore.

Third, time is important. This book examines the preconditions for development that institutional and geographical factors have created over time. Why time? *First*, because it is simply interesting; many remarkable situations of combinations of institutions and geography have already passed away, having played their part. But to forget about them would be wrong. *Second*, the historical process helps us to see how the role of these factors has changed in terms of accelerating or hindering. Let us recall here the "reversal of fortune" argument of Acemoglu, Johnson, and Robinson. Or the consequences of Europe's "blessed" disunity and of China's "harmful" unity in the fifteenth century presented by Diamond. It was European geography (highly indented coastline, mountains, and rivers) that contributed to the evolvement of independent languages, ethnic groups, and governments as decision-making centers. And so the expeditions that discovered new worlds sailed not from China but from Europe.

Third, the role that geographical neighborhood plays for development can change with time as it happened in Europe. For centuries, neighboring European countries fought each other, two world wars destroyed Europe. For Germany and France, neighborhood meant war, and there seemed to be no way to break this "vicious circle." But there was. It consisted not of a common culture (culture came later) but in effectively working institutions of regional integration. And the factor of geographical neighborhood was highlighted in a completely different way – it turned from a driver of conflicts into an important prerequisite for integration.

Fourth, "bad," inefficient institutional decisions can be changed, although it is difficult. Geographical prerequisites for development cannot be changed by a willful decision, but they can change in the course of development and technical progress. "Bad" "geographical institutions" cannot be just abolished. This primarily relates to borders. In Africa, in the process of decolonization, the borders between new independent states not only followed the demarcation lines between the spheres of influence of the European colonial powers, but they also reflected the administrative boundaries within each colonial sphere. Administrative boundaries became intestate borders which were drawn without regard to ethnic and/or tribal identities. The borders between states in Central Asia that were annexed to the Soviet Union in the early 1920s were carried out by "specialists" from Moscow based on "political expediency," without taking into account the settlement system established in these territories. "Bad" boundaries cannot be undone. (Boundaries cannot be completely erased as they remain in the collective memory of the people.) So these borders will continue to create problems, remaining a condition, alas, unfavorable, for their development.

Fifth, geographical factors work in combination, and these combinations affect the operation of similar institutions in different ways. Let's look at Canada and Russia. It is hard to imagine greater differences than the differences in the development trajectories of Canada and Russia than the differences between liberal democracy in Canada and consolidated autocracy mutating toward totalitarianism in modern Russia. Meanwhile, in terms of geographical factors, there are many similarities between these countries. Both are northern countries, both are the largest countries in the world territorially, and both are characterized by great geographic diversity. Constitutionally, both Canada and Russia are federal states. However, in Canada, federalism is embedded in and supports geographic diversity, while in Russia federalism is an integral part of the authoritarian regime, ensuring its legitimacy and survival throughout the country.

Of course, the choice of institutions and their operation is strongly conditioned by legacy. There is no denying the fact that the Soviet legacy proved not only easily reproducible but also extremely unfavorable for Russia in terms of development. However, combinations of geographical factors also play a role in the operation of institutions. Again, the "Northerness" and sheer size of the countries are similar in Canada and Russia, but geography and neighborhood differ. Canada has only one neighbor – a large and economically powerful yet democratic and also federal state, the United States. Canada's north is the harsh Arctic, while the west and east face two oceans. Territorial expansion is thus simply excluded. Russia, too, reaches out to the Arctic in the north and to the Pacific Ocean in the Far East. However, in the west and especially in the south, it reaches out to vast Eurasian continental landmasses that can potentially be absorbed (and the legacy of the Russian Empire and the Soviet Union encourages this). Russia's neighbors are states much smaller and weaker than Russia that are linked to Russia through the legacies of the Russian Empire and Soviet Union.

Sixth, it is not possible to embed geography into institutions, but the opposite is possible. Institutions work better for development if they are embedded in national and local geography. Democratic federalism is a good example to illustrate this point. In Australia, British institutions were placed in the "soil" for which they were not designed in terms of geography. The difference between British and Australian "soils" was geography – location and climate. Later, Australia's own, not borrowed, institutions of federalism were certainly not perfect and did not allow for all of Australia's developmental problems, but they did allow the country to consolidate to the extent possible and develop as a unified community. In addition, it is worth pointing out that the non-embeddedness of institutions into the local geography gives the elites of the country's recipients of reform programs of international organizations the opportunity to argue that reforms do not work because external experts do not know the specifics of the country and their reasoning is too abstract. Such arguments may be populist in nature, but they often make sense. In the second case, it undermines not only the incentives of local elites to implement reforms but also, to some extent, the credibility of international organizations.

I would like to add one more, *seventh*, point, which is important, though not discussed in detail in this book. Geography and institutions are closely related to the nature of the state. In their book *The Narrow Corridor: States, Societies, and the Fate of Liberty*, Acemoglu and Robinson (2019) made a fundamental distinction between a stateless society (Absent Leviathan) that can degenerate into total disorder and a state that can take over the task of maintaining order and turn to repressions and restrict freedom to serve its own interests (Despotic Leviathan). Both are bad for development. Between these two bad situations is the narrow corridor with a Shackled Leviathan, where a state has enough power to maintain order but not so much as to be oppressive. This preserves liberty and facilitates development. This distinction is very much about institutional choices and the operation of institutions. But this is also about geography. A particular combination of geographical factors can encourage the maintenance of an unlimited state – Despotic Leviathan – and undermine any attempt to shackle it. This is the case of Putin's Russia.

Concentrating on geographical factors and institutions as explanations for development outcomes as it is done in this book is important due to their policy relevance. What is needed to increase policy relevance is taking into account the geographical specificities of the territories for which the policy is being developed when formulating institutional recommendations and the premise that institutions always work in combination and influence each other. Besides that, institutions that have proven effective for development in some countries cannot be replicated by other countries. Decentralization actively – and universally – recommended by international organizations for developing countries is a good example. In the early 1990s, decentralization was considered almost a magic formula that would allow all developing countries to achieve accelerated rates of development – and in a short time. Decentralization has advanced considerably in Africa in the last three decades. Since 1990, many African central governments have initiated or deepened processes to transfer authority, power, responsibilities, and resources to subnational (regional or municipal) levels. However, the results of the institutions of decentralization were at best mixed, with considerable achievements in some areas (like local democracy) and more limited advances in others (like accountability and corruption) (Dickovick and Riedl 2010). The difference in outcomes was recorded not only between areas but also between the countries and their territorial units. In addition, it has come to light that countries can only reap the benefits from decentralization when the quality of their governance arrangements exceeds a certain threshold (Nakatani, Zhang and Garcia Valdes 2022).

Critical in the argumentation of Acemoglu and Robinson about Leviathans is the fact that the corridor between the two Leviathans where development is happening is *narrow*. "Getting to Denmark" – a widely used metaphor for the task of transforming countries into prosperous, well-governed, and free – is both hard and long (Denmark is, by the way, a territorially small country). It means that the head of this mythical animal that I mentioned in the introduction is and will remain small for the foreseeable future. But are the two other parts doomed to remain as large as today? Conscious and adequate efforts by international organizations, national governments, NGOs, as well as experts and academic communities are needed to reduce these groups. Being overoptimistic regarding the time horizons of the victory over poverty and underdevelopment, Sachs quite rightly pointed out that

> poverty will not be ended by sheer willpower alone. It will not even be ended by ethical commitment alone, though ethical commitment is essential. It will be ended by bringing the best of our thinking and the best of our science, together with ethical commitment to attend to the very great problems of the world. It will require the thinking of scholars and scientists and committed practitioners from across the range of human knowledge.
>
> (Sachs 2008: 17)

Efforts to reduce spatial unevenness inequalities must continue to increase. As the Berbers say, "the speed of the caravan is determined by the speed of the slowest camel." Humanity – like a caravan – must remain united, and the pace of its development is determined by the pace of the most disadvantaged nation.

Notes

1 The gap between the world's richest and poorest countries is widening | Semafor.
2 Fundamentals of Human Geography – UPSC Geography Optional (wordpress.com).

References

Acemoglu, Daren, and James Robinson. (2019). *The Narrow Corridor: States, Societies, and the Fate of Liberty*, New York: Penguin Press.

Auer, Raphael. (2013). "Geography, Institutions, and the Making of Comparative Development." *Journal of Economic Growth*, 18: 179–215.

Diamond, Jared. (1997). *Guns, Germs, and Steel: The Fates of Human Societies*. New York: Norton.

Dickovick, Tyler, and Rachel Riedl. (2010). *Comparative Assessment of Decentralization in Africa*. Washington, DC: USAID.

Nakatani, Ryota, Qianqian Zhang, and Isaura Garcia Valdes. (2022). Fiscal Decentralization Improves Social Outcomes When Countries Have Good Governance. IMF Working Paper No. 2022/111.

Rodrik, Dani. (2002). "Institutions, Integration, and Geography: In Search of the Deep Determinants of Economic Growth." http://www.tinyurl.com/yyavhdqn.

Ros, Jaime. (2013). *Rethinking Economic Development, Growth, and Institutions*. Oxford: Oxford University Press.

Sachs, Jeffrey. (2005). *The End of Poverty: Economic Possibilities for Our Time*, New York: Penguin Press.

Sachs, Jeffrey. (2008). "The End of Poverty: Economic Possibilities for Our Time." *European Journal of Dental Education*, 12(1): 17–21.

Tang, Kin Boon, and Diya Bundhoo. (2017). "Foreign Aid and Economic Growth in Developing Countries: Evidence from Sub-Saharan Africa." *Theoretical Economics Letters*, 7: 1473.

Wolfensohn, James D. (2002). *Keynote Address Delivered at the Woodrow Wilson International Center*. Washington, DC: World Bank.

Index

Note: Page numbers in **bold** indicate a table on the corresponding page.

Aboriginal people 156, 199–201, 203, 208
administrative borders 61–62; *see also* borders
administrative-territorial divisions: Russia 224–227
Afghanistan 113–114
Africa 124–125; borders and border conflicts in 137–141; colonial legacy 133–135; colonial partition of 126–131; decolonization of 131–133; explaining African statehood 135–137; first political communities in 125–126; geography and/or institutions and development in 143–144; Nigeria as "mirror" of Africa's problems 141–143
Appalachian Mountains 179–180
Argentina 162–163
Asia 102–104; collapse of colonial system and legacy 110–113; development 113–114; European colonization 106–110; fragmentation 113–114, 117–118; geography 104–106, 113–116, 118–121; governability 117–118; institutions 104–106, 113–115, 120–121; interregional disparities 118–120; localized inequalities 118–120; location 114–115; neighborhood 114–115; policies 114–115
Atlantic Europe 85–87; *see also* Europe
Australia 194–197

Baltic Sea Strategy 96
border conflicts 57; Africa 66, 137–141; Latin America 158–165
borderlands 63, 66–68
border regions 51, 66–68, 234
borders 56–57; adjacent territories 66–68; administrative 61–62; in Africa 137–141; frontier as geographic institution and way of life 63–65; as institutions 62–63; interstate 59–61; typology and function of 57–59; why border disputes 65–66
Brazil 163–165
British legacy 7–10; Africa 128–132, 135–142; Asia 104–113; Europe 80, 82–87, 89–90; Latin America 153–155, 162–163; North America 169–176, 180–182, 188–191; Oceania 195–206; Russia 217–220

Canada 187–191
center–periphery relations: Russia 231–232
Central Asia 114–115; *see also* Asia
centralization: Russia 214–216
China 118–1120
choice of institutions and policies 114–115
"collecting of lands" 77, 218–221
Colombia 161–162
colonialism 82–85; Africa 126–135; Asia 110–113; Latin America 154–156
colonization 106–110; Russia 218–221; Spanish–Portuguese 152–154
compromises, institutional 180–185
conflicts, border 57; Africa 66, 137–141; Latin America 158–165
conflicts, territorial 61; Africa 138; Latin America 159
contrasts, territorial: Russia 214–216
control, territorial: Colombia 161–162
cooperation, transborder 95

decolonization 156–158; Africa 131–133
de facto states 115–116
democracy 176–179

development 18–22; Africa 143–144; Asia 113–114; Canada 187–190; European 91–96; Oceania 197–199, 206–207; role of geography in 28–35; Russia 227–230, 233–234
disparities, interregional 118–120
disputes, border 65–66; *see also* borders
disputes, territorial: Latin America 158–165
division 120–121
drivers for European development 91–96
dwarfs, territorial 43

economic characteristics of modern states 44
empire 174–176; Russian 224–226; *see also* colonialism
Eritrea 66, 130–132, 137, 141
Ethiopia 66, 126, 130–132, 137, 140–141
Europe 73–4; ancient period 74–6; Atlantic Europe 85–7; colonialism/colonization 82–5, 106–110; Middle Ages 76–9; New Age 79–82; postwar Europe 90–1; supranational institutions 91–6; territorial–political orders in 96–9; twentieth century 87–90
European Union 34–35, 49–53, 57, 67, 90–98
Euroregions 95
expansion, territorial 180–185; Russia 233–234
"experiment," Korean 120–121

Falkland Islands/Malvinas 162–163
federalism: Russia 224–230
fragmentation: geographic 113–114; governability in a fragmented state 117–118
frontier: as geographic institution and way of life 63–65; Russia 221–224
functions of borders 57–59

geography 17–18, 25–28, 39–41, 120–121; Africa 143–144; borders as geographical institutions 56–68; Canada 191; changing "geographical institutions" 158–165; geographic fragmentation 113–114; geographic location 114–115; geographically localized inequalities 118–120; in the history of Asia 104–106; location of states 47–53; Oceania 197–199; role in development 28–35; Russia 216–218; shape of territory 46–47; territorial size 41–46; uneasy geography of de facto states 115–116; United States 185–187
geopolitics: Argentina 162–163
giants, territorial 43
globalization 51–53
governability 117–118
governing: Russia 224–227

history 7–10; Asia 104–106; Oceania 204–206; Russia 214–216

immigration 199–201
imperial legacy: Russia 231–232
Indonesia 117–118
institutions 18, 21–25, 113–114; Africa 143–144; borders as geographical institutions 56–68; changing geographical institutions 158–165; choice of 114–115; colonial 154–156; compromises 180–185; divided 120–121; in the history of Asia 104–106; inventing political institutions 173–174; Oceania 197–199; Russia 224–230; supranational 91–96; United States 185–187
interregional disparities 118–1120
interstate borders 59–61; *see also* borders

Korean "experiment" 120–121

Latin America 147–151; border conflicts and territorial disputes 158–165; colonial institutions 154–156; decolonization 156–158; pre-Columbian civilizations 151–152; Spanish–Portuguese colonization 152–154
localization: geographically localized inequalities 118–1120
location 47–53; Asia 114–115; Russia 216–218

Malvinas 162–163
Mexico–US 160–161
Middle Ages 76–79
militarization: Russia 233–234
Modernity (New Age) 79–82
modern states 39–41; location of states 47–53; shape of territory 46–47; territorial size 41–46
Mongolia 114–115
Moscow 231–232; *see also* Russia

national development: Russia 227–230
nations, divided 120–121

neighborhood 114–115; Mexico–US 160–161
New Age (Modernity) 79–82
Nigeria 141–143
North America 168–172, 179–180, 187–192; combining territorial size and democracy 176–179; geographic and institutional differences 185–187; institutional compromises and territorial expansion 180–185; inventing political institutions 173–174; problem of empire 174–176
Northern Dimension (ND) 95–96

Oceania: Australia 194–197; British legacy, geographic constraints, and institutional development 197–199; history and territorial structure 204–206; immigration and the Aboriginal problem 199–201; "Pacific paradox" and "Polynesian experiment" 207–209; or the Pacific region 201–204, **202**; specific approaches to development 206–207

"Pacific paradox" 207–209
Pacific region 201–204, **202**; *see also* Oceania
Pakistan 113–114
"parents" 115–116
"patrons" 115–116
periphery *see* center–periphery relations 231–232
policies 114–115
politics: first political communities in Africa 125–126; inventing political institutions 173–174; political characteristics of modern states 44; territorial–political orders in Europe 96–99
"Polynesian experiment" 207–209
Portugal: Spanish–Portuguese colonization 152–154
pre-Columbian civilizations 151–152
Putin 10, 12n3, 213, 228–233

regions: border 66–68; Euroregions 95; Pacific 201–204, **202**; *see also* borders
Russia 212–213, 233–234; administrative-territorial divisions and federalism 224–227; "collecting of lands" and beginning of colonization 218–221; frontier 221–224; imperial legacy 231–232; institutions of federalism and national development in the 1990s 227–230; peculiarities of the geographic location 216–218; Putin's federalism 230; territorial contrasts and centralization 214–216; territorial size 213–214
Rwanda 139

shape 46–47
Siberia 221–224
size 41–46; North America 176–179; Russia 213–214
sociocultural characteristics of modern states 44
Somalia 139–141
South Sudan 138–139
Soviet Union 226–227; *see also* Russia
Spanish–Portuguese colonization 152–154
statehood, African 135–137
states, de facto 115–116
states, fragmented 117–118
states, modern 39–41; location of states 47–53; shape of territory 46–47; territorial size 41–46
structure, territorial: Oceania 204–206
supranational institutions 91–96

Tajikistan 113–114
territorial conflicts 61; Africa 138; Latin America 159
territorial control: Colombia 161–162
territorial disputes: Latin America 158–165
territorial dwarfs 43
territorial giants 43
territorial–political orders 96–99
territory: development of Canada 187–190; Oceania 204–206; Russia 213–216, 224–227, 233–234; shape 45–47; size 41–45, 176–179; strategies of territorial expansion 180–185
transborder cooperation 95
typology of borders 57–59

uneasy geography 115–116
United States 170–172, 185–187; Mexico–US 160–161

variables: and globalization 51–53

war 9–10, 19–20, 40–41, 46–48, 52–53, 57–59; Africa 124–126, 129–138, 141–144; Asia 105–116; Europe 73–74, 80–91, 96–99; Latin America 149–165; North America 174–187; Oceania 195–197; Russia 212–213, 220–222, 229–233
way of life, frontier as 63–65